AF757462

The Politics of Law and Stability in China

The Politics of Law and Stability in China

Edited by

Susan Trevaskes

Griffith University, Australia

Elisa Nesossi

Australian National University, Australia

Flora Sapio

The Chinese University of Hong Kong

Sarah Biddulph

University of Melbourne, Australia

Edward Elgar

Cheltenham, UK • Northampton, MA, USA

© The Editors and Contributors Severally 2014

All rights reserved. No part of this publication may be reproduced, stored in a retrieval system or transmitted in any form or by any means, electronic, mechanical or photocopying, recording, or otherwise without the prior permission of the publisher.

Published by
Edward Elgar Publishing Limited
The Lypiatts
15 Lansdown Road
Cheltenham
Glos GL50 2JA
UK

Edward Elgar Publishing, Inc.
William Pratt House
9 Dewey Court
Northampton
Massachusetts 01060
USA

A catalogue record for this book
is available from the British Library

Library of Congress Control Number: 2014937077

This book is available electronically in the ElgarOnline.com Law Subject Collection, E-ISBN 978 1 78347 387 8

MIX
Paper from
responsible sources
FSC
www.fsc.org
FSC® C013056

ISBN 978 1 78347 386 1

Typeset by Columns Design XML Ltd, Reading
Printed and bound in Great Britain by T.J. International Ltd, Padstow

Contents

Contributors

Sarah Biddulph is a Professor at The University of Melbourne Law School, specializing in researching and teaching Chinese law. Her academic career builds on extensive experience of Chinese-related legal practice obtained whilst working as a lawyer in Australia and in China. Professor Biddulph's research focuses on the Chinese legal system with an emphasis on legal policy, law making and enforcement as they affect the administration of justice in China. Her particular areas of research are contemporary Chinese administrative law, criminal procedure, labour, comparative law and the law regulating social and economic rights. She is the author of *Legal Reform and Administrative Detention Powers in China* (Cambridge University Press 2007).

Ding Peng is a researcher and programme coordinator of the Wuhan University Public Interest and Development Law Institute (PIDLI). His research areas include human rights, access to justice and legal empowerment. He is the co-author of several papers on legal aid in the annual *Blue Book of China's Human Rights* and other publications on multi-disciplinary human rights research.

Xin He is a Professor at the School of Law, City University of Hong Kong. He has published widely in the leading journals in the fields of law and society, and the Chinese legal system. His recent articles are 'Above the Roof, Beneath the Law: Perceived Justice behind Disruptive Tactics among Wage Claimants in China' (with Lungang Wang and Yang Su 2013), 'Pragmatic Discourse and Gender Inequality in China' (with Kwai Ng 2013), 'Black Hole of Responsibility: The Role of Adjudication Committee in a Chinese Court' (2012), all in *Law & Society Review*, and 'Do the Haves Come out Ahead in Shanghai Courts' (with Yang Su 2013), in *Journal of Empirical Legal Studies*. His previous Visiting Professorships include those at New York University School of Law, University of Illinois College of Law, and Southwestern University of Finance and Economics, China.

Fu Hualing is a Professor of Law in the Faculty of Law of the University of Hong Kong. He graduated from the Southwestern University of

Politics and Law in Chongqing and completed postgraduate degrees in Canada. His research interests include human rights and legal institutions in China and he has published widely in those areas. His most recent publication is *Liu Xiaobo, Charter 08 and the Limits of China's Political Reform* (Hong Kong University Press 2012, co-edited with Jean Philippe Beja and Eva Pils).

Guo Zhiyuan is an Associate Professor at the China University of Political Science and Law (CUPL) in Beijing and a research fellow at the Center of Collaborative Innovation for Judicial Civilization with the Ministry of Education (MOE). She specializes in Criminal Procedure, Evidence, International Human Rights Law and Law and Society Studies. She is also a pioneer in empirical research in China. She is Deputy Director of the Center for Criminal Law and Justice, CUPL and a Non-resident Senior Research Fellow at the US-Asia Law Institute, New York University School of Law. Guo was appointed as Guanghua Visiting Scholar at NYU School of Law from 2008–09 and as Sohmen Visiting Scholar at the Faculty of Law, Hong Kong University in 2011. She has published several books in Chinese and has published extensively in academic journals in both Chinese and English languages.

Elisa Nesossi is a Post-doctoral Fellow at the Australian Centre on China in the World (CIW). She graduated from the Department of Oriental Languages and Civilisations in Venice (Italy) and obtained postgraduate qualifications from the School of Oriental and African Studies (SOAS), University of London. Her research interests include Chinese law and institutions, comparative criminal justice and human rights law. She has extensive experience working for NGOs, developing projects on criminal justice and human rights within China. She is the author of *China's Pre-Trial Justice: Criminal Justice, Human Rights and Legal Reforms in Contemporary China* (Wildy, Simmonds and Hill 2012).

Michael Palmer is Dean and Professor of Law at the Shantou University Law School in Shantou, China. He is a former Chair of the Centre of Chinese Studies (CCS) and Chair of the Centre of East Asian Law (CEAL) at the School of Oriental and African Studies, and a former chair of the SOAS Law School. He is now Emeritus Professor of Law at the University of London, a Research Professor in both the CCS and the Law School at SOAS and a Senior Associate Research Fellow of the Institute of Advanced Legal Studies (School of Advanced Studies), at the University of London. Within China, he is also Visiting Professor of Law at Renmin Daxue (People's University, Beijing) Xinan Zhengfa Daxue (Southwest Institute of Political Science and Law, Chongqing), and

Xiamen University Law School. He is joint editor of the *Journal of Comparative Law*, and a barrister practising at Serle Court Chambers in Lincoln's Inn, London and McNair Chambers, Doha. He has in the past served as special advisor to the Attorney-General of Hong Kong, and he is currently a special advisor to the Shanghai Commercial Mediation Centre and to the Shenzhen Court of International Arbitration. He is the author of numerous publications, including (with Simon Roberts) *Dispute Processes: ADR and the Primary Forms of Decision Making* (Cambridge University Press 2005), translated into Chinese and published by Peking University Press in 2011.

Flora Sapio is a Research Assistant Professor at The Chinese University of Hong Kong. Her main research interests include Chinese criminal justice, administrative detention, extra-legal violence and coercion. Her publications include *Sovereign Power and the Law in China* (Brill 2011). In recent years she has been Visiting Researcher at the Centre for Rights and Justice at The Chinese University of Hong Kong, Research Fellow at the Centre for Advanced Studies on Contemporary China (Turin, Italy), Visiting Scholar at the New York University School of Law, and Assistant Professor at the Julius-Maximilians Universität, Würzburg, Germany. She is a founding member of the European China Law Studies Association.

Murray Scot Tanner is a China security analyst at the CNA Corporation. His previous appointment was as researcher at RAND Corporation and before that he served for 13 years as Professor of Political Science at Western Michigan University. He has written extensively on Chinese criminal justice and politics, in particular on policing and internal security, political instability and unrest, the dilemmas of building the rule of law, human rights, lawmaking, leadership politics, and China–Taiwan relations.

Susan Trevaskes is an Australian Research Council QEII Research Fellow at Griffith University, Australia. She is also currently an Adjunct Director of the Centre on China in the World (CIW) at the Australian National University. Her main research interests are in criminal justice, punishment and courts in China. Her recent books include *Courts and Criminal Justice in Contemporary China* (Lexington Press 2007), *Policing Serious Crime in China: From 'Strike Hard' to 'Kill Fewer'* (Routledge 2010) and *The Death Penalty in Contemporary China* (Palgrave Macmillan 2012). She has also published a number of papers on anti-crime campaigns, private security, public security, drug crime, public shaming events, and death penalty reform. As part of her Australian

Research Council fellowship, she is currently examining serious drug crime and the death penalty in China.

Benjamin van Rooij is the John S. and Marilyn Long Professor of US-China Business and Law and academic director of the John S. and Marilyn Long US-China Institute for Business and Law. By affiliation he is Professor of Chinese Law and Regulation at the Faculty of Law at Amsterdam University and director of the Netherlands China Law Centre. Also he is honorary professor at Wuhan University School of Law and long-term Visiting Professor at Yunnan University School of Law. He obtained his PhD with honours in 2006 in Leiden, with his dissertation 'Regulating Land and Pollution in China: Lawmaking, Compliance and Enforcement, Theory and Cases'. His research focuses on processes of lawmaking and implementation of law, with a particular focus on compliance and enforcement. Areas of research include land management and zoning, pollution regulation, labour law, tax collection, and food safety.

Zhang Wanhong is an Associate Professor at the School of Law in Wuhan University, where he is also the Director of Wuhan University Public Interest and Development Law Institute (PIDLI). His research areas include human rights, public interest law, access to justice and civil society. He is the founder of the Access to Justice Project in Rural China (2006). Professor Zhang has recently been awarded an LLM from Columbia University Law School. In 2009 he was Visiting Researcher at the Danish Centre for Human Rights and in 2005 he was the Edwards Fellow at Columbia University School of Law, New York. In the summer of that year, he visited and lectured at the Norwegian Centre for Human Rights in Oslo, Norway, and at the Raoul Wallenberg Institute of Human Rights and Humanitarian Law, Lund, Sweden. He is the author and translator of a number of books, and has published articles in both international and Chinese publications. Zhang was one of the main drafters of China's first National Human Rights Action Plan (2009–10).

Preface*

A functioning system of law whose independence from the state is upheld and respected by both the state and citizens is widely recognized as intrinsic to a strong and stable nation. Law and stability are seen to be not simply coexistent but interdependent; stability is an outcome of a system of law working effectively in a relatively stable society. In contemporary China, however, this law–stability nexus is complicated by Communist Party politics and the political priorities of state development. As we will see throughout this book, in the era of Harmonious Society and Stability Maintenance, Party-state actions have given China's legal institutions an activist role in the pursuit of national stability, a role that stretches the institutions' legal actors into responsibilities that entangle their interests in legal and political outcomes.

This book is about judicial and governmental activism around the issue of managing social instability in China today. The studies in this volume examine the relationship between law and the political imperatives of state development and observe how the stability imperative shapes this interaction. The imposed activist disposition has enabled the Party-state to legitimize important changes in the practices and policies of courts, governments and security organs on the basis of a political narrative about the imperative of social stability. The Party-state in China has deployed this political narrative, expressed particularly through Harmonious Society and Stability Maintenance discourse, to reframe and reformulate justice and security practices to accommodate its own place leading the country through social upheaval that accompanies rapid economic growth and inspires political disaffection among citizens.

We will find in the chapters of this volume that at the local government level, Party and government involvement in achieving the stability imperative through adjudication and dispute resolution makes judicial fairness difficult to attain for many citizens who use the law to protest against land, labour and environmental decisions made by judicial and

* The editors would like to thank the Australian Centre on China in the World at the Australian National University for financial support for the editing of this volume.

governmental authorities. This is because these authorities also often hold a vested financial interest in supporting the cause of local enterprises over the rights of local residents or transient workers. This is evident in cases of land, labour and environmental disputes discussed in this volume.

The legal measures to achieve stability make a life for law in China that is still at the firm hand of Party, politicians and national policy, and so have created a very potent politics of law and stability in the first decade of the 21st century. In the absence of structural reform that would improve government oversight at the local level, law and judicial activism have been deployed as mechanisms to enforce a political morality in China today that is premised on high-speed economic growth as the basis for continuity of the current political arrangements of power. This has been achieved by enhancing the 'combat power' of criminal trials, civil and criminal mediation, parapolicing operations and re-education through labour, which have been used as stop-gap mechanisms for containing social unrest.

The Party-state has articulated social conflicts as the result of 'contradictions among the people'. Yet rather than tackling social contradictions head on through structural reform, authorities have sought to counter areas of dispute and dissent by mounting Stability Maintenance operations to quell unrest and dispute. While this has proven to be effective in the short term in dealing with instability-inducing protests and disputes, it will have long-term repercussions for the prospects of a well-functioning and credible legal system. Rather than cultivating institutional arrangements that would sustain long-term stability by promoting the legitimacy of well-functioning and robust legal systems, authorities have kept law relating to social conflict and disputes in an elastic state, ready and able to respond to political sways.

As many of the studies in this volume make apparent, the political obsession with stability in the first decade of the 21st century has intensified tensions between the agendas of social order and social justice, bringing about a wider societal antipathy towards the prospects for genuine systemic reform. As is made apparent in the chapters that follow, this leads back to the wider issue of law's long-term prospects for delivering the kind of legitimacy that is essential for the future of Party rule.

Susan Trevaskes, Elisa Nesossi, Flora Sapio and Sarah Biddulph

1. Stability and the law

Susan Trevaskes, Elisa Nesossi, Flora Sapio and Sarah Biddulph

INTRODUCTION

Social stability is a top national concern of Chinese authorities. Law is essential to achieving and maintaining stability, in the understanding of these authorities and in practice. This volume therefore explores the place of law in judicial and government activism around managing social instability in China today. In official circles, social stability is understood as the political and social security that accompanies orderly, conflict-free social relations. Instability is manifest in what the Communist Party-state deems unharmonious relations within communities and between individuals and the state, brought about by crime, dispute and protest. Disparity in income distribution,[1] the underdeveloped welfare system and weak governance oversight mechanisms in local areas are the root causes of festering social unrest that has swept the nation for at least the last 15 years. Well over 100,000 collective protests annually make stability a major political preoccupation. How local courts and governments marshal the forces of law to deter and punish crime, resolve disputes and manage protest has become a central socio-political concern for China's governing authorities. Social stability has become a defining socio-political goal because the Party-state sees social disorder as a threat to future prospects for economic growth, hence to its own future. The studies in this volume observe interactions between law and the stability imperative and how politics figures in these interactions.

These studies reach broadly across matters of law in China, including litigation and mediation practices, substantive law, procedural law reform, anti-corruption initiatives, detention centre operations, parapolicing law and administrative law. Running through these studies are two

[1] China's gini co-efficient was 0.474 in 2012.

related threads. One concerns how the political imperative of social stability has reframed approaches to law and justice in the decade of the 2000s to fit the contours of the stability imperative. The second concerns the challenges posed to the legitimacy of the law when the stability agenda of politics overtakes routine law and justice concerns. What links these two strands is the shift in China's justice and security policy to prioritize positive 'social outcomes' (i.e., successfully preventing disorder) over 'positive legal outcomes' (through due legal process) in handling disputes, protest and crime.

Emphasizing substantive over procedural justice has served to reshape legal practices early in the 21st century at a cost to law's legitimacy. Political responses to the stability imperative have challenged the legitimacy of the law in the eyes of many because these responses hamper judges and government decision-makers trying to follow established legal procedure. This undermines their capacity to make judicial and governmental decisions free from the political pressure to act as the Party-state deems necessary to maintain stability.

The stability imperative has compelled the Party-state to reframe legal and justice practices in a way that in many respects runs counter to the Party's own principle of 'governing the country according to the law' (*yifa zhiguo*). Therefore while the empirical focus varies among chapters, the studies in this volume share a common theme: the challenge of maintaining law's legitimacy when at grassroots the stability imperative from Beijing often translates as, in the words of Deng Xiaoping, to 'preserve stability above all other concerns' (*wending yadao yiqie*). This 'whatever it takes' imperative often invites excessiveness when translated into local practice. In these chapters, the authors show the difficulties for those involved when stability trumps all other concerns. For those who administer justice it is balancing the imperatives of crime control and due process; for those who adjudicate civil and criminal cases it is reconciling the achievement of so-called positive legal outcomes and positive social outcomes; and for those in government and courts who deal with labour, land and environmental disputes it is 'harmonizing' the competing rights and interests of participants, especially when one of them is a local government agency.

CONTAINING INSTABILITY AT THE LOCAL LEVEL

The Party-state has conceived of stability as a precondition for successful economic development since Deng's era of open reform began in 1979. Threats such as crime to the stability of communities have since been an ongoing concern (Dutton 1992). Given its prerequisite status, social stability has been put forward to legitimize most of China's criminal justice policies over the past 30 years (Biddulph 2007, Trevaskes 2010, Sapio 2010, Nesossi 2012). However, over the last 15 years or more, official concern for stability has widened considerably to incorporate social actions that now reach well beyond conventional crime to include legal disputes, individual petitioning and collective protests. Social stability began to be transformed into a key political preoccupation after the Tiananmen incident in 1989 but it took until the 21st century for this concern to be fully institutionalized in the justice and security arenas.

Today stability is the primary socio-political concern of the Party-state, which claims that unregulated social action such as protest or legal dispute over socially sensitive matters such as land, labour and environmental issues threatens not only the success of China's economic agenda but also the nation's political life and the Party's future. This preoccupation with stability has reshaped how the Party-state approaches justice and government decision-making practices and security arrangements. Since many protestors and petitioners perceive they cannot obtain justice in their local courts, over the last 15 years or so, millions of petitioners have travelled to provincial capitals or to Beijing to lodge protests, hoping to have court or government decisions overturned. Particularly in the early to mid-2000s, complainants preferred to take their chances petitioning in Beijing or in the provincial capital since they found it difficult to have their administrative suits heard in local courts or to have their grievances heard by the local government (Zhang 2009, Li, Liu and O'Brien 2012).

In response to the petitioning phenomenon and to the escalation in collective protests throughout the first decade of the 2000s, central and provincial authorities have produced a strategy of 'localizing grievances while insulating the Centre' (Mattis 2012). Part of this strategy involves policing protests financed through a 'Stability Maintenance' budget that now runs to over 700 billion yuan (approximately US$120 billion) annually. Another part of the strategy has been for courts to refuse to accept civil cases for litigation and to deal with disputes through mediation practices (Woo 2013). Practices such as mediation can give authorities firmer control over case outcomes, ensuring that relations between competing parties are 'harmonized'. The Party-state has therefore taken steps to make local courts and governments increasingly 'activist' (Zhu 2010) in their decision-making in response to the escalating number of people who use petitioning outside court and government agencies to seek justice.

Courts and other governmental and justice agencies are these days reluctant to allow cases of forced eviction, land-taking and other civil and administrative disputes to go to trial, preferring to solve the issue through meditation. Mediation is attractive to local authorities because when complainants (including those likely to petition to authorities in provincial capitals or Beijing) agree to the terms of a mediation agreement, it is difficult for them to complain legitimately through appeal or petitioning against a decision that they participated in. But Beijing's pressuring of local courts to 'close the case and solve the problem' (*anjie shiliao*) (Liebman 2012, Zhang 2012) before it reaches higher levels of justice administration or before petitioners head off to Beijing to protest, has created a logistical problem for local authorities. It means court time is now clogged with administrative cases that are sometimes difficult to mediate in favour of the complainant. Indeed, according to some Chinese commentators, with the 'petition-ization' (*sifa xinfanghua*) of court work, court time is increasingly taken up with judicial mediation outside courtrooms; up to 80 per cent of administrative cases are now required to undergo mediation rather than litigation (Zhou 2010, Wang 2013).

Other agencies such as local governments have become increasingly activist through mechanisms such as enforcement campaigns against labour unrest that hark back to the era of Maoism (Biddulph, Cooney and Zhu 2012). Other expressions of stability-related activism are present in the 'Stability Maintenance' policing operations, operations entailing mass CCTV surveillance (Bakken 2012), operations requiring the increasing involvement of China's parapolicing forces (Tanner 2007, 2012) and criminalizing the actions of petitioners and protestors (Cai 2008, Sapio 2013). The overriding concern is to contain potential or realized unrest and dissent at the local level so that a dispute or other social problem does not escalate to become unmanageable.

In short, the strategy of containing contention within local areas has been achieved by bringing back Mao-style pre-emptive mechanisms to deal with social problems through means such as mediation. These mechanisms often prevent citizens from exercising their legal rights through court appeal to higher provincial authorities or through petitioning to central authorities in Beijing. As a consequence, the strategy has politicized what was once routine dispute-related judicial and governmental decision-making, which in turn has politicized the ways in which citizens seek to solve social problems through collective action (Fu 2013). In these circumstances, citizens' rights in relation to legal disputes now run thickly with contention and politics. Obsession with instability has reframed the human rights and justice debate within China in the 21st century. For the Party-state law is the central ingredient to these responses, but for increasing numbers of aggrieved citizens it is also the essential ingredient to their actions as citizens increasingly challenge the state-centric view of their rights. These conditions position law in a complex, inextricable and difficult relationship with the national goal of stability.

CITIZEN ACTIVISM, STATE ACTIVISM AND RIGHTS

From the outset of China's open door reforms in the late 1970s with Deng Xiaoping at the national helm, the Party-state linked development of rights directly to its blueprint for economic modernization. Economic and social rights were made the nation's top human rights priority, to be developed in lockstep with increasing national wealth. Official discourse linked commitment to improving rights to subsistence as the nation's primary human rights goal, while to enable the market to function the state gradually withdrew from what had been its Mao-era responsibilities as 'provider'. Subsistence was indeed still a critical problem for many Chinese in the 1980s and early 1990s. The Chinese government's most impressive feat over the last two decades has been to lift out of poverty hundreds of millions of people from rural areas across the nation, an accomplishment of truly historic proportions.

But the social and economic fallout of this feat has challenged many people's social and economic rights. Uneven distribution of wealth, unequal access to justice, and corruption – entrenched throughout a political system characterized by weak oversight mechanisms – have inspired widespread discontent. Many increasingly feel that their health, property and wages are no longer adequately protected by the legal system or government. They are aggrieved when local authorities consistently fail to punish widespread corruption. They are also aggrieved when government and courts protect the economic interests of big and small business over the rights and interests of the Chinese people. They want state action through law and policy to deliver justice by protecting their rights as citizens rather than their roles in what has become a political as well as economic marketplace. Citizens, like the state, have been increasingly activist and strategic about how they approach this activism (Chen 2012, Fu 2013).

The fallout of decades of social and economic inequality and inadequate access to reliable avenues of justice has therefore transformed the rights debate in China's liberal press (*Southern Daily* and *Southern Weekend*) and in social media, which has shifted significantly to the issue of how protests, petitions, appeals and security threats are managed and punished. Crucially this fallout also creates challenges to the legitimacy of the law when the stability agenda overtakes routine law and justice concerns. At the core of the stability obsession is the issue of loss of public trust in the law (Minzner 2013, Chen 2013). Mass protests continue to occur because people have little faith in the commitment and ability of local governments to address their problem or of local courts to deliver fair and independent decision-making, especially when courts refuse to accept socially sensitive cases for litigation. While billions of yuan each year are poured into Stability Maintenance as a budget item (Xie 2013), an additional and arguably more costly aspect to maintaining stability is apparent. It is the loss of regime legitimacy in the public's eyes brought about by changing legal and justice practices to accommodate the stability imperative. Authorities have been unwilling or unable to effectively address two key sources of public anger that fuels social unrest. One is the corruption and apathy towards corruption apparently entrenched at all levels of government, and the other is blocked access to formal justice, that is, the incapacity of many people to use and afford the legal system as an avenue through which they can have their grievances addressed.

The stability imperative follows a political logic legitimized through grand political narratives such as Hu Jintao's 'Harmonious Society'. In the same manner, the rights prescribed by the Party-state for citizens to appeal and protest a legal or governmental decision follow a political ideology, fashioned by political values and by a social system that is a product of nearly 70 years of Party rule. Citizens' actions can challenge government and court decisions but these challenges are circumscribed by what the Party-state sees as regime threatening. And while China's transition has indeed opened a wider space for popular expression over the past 30 years, the scope and nature of this space are intrinsically linked to how far the Party-state is willing to tolerate disunity. This may not be surprising when we consider that in most modern states, the official position on human rights is tailored by how the state validates notions of rights and justice to accommodate the impact of its governance and social control policies. In China, validation is through the concept of 'mutuality of rights and duties'.

'Mutuality of rights and duties', a guiding human rights principle in China, accommodates stability-related policy in implying that rights are inseparable from the duties prescribed by the Constitution and other laws. Stressing the utmost importance of 'social stability' serves to lock on rights to duties and in the process it interlocks the mutual responsibilities of citizen and state. Since the Party-state sees social instability as a threat to economic development and national prosperity, citizens who are not fulfilling their duty to maintain social stability forfeit their rights. Official jurisprudence sees that individual as well as collective protests undermine the rights of the larger collective ('the people') since protests of any size hamper economic development and hence the capacity of all citizens to realize their economic and social rights.

Regardless of how official jurisprudence legitimates state responses to instability, socio-economic disputes relating to land, environmental and labour issues find expression in the over 100,000 collective protests across the nation annually (Mattis 2012). Obsession with instability pushes and pulls citizens' calls for justice through the tight nexus between politics and law. But the problem of how the state prescribes rights and justice is complicated by the reality of weak oversight mechanisms at the local level, which has encouraged widespread corruption, corporate malfeasance and consequently, public mistrust of the law. The people's lack of access to reliable avenues for redressing injustice has exacerbated problems from the speed and depth of social change through economic development, especially the increasing wealth gap separating poor from rich. But rather than identifying root causes to initiate remedial action, the Party-state has cast consequences – the sharp rise in social unrest and protests – as the key problem. It has planted 'social stability' as the key principle to legitimize both changes in justice and security practices and how it exercises authority to govern the nation through this era of increasing social discord.

The chapters in this volume share a number of themes that primarily concern how citizens respond to injustice and how, in turn, justice and security organs have reorganized their practices in response. The volume has three parts. The first, 'Managing Disputes', sets the stage with detail for analysis through introducing both the legal disputes and the government and judicial activist mechanisms that seek to contain these disputes and their social fallout. The second, 'Creating and Sustaining Legal Frameworks', explores the myriad legal mechanisms open to authorities for responding to what they perceive as instability since the authorities have changed laws and legal practices in response to the stability imperative. The third, 'Framing the Discourses of Stability', reflects on the political logic of the stability imperative, discussing the discursive frameworks that support it, particularly 'Harmonious Society', 'Stability Maintenance' and 'Social Management', which are used to embed the stability imperative within the Chinese legal system.

PART 1: MANAGING DISPUTES

Law is the main mechanism for action used by both the Party-state and Chinese citizens in the stability arena. As we noted above, while the imperative of social stability is politically conceived by the Party-state, which responds to instability through a range of legal and governmental mechanisms, the law also provides citizens with avenues for redress. When citizens believe that individuals, the state or private enterprises have done them or their society an injustice, law can become an empowering instrument for them. Citizens have increasingly pursued legal action such as protesting and appealing court decisions to defend their rights and interests. Many have successfully used legal avenues, including administrative and civil law suits, to fight decisions made against their interests by land developers, construction companies, factory or plant owners and local governments. But when citizens push, the Party-state pushes back by readjusting governmental and judicial decision-making practices. As this volume reveals, such use of the law by citizens can have limited success given the close bonds of financial, administrative and political interdependence that link courts to local governments and shape adjudication and mediation practices.

Part 1 concerns how citizens push – and how courts and governments push back – in labour, land and environmental disputes. Collective and individual legal disputes began to draw the Party-state's legal institutions onto the centre stage of politics in the first decade of the 21st century. Equipped with reconfigured political rhetoric and ideology to justify its evolving approach to law and order, the Hu Jintao–Wen Jiabao leadership came to be known for its 'rigid' (Yu 2010) approach to the maintenance of stability, particularly from 2007 to 2012. Front and centre in this surge of public dissatisfaction with abuse of power, economic inequalities and lack of access to formal avenues of justice are the labour, land and environmental disputes. Disputes and protests in these years incarnated people's frustration at being unable to secure their social and economic rights in a society that for the most part has bifurcated sharply into the urban haves and the rural have-nots. Increasingly citizens expressed anger at inequalities, not just of wealth and opportunity but also of access to justice. Part 1 of this volume explores the politics–law–stability nexus in relation to these three types of disputes.

We begin with labour disputes, which Sarah Biddulph's chapter argues the Party-state sees as a serious threat to social and political stability. This study explores the relationship between stability and rights in the regulation of labour protests through examining how Party-state agencies have interpreted and responded to this unrest. Biddulph argues that the upsurge in labour-related protests can be seen as a problem of both rights and stability. Legal reforms and administrative measures have tried to enhance labour stability through addressing failings in the current regulatory regime, but this is not a high priority; the authorities see that other disturbances pose greater political risk. Some labour disturbances start out as a form of rightful resistance but develop more explicitly political overtones. Authorities can quickly characterize violent labour protest as a social order 'emergency' requiring more direct and coercive intervention. Biddulph argues that despite some reforms, the Party-state has been unable and unwilling to address the problems of low wages and work insecurity that arise from both the current economic development model and concomitant inadequacies in the labour regulatory regime.

Forced land-taking by local governments for the purposes of development is one of the most prominent sources of social conflict in contemporary China. Xin He's chapter on 'hard-nail household' disputes explores the process of legal mediation in land-taking cases as a relatively new form of judicial activism aimed to prevent unrest and preserve stability. Policymakers encourage mediation to resolve these disputes because it discourages or even prevents the aggrieved party from appealing or petitioning against the court's decision; the aggrieved party voluntarily accepts the outcomes so is unlikely to appeal, petition or complain. This mode of dispute resolution may seem workable in the short term, but mediation does not guarantee stability. As Xin He points out, when courts fail to support the aggrieved party in mediation, protestors often assume the courts are 'wearing the same underwear' as the local government and developers, which can escalate tensions. Conversely, courts are pressured not to rule in favour of the aggrieved party in land-taking disputes since acquiescing in pressure from the aggrieved party encourages more hard-nail households and others to demand justice through the courts. Case outcomes are thus often skewed to avoid further tensions, regardless of legal merit. Xin He argues that stability concerns overtaking legal procedures such as formal litigation undermines court authority. He questions the sustainability of mediation as a dominant approach to the stability agenda, arguing that it may resolve some disputes, but in the long run weakens the institutional capacity of the courts and results in increased petitioning and resistance.

Further to Xin He's chapter exemplifying stability-related judicial activism in generally urban development disputes, Zhang Wanhong and Ding Peng's chapter illustrates how judicial and governmental activism has also become prominent in rural environmental disputes over use of water. Central to this rural water activism is China's rapidly deteriorating ecological terrain, which feeds into poor sanitation, accelerated relocation of pollution to rural areas, soil contamination, and shortages and contamination of water (Ma 2008). Zhang and Ding focus on efforts to mediate collective disputes over serious infringement of regulations on water, which endangers the lives and livelihoods of rural residents. Here dispute resolution is to ensure that rural social stability is maintained, sometimes at any cost. Through case studies of two areas in rural Hubei province, this chapter documents rural residents' attempts to resolve water pollution problems that gravely affect those living in the vicinity of river-polluting manufacturing plants, who drink the water from the river and use it for their crops. We see that when villagers cannot access the law or courts fail to protect their interests over manufacturers' and developers' interests, villagers may feel forced to organize and participate in 'mass incidents'. As argued in the previous two dispute-related chapters, Zhang and Ding argue that the only lasting foundation of stability in Chinese society is the legitimacy of the law that is manifest in effective judicial remedy and the protection and realization of rights.

PART 2: CREATING AND SUSTAINING LEGAL FRAMEWORKS

The chapters in this part unmask the stability imperative now embedded widely across the practices of administrative, legal and security organs. The scope of the studies here is therefore broad, each homing in on a variety of law and justice sites that illustrate the centrality of the imperative to manage discord, disorder and dispute in the intersection between law and the Party-state's political agenda of stability.

Benjamin van Rooij's chapter sets the scene for Part 2 by reflecting on how regulation itself can produce instability through underdevelopment of the enforcement capacities of China's regulatory regime, which seeks to oversee the activities of state-owned and private enterprises. He argues that weak regulation and social instability are now closely entwined in China, resulting in fragmented and 'irregular' uses of regulation that can damage public trust in the law. Fear of social unrest also plays multiple and sometimes contradictory roles in the development and functioning of regulation. Protests can inspire the state to respond by launching campaigns that crack down on irregularities. The stop–start and short-lived nature of government commitments triggered public pressure to enforce regulatory law but sends mixed signals to the community about the 'stability' of the law itself. It also underscores the need for local and central authorities to take regulatory law much more seriously as a legitimate state instrument for protecting citizens and ultimately preserving stability in China.

Michael Palmer's study in Part 2 expands on Xin He's in Part 1, which acknowledges the renewed dominance of mediation over litigation in settling disputes. Palmer examines how state–society relations are mediated in administrative suits in China today, tracing the rise of mediation as dominant in practice – if not in the official rhetoric – in administrative suits. One of the most serious difficulties facing the legal reform drive immediately post Mao was the need for legal control over the administrative powers of the state. Politico-legal authorities experimented with a system of administrative litigation (*xingzheng susong*) in the 1980s, which was introduced as a national law in 1990. Originally this was a means by which citizens might more effectively challenge the actions of administrative agencies. However, as Palmer explains, it has nowadays been transformed by judicial practice that favours mediation over litigation. Transforming the meaning of administrative litigation – and the relationship between this transformation and official policies favouring socio-political stability and 'Harmonious Society' – is a story both significant and ongoing. Accordingly, this chapter explores two central questions: the nature and significance of the role of mediation in administrative litigation in the PRC, and the most salient current developments in this unfolding tale.

Trevaskes considers a very different and somewhat unexpected site for judicial mediation: the death penalty. Her chapter examines reshaping of death penalty policy and practice to address issues of stability and harmony preservation through propagation by China's Supreme People's Court (SPC) and Supreme People's Procuratorate (SPP) of two types of model cases: 'standard cases' (*dianxing anli*) and 'guiding cases' (*zhidao anli*). By examining the medium and the message of model cases on lenient death sentencing post 2007, Trevaskes investigates how the socio-political role of punishment in relation to maintaining stability is articulated top down from the SPP and SPC to prosecutors and judges in local jurisdictions. Guiding cases are a key means for the SPC and SPP to convey to judges and prosecutors in local jurisdictions what these two top legal institutions construe as correct practice for death sentencing that responds effectively to the political imperatives of Stability Maintenance and Harmonious Society-building. The guiding cases thus exemplify how in homicide cases where death sentencing is applied, judges and prosecutors are to prioritize positive 'social outcomes' driven by the constant political imperative of social stability, over the long-term positive 'legal outcomes' concerned with legal propriety of the nation's civil law system.

Reconciling positive legal and social outcomes was also a keen concern for the drafters of China's latest Criminal Procedure Law (2013) as Guo Zhiyuan explains. Crime control and due process are key imperatives for criminal justice systems worldwide. In China, these two imperatives have informed recent debates on criminal procedure reform and have been an integral part of the legislative drafting process of this newly amended law. China enacted its first Criminal Procedure Law (CPL) in 1979, and substantially revised the law in 1996. Guo examines the most recent reform to the CPL brought into effect in March 2013, arguing that stability is one of the most important goals, through balancing crime control and due process. The crime control imperative requires that the criminal procedure law punishes offenders to protect the public from social harm caused by crime, while the legal imperative of due process requires the criminal procedure law to protect the accused from wrongful proceedings and other abuses of power. Guo argues that due process and crime control are compatible in theory, but in practice they can easily be set in contradiction when stability becomes the overriding politico-legal standard. Criminal law in China is predominantly to protect the collective majority from the minority, a predisposition that suits the stability maintenance agenda and justifies the dominance of crime control as the driving principle of the CPL.

Disciplinary and legal frameworks dealing with corruption and abuse of power are explored by Fu Hualing. One of Xi Jinping's first political statements after ascendancy to the Party throne in November 2012 was to announce yet another anti-corruption drive. Corruption and abuse of power link directly to stability and social order because they are the key sources of community dissatisfaction with China's governance model. Since acceding to the United Nations Convention against Corruption (UNCAC) in 2003, China has implemented a series of anti-corruption initiatives to prevent and reduce corruption and to punish corrupt officials. Fu Hualing's study introduces those initiatives and offers an assessment of their success and limits in containing the spread of corruption and regaining public trust. Fu's study strikes a largely positive note, arguing that for the time being, implementing the UNCAC-based international best practices in China has contributed to the nation's political stability and authoritarian resilience. In the long term, however, the one-Party state may be unable to resolve the deeply entrenched corruption that reaches into every sector of government and is sustained by the existing legal frameworks.

Murray Scot Tanner's chapter explores the law–stability nexus in relation to the People's Armed Police (PAP) in the 21st century. The PAP is intrinsic to the politics of law and stability in China. This paramilitary force has been called upon to supplement the police force in breaking up large-scale mass protests and is therefore seen by the authorities as instrumental in the Party-state's moves to create and sustain social stability in a practical way by preventing or curbing social unrest through armed force. In this context the creation and implementation of law to legally codify the deployment of the armed police forces – where, when, how, why and most importantly by whom – runs thick with politics. Control over the armed police matters very much. In this context, the 2009 PAP Law was designed to legalize organizational control over China's paramilitary police forces, which had been governed primarily by military and police regulations. But the law's text, debated extensively within the National People's Congress Standing Committee, ultimately raised as many questions about control of paramilitary forces as it answered. Tanner's chapter on changes to the PAP Law examines control over the PAP before the law was changed, debates over the 2009 Law and its final text, and subsequent practices under the revised law for mobilizing these forces, which play an increasingly important practical role in China's internal security and maintenance of stability.

PART 3: FRAMING THE DISCOURSES OF STABILITY

The final part of this volume interrogates political rhetoric surrounding the stability imperative and how the prevailing political discourses in 21st-century China relate to stability. Elisa Nesossi's chapter on social management discourse examines the framing of 'Social Management Innovation' that has emerged over recent years in the Chinese criminal justice system and its effects on pre-trial detention. Nesossi assesses how the Party-state sustains a neoliberal rhetoric on rights and justice without weakening emphasis on its own leading and paternalistic role in society. She examines how typically Western concepts like transparency and accountability have been co-opted within the Chinese legal-political discourse on 'social management' and 'criminal justice socialization' to support the line of stability and legitimacy maintenance, which helps sustain Party-state leadership. Illustrating through the place of reform in the system of pre-trial detention, this chapter examines in particular the role of the procuratorate, mass organizations and the general public within detention centres.

Flora Sapio's study of social management theory contemplates this new 'Social Management Innovation' discourse as a recent post-Harmonious Society political programme that rationalizes stability as an imperative of the 'general will' of the masses. Sapio examines the rationales behind this discourse as a new ideological phenomenon in China. Social Management Innovation began life as an add-on to Stability Maintenance but has been given a life of its own since 2010. Sapio's discussion identifies the theoretical role of the 'general will' in Chinese and Western political philosophy to connect Social Management Innovation rationales to Stability Maintenance. Social Management entails selectively adapting neoliberal government techniques to maximize the prospects of social stability and economic growth. This development has been explained as the 'retreat of the state' and the decline of ideology, but as Sapio explains, politics remains supreme in this new programme, just as it has in the Harmonious Society and Stability Maintenance years. She argues that the endogenous intellectual forces that encouraged such a shift in governance in China did not envisage a shift in the relationship between power and the lives of individual human beings. Rather, translated into political praxis, such ideas have induced a continuing emphasis on stability: the undisturbed operation of the laws that regulate politics, the economy, society and the individual.

The final chapter by Trevaskes, Nesossi, Sapio and Biddulph reflects on the political context of the themes explored in the volume, through reappraising the journey to stability obsession in recent years. It considers the discursive frameworks within which China's leadership has reframed justice and security practices to deepen understanding of how and why the stability imperative became the Party-state's number one preoccupation in the decade of the 2000s. It sketches the path of stability's rise to prominence through political programmes and rhetoric linking stability to the national imperatives of economic development and institutional reform.

Stability Maintenance and Harmonious Society are agendas that aim to address the connection between three key ingredients of China's modernization drive: stability, economic development and reform. In the early 2000s, the new Hu Jintao leadership recognized that, long term, they would need to take institutional reform, particularly legal reform, seriously as the ultimate mechanism required to 'govern the country according to the law', to curb corruption, to improve China's weak governmental and legal oversight mechanisms and to sustain the prospects for a moderately prosperous society. But while they recognized that a strong legal system capable of enforcing the law across the nation would be the ultimate guarantee for long-term social stability, it is apparent that they did not believe that, at this juncture in time, the law would be sufficiently robust to create a stable social environment for growth.

This final chapter traces the journey towards stability preoccupation in the late 20th and early 21st centuries, reflecting on how stability came to tie in with the two other key elements of China's modernization goals: institutional reform and economic development. How the Party-state perceived their interrelationship explains why the stability imperative became the central political concern of the first decade of the 21st century in China, while institutional reform ended up as the weakest link in this tripartite chain.

This discussion concludes the volume by reflecting on the erosion of public trust in the law in China, questioning the cost of the stability imperative in relation to the loss of law's credibility in recent times. The Party-state's quest for stability in China has been exercised partly through the law, but not always for the nation's legal system. Therein lies the politics of law and stability in 21st-century China.

CONCLUSION

The Politics of Law and Stability in China examines the nexus between law, politics and stability at this crucial period in the nation's rise to the status of economic superpower. It explores the impact of Party-state rationales for social stability on legal reform, judicial decision-making and justice system policy relating to institutions such as courts, the PAP and detention centres and the handling of civil disputes and social unrest. This volume presents politico-legal approaches the Party-state has used to manage (and in some cases, to punish) the behaviour of Chinese citizens in response to what it sees as destabilizing or potentially destabilizing social action. The studies in each chapter digest how in the first decade of the 21st century the stability imperative has driven the reframing of approaches to law and justice practices, impinging upon the legitimacy of the law when it has overtaken routine law and justice concerns. Many of the Party-state's changes in legal and justice practices in response to the stability imperative challenge law's legitimacy because their results contradict the idea of 'governing the country according to law', which the Party-state wants to promote and practise at this stage of China's socio-economic development. Excesses also register below the national level, as local governments and court workers can be penalized for not containing dissent locally.

The Party-state attributes the rise in legal disputes, protests and other public disturbances, particularly since the beginning of new century, to the social and economic fallout of rapid economic growth. If it recognizes these public expressions of resistance, dissent or conflict also as products of the nation's one-Party political system and the corruption entrenched within it, it does not publicly acknowledge them. Rather than dealing head on with the causes of the problems, it has cloaked disputes in rhetorical garb as destabilizing and potentially dangerous to society. By implication, of course, disputes also threaten the Party's prospects for long-term rule. The price that the nation now pays for the Party-state's unwillingness and/or incapacity to deal head on with structural and political weaknesses is an increasingly unharmonious Chinese society, which lacks trust in the Party's commitment to 'governing the country in accordance with the law'. It creates a very potent politics of law and stability in 21st-century China.

REFERENCES

Bakken, Borge (2012), 'The Chinese surveillance state: the rationalities of "social management" in China'. Paper delivered at the Conference on Stability and Law, Australian National University, Canberra, 8–9 November.

Biddulph, Sarah (2007), *Legal Reform and Administrative Detention Powers in China*. New York: Cambridge University Press, 2007.

Biddulph, Sarah, Cooney, Sean and Ying Zhu (2012), 'Rule of law with Chinese characteristics: the role of campaigns in lawmaking', *Law and Policy*, 34/4: 373–401.

Cai, Yongshun (2008), 'Local governments and the suppression of popular resistance in China', *The China Quarterly*, 193: 24–42.

Chen, Xi (2012), *Social Protest and Contentious Authoritarianism in China*. New York: Cambridge University Press.

Chen, Xi (2013), 'The rising cost of stability', *Journal of Democracy*, 24/1: 57–64.

Dutton, Michael (1992), *Policing and Punishment in China: from patriarchy to the people*. Cambridge: Cambridge University Press.

Fu, Hualing (2013), 'Politicized challenges, depoliticized responses: political monitoring in China's transitions', University of Hong Kong Faculty of Law Research Paper 2013/014.

Li, Lianjiang, Liu, Minxing and O'Brien, Kevin (2012), 'Petitioning Beijing: the high tide of 2003–2006', *China Quarterly* 210: 313–34.

Liebman, Benjamin L. (2012), 'Professionals and populists: the paradox of China's legal reforms', in Timothy B. Weston and Lionel M. Jensen (eds.), *China in and Beyond the Headlines*: Lanham MD: Rowman and Littlefield, pp. 214–30.

Ma, Tianjie (2008), 'Environmental mass incidents in rural China: examining large-scale unrest in Dongyang, Zhejiang', *China Environmental Series (CES10) (2008/2009)*: 33–56, http://www.wilsoncenter.org/sites/default/files/CES%2010%20 Feature%20Article,%20pp.%2033-56.pdf. Accessed 8 August 2013.

Mattis, Peter (2012), 'The foundations of China's future stability', *Asia-Pacific Bulletin*, 149, http://www.eastwestcenter.org/publications/foundation-chinas-future-stability. Accessed 30 January 2013.

Minzner, Carl (2013), 'China at the tipping point?: The turn against legal reform', *Journal of Democracy*, 24/1: 65–72.

Nesossi, Elisa (2012), *China's Pre-trial Justice: criminal justice, human rights and legal reforms in contemporary China*. London: Wildy, Simmonds and Hill Publishing.

Sapio, Flora (2010), *Sovereign Power and the Law in China*. Leiden/Boston: Brill.

Sapio, Flora (2013), 'Legal erosion and the policing of petitioners', in Mike McConville and Eva Pils (eds.), *Comparative Perspectives on Criminal Justice in China*. Cheltenham UK/Northampton MA.: Edward Elgar, pp. 345–69.

Tanner, Murray Scot (2007), 'Chinese Communist Party strategies for containing social protest'. Paper delivered at 2nd Berlin Conference on Asian Security (Berlin Group).

Tanner, Murray Scot (2012), 'Internal security', in Chris Ogden (ed.), *Hand of China's Governance and Domestic Politics*, Florence, KY: Routledge, pp. 88–96.

Trevaskes, Susan (2010), *Policing Serious Crime in China: from strike hard to kill fewer*. London: Routledge.

Wang, Qinghua (2013), 'Sifa xinfanghua qushi zhide shensi' (Petition-ization of justice is worthy of deeper attention), *Nanduwang* (Southern Daily online), 6 February, http://ndnews.oeeee.com/html/201302/06/22518.html. Accessed 13 February 2013.

Woo, Margaret Y.K. (2013), 'Bounded legality: China's developmental state and civil dispute resolution', *Maryland Journal of International Law*, 27(1): 235–62.

Xie, Yue (2013), 'Rising central spending on public security and the dilemma facing grassroots officials in China', *Journal of Current Chinese Affairs*, 42(2): 79–109.

Yu, Jianrong (2010), 'Holding tight and not letting go: the mechanisms of "rigid stability"', *Global China* 5/2, http://www.globalasia.org/Issue/Detail/13/inside-china.html. Accessed 13 February 2013.

Zhang, Taisu (2009), 'Zhongguoren zai xingzheng jiufenzhong weihe pianhao xingfen?' (Why the Chinese Public Prefer Administrative Petitioning over Litigation), *Shehuixue yanjiu* (Sociological Studies), 3: 139–62.

Zhang, Taisu (2012), 'The Pragmatic court: reinterpreting the Supreme People's Court of China', *Columbia Journal of Asian Law*, 25: 1–61.

Zhao, Suisheng (2011), 'The China model and the authoritarian state', *East Asia Forum*, 2: 12–13, http://www.eastasiaforum.org/2011/08/31/the-china-model-and-the-authoritarian-state/. Accessed 15 September 2013.

Zhou, Kaili (2010), 'Sifa xinfanghua qushi yinfa danyou' (Trend in the petition-izing of justice becoming an increasing concern), *Caixin*, 2 December, http://china.caixin.com/2010-12-02/100203981.html. Accessed 2 July 2013.

Zhu, Suli (2010), 'Guanyu nengdong sifa yu datiaojie' (On judicial activism and grand mediation), *Zhongguo faxue* (Legal Science in China), 1: 5–16.

PART 1

Managing disputes

2. Management of stability in labour relations

Sarah Biddulph

INTRODUCTION

Workers occupy a central position in the ideology of the socialist state. In theory they continue to occupy the position of 'masters' of the country. They enjoy a range of constitutionally protected labour rights such as the right and duty to work; freedom of association, procession and demonstration; and the right to rest and to receive material assistance from the state and society when they are old, ill or disabled. Women and men enjoy equal rights. Workers' rights are defined and given specific form by legislation and to a great extent are dependent upon state action for their fulfilment. Private civil law enforcement mechanisms exist, but in important respects are of limited scope and are ineffective to pressure for broader structural changes in either economic policy or the labour market.

The right to subsistence and development underpins these rights. In the case of workers this right is articulated as a right to share the benefits of economic reform and development. The 12th Five Year Blueprint on Economic and Social Development (12th Five Year Plan) launched in March 2011 reaffirms that the ultimate objective of economic reform and modernization is to improve the people's livelihood (Chapter 2: Fundamental Principles).[1] This improvement is the explicit objective of establishing a moderately well-off society (*xiaokang shehui*), and in turn is understood to be key to underpinning social stability. The Harmonious Society Policy also articulates this idea; social stability is promoted through enabling all people to share the benefits of economic reform and

[1] http://news.sina.com.cn/c/2011-03-17/055622129864.shtml. Accessed 10 June 2011.

development.[2] The objective of promoting social stability is connected explicitly to all talk of rights protection and may be understood as integral to any analysis of the rights afforded to labour. China's unions, for example, articulated the linkage as one where protection of the right to participate in the benefits of economic development is for the purpose of promoting stability in labour relations (Wang 2001).

But the privileged rights-bearing position occupied by workers in theory and the promise that they will have an opportunity to share in the benefits of economic development is not matched by the reality of life for the vast majority of China's workers. Transformation of the economy has brought about stark and growing inequality in the distribution of benefits of economic growth between government and enterprise on one hand and workers on the other. There is also a vast inequality within the labour market itself, with the lowest levels of the labour market, such as migrant workers and labour hire workers, obtaining a disproportionately small share of total wages. And, unsurprisingly, the goal of industrial and social stability also remains remote.

Throughout the 1990s and the 2000s there has been a dramatic increase in strikes, go-slows, mass petitioning and even large-scale, violent protests (Lee 2005). The number of officially recorded labour disputes rose from 135,000 in 2000 to 314,000 in 2005 (Quan and Li 2012: 188). Low wage levels and employment insecurity exacerbate other insecurities created by the current model of economic reform, including limited access to and cost of education, lack of affordable and reliable healthcare, and land and housing insecurity. The systematic failure of China's industrial relations system to protect workers from abusive practices and to ensure a basic level of subsistence, along with the consequent surge in labour disputes and protests, raises the issue of the extent to which this increase in protest might develop into broader social and political instability (Li 1999, Chung et al. 2006).

This chapter focuses on one aspect of the multi-pronged approach adopted by the Party-state to deal with the problem of industrial unrest, that is, labour unrest as a problem of social order. It discusses the different interpretations by state agencies of the nature of labour-related disputes and protests, the degree of risk they are seen to pose to social order (or vested interests), and the range of official responses to deal with

---

[2] The Harmonious Society policy was formally adopted at the close of the Sixth Plenary session of the 16th CPC Central Committee meeting on 11 October 2006 in the Resolution on Major Issues Regarding the Building of a Harmonious Socialist Society, http://www.china.org.cn/english/report/189591.htm, accessed 18 September 2013.

labour protests in both the short and long term. We see that a few of those responses are to strengthen law and law enforcement. More commonly, both short and long term administrative measures are adopted. In some cases the aim is to rectify the worst abuses, with 'rights protection' serving as a means of promoting social stability. These reform measures have included legislative and policy reforms to improve both wages and the conditions of work.

However, the over-sensitivity of the Party-state to publicly disruptive conduct means that labour protests are often characterized as social order 'emergencies' that require some more direct form of intervention – to deal with the actual incident and to strengthen the state's early warning mechanisms and its capacity to forestall escalation of disputes. These strategies focus squarely on the problem of restoring order in the short term. Protesting workers thus readily fall within the purview of the state's social order protection policies and the mechanisms that have been developed to address problems of crime and other unlawful or socially disruptive conduct. Like the Comprehensive Management of Public Order that preceded today's comprehensive social management policies, these policies pretend to be comprehensive at a time when the pluralization of both state and social interests makes a comprehensive and coordinated, state-led approach to management of social order difficult to achieve. We see deployment of a range of interlinking approaches that involve mobilization of Party, state and other agencies to implement a range of administrative measures. These measures may in some cases improve law enforcement but in other cases circumvent or act as a substitute for formal legal channels of dispute resolution. Finally, where a protest is large and violent, a punitive approach is taken to suppress the protest and punish its leaders.

These features of the Party-state's response to industrial unrest illustrate a number of the broader themes developed in this volume. Three are mentioned here. The first is the prevailing view of social stability as a form of 'rigid stability', which prominent scholar of rural development Yu Jianrong asserts depends on the coercive power of the state and requires absolute social order. That is, social stability is understood as the existence of an 'orderly and non-conflictual' social sphere discussed in the introductory chapter to this volume. Such a form of stability eschews many forms of disruption and protest as pathological and as posing a direct threat to social stability. From there, it is a short step to see these disruptions as undermining political stability. From such a standpoint, mass protests and strikes are readily interpreted as a social order crisis. Yu Jianrong poses an alternative view of stability, which he labels resilient or flexible stability. A core feature of a system that has resilient stability is a functioning legal system that provides a mechanism for the peaceful resolution of disputes. The functioning legal system on which resilient stability is based enables disputes, the vast majority of which are over material interests, to be aired and resolved with finality as part of the ordinary processes of governance. Such a view of stability is less ready to view disputes and other forms of social disruption related to dispute settlement (such as strikes) as a direct threat to political stability (Yu 2009). This chapter traces a number of occasions where protest and labour unrest has been characterized as a social order emergency, illustrating the ready extrapolation from protest to a conclusion that social stability is imperilled and reinforcing the rigid stability view.

The second theme is connected to the first, which is the willingness of the Party-state to bypass legal processes at times of perceived social order crisis. This chapter documents a range of administrative measures including early warning, enforcement campaigns and emergency response used at times of perceived crisis. Whilst these measures are not themselves illegal, they often circumvent legal processes, or impose administrative overlays on top of legal processes. These responses perpetuate a political-administrative approach to law making and enforcement and the preference for top-down, state-led law enforcement (Biddulph et al. 2012).

The third theme is the state's demand to keep disputes and protests localized. A consistent approach of the Party-state has been to assign primary responsibility for dispute resolution or dissolution to local governments, to ensure that disputes, protests and petitioners do not leave the local area. In particular, in the area of labour, the union movement has implemented policies and programmes to increase the number of working people organized under the union umbrella and improve delivery of services in part to circumvent other forms of independent organization they may undertake.

DISPUTES, DISPUTE RESOLUTION AND INSTABILITY

How is the rising level of labour unrest understood by state actors? The answer becomes a significant factor in determining the range of state responses to protests, which range from accommodation to violent suppression. Before examining different types of labour unrest, it is necessary to set out some brief points about the regulatory framework governing labour relations since this framework shapes, even produces, the ways in which labour grievances are vented.

The existing regulatory regime has individualized labour relations by way of the labour contract, which in turn has tended to individualize and privatize disputes. Opportunities to exercise collective labour power, either to bargain or to seek redress for grievances, have also been severely circumscribed. The authorized union movement has been unwilling and unable to act as a strong advocate for workers and the state has been implacably opposed to attempts to establish independent unions or worker representative organizations. Given a reasonable opportunity to pursue a grievance, workers have demonstrated a willingness to use legal dispute resolution channels of arbitration and litigation. For example, after passage of the Labour Contract Law and the Labour Disputes Mediation and Arbitration Law (LDMA), the number of labour arbitration and litigation cases increased dramatically. In fact, after 2008 the bulk of labour arbitration cases threatened to overwhelm the capacity of the labour arbitration bureau to deal with them.[3] However, there are many types of grievance that cannot be addressed adequately through individual dispute resolution channels. Wage-setting disputes are one. Another involves worker complaints against corrupt misappropriation of enterprise assets by company managers, which prejudices the viability of the company hence employment and pension entitlements.

Many protests have arisen where workers are laid off due to state-enterprise bankruptcy or reorganization, without being paid and/or without receiving entitlements and pensions as required. Other protests relate to low wages, unpaid wages, workplace disciplinary violence and failure to provide medical or accident insurance or compensation. Popular protests such as strikes, sit-ins and petitioning generally share the characteristics of being fragmented, narrowly framed and arising in response to the immediate complaint. Protesters do not generally challenge the legitimacy of the central state or the leadership of the Communist Party of China (CPC). Neither do they seek to include any expansion of participation by people with similar complaints but from different enterprises. Ching Kwan Lee has labelled this form of fragmented and narrowly framed protest 'cellular activism' (Lee 2007).

Protesters are mostly careful to avoid framing their complaints and demands in a manner that could be interpreted as political (Chen 2007: 274). At most, protesters might challenge the legitimacy of local government where it is implicated in corrupt dealings of local enterprise managers, as was the case in the Liaoyang Ferro-Alloy Factory dispute

---

3 For an extensive discussion of these points see Cooney et al. (2013).

(Lee 2007: 241–2). Many collective actions, even those that are disruptive, are framed as a form of 'rightful resistance'; to stay close to lawful channels of dispute resolution and to employ officially authorized language to legitimate their claims (O'Brien 1996: 33, Chen 2007: 255).[4] These types of protest, which often progress through formal to informal and then back to formal channels of dispute resolution, illustrate the porous boundary between institutionalized dispute resolution and non-institutionalized conflict resolution (Lee 2007: 231). They also illustrate a significant failing of the current institutionalized dispute resolution mechanisms to provide a final resolution to grievances that is acceptable to all parties.

From a policing perspective, these large-scale public protests, strikes, mass petitioning and other forms of public action are characterized as 'mass incidents', which require the government to take a leading role in their resolution (Ren 2005: 49). The police are often called to the front line to deal with these protests. Many police officers see these protests as based on a legitimate grievance and even feel some sympathy for the protesters (Chung et al. 2006, Li 1999). In many instances the police do not use violence to disperse crowds. Police research into mass incidents characterizes this type of conflict as a predictable outcome of economic reform and development. They are seen as conflicts between different interest groups over material interests (Ren 2005: 49). It is significant that these types of protest are characterized as non-antagonistic contradictions, as in principle they should be addressed without resort to violent suppression and ideally through the use of education and persuasion to defuse the situation. However, when these conflicts become 'confrontational' in form, policing responses are affected (Ren 2005: 259–63).

Over time ever more protests are becoming larger, better organized and more violent as the underlying grievances are not satisfactorily resolved (Wang 2001). However, police also view the increase in this type of dispute as carrying a high degree of political risk. If such disputes are handled appropriately they can contribute to social stability. If, however, they are handled inappropriately, what is in essence a conflict over material interests has the potential to intensify, to become increasingly confrontational and to seriously undermine social stability (Ren 2005: 49). Police see this type of incident as difficult to manage, or 'complex' because of the large numbers of people often involved in different

[4] O'Brien (1996: 36–9) has labelled the range of conduct from non-cooperation, to petitioning and protest as 'rightful resistance' as it does not seek to oppose the state but to elicit state assistance to correct local wrongdoings.

capacities (Ren 2005: 263–4, Tanner 2004: 140–2). In protests that involve large numbers of people or touch on politically sensitive areas, or that are confrontational or violent, the boundary may easily be crossed from a protest dealt with as a non-antagonistic contradiction to one where the response is to use force. For these types of protest, characterized as a riot or as a contradiction that should be seen as essentially antagonistic, employment of state violence to quash the protest is seen as necessary.

There is thus a risk that disputes framed to fall within the bounds of 'rightful resistance' may become characterized as political, or if they become confrontational, may bring down the state's repressive violence on the heads of the people identified as ringleaders, especially where the interests of the local government are challenged. One of the best-known illustrations of a protest framed as 'rightful' that resulted in the use of violence to suppress it was the extended protest by workers in a number of factories in Liaoyang, Liaoning province. It started with those employed in the Liaoyang Ferro-Alloy Factory and culminated in 2002. That enterprise was bankrupted in 2001 following several years of corrupt misappropriation of enterprise funds and assets by the enterprise director. This left little prospect that workers owed back wages, pension payments, welfare, medical and housing subsidies or severance pay under law would recover their entitlements. Workers at that factory organized mass protests and sit-ins. In addition to demanding their pay and other entitlements, they demanded removal of corrupt enterprise directors and the Provincial congressman believed to have been implicated in the corruption from their positions (Lee 2007: 238–43).

The state's crackdown on the protests and those identified as its leaders was harsh. Yao Fuxin and Xiao Yuanling were accused of organizing the unrest and were charged and convicted of subverting state power. They were sentenced to seven and three years' imprisonment respectively (Kent 2007:199–202). This case created an international outcry resulting in the International Confederation of Free Trade Unions (ICFTU) and the International Metalworkers Association (IMA) bringing a case to the International Labour Organization's Committee on Freedom of Association (CFA). Their case, Case 2189, was in respect of the intimidation, arrest and beating of workers accused of leading worker protests in Liaoning, Heilongjiang, Sichuan and Shanxi in 2002.[5] In its interim

[5] Case No. 2189, Report No. 333 (China): Complaint against the Government of China presented by the International Confederation of Free Trade Unions (ICFTU) and the International Metalworkers' Federation (IMF), http://www.ilo.org/public/english/standards/relm/gb/docs/gb289/pdf/gb-9.pdf, accessed 18 September 2013.

report, the CFA requested that an independent investigation be conducted into allegations of violent police intervention in the protests, torture, beating and mistreatment of worker representatives. It also requested that charges of terrorism, sabotage and subversion be dropped in respect of protests at the Liaoyang Ferro-Alloy Factory. However, China disregarded 'essentially all of [the CFA's] previous recommendations'.[6] This case is illustrative of China's domestic and international posture on protests that are perceived by the state to touch on politically sensitive issues of social order and independent union organization.

Other large-scale violent protests have arisen in the context of accumulated grievances but were never framed as 'rightful'. Two well-known recent examples illustrate this. On 6 June 2011, after a factory manager seriously wounded a migrant worker and his father after they confronted him seeking payment of wages owed, a violent mass protest erupted in Chaozhou, Guangdong province. Reportedly over 200 migrant workers gathered in front of government buildings and, in the ensuing violent confrontation with local residents and police, cars were smashed and burned (Qiu 2011). In the second incident, on 13 June 2011 the *South China Morning Post* reported that over 1,000 migrant workers had been involved in rioting over a three-day period, sparked by security guards' harassment of a pregnant migrant worker peddling goods outside a supermarket in Dandun village, Xintang, Zhencheng, central Guangdong (Lau 2012). This protest was subsequently labelled a 'riot', which provided an official justification for using harsh repressive measures against the 'small number of elements who created chaos'.[7] Apparently in dealing with the riot in Xintang, the authorities were instructed to take severe repressive measures and to make an example of the leaders of the protest.

As we have seen with other major violent incidents, such as the Weng'an Incident,[8] identifying a small number of instigators enables the authorities to use extreme force, but at the same time attempts, in public

[6] Case No. 2189, Report No. 333 (China) paragraph 384.

[7] Guangzhou Xintang 'Baoluan' gaocheng xialing yanli zhenya youren haozhao chetui bagong (Senior leaders order a harsh crackdown in Guangzhou Xintang 'Riot', some people call for a retreat from the strike) 13 June 2011, http://boxun.com/news/gb/china/2011/06/201106131100.shtml. Accessed 17 June 2011.

[8] In June 2008 tens of thousands of residents in Weng'an County, Qiannan Buyei and Miao Autonomous Prefecture, in the Guizhou province of Southwest China smashed government buildings and torched several police cars to protest against an alleged police cover-up of a girl's death, see Fewsmith (2008).

at least, to divert attention from the broader nature of the underlying grievance. Where a protest, such as the one in Xintang in June 2011, is reclassified as a riot and so an antagonistic contradiction, serious punishment or techniques of suppression are seen as not only justified but required.

RESPONSES: ‘RIGHTS PROTECTION’ FOCUSING ON STABILITY

The description above suggests that labour protests arise out of an accumulation of grievances, including the multiple failures of the legal and institutional structures to protect basic living standards of workers. Acknowledging the systematic institutional and legal failings that give rise to these grievances, the state has adopted a range of strategies to take both short- and longer-term measures to rectify the worst shortcomings and abuses (Lum 2006: 8–9). These responses are explicitly aimed at promoting industrial and social harmony and are often framed in terms of rights protection. They suggest that the state sees rights protection as serving the primary national objective of protecting stability. These measures include increasing the minimum wage, expanding unionization of ‘vulnerable’ groups such as migrant workers, legislative reform to address some of the most glaring deficiencies in the legal regime, improving accessibility of formal dispute resolution mechanisms such as arbitration and litigation, strengthening union programmes to focus on ‘rights protection’, expanding the reach of collective consultation and collective contracting, and even experimenting with ways of bypassing the enterprise union in doing so (see Cooney et al. 2013, Biddulph 2012).

However, rights are articulated in a very particular way: as an undertaking by the state to adopt measures to protect subsistence rights and provide citizens an opportunity to participate in the benefits of a ‘moderately well-off society’. None of the reforms goes so far as to change the basic regulatory framework for labour relations. They preserve the existing characteristics of state-centric regulation and law enforcement, and do not loosen existing constraints on the development of decentralized or coordinating mechanisms, such as collective bargaining. There remains some degree of wariness about expanding law enforcement through civil dispute resolution mechanisms, especially about advice and assistance that may be provided to claimants by labour NGOs and unlicensed lawyers. One feature of the state’s response to perceived crises has been to employ administrative mechanisms to address failures in law enforcement or to deal with instability that arises as a result of those failures. Some mechanisms supplement the law and others circumvent it (Biddulph et al. 2012). To the extent that they circumvent formal legal processes, they weaken long-term legitimacy of the law as an institution for social ordering and dispute resolution.

A range of responses deals with public protests purely as a problem of managing social order. Whilst the police are often the frontline agency called on to deal with protests, other local agencies, including the local government, labour bureau, courts and unions also play a role in pre-empting or preventing escalation of the protest. As noted above, police are acutely aware of the underlying grievances that give rise to public protest and are often sympathetic to these protesters' claims. In many cases these views shape police responses to dealing with protests. However, police capacity to act on this understanding is limited where the protest becomes confrontational, or where there are conflicting demands by local governments. The interests of local governments are often in conflict with those of workers through local government ownership of, or collusive relationship with, local enterprises (Oi 1992).

But dealing with protests is not limited to police responses. Local residents' committees, government agencies and unions have also been tasked with early discovery of discontent. Early warning mechanisms have been established at the local level to discover potential sources of unrest and a range of strategies have been adopted to prevent escalation of those grievances or disputes. Coordinated dispute resolution mechanisms such as grand mediation have been established to tackle labour-related grievances and to assist in circumventing problems.

MANAGEMENT OF STABILITY: EARLY WARNING AND EMERGENCY RESPONSE MECHANISMS

Labour instability is one of the core concerns of the Party's Protection of Stability Committee. One report indicates the CPC Central Committee first established a multi-agency stability protection mechanism in the late 1990s to respond to the social unrest arising from restructuring and bankruptcy of state-owned enterprises (Liao 2009). It has since evolved into the Central Committee's Office of the Leadership Small Group for Protection of Social Stability Work (Stability Protection Office). This office, in which the trade unions are also represented, plays a central role in developing labour policy, coordinating social management and coordinating responses to mass incidents, to prevent, minimize or deal with protests. For example, momentum to strengthen establishment of union and Party grassroots organizations in foreign investment enterprises came from Hu Jintao's speech, 'Analysis of the Factors Leading to Instability in Foreign Investment Enterprises in China's Coastal Areas and Recommended Countermeasures', which he delivered at the Central Committee's Stability Preservation Office on 14 March 2008. In this speech he recommended 'improving legal regulation, strengthening coordination mechanisms between labour and capital, and strengthening establishment of Party and union organs in foreign investment enterprises' (Liao 2009). A characteristic of this style of management is the coordination of a range of organizations – state, Party and other mass organizations – under the leadership of a high-level Party committee using tools reminiscent of central planning. It is also characterized by the flexible use of a range of policy, administrative and legal tools to achieve desired outcomes.

Responses to Perceived Crises

The policies adopted to deal with the destabilizing effects of the global financial crisis (GFC) on industrial relations, particularly between the first quarter of 2008 and the third quarter of 2009, provide a recent illustration of state responses to a perceived labour crisis.[9] The GFC did not have a deep or lasting effect in China, but this outcome was not apparent at the onset of the crisis. The difficulties facing export-oriented enterprises during this period gave cover to some enterprises for unlawful and abusive practices such as delayed payment of wages, and failure to pay wages, overtime and social insurance payments (Yang 2009: 1). The 2008–09 period thus saw a significant increase in labour disputes, petitioning and mass protests, alongside enterprise closure, wage arrears, and some managers even locking the factory door and running away, leaving wage and other commitments unmet (Yang 2009).

At the time there was a perception that the risks of social instability arising from the GFC were high. In Guangzhou in 2009, for example, labour disputes accounted for more than 70 per cent of cases heard by the Number 1 Civil Division of the Guangzhou Intermediate People's Court.[10] Concern about the increase in labour disputes from 2008 spurred

---

[9] '2009 Nian laozi maodun beijing: Guoji jinrong weiji' (The background to labour conflicts in 2009: the Global Financial Crisis), 14 December 2009, http://news.sina.com.cn/c/sd/2009-12-14/094219255581_2.shtml. Accessed 30 May 2011.

[10] Guangzhou: Laozi Jiufen Chengwei Yinxiang Shehui Wending Di Yi Yinsu (Guangzhou: Labour disputes have become the number one factor affecting social stability) http://acftu.people.com.cn/GB/11177287.html. Accessed 20 May 2011.

multi-agency meetings and programmes to address labour instability. One meeting convened on 18 March 2010, for example, comprised representatives of the political-legal committee of the Party, government, court, procuratorate, lawyers' association, industry association, unions and academia.

Nationwide, a number of short-term administrative measures were adopted in late 2008 to deal with the GFC. These included instituting a temporary freeze on the minimum wage (Yang 2009) and adoption of a range of measures to underpin the viability of enterprises and to prevent employee layoffs.[11] Funds earmarked for unemployment benefits were diverted to employment preservation and expanding wage guarantee funds. Workers were encouraged to cooperate with companies, support flexible working hours, improve productivity and reduce cost. Special emphasis was placed on setting up effective early response mechanisms to emergencies from large-scale or violent mass incidents through strengthening information sharing between unions, enterprises and government, and taking concerted action in serious cases.

In some local areas, special measures were adopted to minimize the potential for escalation of disputes. These involved coordinated responses from all agencies that have a role in labour dispute resolution. For example, from the end of 2007 until the end of 2008 in Jinjiang, Fujian, a city with 5,500 registered small and medium-sized enterprises mostly in the footwear, clothing, textiles and food products sectors and with a concentration of migrant workers, the number of disputes over pay, workers' compensation and labour insurance payments more than doubled. This increase was attributed to difficulties arising from the changing terms of export trade, which were exacerbated by the GFC. To limit the social disruption caused by these disputes, the local government and court set up a specialist labour disputes division with an associated labour rights protection centre. This centre comprises a one-stop service staffed by representatives of the government, court, justice department, unions, chamber of commerce, industrial and commercial bureau and the police to work together to deal with labour disputes more quickly and effectively. Its motto was 'Don't let one migrant worker fail to receive protection of their lawful rights and interests'. As in other places, the city government established an 'Enterprise Wages Protection Adjustment

---

[11] Vigorously implement the 'Mutually Agreed Action' between Trade Unions, Enterprises and Employees to promote unity and to mobilize the broad masses of workers to contribute to stable and rapid economic development 30 December 2008 at http://www.npc.gov.cn/npc/xinwen/syxw/2008-12/30/content_1465498.htm. Accessed 28 May 2011.

Fund' to ensure that demands for payment of unpaid wages could be met if they could not be recovered from the employer (People's Daily Online 2008).[12]

Actions taken during this period of perceived crisis illustrate the state's ready resort to the use of coordinated top-down administrative measures as a means to allocate tasks and responsibilities to respond to problems of labour unrest. In this situation, workers were called upon to make sacrifices in their conditions of employment to preserve the viability of their employers, whilst employers received payments and benefits on the basis of undertakings to maintain employment rates.

The Enforcement Campaign

Another striking illustration of the ready resort to coordinated political-administrative responses to address perceived crises was the three-year wages campaign waged between 2004 and 2007. This campaign was launched in response to escalating worker protests arising from serious and systemic failure to pay wages earned and owing to workers in certain sectors of the economy. Impetus for the campaign was the systemic and chronic abuse of migrant workers' rights to be paid their wages, particularly in the construction industry. The reach of the campaign ended up being much broader. The campaign in form was modelled on earlier campaigns, extending for a total of three years and divided into annual stages. It was overseen by a specially created Leadership Small Group under the leadership of a Vice-Premier. Performance targets were allocated to all relevant government agencies, to the courts and to mass organizations such as unions. They were backed up by regular reporting requirements and random inspections to ensure that reported achievements were, in fact, real (discussed in detail in Biddulph et al. 2012). Requiring that priority be given to passing rules to resolve structural problems and to enforcement in this area has made the political-administrative nature of the campaign explicit. This campaign did manage to overcome barriers to enforcement resulting from lack of both resources and will and from the detrimental impact of the 'silo' mentality of government agencies. However, it arguably had a detrimental long-term impact on development of stable and robust legal mechanisms for dealing with such problems. (The campaign and these issues are discussed in detail in Biddulph et al. 2012.)

---

12 See also Su, Yang and He Xin (2010) discussing the establishment of 'stability maintenance funds' in an unnamed county in Guangdong.

Early Warning Mechanisms

At the local level, governments and unions have adopted a range of early intervention strategies that seek to deal with disputes early and prevent their escalation. From the early 2000s (Wang 2001), the unions have established and headed up nationwide tripartite Labour Disputes Early Warning and Emergency Management Organs, with their mission being 'early discovery, early reporting, early involvement, and early coordination' of a response to minimize labour disputes and prevent intensification of a dispute into a mass incident (Lu 2009: 48). Failure by union officials to carry out their responsibilities diligently or to discover and report the 'seeds' of a mass incident will be punished (Sun 2001). As at 2005 there were reported to be 5,088 such organs nationwide (Zhong 2006).

As part of their efforts to resolve disputes before they escalate, unions in a number of areas have established complaint hotlines and information centres, and have sought to improve mediation and their handling of complaints lodged by letter and office visit and to strengthen mediation (Zhong 2006, Lu 2009: 48, Sun 2001). However, unions have played an ambiguous role in dispute resolution, acting as an intermediary between the parties and giving priority to obtaining a return to work over representing worker demands. As many strikes are wildcat strikes, unions are often last to find out about the dispute (Chen 2010: 110).

The continuing high level of strikes and violent conflict demonstrates that the early warning mechanism and the regularized dispute resolution channels of arbitration and litigation have failed, in part at least, to resolve labour disputes. The wave of highly publicized suicides at the Foxconn Group Shenzhen plant and extended strikes at three Honda plants in early and mid-2010 highlighted the inability of unions to forestall industrial action and the fundamental weakness of unions not organized by the workers themselves (Feng 2011:167). They also made very public the crisis of legitimacy facing the unions (Rulliat 2010).

Where early warning mechanisms fail to prevent a dispute escalating, local governments are responsible for ensuring that it does not intensify. When a labour-related 'mass incident' occurs, responsible leaders from the Party, government and union are required to attend in person to supervise its handling and early resolution. Under the PRC Emergency Response Law, local governments have primary responsibility for handling major strikes or protests (Article 7, see also Chen 2010: 109). Again, failure to respond adequately can result in punishment for the responsible officials, whose performance appraisal depends upon preventing the occurrence of mass incidents (Wang 2001, Sun 2001). Some mass incidents, especially grievances over failure to pay wages, can be resolved by payment of some, or all, of the outstanding claim. As Su and He (2010) have documented, the process of negotiating a settlement in some cases is carried out by the court on an ad hoc basis, outside the bounds of ordinary litigation procedures.

The discussion above illustrates the extent of cooperation between government and other agencies in establishing special emergency response mechanisms not only to give priority to dealing with labour disputes, and wage disputes in particular, but also to ensure unpaid wage claims can be met. It also highlights the extent to which wages and labour disputes have become perceived as a problem of social order and much more serious and widespread than the Party-state feels it can afford to leave to individually accessed mechanisms to resolve. In fact, the state may have no choice but to intervene, as many violent protests may start as a dispute over wages or conditions, but, especially in the case of migrant workers, very quickly become public expressions of pent-up anger over long-term and broad-ranging discrimination and mistreatment.

Multi-agency collaboration is illustrative of the regulatory approach to supervision and of the enforcement of policies and legal standards that remains concentrated in the hands of state agencies. In situations of crisis, the courts, unions and industry representatives are expected to act in strict concert with government and Party agencies and to form a relatively seamless part of the administrative arrangements put in place. This regulatory model risks creating a vicious cycle where the Party-state concentrates power in its own hands to deal with crises. And in preventing any meaningful empowerment of unions to focus on representation of worker interests, or of workers to take action to protect their own rights, this model ensures that demands will continue to be made to the state to rectify these problems.

Reactive Strategies: Responding to Mass Incidents

The continuing high level of strikes, petitioning, mass incidents and violent conflict demonstrates that early warning mechanisms and the use of regularized dispute resolution channels of arbitration and litigation have failed, in part at least, to resolve labour disputes. When strategies to prevent a protest fail, or simply fail to identify a potential problem, the police, or if the protest is very serious the armed police, are commonly the agency called to respond. Once this happens, violence is not uncommon (Chan 2011). From the late 1990s the number of mass incidents arising out of labour disputes has increased significantly, with reports of an average annual increase of 30 per cent in the number of labour disputes over the period 1997–2003 (Ren 2005: 59). In general this type of protest is characterized as 'non-antagonistic', as it relates to conflicts over material interests. However, their confrontational nature has led to divergence of opinion about the best approach to dealing with them.

Conduct that disrupts public order such as petitioning, strikes and mass incidents may be punished under a range of legal instruments. A wide range of petitioning conduct has recently been classed as 'abnormal' if it is not compliant with the forms of petitioning authorized in the 2005 State Council Regulations on Letters and Visits. A person or group carrying out 'abnormal' petitioning may be liable to 'retrieval' and/or punishment (Sapio 2011: 213–20).[13] Failure to conform to the restrictive scope of permitted petitioning set out in the 2005 State Council Regulations on Letters and Visits renders a person liable to punishment under the Security Administrative Punishments Law (SAPL), or, if the matter is serious, under the Criminal Law.[14] They may also be designated as part of the focal population and then subjected to intensive local surveillance (Biddulph 2007: 116–17, Wang 2005).

Local government retrieval policies and practices have received a great deal of critical attention as they involve imposition of unlawful detention and other unauthorized punishments. Whilst formal legal authority to punish petitioners is only just emerging, police have clear powers to impose administrative punishments on those who engage in strikes and public protests that breach the 1989 Law on Assemblies Processions and Demonstrations,[15] or otherwise disrupt public order under a range of powers, including the SAPL and the Criminal Law.

The arrest in October 2010 of two executives of the Anyuanding private security company in Beijing and the launch of a six-month police crackdown on illegal activities of private security companies threw the practices of private security into the spotlight. The case of Anyuanding illustrates the extent to which private enterprise and the market have penetrated the policing of social order. Local governments anxious to

---

13 An example is the 2009 Shenzhen Notice on Handling Abnormal Petitioning According to the Law, issued jointly by the Shenzhen Intermediate People's Court, People's Procuratorate, Public Security Bureau and Justice Bureau.

14 Ministry of Public Security, Guiding Opinion on the Relevant Law for Handling Unlawful and Criminal Conduct in Letters and Visits Activities, 2008.

15 Articles 28, 29 and 30 provide for the issue of a warning or punishment of up to 15 days' administrative detention under the SAPL, or punishment under the Criminal Law, for carrying out demonstrations that contravene the law and disrupt social order.

retrieve petitioners before they can blot the social order record of the local government have used a range of coercive retrieval practices. One of long standing was to contract out retrieval work to private security firms, which intercepted, detained and forcibly repatriated petitioners for punishment in their home place.

Violent Protests

There are now significant numbers of cases where an incident triggers widespread and extreme violence. In particular the long-term mistreatment of groups of migrant workers by local governments and employers has resulted in large-scale violent riots where government buildings and cars are smashed and burned. Whilst some might argue that these are not labour disputes, I would argue that they are quintessentially grounded in the failure to protect basic labour rights. In Guangdong, for example, the 2011 Xintang and Chaozhou riots involved migrant workers from Sichuan who were able to rally support from large numbers of other Sichuanese workers through the use of new information technology.

Apart from the violence of these protests and the subsequent confrontations with authorities, it is of significant concern to authorities that such a large number of people who had not been involved in the actual dispute, or who were not based in the same town, came to support the protest. Arguably these types of protest differ from the form of cellular activism described by Ching Kwan Lee, which is spontaneous protests arising in response to 'local and work unit based' issues (Lee 2007: 238). Whilst the protests themselves were triggered by a local or work unit-related incident, participation in the riots quickly spread beyond those immediately involved. In the case of Xintang, tweets were sent out calling on other Sichuanese to join the protest and many did, or sought to travel to Xintang. Willingness to participate in such a protest could be understood as motivated by solidarity with people from one's home place coupled with a shared antagonism born of common experience of discriminatory and unfair treatment.

The local state is not unmindful of the dangers that a large population of disenfranchised migrant workers poses to long-term social stability. In some areas efforts have been made to include migrant workers in positions within local government. Such programmes remain small and tentative. Much more is required to integrate migrant workers into urban communities. Other sources hint that the number of exceptions to the predominant form of labour protests described by the model of cellular activism is growing. Research by Chris Chan and Pun Ngai (2009) on the organization of industrial action including strikes in the factories of the

Pearl River Delta suggests that the work experience of second generation migrant workers has characteristics of a newly emerging class consciousness. Their research documents the ways in which workers take their industrial disputing experience to other factories and that workers are no longer fragmented into individual factory groups.

CONCLUSION: WHAT IS THE RELATIONSHIP BETWEEN RIGHTS AND STABILITY?

Labour is one of the areas where there is a clear acknowledgment that the failure to protect rights links directly with social instability. Yet even here we have seen only partial embrace of legal mechanisms by the state as a way of better protecting workers' rights. The Party-state has largely bypassed the opportunity to strengthen civil enforcement mechanisms, for example through allowing labour NGOs greater freedom to provide education and litigation support to workers. It has also put on hold the opportunity to enable adjustment of the interests of labour and capital through reforms that would enable development of more adversarial approaches to collective bargaining. Relaxing the prohibition on creation of independent unions is beyond the realm of possibilities under the current political system. Instead, in dealing with perceived crises there has been resort to shorter-term administrative mechanisms that are not unlawful, but are extra-legal, such as establishing local funds to meet demands from migrant workers for unpaid wages.

Cooperation between government and other agencies illustrated above highlights the extent to which labour disputes are treated as a problem more of social order than of rights. These problems are seen as much more serious and widespread than the Party-state feels it can afford to leave to private mechanisms to resolve. That perception is correct at a number of levels. First, private interest adjustment and civil dispute resolution mechanisms currently cannot adequately address the institutionalized imbalances between labour and capital. Second, many perceive that the ultimate responsibility for their plight somehow lies with the state, either indirectly through failure to establish a trustworthy and fair regulatory regime, or directly through corrupt or other improper relationships between enterprises and local government. Local Party and government officials may therefore have no choice but to intervene in disputes when they arise. As we have seen in Chaozhou and Xintang in 2011, protests may start as a dispute over wages or harassment for peddling goods in the street, but very quickly escalate into public expressions of pent-up anger over longer-term mistreatment.

Part of the problem may lie in the Party-state's willingness to view many forms of disruption as an emergency. It illustrates the lack of confidence in the existing regulatory framework to deal with conflict, a lack of confidence that may be warranted. Another part of the problem may be that the current stability protection mindset is unable to distinguish between different types of social upheaval, seeing them all as a threat to political stability. As Professor Yu Jianrong has explained, desire for a form of 'rigid stability' eschews social upheaval, but ultimately this stability cannot be achieved. The tentative reforms to improve the stability and resilience of the legal regulatory system, that is to promote a model of flexible stability, have so far at least been unequal to the task.

REFERENCES

Biddulph, Sarah (2007), *Legal Reform and Administrative Detention Powers in China.* Cambridge: Cambridge University Press.

Biddulph, Sarah (2012), 'Responding to industrial unrest in China: prospects for strengthening the role of collective bargaining', *Sydney University Law Review*, 34: 35–63.

Biddulph, Sarah, Cooney, Sean and Zhu, Ying (2012), 'Rule of law with Chinese characteristics: the role of campaigns in law-making', *Law & Policy*, 34 (4): 373–401.

Chan, Anita (2011), 'Strikes in China's export industries in comparative perspective', *The China Journal*, 65: 27–51.

Chan, Chris King-Chi and Pun Ngai (2009), 'The making of a new working class? A study of collective actions of migrant workers in south China', *The China Quarterly*, 198: 287–303.

Chen, Feng (2010), 'Trade unions and the quadripartite interactions in strike settlement in China', *The China Quarterly*, 102: 104–24.

Chen, Xi (2007), 'Between defiance and obediance: protest opportunism in China', in Elizabeth Perry and Merle Goldman (eds.), *Grassroots Political Reform in Contemporary China.* Cambridge, MA and London: Harvard University Press, pp. 253–81.

Chung, Jae Ho, Lai Hongyi and Xia, Ming (2006), 'Mounting challenges to governance in China: surveying collective protestors, religions sects and criminal organizations', *The China Journal*, 56: 1–31.

Cooney, Sean, Biddulph, Sarah and Zhu, Ying (2013), *Law and Fair Work in China.* London: Routledge.

Feng, Tongqing (2011), *Gonghui fa-dangdai zhongguo gonghui lilun* (Trade union law – contemporary Chinese trade union theory). Beijing: Zhongguo ladong shehui baozhang chubanshe.

Fewsmith, Joseph (2008), 'An "anger venting" mass incident catches the attention of China's leadership', *China Leadership Monitor*, 26, http://media.hoover.org/sites/default/files/documents/CLM26JF.pdf. Accessed 24 October 2013.

Kent, Ann (2007), *Beyond Compliance: China, international organizations, and global security.* Stanford: Stanford University Press.

Lau, Mimi (2012), 'Angry migrant workers riot for the third day', *South China Morning Post*, 14 August.

Lee, Ching Kwan (2005), 'Livelihood struggles and market reform (un)making Chinese labour after state socialism', *UNRISD Occasional Paper*, February.

Lee, Ching Kwan (2007), 'Is Labor a political force in China?', in Elizabeth Perry and Merle Goldman (eds.), *Grassroots Political Reform in Contemporary China*. Cambridge, MA, London: Harvard University Press, pp. 228–52.

Li, Wei (1999), 'Ruhe yufang he kongzhi qunzong jiti shangfang' (How to prevent and control the masses engaging in collective petitioning), *Mishu zhi you* (The Secretary's Friend), 34–5.

Liao, Haiqing (2009), '"Weiwenban" zoushang qiantai' (The 'stability preservation office' takes the front stage), *Nanfang chuang* (Southern Window), 14 April.

Lu, Zhaomin (2009), 'Gonghui xinfang gongzuo yu falü fuwu jiehe zi chutao' (A preliminary study of the linking union letters and visits work and legal services), *Zhongguo gongyun* (Chinese workers' movement), 4: 47–8.

Lum, Thomas (2006), 'Social unrest in China', *Congressional Research Service: reports and issue briefs*, Washington, DC.

O'Brien, Kevin (1996), 'Rightful resistance', *World Politics*, 49: 31–55.

Oi, Jean (1992), 'Fiscal reform and the economic origins of local state corporatism in China', *World Politics*, 45: 99–126.

People's Daily Online (2008), 'Fujian jinjiang: laozi jiufen pinfa cuisheng "laodong zhengyi fating"' (Fujian Jinjiang: the frequent occurrence of labour disputes gave birth to the 'Labour Disputes Tribunal'), 25 December, http://qingyuan.people.com.cn/GB/14748/8576454.html. Accessed 27 May 2011.

Qiu, Quanlin (2011), '9 Detained over violent wages dispute' *China Daily*, 8 June 2011, http://www.chinadaily.com/china/2011-06/08/content_12654074.htm. Accessed 24 September 2013.

Quan, Heng and Li, Ling (2012), 'Hongguang jingji shidu xia de zhongguo laodong li shichang zhuanxing yu neishengxing liyi baohu qushi' (Transformation and endogeneity of China's labour market from a macroeconomic perspective), in Yang Pengfei (ed.), *Laodong guanxi jiti xieshang zhidu yanjiu* (Research into the system of collective negotiation of labour relations). Shanghai: Shanghai Academy of Social Sciences Press, pp. 187–201.

Ren, Hongjie (2005), *Shehui wending wenti qianyan tansuo* (A preliminary exploration of problems of social stability). Beijing: Zhongguo renmin gong'an daxue chubanshe.

Rulliat, Anne (2010), 'The wave of suicides among Foxconn workers and the vacuity of Chinese trade unionism', *China Perspectives*, 3: 135–7.

Sapio, Flora (2011), 'Legal erosion and the policing of petitions', in Mike McConville and Eva Pils (eds.), *Criminal Justice in China: comparative perspectives*. Hong Kong Faculty of Law, The Chinese University of Hong Kong, pp. 203–24.

Su, Yang and He, Xin (2010), 'Street as courtroom: state accommodation of labour protest in south China', *Law & Society Review*, 44 :157–84.

Sun, Fuhai (2001), 'Shandong Jianli qiye laodong guanxi yujing jizhi' (Shandong sets up a labour relations early warning mechanism), *Gongren ribao* (Workers Daily), 20 June: 5.

Tanner, Murray Scot (2004), 'China rethinks unrest' *The Washington Quarterly* 27: 137–56.

Wang, Feiling (2005), *Organizing Through Division and Exclusion: China's hukou system.* Stanford: Stanford University Press.
Wang, Huaiai (2001), 'Guanyu jianli laodong guanxi xietiao yujing jizhi de sikao' (A reflection on establishment of a labour relations early warning mechanism), *Gongren ribao* (Workers Daily), 9 October: 5.
Yang, Lin (2009), 'Zhuazhu zhongxin shen shi laozi geju, xiaochu laozi maodunzhe yinchong, tiaozheng laogong zhengci de jihui' (Seize the opportunity to re-evaluate labour relations, eliminate potential labour problems, and reformulate labour policy), *Liaowang* (Eng transln), 16 December.
Yang, Pengfei (2009), 'The dilemmas and countermeasures of trade union under the financial crisis', *Gonghui lilun yanjiu* (Labour Union Studies), 4: 1–4.
Yu, Jianrong (2009), 'Rigid stability: an explanatory framework for China's social situation', *China Digital Times*, 26 May.
Zhong, Angang (2006), 'Jiaqiang yujing jizhi: quanguo gonghui laodong zhengyi tiaojie zuzhi da 23 wan' (Strengthening early warning mechanisms: nationwide union dispute mediation organs have reached 230,000), *Legal System Web*, 20 August.

3. 'If we award this case to you, all the Chinese people would come to us for justice!' Land-taking cases in the shadow of social stability

Xin He

INTRODUCTION

Despite recent legislation and regulations to protect homeowners' rights, land taking is probably the most important source of violent conflict in China today. Laws allow people to own their homes, but the land on which homes are built remains the property of the state.[1] Over the last decade, local governments intent on acquiring revenue through land development have appropriated vast amounts of residential and farming land. Buildings are demolished, frequently against the will of those who have built their lives and livelihoods on an understanding of their entitlement to land and home. In many instances, legal procedures for eviction and compensation are not followed properly. Farmers and homeowners receive only a fraction of their legal due; all too often the local government and its corrupt officials take the bigger slice. Gross disparity between the losses of aggrieved individuals and the gains of real estate developers and city officials only exacerbates dissatisfaction (Upham 2011: 257–60). The number of often violent 'mass incidents' has continued to increase for well over a decade (Chongqing Municipality 2010). According to one estimate, of the 180,000 collective actions in 2010, the number caused by forced evictions was greater than that based on all other causes of actions combined (Jacobs 2011).

[1] The 2004 Constitution provides for the power of eminent domain. The state may 'for the needs of the public interest, expropriate or requisition land, and pay compensation in accordance with the law'. Homeowners are entitled to compensation amounts based on their use rights and ownership of fixtures on the land. See Erie 2012: 40.

Homeowners have drawn from a repertoire of resistance actions including protests, demonstrations, petitioning to higher-level governments, and point blank refusing to move out – the so-called 'hard nail households' (*dingzihu*) (see Erie 2012). In recent years more and more owners have resorted to litigation to resolve land-taking issues, which in some courts now exceed 20 per cent of all their administrative litigation cases. The primary goal of the aggrieved individuals is economic compensation. Yet the reasons for filing cases, civil and administrative, vary from redressing outrageous unfairness to pursuing due process of law and forcing disclosure of government information.

Here the courts are placed at centre stage with their every move linked to the sensitive nerve of wider social conflicts. On the one hand are laws and legal requirements; on the other are court decisions with significant implications for social stability. This is the context in which a court president uttered the quote in the title, explaining the decision of his court to a group of petitioners whose apartments were demolished: 'If we awarded the case to you, all the Chinese people will come to us for justice!' This exculpation from the court president was sympathetic to the position of the petitioners but understood the political as well as the legal requirements. A decision that could lead to further social instability was simply out of the question. The statement reveals not only the difficult position in which the court is caught but also a broader tension between the laws and political requirements in relation to the 'stability' imperative.

This chapter explores how the courts have handled land-taking cases in the shadow of mounting social instability. Social stability is the paramount concern of the ruling Communist Party, with a budget allocation exceeding the official annual military budget. Concern for social stability is widely seen to play an important role in the operation of the nation's courts (Su and He 2010, Chen and Xu 2012). But how this concern factors into the case handling process in practice, especially in decision making, is rarely addressed in the literature. Drawing from fieldwork investigations and interviews with judges who specialize in this type of case,[2] this chapter shows how having to address the social stability concern makes the process for handling this type of case different procedurally and substantively from that for regular cases. The chapter then analyses the consequences of such an approach and its implications.

[2] The author interviewed a number of judges from southern and eastern China in 2011 and 2012.

THE CONCERN FOR SOCIAL STABILITY

What is the meaning of social stability? At the political centre it means the absence of protests or other social unrest that affects the security of the regime. For officials at the grassroots level, however, by and large this unrest is reified in three forms: petitions, collective action or mass incidents, and 'vicious' (*exing*) violent events.

Petitions figure prominently in government measurement criteria to assess officials' job performance. According to one local government document (Yuexi County 2011), of the 100 possible performance points, 20 can be deducted for an incident of petition to government in Beijing, 10 for this incident at the provincial government, seven at the municipal government, and five in the county or township government. A second basis for assessment is the number of mass incidents that occur in the area, while any demonstration or protest with more than ten people counts as an incident. The third and usually most serious basis is death or personal injury resulting from social conflict. One such death may lead to termination of a top local official's political career. The most serious incidents affecting social stability are all related to death. Partly this is because claiming a life may trigger further collective actions; the agitated masses often want to hold some officials responsible and demand compensation and even political concessions on that basis. The most sensational collective actions always relate to the death of a protestor. The most widely reported recent example is the so-called Siege of Wukan in late 2011, which began as an anti-corruption protest in this southern village and escalated with the villagers expelling officials, police seizing the town, and subsequently with détente (Wines 2012). Local officials have thus been extremely cautious in preventing vicious incidents and especially death.

Courts and judges are subject to performance measurements and pressures similar to those of local government officials. In 2002 the Supreme People's Court (SPC) issued a notice instructing all courts nationwide to emphasize resolving complaints raised by petitions; handling these petitions is as important as handling cases through trial. The SPC instructed lower courts to follow through with letters and visits in the process of handling cases, to persuade and guide petitioners, and to change judgments in which they had erred. As a result some courts, like government departments, set targets of 'zero petitions'. The SPC itself has as many as 80 judges working on letters and visits (Liebman 2011: 295). Similar measurements relating to the number of incidents in which people have been killed and other types of vicious incidents are also in the performance assessment criteria for judges at grassroots level (cf., Panyu Court 2004). Of course, any escalation of protest and the resultant attention of the media are also counted against the performance of a court and its judges.

Consequently even though judges may not toe the line with local officials, they share the officials' concerns, or at the very least have to keep these concerns in mind when dealing with the issues. Although courts can carve room for autonomy from extra-legal influences, the pressures faced by courts and judges appear striking insofar as they interfere with and influence the handling of land-taking cases, which are often fraught with conflict. Below is a brief examination of a number of court tactics and activities in place to protect courts from potential political fallout of handling land-taking disputes.

HANDLING CASES IN THE SHADOW OF CONCERN FOR STABILITY

Faced with increasing numbers of cases, many of which have multiple plaintiffs and are accompanied by popular protest, courts often first respond with temporary techniques. To reduce public pressure, for example, courts across the country often break up a collection of multiple plaintiffs into smaller groups, provide a spokesperson to meet with the groups, and encourage conciliation, settlements and even withdrawal of the case (Li 2011, Chen and Xu 2012). In most situations, the courts are reluctant to allow cases to be accepted for trial. The reason is straightforward: as long as the courts are not involved, they will not be held responsible for any mishandlings. Significant pressure may not always generate the desired effect. Similar to other bureaucrats, when judges are subjected to tight controls they may work harder, or they may avoid difficult tasks or even sabotage a programme (Brehm and Gates 1997). That is why many courts have devised tactics to push disputes outside the gate of the courts, especially in administrative cases. Many courts will not accept such cases until approval of the senior court officials is obtained and only after some communication or even consensus has been reached between the courts and the related administrative agencies. Wang and Yin (2010) aptly term this 'the politics of case filing'. The point is that the courts accept only the cases they are able to handle or are well positioned to control (He 2007). They leave difficult cases to other institutional channels or simply refuse to offer judicial remedies.

But as courts are the formal and the most important dispute resolution organization, they sometimes find it difficult to reject petitions. For petitions with clear legal basis, an outright rejection would only lead to appeal at the upper-level court and eventual return of the case to the original court. For other petitions, the Party and the government place expectations on courts to resolve the dispute to reduce pressure on the Party-state (He 2007, Su and He 2010). This is especially true in administrative cases of compulsory enforcement, the majority of which are housing demolition cases. In these cases, the government or the land developer has already obtained the licence to demolish, which gives them the legal right to require the courts to implement the licences for them under law. The government also wants to take advantage of the legitimacy vested in the courts to justify government actions. Once a case enters the legal process, courts and judges have to be extremely cautious. In short, the Party-state's concern for social stability has profoundly impacted the case-handling process by the courts, both procedurally and substantively.

Adjudication Committees

Adjudication committees are organizations within each court comprising senior court officials whose task is to decide on difficult or sensitive cases. In contrast to other types of cases that are generally free from concerns about social stability, almost all land-taking cases are placed on the agenda of the adjudication committee, the highest decision-making body of the Chinese court. This suggests that courts and judges are cautious and careful in handling this type of case, which they want the most senior court officials to decide. Adjudication committee members are bureaucrats with years of experience so they are particularly alert to political concerns and the social impact of sensitive issues, an aspect of court work in which some junior judges may lack experience. Having the adjudication committee decide the case also serves an important function for the judges and the court at large: once the case is discussed and determined by the committee, responsibility for making decisions is diluted, and almost no single judge will be held responsible for any potential vicious incidents consequent to that decision (He 2012). Collective responsibility simply means no one in the court is responsible for the court's decision.

The intention to avoid responsibility for making decisions is evident in the minutes of an adjudication committee of a local court. As documented by He (2012), in a case in which the local government was sued for a demolition arrangement, the court president made the following comments after reaffirming the government's action: 'We recommend the municipal intermediate court asks the provincial higher court for a retrial and makes it clear to the government that if the plaintiff seeks to petition in Beijing, the local government will bear the full responsibility. Second, we recommend that the intermediate court enforce the case.' In another case involving a compulsory enforcement petition relating to a housing demolition by the local government, the court president announced: 'Compulsory enforcement is approved; prepare the decision, but wait for further instructions from the district Party Committee.' These examples, along with many other requests to the intermediate court for instructions, indicate that the court president's tactic is to avoid taking responsibility and simultaneously maintain a good relationship with the local government and the Party.

The Ma Xiwu Approach Restored

The Ma Xiwu approach is an old Maoist approach to delivering justice. It emphasizes that judges take the initiative in participating in pre-trial investigations, before persuading the litigation parties into a settlement. This approach was praised and promoted by Mao in part because it is consistent with his thoughts on 'correctly handling contradictions among the people'. This approach was largely abandoned in the post-Mao period when adjudication took over as a primary method of dispute resolution. Partly to relieve the heavy burden incurred by the inquisitorial process, the state revised court procedures, placing more responsibility on individual litigants to provide evidence that would prove a case in their favour (SPC Report 1996).

The policy slogan in the Chinese courts is now *dangshiren zhuyi* (litigant as the centre). The burden of proof is now on the litigants, not on the judge's assessment of evidence (Woo 2003). In most trials, mediation takes place immediately following the court investigation and discussion, within the same court session. The current Civil Procedure Law stipulates that the court may or may not conduct mediation after court discussion. Indeed, during most of the period when the president of the SPC was Xiao Yang (1998–2008), an advocate of Western-style judicial reform, the judiciary emphasized formalism and adjudication. Most court decisions in civil and commercial areas were adjudicated without much effort given to mediation (Fu and Cullen 2011). Judges ruled primarily based on the admitted evidence provided by the litigation parties and the examination of witnesses during court hearings. Even in family-related cases where mediation was legally mandatory, mediation as a practice was conducted only summarily (He 2009).

But in land-taking cases affecting social stability, the traditional Ma Xiwu approach has been restored. The judges and the courts not only conduct thorough investigations before the trial, they also speculate on the possible reactions of the affected households and accordingly provide counter-measures that the courts and the governments can take. Obviously this practice is in place to prevent any escalation of conflict in general and vicious incidents in particular. This approach has been applied in both the approving and implementing stages. In approving a compulsory demolition request of the housing authorities, for example, one particular court report stated (Chixi Court 2012):

> We request that the administrative agencies provide facts, evidence and the legal basis for their decisions. We not only examine the lawfulness of the decisions, but also focus on compensation, relocation and fairness, as well as whether the compensation has materialized and whether the decision has infringed the lawful rights of the affected individuals. We try to … meet the justice expectations of the masses.

As the minutes of the committee meeting revealed, the court president even suggested a retrial at the intermediate court. Adjudicating judges at the very least have to examine the site in question and talk to relevant parties before the hearings.

This approach becomes even more obvious at the implementing stage. In one case involving thousands of plaintiffs and several petitions, in May 2001 an intermediate court in central China did not dare to issue its judgment favouring the government immediately after the court hearing. Instead, the court worked very hard to convince other government agencies to provide tangible remedies for the litigants in advance of issuing the judgment. On the day of issue, detailed pre-emptive actions were implemented to prevent mass incidents (Liaowang Newsweek 2006). In another jurisdiction, a court report issued with the objective of sharing experiences in successfully implementing a compulsory demolition stated (Chixi Court 2012):

> In accordance with the risk assessment reports prepared by the administrative agencies, the court's enforcement bureau formulated detailed measures to deal with all kinds of possible reactions, with clear division of labour and responsibility among relevant personnel to ensure the personal safety of relevant parties. Particularly in cases when it is considered that the affected individuals may potentially take radical action, we contact relevant authorities immediately to take appropriate measures to soften the confrontation and pacify the conflict.

Mediation Pursued

In response to mounting social conflicts and as a result of the continued dominance of the ideology of social harmony, mediation has been re-emphasized generally in all sectors of dispute resolution since the mid-2000s. This process is called 'Grand mediation', a kind of mediation writ large that involves multiple government departments, to nip social disputes in the bud before they escalate (Fu and Cullen 2010, Minzner 2009, Hand 2009). Under the pressure of such a political push and as part of its own drive to reduce petitions arising from adjudicated cases, China's judiciary now once again emphasize judicial mediation. Political levers are visibly relied on in handling disputes involving collective protests (Su and He 2010, Chen and Xu 2011). Financial incentives are introduced and standards of promotion are altered to encourage judges to mediate, rather than to adjudicate, cases (He 2009, Minzner 2011).

If the discussion above suggests only a general trend towards mediation, the emphasis upon mediation is most conspicuous in land-taking cases affecting social stability. No judge wants be implicated in cases involving violence, petitions and vicious incidents, and mediation is recognized as the best way to achieve resolution so long as the parties consider a settlement. This is because mediation by its very nature indicates that relevant parties have accepted at least the potential of considering a proposed arrangement, which means they are unlikely to appeal, petition or complain. The problem for the judges, however, is how to obtain the consent of the affected individuals when the government position in land-taking cases is often inflexible. The task of the judges, then, is to devise ways to persuade, cajole or even coerce the affected individuals to 'accept' a deal voluntarily.

A report by a Langxi court in Anhui province describes how a judge successfully mediated a land-taking case in which the family refused to move house. The affected household in the case was in grave financial difficulty: a man of the household had been diagnosed with an incurable disease. There were elderly parents and toddlers in the family, all of whom needed financial support. While all their neighbours had moved, they simply refused to move unless they were compensated with much more money than originally offered to them, as well as acceptable relocation housing convenient for the elderly and the sick members of the family. The family believed that they had made the request based on their actual needs; after all, the demolition had worsened their already dire situation. Since their two requests were out of the question in terms of what the law could do, according to the court report (Langxi Court 2012), the judges:

> adjusted their working philosophy and bettered working tactics and methods. They approached the household with a warm heart, patiently explaining the demolition policy to the family members, forgetting their positions as judges. They repeatedly paid attention to the health of the affected family member and other factors involving the well-being of the family, and on numerous occasions contacted the relevant authorities to help them appreciate the family's requests. They placed themselves in the shoes of the affected household, and found replacement housing that suited the family's requirements. Eventually the household was touched by what the judges had done for them. They withdrew their 'unreasonable requests' and signed the demolition agreement with the demolition company.

The court and the judges thus prevented a potential vicious incident from occurring because 'an oversimplified legal enforcement was likely to have led to confrontation, and members of the affected household, feeling hopeless because of the illness and the demolition, may have injured themselves or resisted violently'. The court report stated that the key for successful mediation is to find suitable business premises for the affected household so the household can continue their retailing business after being relocated (Langxi Court 2012).

Duration Lengthened

With the exception of some cases that pose an immediate threat to social stability, an inevitable outcome of taking the above approach is that the duration of the case-handling process is lengthened significantly. Investigation and persuasion take a significant amount of time and energy, so that cases where they are pursued take much more time than other cases to be completed (Liaowang Newsweek 2006). It is not uncommon for mediated cases to last for two to three years, even though the statutory adjudication period is normally six months. The Langxi court case discussed above also indicates that judges contact the relevant authorities on numerous occasions. They speak to the households until, figuratively, 'their throats are burning and their shoes are worn out'. In the above-cited minutes of the adjudication committee, the court president even suggested that the intermediate court retry the case, which would obviously take more time to complete. In one Taizhou city case where the housing authorities adopted an outdated compensation standard, the intermediate court, fearful of taking any responsibility, simply remanded the case back to the district court for retrial. After the retrial, the affected households appealed again. Six months after the case had been sent for appeal, the adjudication committee of the appeal court (the intermediate court) discussed the case on three separate occasions. The responsible judge wrote numerous reports to relevant authorities, and the court president in charge of the case met with the district Party head several times. At the time of writing this chapter, the responsible judge still had no idea what the outcome of the decision would be.

Outcome Skewed

When parties do not agree to settle, courts have to award a judgment that supports or rejects the plaintiffs' claims. O'Brien and Li (2004) argue that in the face of possible petitions and other tactics of resistance, the courts are likely to react favourably to the plaintiff in the administrative litigation. Su and He (2010) also speculate that a big protest often places the litigants in an advantaged position to obtain a favourable outcome. Liebman (2011) suggests that the courts overreact to petitioners whose claims lack merit and thus there is a 'populist threat' to China's courts. But my interviews suggest the picture is less straightforward. I have found that in most instances, the courts support the positions of the government and the land developers when social stability is at stake. In protest-supported litigation, a decision favouring the plaintiffs will only open the floodgates for more litigation. The courts appear motivated by concerns that protests may spread to a wider group. Resolving one litigant's grievance therefore becomes problematic if satisfying their demands encourages others who have suffered the same mistreatment to begin litigation or petitioning.

In one case, for instance, the government persuaded villagers to sign a demolition agreement by promising that under various scenarios any increase in monetary compensation for those who signed the agreement at a later date would be applied to those who had signed earlier. Most households in the area signed except for nine hard nail households. So that the extended line of a highway could be completed as planned, the government later agreed to compensate each of the nine households an extra 80,000 yuan. This enraged the households that had signed earlier and they claimed for the same treatment in court and petitioned in Beijing. A judge in Nantong noted that in one case, a plaintiff should have been compensated more than others because the demolition company had indeed without authorization cut into the land on which the plaintiff had built his house. But the judge dared not offer the plaintiff compensation lest other households protest. The plaintiff ended up appealing and petitioning.

Concern for social stability handcuffs courts facing entirely reasonable compensation demands. In many situations, the court adamantly refuses to offer any help to the plaintiff, even though it has admitted that the plaintiff's demand was not unreasonable and the compensation requested was a relatively small sum. The judge's statement in the title of this chapter indicates the bind the court is in: it cannot decide a case in favour of an aggrieved household when it recognizes that such a decision may inspire more cases and petitions. In another case documented by Erie (2012), the plaintiff was awarded what was seen to be appropriate compensation, but this was never recorded in the court decision because the authorities did not want to set a precedent. A judge in Nantong explained his restraint: 'I was willing to compensate a victim for demolition of his property if the extra compensation to him was not disclosed. But how could I be sure of that? People all want to spread the news of their victory.'

During their interviews with me, many judges from developed areas said that both government and Party rarely instructed the courts in detail about how a case should be decided, but the judges are still concerned with the consequences of their decisions. Typically these judges questioned, 'Will the decision withstand scrutiny under both the laws and the political requirements of social stability? If the government and the Party raise questions about the case, how shall we respond?' A female judge specializing in administrative law acknowledged: 'In many cases we are adopting a temporary treatment (*guxiliaofa*), staying in line with the government regardless of the long-term impact. We cannot do much to [affect] the macro political environment.' A judge in Beijing despaired that in many cases the court was held hostage by the government because the government's unlawful practices were so widespread. Declaring government practice illegal would surely cause social instability. In Jiangsu province, about half of the plaintiffs won their house demolition cases against the government, but none of the 10 most significant cases published by the courts relates directly to multiple plaintiffs or social stability.

In some situations, however, the court and the local government make compromises and provide extra compensation for the affected individuals. Usually this is in cases involving a few households where it is highly likely a vicious incident would follow without such official accommodation. The rationale for this compromise is that when only a few households are involved, the money needed to buy off them is relatively small and thus the compensation is feasible. As Su and He (2010) explain, as long as the officials and judges can erase potential elements that may lead to social instability, especially when others' money is involved, they will gladly do so.

In the Taizhou city case mentioned above, the nine hard nail households were eventually offered 80,000 yuan more than households that had earlier signed compensation agreements. This was to rescue the government from complaints of ineffectiveness because the highway construction that was the cause of the complaints was years behind schedule. In Chongqing, in what is recognized as one of the 'hardest' hard nail household cases, the government backed down and offered more compensation to prevent compulsory demolition. In the successful mediation case mentioned above relating to the householder who had a terminal illness, the key was to find 'suitable replacement housing and in some cases, commercial premises for the affected households'. Here the judges were willing to make an extra effort because the aggrieved individual was already very ill and there was a realistic possibility he would injure himself or take radical action to resist.

In one case documented by Erie (2012), a household was offered extra compensation after their home was demolished before the 2008 Olympics, obviously to diminish the likelihood of confrontation between the household and the housing authorities and thus lowering the chance of petition or the like. In another case the aggrieved individual was a woman in her seventies who moved into the doorman's quarters of a court, refusing to move until the court offered her extra compensation for her demolished home. The court was reluctant to respond until half a year later. Her moving in to live at the court attracted media attention and prompted an inquiry of the people's congress (author's interview with a judge in 2012). To maintain its reputation as a 'judiciary for the people', the court eventually said yes to her request, a decision that, according to relevant legal stipulations, was totally groundless. To resolve this type of dispute, some courts even have dedicated funds available for paying petitioners.

CONSEQUENCES

Handling land-taking cases in these ways has consequences. Most conspicuous is the generation and reproduction of more hard nail households. In China nowadays the squeaky wheel truly does get more grease in all types of cases (He 2009), even more obviously in land-taking cases. As discussed above, to avoid being involved with so-called vicious incidents, courts and judges tend to award decisions in favour of hard nail households, especially when the possibility of consequential protests and other incidents is high. Governments and land developers are also willing to make compromises to prevent or shorten delays in construction. All these possibilities encourage aggrieved citizens to become hard nail households, some of which proceed with ever more creative hold-out responses.

In Taizhou, a dramatic picture appeared in the news of a house standing in the middle of a highway. The owner was a 75-year-old grandmother. More than 10 security cameras were installed in the house to cover different angles. It is said that the elderly owner changed her mind after signing the demolition agreement 10 years earlier. When asked by the media, the relevant officials responded only that 'the situation is complicated' (Sina News 2012). A judge whom I interviewed told me of another case involving an elderly hard nail householder in Nanjing. The old man employed a creative strategy to deal with potential compulsory demolition by removing all the valuables from the home then sealing the doors, leaving only a small window as the channel for his family members to pass in his food. He claimed he would stay inside the house as long as the developer refused to meet his request. No developer would be able to sustain such a contest. As these examples reveal, forced removal encourages strategic behaviour by the aggrieved parties because they now have precedents for hold-out behaviour being rewarded with more benefits.

The second consequence of these ways of handling disputes is the increase of petitions and other forms of social protest. When the decision is in favour of the government, which is often the case, the aggrieved individuals are dissatisfied or even angry. Losing the case prompts litigants to depict courts and judges as corrupt and incompetent, or simply 'wearing the same underwear as the government'. When the court as the formal channel for dispute resolution has effectively been blocked by political imperatives, aggrieved individuals adopt methods such as petitions and other means of protest that they perceive to be useful. Petitions related to land taking have therefore surged, becoming probably the most important type of petition. Protest-supported litigation has also skyrocketed recently. In some courts, protest-supported cases comprise more than 20 per cent of all administrative litigation cases received. The plaintiffs in these cases number in the hundreds, if not thousands. They are farmers from several villages or residents from a block in the old city district. These litigants believe they cannot rely on litigation alone or on their personal actions alone. They employ various means of public protest collectively to exert more pressure on the court and the government.

As some examples discussed here reveal, handling disputes can place the courts and judges in an embarrassing situation and can become extremely troublesome and time consuming for both. The adjudication committee may have to discuss cases several times before a decision is made. As said, the shoes of the responsible judges are virtually worn out by the time the aggrieved households accept a proposed arrangement. The rewards given to the hard nail households encourage more strategic resistance behaviour, which makes the judges' task of obtaining settlement inside or outside the court even more difficult (Mnookin and Kornhauser 1979).

Finally, a court decision favouring the government may trigger escalated collective protest. In a land-taking case mentioned earlier, an intermediate court in central China took a comprehensive series of actions to prevent mass incidents before issuing its judgment favouring the government (Liaowang Newsweek 2006). This story was reported in the public media to show that the court performed its job effectively in solving social conflicts, but it also portrays the embarrassing situation of the court.

According to some of my interviewees, more than 30 per cent of this type of land-taking case have been appealed, an appeal rate much higher than for other types of administrative litigation. The original conflict is between the households harmed by the demolition policy and the developers and/or the housing demolition authorities. Yet the way in which courts handle these cases appears to shift the blame, so it seems to some that courts take sides with the government and the land developers. The courts are therefore often regarded as an opponent of the plaintiffs, rather than as the judgment maker of the legal case. As a result, courts and judges are blamed for the animosity that accumulates in these conflicts toward the developers or the housing authorities.

CONCLUSION

This chapter has examined why and how the courts handle land-taking cases, which are recognized by the Party-state, the court system and beyond for their capacity to abrade social stability. This analysis speaks volumes about how politics has permeated the legal process and its outcomes. Although the boundary between law and politics has never been clearly delineated (Thompson 1975, Upham 2011), the situations described above prompt us to question whether there is any border between them at all. It seems that any action is permissible when courts are influenced by social stability concerns. Courts want to prevent at all cost conducting cases in a way that escalates conflict or generates other incidents affecting social stability.

The embarrassing situation in which the courts find themselves also begs the question: is such an approach sustainable? As shown in the discussion above, once the court is overwhelmed by stability concerns, its way of handling cases becomes hardly recognizable as legal remedy. When the courts operate in this way are they still courts, and are their judges still judges? Courts and judges invest tremendous energy and time in land-taking cases, but their efforts seem only to form a vicious circle, generating more petitions and protest-supported litigation that may, in turn, threaten social stability even further.

Moreover, the court's authority is undermined by the very fact that concerns for social stability as made clear by the Party-state have replaced the law in the handling of court cases. When courts do not support the cause of the protestors, the protestors believe that the courts, the government and developers are wearing the same underwear; when the courts cave in to pressure by the protestors, the action encourages more hard nail households and other types of resistance that worsen social instability. This strategic myopia leads to actions that appear to be effective in the short term but are more hazardous in the long term. Lack of public confidence in the legitimacy of legal procedure only becomes more serious. Indeed, recent developments already suggest that some courts have been trying to break from this embarrassing situation and take strategies to rein in the housing authorities. In the current political environment, as the quote in the title suggests, aggrieved Chinese citizens across the country will flock to a court if the court dares to stand up for justice. Only when all courts make a decision involving greater commitment to the elements of law, to the facts of a case and to justice, can the vicious circle be broken. If China is serious about maintaining social stability, it should thus aim at a more independent and powerful judiciary.

The analysis in this chapter also casts doubt on the conventional wisdom that the local government is dominant in all state–society relationships in China. Local governments are surely still powerful and can manoeuvre various resources to achieve their goals. But the mushrooming of hard nail households has become an ever more serious challenge to local government authority. That a fragile grandmother could delay the building of a highway for years was once unimaginable in China. Protest-supported litigation may also paralyse the functioning of the courts and the government. When concerns for stability overshadow every aspect of the government's operations, it is questionable whether the local government is more powerful in protest situations than those citizens with few resources at hand. The citizen's resistance, even though often unsuccessful, nevertheless offers a vantage point to view the changing dynamics among the players in the state–society relationship in China today.

REFERENCES

Brehm, John and Gates, Scott (1997), *Working, Shirking, and Sabotage*. Ann Arbor, Michigan: University of Michigan Press.

Chen, Feng and Xu, Xin (2012), '"Active judiciary": judicial dismantling of workers' collective action in China', *China Journal*, 67: 87–107.

Chixi Court (2012), 'Chu fayuan wei chaiqian gongzuo baojia huhang' (The district court is facilitating the demolition activities) available at http://jbxww-old.cnnb.com.cn/gb/node2/node114/node115/node471/node914/node940/node941/userobject1ai11410.html. Accessed 18 March 2014.

Chongqing Municipality (2010), 'Jiceng fanying zhengdi chaiqian zhong beichaiqian qunzhong chuanlian' xianxiang tuchu yingyu gaodu zhongshi' (Trans-local association among residents stands out in housing demolition and deserves special attention), Jiangbei District Stability Maintenance Office, Chongqing Municipality, 14 May 2010, http://www.pacq.gov.cn/platform/news_view.asp?newsid=2070. Accessed 26 October 2010.

Erie, Matthew S. (2012), 'Property rights, legal consciousness and the new media in China: the hard case of the toughest nail-house in history', *China Information*, 26: 35–59.

Fu, Hualing and Cullen, Richard (2011), 'From mediatory to adjudicatory justice: the limits of civil justice reform in China', in Margaret Y.K. Woo and Mary E. Gallagher (eds.), *Chinese Justice*. New York: Cambridge University Press, 25–57.

Hand, Keith J. (2009), 'Citizens engage the constitution: the Sun Zhigang Incident and constitutional review proposals in the People's Republic of China', in Stephanie Balme and Michael Dowdle (eds.), *Building Constitutionalism in China*. New York: Palgrave Macmillan, 221–42.

He, Xin (2007), 'Why did they not take on the disputes? Law, power and politics in the decision-making of Chinese courts', *International Journal of Law in Context*, 3: 203–25.

He, Xin (2009), 'Routinization of divorce practice in China: institutional constraints' influence on judicial behaviour', *International Journal of Law, Policy and the Family*, 23(1): 83–109.

He, Xin (2012), 'Black hole of responsibility: the adjudication committee's role in a Chinese court', *Law and Society Review*, 46(4): 681–712.

Jacobs, Andrew (2011), 'Harassment and evictions bedevil even China's well-off', *New York Times*, 28 October, A4.

Langxi Court (2012), 'Langxi fayuan liuxiang cuoshe tuoshan banli fangwu chaiqian anjian' (Six measures in handling housing demolition cases Langxi court), http://www.ahxccourt.gov.cn/Article/Article.Asp?ID=3352. Accessed 13 October 2013.

Li, Li (2011), 'Strategies for judicial restraint in Chinese group action cases: a realistic reaction to judicialization', http://ssrn.com/abstract=1789564 or http://dx.doi.org/10.2139/ssrn.1789564. Accessed 13 October 2013.

Liaowang Newsweek (2006), 'Zhongguo jiceng fayuan mianlin gaoyuan anjian dafu zengzhang susong yali' (Caseload pressures in administrative litigation mounted for China's basic-level courts), http://news.sina.com.cn/c/2006-04-22/12159690235.shtml. Accessed 21 November 2011.

Liebman, Benjamin L. (2011), 'A popular threat to China's courts?', in Margaret Y.K. Woo and Mary E. Gallagher (eds.), *Chinese Justice*. New York: Cambridge University Press, pp. 269–313.

Minzner, Carl (2009), 'Riots and cover-ups: counterproductive control of local agents in China', *University of Pennsylvania Journal of International Law*, 31: 53–123.

Mnookin, Robert and Kornhauser, Lewis (1979), 'Bargaining in the shadow of the law: the case of divorce', *Yale Law Journal*, 88(5): 950–97.

O'Brien, Kevin J. and Li, Lianjiang (2004), 'Suing the local state: administrative litigation in rural China', *China Journal*, 51: 75–96.

O'Brien, Kevin J. and Li, Lianjiang (2006), *Rightful Resistance in Rural China*. Cambridge, UK: Cambridge University Press.

Panyu Court (2004), 'The stipulation with regard to post responsibility of Panyu District Court, Guangzhou Municipality (Trial)', in *The Compilation of Regulations and Institutions of P. District Court, Guangzhou Municipality*, Volume 1, 181–8, June 2004 (no press or ISBN series number).

Sina News (2012), 'Zhejiang taizhou dingzihu malu zhongjian duanshui shenghuo shi yu nian' (The nail-household sustained for more than 10 years in the middle of highway in Taizhou Zhejiang), http://slide.news.sina.com.cn/c/slide_1_2841_28147.html. Accessed 26 May 2013.

Su, Yang and He, Xin (2010), 'Street as courtroom: state accommodation of social conflicts in south China', *Law & Society Review*, 44: 157–84.

Supreme People's Court (1996), 'Zuigao renmin fayuan gongzuo baogao 1996 nian' (Supreme People's Court Working Report 1996), http://www.gov.cn/test/2008-03/27/content_929938.htm. Accessed 12 March 2014.

Thompson, Edward P. (1975), *Whigs and Hunters*. London: Allen Lane.

Upham, Frank K. (2011), 'Reflections on the rule of law in China', *Taiwan University Law Review*, 6(1): 251–67.

Wang, Qinhua and Xin Yin (eds.) (2010), Zhongguo jiceng xingzheng zhengduan juejue jizhi de jingyan yanjiu (*An Empirical Study of Administrative Dispute Resolution in Grassroots China*).

Wines, Michael (2012), 'Revolt begins like others, but its end is less certain', *New York Times*, 17 December, A6.

Woo, Margaret (2003), 'Shaping Citizenship: Chinese Family Law and Women', *Yale J. Law & Feminism*, 15(1): 99–134.

Yuexi County (2011), 'Guanyu zhiding changpuzhen xinfang weiwen gongzuo kaohe banfa de tongzhi' (The notice on the measures of performance on petitions and stability maintenance by changpu township government), http://cpz.ahyx.gov.cn/gwgk/bmfw/201105/50130.html. Accessed 6 May 2013.

4. Ripples across stagnant water: stability, legal activism and water pollution disputes in rural China

Zhang Wanhong and Ding Peng*

INTRODUCTION

Law penetrates almost every aspect of social life in China today. Indeed, in November 2011 the Chairman of the NPC (National People's Congress) Standing Committee declared that a socialist legal system with Chinese characteristics was fully established in China, providing a legal basis for all sectors of social life (Xinhua News Agency 2011). Great strides in legislation over the past 30 years have been accompanied by promotion of activism in the judicial field (Wang 2009). 'Judicial activism' has become an important route for pursuing social stability in the present political climate where stability is the nation's foremost socio-political goal. This activism is particularly manifest in dispute resolution conducted through 'grand mediation' (*da tiaojie*) (Liu 2012) and to a lesser extent through government legal aid departments for those who are eligible.

In rural areas judicial activism also operates through local governments, aiming to resolve disputes between citizens and local industry or government in a way that ensures social stability is maintained among rural populations. Traditionally rural China was beyond the reach of law; now it is under the vast net of justice administration accomplished through national policies, law popularization drives and 'sending law to the countryside' (*song fa xiaxiang*). This chapter documents the tales of

* The authors extend warm thanks to Professor Benjamin van Rooij for his intellectual inspiration and support. They also acknowledge with thanks the financial support received for research informing this chapter, provided by the Netherlands Organization for Scientific Research (NWO) and the Chinese Education Ministry's Fundamental Research Funds for the Central Universities.

two areas in rural Hubei Province where residents have struggled to resolve problems that have gravely affected the lives and livelihoods of people residing in the vicinity of manufacturing plants that pollute local rivers. We explore the legal activism of these people to resolve water pollution disputes and the place of the quest for stability in their pursuits.

DISPUTE TYPES, STRATEGY SELECTION AND STABILITY WHEN LAW REACHES THE COUNTRYSIDE: AN OVERVIEW

Some legal elites in China have tended to assume that the 'common people' in rural areas are ignorant of law, and in some cases peasants themselves agree with this assumption. Yet rather than law per se, this ignorance is more to do with the minutiae of law texts and the complicated divisions of power between and within legal organizations. In reality, most people in rural areas are aware of the general concepts of law manifest in ideas such as 'the law of the state' (*wangfa*) and 'law of officialdom' (*guanfa*), and they know of the existence of lawyers. It is true that the common people usually feel reluctant to litigate (*da guansi*), particularly since law tends to be subordinated to authorities (*quan dayu fa*) due to the traditional practice of government officials (*guan*) taking charge of justice administration and to the high cost of activism and unexpected risks involved. They have also witnessed real life cases that have cost litigants large amounts of money and have negatively affected people's daily lives and interpersonal relations. A vast number of television programmes, news stories and local cases have magnified the idea in people's minds that litigation is indeed an option, but while law is not an unfamiliar concept to rural residents, only where vital interests are at stake and there is no alternative will peasants mobilize themselves in groups, acquaint themselves with relevant legal knowledge, and take advantage of law to defend their rights.

Numerous cases exemplify this. In terms of sheer volume of cases, legal workers at basic levels have to provide a great deal of legal consultation and representation for peasants. Hubei Province is an example. In one township alone, with a population of 80,000 to 100,000, a Justice Bureau chief deals with about 15 legal aid cases on average in a year. Litigation accounts for around half the workload since dozens of mediation cases are also handled simultaneously. Even more disputes have been solved through less formal means by the village leaders and so do not go through the Justice Bureau system as formal disputes. They entail mediation sessions usually mediated by the chief of the village Party committee or the public security head, both of whom hold concurrent posts as directors of village mediation. These cases are not under the purview of the Justice Bureau. The authors' field research finds that village leaders use legal knowledge to a large extent through the mechanism of mediation, for instance in the requirements for establishing a marriage, mediating agreements on a couple's joint property, in civil cases of at fault liability, for compensation in personal injury incidents and so forth.[1]

Dong Leiming's research on the Song Village (Dong 2008: 150–3), as well as observations and research by many other social scientists and anthropologists, concurs with the above observations. As to the prevalence of mediation in rural areas, it is commonly held that 'Law is the main principle, while due consideration should also be given to human sentiment and connections (*renqing*)'. This eclectically held and rather expedient attitude means that customary law has incorporated some traditional ideas of village communities towards 'emotion and reason' (*qingli*). These ideas are not necessarily in conflict with national laws, since people usually employ 'emotion and reason' within a legal framework; local knowledge and norms have actually been well accommodated with national law in people's minds, which is reflected in the status of customary law operating in many villages including the Song Village. In many villages, people are now more or less aware of some modern legal knowledge through government drives to popularize law, media publicity and other indirect channels. However since the people rarely use this legal knowledge in daily life, it is usually in hibernation or semi-hibernation in their minds. Once they realize that the national power backing the law may intervene, people usually activate this hibernated knowledge and it can strongly affect the actions they take (Dong 2008:150–3).

While this is the case generally, decisions by villagers to take legal action and the extent to which they use law and rely on lawyers differ depending on the types of dispute at hand. In cases regarding marriage and family, mediation directors and chiefs of justice bureaus have informed us that they rarely receive complaints about domestic violence. The adage 'don't wash your dirty linen in public' is still very influential in China. A local chief of a Justice Bureau who has dealt with cases of domestic violence advised that these cases are usually handled by issuing

1 Authors' interviews during field visit in L County, Hubei Province in July 2011.

police warnings or they end up in divorce. On issues of adjacent rights, housing, and neighbourhood or village water disputes (even between siblings), if villagers are dissatisfied with the village mediation, they tend to move easily into litigation and to seek consultation from lawyers. In these cases the court may deliver the same judgment as the mediation officer but with different reasoning, and the suing party tends to obey the court judgment.

In traffic accident cases, the general trend is for traffic police to decide on liability and personal injury compensation standards, which is generally regarded as a clear and speedy approach. In some cases law has been abused by police imposing greater liability on car owners who are insured, to prevent uninsured motorcyclists from making trouble through petitioning (*shangfang naoshi*). Traffic police sometimes 'force' a car owner to take responsibility for an accident, thus rendering compulsory insurance an external cost of stability maintenance.[2] In these types of situations, it would not be unfair to say that the police and the people are in alliance against the interests of insurance companies – ensuring these companies contribute to the bill for stability maintenance.

The dispute types mentioned above occur frequently within families or among neighbours in rural communities. Another type of dispute is between villagers and the external world, mostly in cases of occupational injury and pollution. Occupational injury cases are more likely to be compensated through litigation or mediation, where the damages, causality and legal basis are on more solid ground. These cases are considered relatively serious because they concern people's lives and livelihoods, so they can usually be solved quite promptly. But there are still scenarios where a particular enterprise takes advantage of its power or standing to bully the injured party, particularly with migrant workers who have to compromise and accept whatever money they can get as soon as possible to end the dispute quickly (Zhou and Zhu 2009). In pollution cases, neither the amount of damage nor the causal relations may be clear cut, and as big tax payers, enterprises may gain more support from the government than other parties. These types of cases are more likely to evolve into confrontation between pollution victims and the government. In cases such as land expropriation and eviction, which involve damages initiated by the government and usually big loss to affected citizens, the confrontation becomes even more intense.

---

[2] Authors' interviews during field visit in L County, Hubei Province in October 2011.

In summary, in cases where power between the parties is balanced and the government is relatively impartial, such as those involving divorce (including domestic violence), loans, traffic accidents and even occupational injury, the law tends to attract greater enforcement authority and lawyers are given full play to use the law to protect their clients' rights. In cases of traffic accidents and medical disputes, judges and lawyers may sometimes even take the side of the disadvantaged party to ensure they do not take the matter further. In doing so, they arguably abuse the law and their office to take advantage of 'the rich' or those with deep pockets, a practice well beyond proper legal standards. They do so to prevent the disadvantaged party taking further action through petitioning, which is seen as making even greater trouble. Most individual petitioners who are persistent but controllable, and whose complaints stand no chance of a proper solution through judicial channels, are seen not to constitute a direct threat to stability. Nevertheless, with the logic of cost–benefit analysis, when all other repressive measures are exhausted, authorities sometimes provide petitioners with extra-legal interests to buy them off and 'tie up their tongues', at least for a period of time.

When government and citizens confront each other in disputes – for example, when peasants' interests and demands may affect government interests in relation to tax, land development, investment initiatives and political performance – the government's usual strategic response is to shut down all official forms of legal remedies. But doing so creates a vicious cycle. Being unable to seek remedies through formal justice forces villagers to take 'extra-legal' collective action, which can evolve into petitioning and so-called 'mass incidents' that are considered threats to social stability. The government will consequently adopt a more direct 'stability maintenance' mode. Put simply, local governments are often unwilling or unable to accept judgments decided in accordance with law, instead favouring tough measures that include tactics such as buying out the protest leaders, setting members of the collective against each other in 'divide and conquer' strategies, coercion and arrests, which are powerful responses and can be seemingly endless.

The local governments believe these measures can make the people involved step back to become more aware of the whole situation, and in so doing, the people will stop their confrontational actions and the local governments will thus achieve 'stability'. The news and academic research have exposed thousands of collectively organized protests in rural areas, which demonstrate how and why the stability maintenance mode has been strengthened and toughened in recent years. Unfortunately for members of rural communities, most of the time this hard-line strategy is effective for stability maintenance in the short term, despite greater frequency of mass incidents, higher costs of stability maintenance, and lack of sustainability in using this mode. Below we examine these issues in more detail in relation to two pollution cases in Hubei Province.

The Zhaiwan Case

The overall situation

On the border between Hubei Province and Henan Province and to the east of the Bai River (a Tangbai River tributary) lies Zhaiwan, a village in Zhuji Town, Xiangyang District, Xiangfan City,[3] Hubei Province. It has five villager groups, 720 households, more than 3,400 people and a working population of 1,200.[4] The village has 3,800 *mu* (253.3 hectares) of farmland, including 800 *mu* (53.3 hectares) of paddy fields. Water for production and daily life comes from the Bai River. The Bai River rises in Funiu Mountain, running through cities and towns like Nanyang to Xiangfan City. Its main stream is 328.2 kilometres long, with 200 kilometres in Henan Province and 28 kilometres in Hubei Province. The Bai River and Tang River, which both have their source in Henan Province, meet at Xiangwangying in Xiangyang District and form the Tangbai River. The Tangbai is the biggest tributary downstream of the Han River, with a river basin of 24,500 square kilometres, running through Henan and Hubei Province. The Tangbai River is joined by the Gun River flowing from Zaoyang at Sunwangying in Hubei Province. It then runs 22.6 kilometres southwest to Zhangwan in the Xiangyang District before joining the Han River, with a basin covering another area of 991.1 square kilometres. The quality of the Tang River is normally at level III standard, but over roughly the past ten years heavy pollution in the Bai River where the Tangbai River arrives in Hubei Province has worsened the quality to a standard level of V minus or even lower.[5]

---

[3] In 2012 Xiangfang City was renamed as Xiangyang City, while the Xiangyang District was renamed as Xiangcheng District. The highly costly renaming of the city involved the approval of the central government, and was partly driven by the local government's plan to develop tourism. Xiangyang has been a long-used and famous name since the period of Three Kingdom (AD 220–80). In this text, the authors still use the previous name, in use when the field study was conducted.

[4] Authors' interviews during field visit in Xiangyang, Hubei Province in April 2010.

[5] The Environmental Quality Standards for Surface Water (GB3838–2002) set five levels based on function and purpose of protection and specifying what

Shallow groundwater is contaminated by pollutants in the heavily polluted Bai River. Zhaiwan Village lies on an alluvial plain of sand with well water connected to the river. When pollution is heavy in the shallow groundwater, well water pumped out is yellow and putrid. Sometimes the water may look normal, but after being boiled it becomes like mud and contains black sediments. Rice boiled in the water also turns yellow in Well No. 1, the closest well to the Bai River (Zhan and Zi 2005); the permanganate index was 2.96 mg per litre, close to level III groundwater quality standard, and the nitrite index was 0.05 mg per litre, 1.5 times higher than this standard. Other tests at this time showed that water in three other wells in the village contained chromium-6, benzene and toluene, which are all carcinogenic.

These carcinogenic chemicals are mainly used or produced by paper mills that use straw to make paper pulp, or are produced as wastes during industrial processes such as methanol extraction. Statistics show there were once hundreds of paper mills upstream of the Bai River in Nanyang in Henan Province, five of them in the village closest to Zhaiwan, which is Mazhuang Village in Wuxing Town, Xinye County. Xinye County still has no sewage treatment plants and all waste water flows directly into the Bai River. In Nanyang, 300,000 tons of domestic waste water are produced every day, but the city has only one sewage treatment plant with capacity of a mere 100,000 tons. The remaining 200,000 tons of waste water is dumped into the river (Zhan and Zi 2005).

In April 2005 the Department of Health in Xiangyang conducted a study on the causes of death in Zhaiwan Village (with a population of 3,400). The study showed that in the previous ten years more than 150 villagers had been diagnosed with cancer and 109 had died. The death rate was more than twice the average death rate of Xiangfan City in Hubei Province and the incidence of cancer was 80 times higher than the average level in China. Types of cancer diagnosed in the village include

---

the water is mainly suitable for: Level I, water sources and national nature reserves; Level II, first class protection areas of concentrated drinking water sources, fish breeding areas, habitat areas of rare aquatic organisms and feeding areas for young fish; Level III, second class protection areas of concentrated drinking water sources, fishery areas including wintering grounds, migration channels and areas of aquafarming, as well as swimming areas; Level IV, common industrial water sources and areas used for recreation where water does not directly touch human bodies; Level V, agricultural use and water areas in common landscape areas. Waters worse than Level V are not suitable for agricultural use and do not meet the requirements for water areas in common landscape areas.

oesophagus, bladder, colorectal, brain, breast, cardiac and leukaemia. Villager Group No. 3, for example, recorded 36 deaths from 1995 to 2005, with cancer accounting for 69 per cent and heart disease for 22 per cent. Of deaths caused by cancer, gastrointestinal cases accounted for 69 per cent, and respiratory cases for 31 per cent.

Victims of pollution in the village were not only the old. Zhai Junjun died of leukaemia aged 16 years. Zhai Yunsheng lost his father, mother, elder sister and younger brother to cancer. As an 18-year-old orphan, he left to work outside the village and the sight of his deserted house cut deeply into the souls of the local people. Most who died of cancer could not afford medical treatment; they simply went to the hospital for a diagnosis and then returned home, waiting in pain for their life to end.

Water pollution has also had a severe effect on primary production, in particular in crop plantation, animal husbandry and fishing. Rice yield, which was once more than 1200 *jin* (600 kilograms) per *mu*, was subsequently reduced to roughly 800 *jin* per *mu*. Now villagers plant on dry land, refusing to use water from the river. People can no longer breed sheep and cows because there is no longer grass on the river bank and cattle die from drinking river water. And with pollution worsening and no fish in the river, fishermen turn to work in other industries or work outside the village.

Ten years of salvation efforts

Villagers began to notice the high incidence of cancer and suspect the Bai River pollution as its cause in 1995. But because the Bai River and its pollution came from Henan Province, for bureaucratic reasons it was difficult to coordinate a response, making cross-province water pollution almost irremediable. In previous years, authorities of Hubei Province and Xiangfan City had made several attempts to coordinate activities with the relevant government departments, but results were not as good as expected. A turning point came, however, with establishment of an environmental organization, Hubei Province's first environmental NGO, commonly known as Green Han River (*Lüse hanjiang*).

Establishment of Green Han River

The founder of Green Han River, Yun Jianli, had been a member of the municipal Chinese People's Political Consultative Conference (CPPCC)[6]

[6] The CPPCC is a political advisory body of the Chinese government (from central to city or county level). Membership of this conference usually means the person has a high reputation in his/her profession or community and is

for a considerable period of time. In 2000 she noticed a sewage outlet under the Han River Bridge when she was passing by on a bus. One passenger told her that the pollution was even worse upstream in the Gun River. Yun then went to the Gun River to investigate for herself. In April 2000 she travelled more than 2,000 kilometres and spent one month investigating 24 sources of pollution into the four tributaries of the Han River in Xiangfan: the Nan, Bei, Man and Xiaoqing Rivers. Based on this investigation, she wrote 'An Investigation Report on Water Pollution of the Han River in Xiangfan', and presented it at a meeting of the CPPCC Standing Committee. Through her initiatives and community efforts, the pollution in the Han River finally attracted the attention of government officials and relevant authorities.

Yun then began to focus all her energy on environmental protection. She travelled more than 36,860 kilometres on 246 separate occasions to investigate the sources polluting the Han River and its tributaries in Xiangfan and gained considerable first-hand information. Later she made many proposals and wrote several reports with titles such as 'Act Now for Water Treatment', 'The Disturbing Reality of Air Quality in Urban Areas' and 'Do not Turn Industrial Parks into Pollution Sources'.

In March 2002 Yun learned from a television report that the Xiang River and Chang (Yangtze) River Environmental Organization in Hunan Province had organized for college students to come together to remove garbage from the rivers. The news inspired her to set up an environmental organization in Xiangfan. After obtaining permission from relevant authorities, Yun and several other members of the CPPCC set up Xiangfan Environmental Organization (*Xiangfan huanbao xiehui*), otherwise known as the Green Han River (*Lüse hanjiang*). Not only was it the first environmental NGO in Hubei Province, it remains the only environmental NGO in the Han River area. The organization's three full-time volunteers – Li Zhihe and Yun Jianli in their mid-sixties, and Ye Fuyi in her mid-fifties – did not earn a penny due to the organization's lack of financial support. Funds for events and training came from donations that

recognized by the government as an appropriate person to conduct consultations representing this profession or community. The influence of such a status is likened to being a member of the local People's Congress, but their power is much more limited. Ms Yun was a local high school biology and chemistry teacher for more than 20 years and was retired. She had been a member of the CPPCC since 1985 and maintained her status in the CPPCC for close to 20 years. She took up the investigation and used her status to bring this issue to the municipal government decision makers through the mechanism of the CPPCC.

Yun worked hard to obtain, and funds for producing pamphlets and reading materials were all donated by other environmental entities.

The operation: cooperation with government

Yun was aware of how to cooperate effectively with the government and obtain cooperation from it since she was a member of the municipal CPPCC. She views environmental NGOs as an important complement to the government and a bridge between the government and the public, so she recognizes it is important for these NGOs to win support from relevant authorities. Green Han River's efforts won recognition from both the municipal government and the municipal CPPCC of Xiangfan. Yun was invited to give speeches to many government bodies in Xiangfan and many government officials became volunteers in Green Han River.

The solution: a drinking water project

The people were convinced that the high prevalence of cancer caused by contaminated water could be reduced through a drinking water project. The whole project was estimated to cost 1.3 million yuan, 1.17 million of which would come from government offices: the Water Resources Department of Hubei, the municipal government of Xiangfan and the local government of Xiangyang. Villagers of Zhaiwan would have to pay the rest through the villagers' committee. Yun obtained a US$30,000 (approximately 220,000 yuan) donation from the China Development Marketplace of the World Bank. The project, designed and run by the Water Resources Office of Xiangyang, was launched in September 2005.

This project involved drilling a well 130 metres deep and 800 metres away from the Bai River. The well would go through the polluted shallow groundwater layer and provide safe water to every household, with the help of a water tower and water treatment facilities. On 27 March 2006 the project was completed. After drilling of the well was completed, the polluted shallow groundwater layer was sealed to avoid potential contamination. Water tests identified that the well water met the standard of safe drinking water and by June 2006 all villagers in Zhaiwan had access to safe drinking water. The well even produced sufficient water for more than 6,000 villagers in Wangji and Huanggang Villages as well. From 2007 to 2008, the Xiangyang Water Resources Office drilled more wells for other riverside villages, providing drinking water for up 25,000 people in more than 20 villages within two kilometres of the banks of the Bai River.

After the project was completed coordinated by Green Han River, Yun received a 10 million yen grant from the Japanese government for a Peoples-benefit Project to launch a Drinking Water Project in Liuwan

Village in Zhuji Town, also in Xiangyang District. With another 2.93 million yuan from local government, Yun and Green Han River were instrumental in the building of water works with a daily capacity of 2,000 tons, which provides water to more than 10,000 people in six villages in Zhuji Town, Xiangyang District: Liuwan, Sanhe, Yuanwan, Haowan, Panwan and Luzhuang.

Other benefits

These projects described above and the processes through which they were brought about had profound positive, practical and political impacts – on the lives of the villagers in the rural areas where the projects were implemented, on Green Han River as an NGO, and on the governments at local level that were involved. Through these processes, the villagers, the organization and the local governments learned more effective ways to negotiate and collaborate with each other towards overcoming conflict. Eventually they could resolve at least the problem of securing safe village drinking water in the wake of companies polluting the local rivers. Although many of the offending companies retained their political power and continued to operate as they wanted, the authorities did respond to aggrieved villagers exercising their more powerful political voice, which Green Han River helped to unify, activate and steer.

Villagers became more aware of environmental protection and were willing to fight for their environmental rights. They began to take note of environmental violations and report pollution cases. Regaining strength for life, they now have a greater love for their village and there are fewer complaints. Some villagers who had left returned to build houses and young people are able to have a family. Importantly, the villagers learned about political activism. They learned from each other about how to do politics together to achieve their desired goals, as individuals collectively and through establishing a more formal organization such as the issue-focussed NGO. They learned to take initiative, collaborate and pursue alternatives to build collective power in their relations with the authorities and offending companies. They learned not just to achieve desired results but to reach further, to apply and pass on their lessons to help other communities solve similar problems.

At the initiative of activist Yun Jianli and as the result of efforts by Green Han River as an active NGO, this may be a model for others in similar circumstances to pursue political activism to address community concerns. Green Han River has enhanced its ability to handle large projects, with more volunteers and greater influence. Full-time volunteer Li Zhihe claimed that through the Zhaiwan Project their organization's experience in cooperating with the relevant government authorities was positive and the organization's members gained more power over the situation. Volunteer Ye Fuyi noted that the World Bank and other organizations not only brought benefits to the people of Zhaiwan, but also strengthened the organization's capacity as an NGO. Members learned a great deal, from making project proposals to final assessment. Green Han River gained public confidence the hard way, through a rough journey. At the end of 2013 the organization had 66 institutional members, 160 individual members and more than 30,000 volunteers. They included officials from the local People's Congress, the CPPCC and government offices, environmental authorities, the traffic police and even prison management, as well as teachers, students and people from the media.

As well as the political lessons for the villagers, the local governments learned to respond more effectively to the needs of people in the rural areas they govern. They learned to implement policies that not only address local tensions but achieve valuable practical outcomes. To a limited extent, they learned to actually enforce the laws and regulations established to serve village or larger local needs. After launching the initial project in Zhaiwan Village, the authorities in Henan constructed more pollution treatment plants and began punishing high-pollution companies. Authorities in Xiangfan ordered high polluting companies to reach environmental standards within time deadlines or their operation would be shut down and some offending companies were actually closed down. In Zhaiwan and some other villages the projects also presented development opportunities. The Villager Committee of Zhaiwan, for example, renovated its office building, paved cement roads, installed high voltage power transmission lines and helped establish a medical care system for major illnesses.

Still a long way to go

Certainly local activism inspired some improvements to the polluted drinking water and beyond. But both practical and political problems still need resolution. With cross-province cooperation and the iron hand of Xiangfan Environmental Protection Bureau (EPB), pollution produced by some companies was mitigated and the water quality of the Tangbai River was improved from level-V to level-IV by 2006.[7] But this was still not sufficient to completely solve the pollution problem and satisfy

[7] This was stated in the news at the end of the 'hot period' when national media was concerned with this cancer village in 2006. According to the recent official report, the water quality went back and forth after the year 2005. Even in 2011 and 2012, the Tang branch of the river was level-IV, the Bai branch was

aggrieved villagers. When interviewed by a journalist in 2005, authorities in Xinye County Henan province said that by 2004 they had shut down all small paper mills to treat pollution in the Bai River. Xinye EPB Vice Director Gao Shuyun advised, 'One new paper mill has the approval to produce, but it hasn't started production'. Chief engineer of Nanyang EPB in Henan, Lei Qinghe, echoed this view, stating, 'In Nanyang, 100 paper mills have been shut down. Now, there are only five left' (Yuan 2005).

However, law enforcement clearly remained a problem. Pictures taken by some reporters at Mazhuang Village in Wuxing Town, Xinye County on 23 April 2005 reveal that some paper mills were in fact still operating. In July 2005, some reporters came to Wuxing Town to interview local people. The reporters discovered that some paper mills had actually increased their production. Officials at environmental authorities in Henan found their hands tied. As Gao Shuyun remarked, 'Law enforcement is not effective enough. For example, after being identified as a high-polluter, one offending company was given three months to rectify the situation before being shutdown. But three months is a long period to allow companies to keep discharging waste water. And we can do nothing about it'. In the second half of 2005, the Ministry of Environmental Protection sent officials to investigate. They found that some paper mills upstream had been shut down, but many were still running. The pollution level was only slightly lower than it had been before the local activism. Sewage discharge upstream began around 10 o'clock each night. By day, the heat of the sun made the water putrid and by night, the whole river was black.

Before the environmental organization Green Han River's initiatives, all sewage in Xinye County in Henan province was discharged directly into the Bai River. At the time, under pressure from environmental organizations and the media, the sewage was discharged into the Bai indirectly, via the Li River. A disgusting smell was everywhere along the banks of the Li. Sewage from eight paper mills in Mazhuang Village was discharged directly into the river and the polluted river water ran into Xiangfan in Hubei Province. However, in 2006, when volunteers of Green Han River and reporters from Xiangfan went there to investigate, some villagers tried to stop them through violent force. These developments suggest the market economy had corrupted the earlier morals of

level-V in 2011 and improved to level-IV in 2012. See the interview of the deputy chief of the Xiangyang EPB on 5 June 2013 (Xiangyang Government 2013).

some villagers. Some in the neighbourhood believe that offending companies have an effective way to deal with those who are supposed to supervise their activities by paying off the 'guard' at the entrance to the village and anyone who tips off the companies about incoming EPB officers, journalists and others.

In short, as a Green Han River volunteer observed of this organization's work, the outcome amounted to 'Drilling one well, shocking two provinces and saving three villages'. The practical outcomes of their efforts contributed not only to curbing some of the destructive water pollution by powerful offending corporations, but also to restoring villagers' access to essential drinking water, to saving villagers' lives and to stimulating the local economy. Political outcomes included empowerment of the villagers, particularly through their enhanced knowledge of how to do grassroots politics collectively and to pursue legal activism effectively. They could actually see – and taste – the success of their efforts. But perhaps the most important political outcome, at least for governments right through from village to national level, was that resolving the problem of polluted drinking water curbed the social unrest that the problem inspired and hence achieved stability that reigns in national policy priorities.

A Second Dispute: Luotian County, Hubei Province

Luotian County is located in east Hubei at the southern foot of the Dabieshan mountain. It is bordered by Yingshan County and Xishui County in the east and the south, neighbouring Tuanfeng County and Macheng City in the west, and adjacent to Jinzhai County (Anhui Province) in the north. With an area of 2,144 square kilometres and a population of 600,000, the county stretches 105 kilometres from north to south and 54.7 kilometres east to west. With mountains, hills and rivers in its proximity, Luotian has pleasant views of nature and rich resources. It is well known as the home of silkworms, chestnuts, poria cocos and persimmons.

Yishuihe River originates from the Fengshupu and Tanghe Rivers. Its upper streams are named according to where they are situated in relation to the Baimiaohe, Changhe and Lianghekou Rivers, while its downstreams are the Zhongjieehe, Xiajiehe, Youzhahe and Fengshuhe Rivers. It confluences with the midstream of the Bashui River as the Youhe River, goes southwest and finally falls into the Bahe River. The river is 78.2 kilometres long, flowing through towns such as Baimiaohe, Dahe'an, Beifeng, Sanliqiao, Sanlifan and Fengshan. The riverbed is 80–220 metres wide, with drainage of 765 square kilometres. It has 215 tributaries that vary in size; 17 are Level I tributaries. The population within this area is 170,000. Paddy fields account for 34 per cent of the county's total cultivated area and grain accounts for 50 per cent. This area is therefore called the 'granary of Luotian'.

Hongyuan Pharmaceutical Company (hereafter Hongyuan Company) was established in 2002 and is located in Luotian County. With nine years' operating experience, it had become one of the province's top 100 private enterprises and top 100 high-tech enterprises. Hongyuan Company is the biggest taxpayer in Luotian County. The company has three main production bases (the old production zone, a pharmaceutical zone and a chemical zone), all of them beside the Yishuihe river and covering an area of 360,000 square metres. The old production zone is in the suburban area of the county in Hejiafan Town, while the other two zones are both located in the Luotian Industry Zone in Lizi'ao Town. The production zone produces mainly Glyoxal, Glyoxylic acid, Dimetridazole and other chemicals; the pharmaceutical zone produces mainly Metronidazole, Metronidazole Benzoate, beverages, health care products and so forth. The chemical zone mainly produces food additives, new energies, fine chemicals and other products. The annual output of Glyoxal and Metronidazole at 70,000 tons and 5,000 tons respectively makes Hongyuan the world's number 1 producer of those chemicals mentioned above.

The Hongyuan Company moved to the Luotian Industry Zone, only 200 metres away from the confluence of the Bashuihe and Yishuihe rivers, after 2009. Xujiachong village is located across the river and has a population of 900, only 500–600 of whom are permanent residents. Most of them are elderly, children and women, since young and middle-aged men are usually working in other areas out of town. People in Xujiachong Village used to access their water from the Bashuihe River. Since the river has been polluted, some of them have to dig wells, while others take water from ponds.

After Hongyuan Company moved into the industry zone, it expelled waste water into the Bashuihe River without any pollution mitigation in place. Gases it expels from the manufacturing areas are yellow or brown, and their smell, which is bad during the day, worsens at night. Villagers reported the pollution problem to the Village Committee and at the same time attempted to negotiate with the company. After villagers' reporting, the local government required Hongyuan Company to halt its production for a short period. However, production soon resumed. The company no longer discharged waste water directly into the river and instead expelled it from underground. But that worsened rather than mitigated the pollution problem, causing die-off of fish and shrimp. The situation further outraged the villagers.

Recognizing no alternative, villagers in Xujiachong felt forced to organize and act in protest. On 8 January 2011 (immediately after the Chinese new year holidays), villagers went to Hongyuan Company to protest. They carried excrement from the river and protest banners. They sat in front of the factory gate blocking entry and called for a halt to production to at least abate the pollution. The county government sent a large number of police to deal with the incident, but since the police had clearly taken sides with Hongyuan Company, villagers were furious and collided with the police. The police took no further action and left the scene. At around 2 o'clock the following morning, more than 200 policemen rushed into Xujiachong, breaking into people's houses and dragging them out of bed. The police took away three villagers and detained them for 'obstructing official business'; one was a man aged around 70 and two were women, one of whom had not long ago given birth. Villagers asked the Village Committee and town leaders to plead before the Public Security Bureau for their release. The Procuratorate ended up not formally charging the detainees and released them on the condition that the Village Committee would ensure there would be 'no more trouble'.

After the three villagers were released, the local government, the Hongyuan Company, the Village Committee and villagers participated in multilateral negotiations. It was eventually agreed that Hongyuan Company would pay each household 400 RMB (yuan), which they could use to dig wells. After making the agreement, the Hongyuan Company continued discharging harmful wastes, but no one dared to stand up and object.

CONCLUSIONS AND DISCUSSION

Since 1996 the number of mass incidents over environmental concerns has continued to increase, on average by 29 per cent each year (Wang 2012). The frequency of major environmental incidents is high. Since 2005 the Ministry of Environmental Protection has been directly involved in dealing with 927 incidents, 72 of them major. In 2011 the number of major incidents increased by 120 per cent on the previous year's number. The frequency of environment-related protests in 2011 is largely due to the higher levels and volume of heavy metals and dangerous chemicals polluting the environment through industrial production. In recent years the media has relentlessly reported major mass incidents protesting against environmental pollution. These include protests against PX projects[8] in 2007 by Xiamen citizens, dubbed the 'walking' (*sanbu*) protests, in 2011 by Dalian citizens and in 2012 by Tianjin citizens – and later in 2012, incidents in Shifang, Qidong and Ningbo. These mass incidents show that Chinese people are more willing than before to take to the streets expressing their dissatisfaction, and sometimes they are able to win by forcing the government to give in. Importantly, these widely reported incidents all took place in cities, not in rural areas.

The particular circumstances relating to the two rural pollution cases discussed in this chapter were different from the well-documented cases mentioned above. The first ended without any major incident, largely due to the intervention of an ex-government official who could effectively persuade the municipal government to take measures within the context of national media concern and pressure from the central government. The second involved some official action to mitigate the pollution though it did not end up improving the situation for both villagers and the village rivers. Power relations among the major players remained intact. In both of these rural cases, the grievances of the residents and the outcomes of the disputes were politically akin to a breeze wafting past, similar to stones thrown across water causing momentary ripples, with the water then returning to calmness. But beyond the metaphors, the water of these village rivers did not return to cleanliness – to the potable condition it was in before the industrial pollution poured in by the large businesses inspired the villagers to take to the streets for their momentary ripple in the social stability of their village. Neither did the villages, at least in the second case, really return to calmness. The people's protests in Xujiachong were coercively removed from the streets, but it is likely that their unresolved grievances and anger fester in other less public ways.

Time passes and life goes on. Common adages such as 'water is the source of life' and 'food is the first necessity' seem like weak words from a time past when confronted with the discourse of 'development is the absolute principle' and 'stability is the top priority'. The government wants to keep large corporations onside and as a result, year after year,

---

[8] PX is the abbreviation for para-xylene. Exposure of para-xylene in humans can cause headache, fatigue, dizziness, listlessness, confusion, irritability, gastro-intestinal disturbances including nausea and loss of appetite, flushing of the face, and a feeling of increased body heat. It is used in many industries for the production of goods for people's daily necessities and large profits can be made for both companies and local governments. Local residents were angry that they were not informed about the programmes and particularly about the lack of disclosure about the effects of PX on health.

industrial pollution has been penetrating directly into the lives of villagers. It inhabits and harms the natural environment without government or the corporations taking precautions until – and in rural areas, despite – public protest against this pollution, through mass incidents that destabilize society. When people are alienated and forced underground, villagers suffer greatly. This happens when authorities seek to achieve social stability by coercive force, containing mass incidents where people express their unaddressed grievances, rather than by addressing these grievances directly through prohibiting the polluting actions of the offending companies. Governments at all levels behave as if beholden to these companies, despite the law and the people whom the law is to serve.

The rural environmental tragedies in the two cases discussed above are an outcome of both the supremacy of GDP growth as a top national priority and the negative effects of marketization upon people and places. But they can also be attributed to the indifference of policymakers, local authorities and polluting enterprises to villagers' interests. The difference between rural areas and cities in their responses to pollution is that villagers generally have less opportunity and capacity to voice their rights. Because the scale of villagers' public protests is much smaller, they cannot have the political clout of city protesters whose recognizably 'mass incidents' – and thus capacity for expanding social instability – draw large-scale media coverage and consequently responses from the authorities towards remedying the problem and restoring social stability.

Aggrieved villagers also usually require the duty-bearer – the company creating the pollution and also the authorities as guardians of the common good – to take responsibility for the problem. Villagers first became aware of escalation in the incidence of cancer in Zhaiwan around 1995, but they could not make their protest voice heard because they lacked both the capacity for self-help and the negotiation skills required for dispute resolution. They also did not have access to some of the information they needed to negotiate or to obtain advice from professionals and law practitioners. It was not until 2000 when Yun Jianli discovered the issue by accident that she was able to mobilize supporters and push their sufferings into the spotlight, which brought villagers the hope for resolution.

Because the villagers did not have medical insurance, after they were diagnosed with cancer, the elderly would simply return home and wait for death. The younger ones as main breadwinners of the family would receive some medical treatment for a while and then would die with unpaid debts. The pollution remained rampant, and in claiming many lives it made the challenges increasingly tougher. Villagers find that they are not in a position to take advantage of concepts such as 'fighting according to law' (Li and O'Brien 1997) and 'using the law to fight your battle' (Yu 2004).

Villagers are after all 'reluctant fighters'; overwhelmed by interconnected powers and business interests (Wu 2007), they usually suppress their anger. Regardless of the situation, they expect justice from officials and a social conscience from the polluters, hoping the problem will be resolved before things turn ugly. Because they lack organizational and political savvy, their actions are not well organized or politically astute. When their voice is weak, they are easily fobbed off; if their shared anger erupts, their actions are then classified as a 'mass incident', which is often brutally suppressed. But villagers are not timid and they are more sophisticated than is usually imagined. They have many clever ways to fight. However, in the face of rampant, even lethal pollution and conspiracy between polluters and officials, villagers' spontaneous, emotional and scattered actions can easily fail. Failure usually brings long-term frustration to the villagers,[9] making them indifferent to authority, order and values.

Pollution in the rural village river in this chapter's second case, in Xujiachong, created problems in recent times – ten years after the first case in Zhaiwan. During this period, villagers have become more aware of their rights. More importantly, they are now more likely to obtain external support, and from their constant struggles they have gained knowhow and experience. They have gradually figured out the government's 'tricks and strategies' so in some cases they can take action more effectively. The 'tricks and strategies' of the government can be summarized: when the law complements the will of government authorities, legal discourse will be applied and disputes will be solved on a legal basis. But when application of law conflicts with a particular government agenda, law will be used only to hide what is really going on backstage or it will be discarded entirely.

These two 'governance' modes are becoming increasingly incompatible. It appears that legal discourse, long parasitic and subordinate to government authority, has begun to be replaced by the discourse of socialist construction and one-party rule. In this situation, 'the stronger the maintenance [of stability], the less likelihood there is for stability' (*yue wei yue buwen*). This is true in situations where the hypocrisy and

[9] 'Before drilling the well, we went to interview the people. Villagers were very indifferent and said, "Everyone asks us about this and that, but nothing is solved."' Cited from 'The Final Assessment of the Drinking Water Project in Zhaiwan Village'. See Lüse hanjiang (2007).

weakness of law are revealed to those who need the law to protect them. These people have become despondent and disappointed. For them, authority prevails over law, and they 'put their faith in petitioning rather than law' (*xinfang bu xinfa*). They would rather organize collective action than seek help through law. They recognize that within the framework of stability maintenance, they may be able to draw support from the government and change the will of the local authorities by 'making trouble' to draw the attention of higher authorities. Ultimately, to avoid stability maintenance practice backfiring on the government, the only way forward to build and maintain a stable Chinese society is to protect and realize people's rights with an effective judicial remedy system, which is, after all, the foundation of stability.

REFERENCES

Dong, Leiming (2008), *Songcun de tiaojie: jubian shidai de quanwei yu zhixu* (Mediation in Song Village: Authority and Order in the Era of Great Change). Beijing: China Law Press.

Li, Lianjiang and O'Brien, Kevin (1997), 'Dangdai Zhongguo nongmin de yifa kangzheng' (Villagers' rightful resistance in contemporary China), in Wu Guoguang (ed.), *Jiuqi xiaoying* (*The 1997 Effect*). Hong Kong: The Pacific Century Institute, pp. 141–70.

Liu, Yutian (2012), 'Da tiaojie cujin da hexie' (Grand mediation promotes grand harmony), *Renmin fayuan bao* (People's Court News), 11 August: 4.

Lüse hanjiang (Green Han River) (2007), 'Zhaiwancun cunmin anquan yinshui gongcheng zhongqi pinggu baogao' (The Final Assessment of the Drinking Water Project in Zhaiwan Village).

Wang, Shengjun (2009), 'Nengdong sifa shi renmin fayuan fuwu daju de biran xuanze' (Judicial activism is the inevitable choice of the people's court in serving the overall situation), Xinhua wang, http://news.xinhuanet.com/legal/2009-09/01/content_11974701_1.htm. Accessed 12 November 2012.

Wang, Shu (2012), 'Jianyu fa deng 7 bu falü xiugai 18 chu' (Seven laws including the prison law have been revised in relation to 18 issues), *Xinjingbao* (The Beijing News), 27 October: 5.

Wu, Yi (2007), 'Quanli-liyi de jiegou zhi wang' yu nongmin quntixing liyi de biaode kunjing' (The net of power and interest and the difficulty of expressing farmers' interests), *Shehuixue yanjiu* (Sociological Studies), 22: 21–43.

Xiangyang Government (2013), 'Xiangyangshi huanjing zhuangkuang jieshi' (Explanations of the current situation relating to the environment in Xiangfang), Xiangyang government website, http://www.xiangyang.gov.cn/network/zxft/ft/hjzk/. Accessed 20 October 2013.

Xinhua News Agency (2011), 'Zhongguo tese shehuizhuyi falv tixi yijing xingcheng' (Socialist legal system takes shape in China), *Zhongguo falü* (Law in China), 1: 1–2.

Yu, Jianrong (2004), 'Dangqian nongmin weiquan huodong de yige jieshi kuangjia' (An interpretation framework for villagers' rights campaigns), *Shehuixue yanjiu* (Sociological Studies), 2: 49–55.

Yuan, Zhe (2005), 'Xinhua zonghenh wushi liuguo de cunzhuang' (Villages that have been affected by the spread of sewage into waterways), *Xinhua News*, 16 August, http://news.xinhuanet.com/video/2005-08/16/content_3362578.htm. Acesssed 20 October 2013.

Zhan, Guoqiang and Zi, Hongqi (2005), 'Baihe zenme chengle "chiren" he, shinian duozou jin bai cunmin shengming' (How did the Baihe become a river of 'eating people' and take hundreds of villagers' lives over a 10 year period), Xinhuawang, http://news.xinhuanet.com/focus/2005-08/21/content_3377045.htm. Accessed 11 November 2012.

Zhou, Lingang and Zhu, Changhua (2009), 'Shangcan nongmin'gong "shiliao" de ququan jizhi fenxi' (Analysis of the mechanism of disempowerment in cases of 'private settlement' with injured and disabled migrant workers), *Gansu shehui kexue* (Gansu Social Science), 1: 20–23.

PART 2

Creating and sustaining legal frameworks

5. Regulation by escalation: unrest, lawmaking and law enforcement in China

Benjamin van Rooij

INTRODUCTION

Since 1978 the rise of a private or semi-private market in China has coincided with a growth of regulatory rules and institutions. These have now formed into a complex system that seeks to regulate most forms of economic behaviour. This chapter aims to understand how the development and actual functioning of regulation fits with China's resilient (cf., Nathan 2003) authoritarian settings, and more particularly how China's form of regulation interacts with actual and potential unrest.[1]

Regulatory theory offers two key perspectives that help us to understand why regulation has become such an important part of China's authoritarian mode of governance. The first is public interest and market failure theory, which explains how the development of a market and the move towards a market from a planned economy require regulation to deal with failures of such markets. The predominant paradigm of this perspective is one of broad public interest or utilitarianism, namely that regulation helps to change market behaviour that does not serve the public interest and as such helps to sustain economic growth (Baldwin and Cave 1999, Morgan and Yeung 2007). Regulation can help developing markets deal with market failures such as monopolies, externalities, information asymmetries or inequality. The second perspective is private interest theory, which holds that regulation is a product of the interests of the regulators who can use it as a source of rent seeking (Baldwin and Cave 1999, Morgan and Yeung 2007). This theory seems very plausible

[1] This chapter takes a broad view of unrest, defining it as any event that is or could be perceived as undermining stability and the position of those in power.

in the case of China, especially given the immense rent seeking opportunities a combination of economic transition and oligarchic authoritarian political structure holds (Liew 1993, Lu 1999, Wedeman 2003, Ngo and Wu 2009).

This chapter combines the public and private interest view of regulation into a third view that is especially relevant for an authoritarian state such as China. This third view focuses on the role that regulation plays in maintaining authoritarian power and reducing market-driven risks that can cause social unrest and undermine the legitimacy and ultimately the rule of the authoritarian regime. As such, regulation serves both a private interest (namely maintaining the position of those in power) and a public interest (doing so by preventing causes of unrest). In this authoritarian view of regulation, the prevention of unrest becomes the overriding objective of regulation.

To understand the development and functioning of regulation in China, this chapter focuses on the relationship between regulation and unrest. It looks at how Chinese characteristics of authoritarianism converge to shape the formation and functioning of regulation, and how such regulation interacts with perceived and real forms of unrest. The chapter finds that unrest or the fear thereof has played a multiple role in the development and functioning of regulation. Real and potential unrest and sources of unrest have helped create and revise increasingly stringent regulation, while at the same time they have also encouraged more socially responsive forms of regulation. Unrest itself has also has become a form of regulation enforcement in the sense that protests often spur on regulators to enforce compliance with the law.

Yet at the same time, fear of unrest has created a form of public management that is quite opposed to social responsiveness and itself undermines resultant societal-based forms of regulation. Ultimately this reaction will not help regulation to reduce the risks that may cause future unrest. The result of this unhealthy nexus between unrest and regulation is that China's regulatory authoritarianism works through escalation. This is because regulation tends to become more successfully adopted and implemented only when matters get out of hand, while prior to such escalation regulation fails to curb risks that will spur public dissatisfaction and unrest and thus escalation.

The chapter first qualifies China's authoritarian settings. It continues with a look at how regulatory law developed and what role unrest played in that development. We then go on to look in more depth at the influence of unrest first on administrative enforcement of regulatory law and then on private enforcement by citizens.

AUTHORITARIANISM WITH CHINESE CHARACTERISTICS

Before we can analyse how unrest shapes regulation, we need to take into account the nature of China's authoritarian setting, particularly how Party-state expressions of authoritarianism are linked to perceptions of stability threats. Therefore, before we begin to explore the relationship between regulation and unrest in China's authoritarian setting, this setting itself requires qualifying.

A number of observations can be made in respect to China's current political environment. First, China's form of authoritarianism is increasingly one that involves institutions and legal rules. China has left behind the Maoist personal rule-based past for an increasingly rule-based, formal rational and institutionalized form of authoritarian rule by law (formal rational authoritarianism) (cf., Peerenboom 2002). Second, in relation to this first point, the Party-state increasingly uses merit-based and performance-based cadre selection and evaluation criteria (Edin 2003, Heimer 2006, Landry 2008, Minzner 2009, Wang 2013). Government administration thus carries some of the hallmarks of an increasingly competitive form of authoritarianism (Levitsky and Way 2002, 2010).

Third, Chinese governance has become a form of fragmented authoritarianism, where power in the Party-state is fragmented along vertical and horizontal lines (Lampton 1987, Lieberthal 1992, Shirk 1993) and is also increasingly shared between the Party-state and societal and market actors (Mertha 2009). Fourth, China's form of governance has retained strong experimental elements with areas of new policy or implementation first tried in certain localities or for short periods of time before being scaled up (Heilmann 2008), in a form of guided experimentalism.

Fifth and finally, China's brand of authoritarianism is increasingly responsive. In China's emerging form of 'responsive authoritarianism' (cf., Cai 2004, Weller 2008, He and Warren 2011, Reilly 2011), there is now space for societal input, including direct local elections, public hearings, access to courts, social media, and even protest, which act as feed-back mechanisms and tools for Party-state coordination (cf., Minzner 2005, Lorentzen 2013, Stockmann 2012, van Rooij 2012). Under responsive authoritarianism, the Chinese government walks a fine line between tolerating (and sometimes even encouraging) expression and controlling society (cf., Stockmann 2012).

UNREST AND THE DEVELOPMENT OF REGULATION

Before 1978, China could hardly be said to have had much regulatory law. This is not surprising as most of the economy was in the planned state and collective system, and the private market was highly limited. As the reform programme initiated under Deng Xiaoping took off, and especially since the early 1990s, as China embraced its own form of market economy, regulatory law began to flourish. As such we have seen the development of environmental, arable land protection, food safety and labour regulation (van Rooij 2012).

We could view the development of these and other regulatory laws through the perspective of the rise of the market and the necessity for the state to adopt rules to deal with market failures, or through the lens of the private interests of those in power who stand to make much money from the rents some of the regulatory laws could bring them. Here, however, we seek to explore the rise of regulatory laws, and especially the risk-related regulatory laws on labour, land, environment and food safety, from the perspective of regime stability and prevention of real or potential forms of unrest in the broadest sense.

When we look at the legislative histories of Chinese risk-related regulatory laws, we see that in many cases fear of unrest or potential sources of unrest have interacted with the lawmaking processes. The 2009 Food Safety Law is a good recent example to observe in some more depth. Its amendment process, which had been ongoing since 2004, came to its final phase in 2008 just at the time of the Melamine food scare, when a number of children died after developing kidney stones as a result of drinking milk laced with poisonous Melamine (Editorial 2008). Already in the explanations and discussions of earlier versions of the draft law, actors involved in the legislative process expressed the view that concern over popular sentiment about food-related risks and incidents was a key driver for the development of the new law. The State Council Legal Affairs Office (*fazhiban*) stated, for instance, in its introductory section of its explanation to the first formal draft of the new law in 2007: ‘The problem of food safety remains unresolved. Many food products continue to have safety hazards and food safety incidents keep occurring. The general population lacks a sense of safety in relation to food products … Our general population has strong [negative] opinions about this’ (Xin 2009: 286).

At the time there was already a strong indication from surveys conducted among the general population that most Chinese were very worried about the safety of their food (Xinhua News 2009), recording levels of up to 80 per cent of Chinese fearing the safety of their food. So already in the earlier phase of the drafting process, societal fears about unsafe food and negative opinion of this were a key driver in developing a more comprehensive and stronger regulation relating to food safety. Key new rules introduced in the first and second drafts included a stronger permit system, stronger sanctions, improved standards, a risk evaluation system, a producer responsibility system, access to information, the right to report accidents, and stronger civil remedies including a form of punitive damages (Xin 2009: 289–94, 302). With the second draft, a system of coordination and unified responsibility for local-level implementation of food safety law was also introduced, which was largely a response to concerns voiced by those participating in the drafting that the original draft would not be well implemented because of fragmented responsibilities and authorities (Xin 2009: 361).

When the Melamine milk scandal occurred the support for such a stronger law gained direct momentum, just as a third and final draft was being prepared by the National People's Congress Legal Commission. In its notice explaining this third draft, the Legal Commission made direct and explicit reference to the Melamine scandal, which at the time was still playing out, creating a strong negative effect on popular trust in the Party-state rule, a situation that continues even today.[2] The Legal Commission stated:

> Since the Sanlu baby milk powder accident happened, there is even more concern in society about food safety. And the Legal Commission and the [NPC Standing Committee] Legislative Affairs Committee have again conducted earnest study on how the law can help prevent such serious food safety accidents, and have used this to amend the second version of the draft (Xin 2009: 364).

The resultant third draft food safety law introduced a number of measures including more stringent standards for food additives such as the Melamine that had caused the scandal ongoing at the time, as well as measures to strengthen food recalls and accident reporting. While these legislative changes were a direct response to the accident, the concern for food safety was also used to further strengthen rules introduced in the second draft that sought to overcome the fragmentation of regulatory authority, by making the coordination and unified responsibility of local

---

[2] See http://www.wantchinatimes.com/news-subclass-cnt.aspx?id=20120109000012&cid=1103 indicating that 80 per cent of Chinese worry about the safety of their food. Accessed 24 March 2013.

governments more explicit as well as mandating stronger coordination between the various specialist food safety departments involved (Xin 2009: 364–5). The third draft was well received by NPC Standing Committee tasked with reviewing the draft food safety law, who discussed it while explicitly referring to anger and negative sentiments the Melamine scandal had caused (Zhongguo Renminwang 2008).

The Melamine incident thus came to legitimize the proposed rules and to stimulate the development of further rules seeking to curb food-related risk. Delegate Nan Zhenzhong stated, for instance, that after the incident many Chinese expressed worry about food safety and were calling vigorously for a stronger regulatory system (Zhongguo Renminwang 2008). Delegate Li Lianning stated that the Melamine incident was not just a matter of 'economic costs', but also of 'moral and political costs', affecting the reputation of the government. In the light of the Melamine scandal he expressed strong support for the new draft and hope that its measures could help reduce future food related risks (Zhongguo Renminwang 2008).

In the years preceding the Melamine incident, a number of other legislative processes of risk regulation had been similarly driven by concern for matters that could potentially give rise to negative popular sentiments and unrest. The 1998 Land Management Act amendment introduced stringent measures to protect arable land and food security (by maintaining sufficient quantity of food) as well as maintaining low food prices. This followed directly from the publication of a widely quoted study (Brown 1994) that China would at some point be unable to feed itself and a resultant national level investigation initiated by then premier Li Peng (van Rooij 2006: 50). Another example relates to land rights. As the NPC Legal Commission explained in its report introducing the draft, maintaining village stability (Hu 2002: 173) was a key rationale for the introduction of legislation to further strengthen rural property rights in order to address the increasing concerns of the many farmers who were angry because they had lost land without proper compensation (Prosterman et al. 2000, Guo 2001).

Environmental lawmaking processes provide yet another example of how concern for popular worries spurred the development of stronger regulatory rules. By the late 1990s and early 2000s a series of widely reported pollution incidents and more direct exposure to increasingly alarming levels of pollution had shaped a popular and also governmental concern for the environment. This enabled pro-environment lawmakers to introduce stronger regulatory rules in, for instance, the 2000 Air Pollution Prevention and Control Law, the 2002 Environmental Impact Assessment Law, and the 2008 Water Pollution Prevention and Control Law, which had not been possible in the 1996 Water Pollution Prevention and Control Law (Alford and Liebman 2001, van Rooij 2006).

Finally, in the field of labour law we see that by the second half of the 2000s there was sufficient concern in the Party-state about the rising gap between rich and poor and the lack of rights of an increasingly broader mass of urban workers, to introduce rules strengthening labour rights. This came with the introduction of the 2007 Labour Contract Law, as explained in the formal legislative commentary of this new law: 'In implementation of the labour contract system [in the period prior to the new law, since 1994–2007] problems have arisen … which have been harmful for the interests of the workers, and also for the harmonious stability of labour relations, harming overall social stability' (Xin 2007: 2).

Concern for stability and forms of real or potential unrest have thus precipitated the development of regulatory law. It has given rise to more stringent and often also more certain and well-defined forms of legal rules to help prevent and control risks from economic activities. We also find that especially in laws passed after 2000, legislators not only began to strengthen the enforcement powers of administrative enforcement agents, but also increasingly turned to societal actors to help with implementation by granting stronger (even quasi-punitive) rights to compensation and injunctions to end violations, as well as rights to access information about risk and regulatory violations, and the right to voice complaints (van Rooij 2012).

In China today we find that environmental, property, food safety or labour risks continue to potentially undermine regime stability, and the rationale for the development of regulatory laws remains as before. A recent survey among citizens in 16 urban centres found five main sources of negative feeling about one's safety: environmental problems (44 per cent), unsafe food (35 per cent), social conflicts (28 per cent), increasing gap between rich and poor (23 per cent), and seeing violations of law (22 per cent) (Xiaokang News 2012). We also find that the social problems for which regulatory laws were first developed remain major sources of real unrest. According to a 2012 study of social incidents conducted by the *Legal Daily*, 23 per cent of citizen protests involved forced land takings, 9 per cent involved environmental concerns and 24 per cent were about social conflicts, which most likely include labour law-related disputes (Legal Daily 2012).

This is not surprising as China's incredible economic rise continues to generate immense environmental, food safety, construction safety, property and occupational safety risks. According to recent estimates, for instance, pollution causes 750,000 premature deaths in China annually

(World Bank and SEPA 2007). About 300 million Chinese drink contaminated water on a daily basis, and 190 million of them suffer from related illnesses (OECD 2007). According to a 2011 Chinese study more than 94 million people become ill annually from bacterial food-borne diseases alone, causing about 3.4 million hospitalizations and more than 8,500 deaths (Mao, Hu and Liu 2011).[3] Many farmers and urban dwellers continue to have land and housing taken from them without proper compensation (Chen 2003, Phan 2005), and 80 per cent of all new land development in eight major urban centres is still not conducted according to legal procedures (Liu and Jiang 2009: 121).

It can be argued, therefore, that laws introduced to control risks that might undermine regime stability and cause unrest do not yet seem to have that effect. One explanation may be that the conditions under which the laws have been made in response to social concerns about risks and incidents arising out of economic growth might cause lawmakers to adopt so-called symbolic laws. These are laws that seek to signal that the Party-state desires to make an effort to address serious social concerns, rather than being laws meant to create a real change (cf., Aubert 1967). And while arguably even symbolic laws can have a long-term communicative effect that helps reframe social problems and create opportunities for better discussion and eventually a resolution (Zeegers, Witteveen and van Klink 2005), their immediate and mid-term function may be politically driven – to push complex problems off the political agenda and to maintain regime legitimacy (Aalders 1984).

Indication of such symbolic lawmaking is evident in the recent amendments of China's risk regulation. On at least several occasions, actors involved in the lawmaking process complained that proposed rules were too ambitious and could not be implemented in practice (Xin 2009: 296, van Rooij 2006). And indeed each time many of these rules were adopted, they proved to be unable to be implemented (van Rooij 2006). Symbolic regulatory lawmaking fits within a paradigm of regulation to prevent unrest, when lawmakers hope to send a signal that they are addressing a particular risk in order to reduce societal concerns even though they will likely be unable to reduce such risks in practice. The danger, however, is that at some point citizens lose trust in the Party-state and its lofty laws, as they do not see much change in practice.

---

[3] These numbers are actually below even those of the US. However the Asian Development Bank estimates the number of bacterial food-borne diseases is much higher at about 300 million per year (Asian Development Bank 2007). Higher numbers seem plausible given China's weak surveillance system (Alcorn and Ouyang 2012).

While Chinese lawmakers have introduced some regulatory laws that are surely symbolic, they have also introduced various measures aimed directly at overcoming problems in implementing laws and have thus moved beyond a mere symbolic role in lawmaking. Examples include moves towards better coordinated and unified enforcement of food safety law, the introduction of minimum penalties in environmental law, and the introduction of private citizen-based enforcement mechanisms such as the quasi punitive damages in food safety law and the right to double income for workers without employment contracts.

The failure of regulatory laws to prevent causes of potential and actual unrest is thus not just a matter of failed or purely symbolic lawmaking, but should be understood also in terms of failed implementation of such laws. To understand the relationship between regulation and unrest in China's authoritarian setting we must therefore also look at how such regulation is enforced in practice. The discussion below looks at enforcement by administrative authorities while the section following this discusses enforcement by citizens.

UNREST AND ADMINISTRATIVE ENFORCEMENT OF REGULATION

Weak administrative enforcement of regulatory law is one of the most important reasons why Beijing's regulatory laws have been unable to curb risk and prevent and control forms of real and potential unrest. As documented elsewhere in more detail (van Rooij 2012), the administrative enforcement authorities who have been tasked with enforcing such laws have had trouble creating a deterrent effect sufficient to reduce environmental, property, health or other risks of economic activities. Administrative agencies have found it difficult to uncover violations of law since they lack sufficient detection capacity and face a tremendous workload of possible offenders (Mertha 2005, van Rooij 2006, Cooney 2007: 417, World Bank 2007, Roth et al. 2008, Dimitrov 2009, van Rooij and Lo 2010, Wang 2010: 8, Liu 2011, van Rooij 2011). Cooney noted in 2007, for instance, that China's 40,000 labour inspectors were supposed to inspect an estimated 30 million business entities (Cooney 2007: 417). Moreover, the inspectors have had to face direct resistance from regulated firms that have tried to hide violations or obstruct inspectors (An 2009, You 2009, van Rooij and Lo 2010, Wang 2010: 45).

Some inspectors have even had to fear for their safety. Labour inspectors have reportedly been beaten and seriously harassed while investigating violations of regulatory law on site (Editorial 2011). Even when they are able to detect violations, administrative agencies have tended to issue relatively mild sanctions. For instance the average environmental fines in 2006 were still only 10,000 RMB or about 1,100 euro (SEPA 2007). Sanctions are weak not just because the maximum fines remain quite low, but more importantly because of China's fragmented governance structure in which locally managed and funded enforcement agents are unduly influenced by their local governments not to strictly enforce those national laws that run against local interests (Andrews-Speed et al. 2003, Li 2003, Pringle and Frost 2003, Zhang 2003, Wright 2004, Mertha 2005, van Rooij 2006, Dimitrov 2009).

Enforcement agents can also be obstructed when local industries or people under their employ harass or threaten agents executing sanctions on site. Dimitrov provides telling examples where armed locals threatened tobacco regulators who sought to destroy locally produced illegal cigarettes while local police stood by as villagers destroyed the inspectors' car. In another case a regulator who had been working undercover was 'blindfolded and abandoned in a mountain cave' while his four colleagues were surrounded by a mob of villagers, angry at the inspectors who had come to destroy their illegally produced cigarettes (Dimitrov 2009: 212).

We can make several observations about the relation between unrest and regular administrative regulatory law enforcement. We clearly see that weak enforcement undermines the implementation of regulatory law and thus challenges the prevention and control of risks that can give rise to unrest. However, unrest also shapes enforcement. First, the way in which unrest has spurred the creation of national-level laws that were increasingly ambitious has created a context where lawmakers often care too little about whether there is sufficient local capacity and support to enforce such laws. Second, local protectionism obstructs strong sanctions not just because local governments protect local business leaders, but also at times because it is feared that use of strong sanctions could give rise to broader social grievances, for instance workers who stand to lose their job if polluting factories are ordered to close down or if their operating licence is revoked (e.g. van Rooij 2006).

Third, unrest also shapes enforcement through the prioritization practices that the enforcement bureaus have developed to make the most efficient use of their limited detection capacity. Cheng's research on such practices in environmental protection bureaus has demonstrated that local officials will dedicate most of their time to those types of pollution that have created the largest response from local citizens and local authorities. These need not necessarily be the ones that have inflicted the greatest environmental harm, but rather, those that have inflicted the most observable harm and are most directly related to citizens with the capacity and connections to make successful complaints (Cheng 2011). Fourth and finally, we see that unrest organized by the regulated firms directly obstructs enforcement work, be it inspections or the execution of sanctions. The result has been that enforcement agents have had to deal with unrest in their work and have come to fear carrying out inspections at some firms (e.g. van Rooij and Lo 2010).

Unrest has shaped enforcement in an even more fundamental way. A key response in China to the weakness of structural administrative enforcement of regulatory law and resultant inability to mitigate risk and prevent unrest has been the deployment of enforcement campaigns. During these campaigns, for a short period of time national ministries collaborate to set and verify enforcement targets for local-level enforcement agencies. During such periods local-level agencies are expected to carry out extra inspections with a focus on particular violations and violators, to be followed by issuing stricter sanctions (van Rooij 2009).

Campaigns are closely linked to concerns about stability and unrest, often at the highest level of administration. Consider, for instance, the joint notice issued by the CCP Central Committee and the State Council in 1997, launching a campaign to enforce arable land protection laws, which explained its rationale in the following way: 'The loss of arable land not only affects food production and agricultural development, but also influences the whole national economic development and social stability' (CCP Central Committee and State Council 1997). Or consider what China's chief environmental regulator stated in 2001 when launching a pollution-related enforcement campaign: 'Environmental violations are still an acute problem. If acute measures are not taken this may actually mean that the results of the ninth five year plan will be endangered, as well as even social stability and modernization as a whole' (Editorial 2001). A year later, launching a similar enforcement campaign, the same chief regulator said:

> From this year, the problem of environmental pollution created by the illegal emissions of certain industrial and mining enterprises is worsening. This has left the masses extremely dissatisfied and has had an influence on social stability … This time the emphasis of the campaign should be on inspections and sanctions for those environmental problems about which the masses have strongly complained and which have an impact on social stability (Editorial 2002).

Major incidents or scandals involving violations of law that receive wide media coverage and are thus potentially a cause for unrest also spur the deployment of enforcement campaigns. In 2007, for instance, media coverage of a petition by 400 parents in Henan Province calling for help in rescuing their kidnapped children from forced labour conditions in small brick kilns spurred a nationwide campaign against forced labour. The campaign (launched by the Ministry of Labour and Social Security) inspected 277,000 enterprises employing 12.67 million people. During the campaign 1,340 people were rescued from forced labour conditions, 147 people were arrested, while 98,000 enterprises were ordered to sign labour contracts with 1.5 million workers and pay overdue salaries and compensation to a total amount of 130 million yuan (Xinhua News Agency 2007).

The campaigns against illegal food additives, launched with the support of the country's highest leaders including (then) premier Wen Jiabao and vice-premier Li Keqiang have been conducted annually since the 2008 Melamine baby milk scandal. This is a further example of how incidents spur campaign-type ad hoc enforcement. As such, the campaigns, which have become a key element of administrative enforcement, are triggered by escalation of social unrest, as they are often prompted only when the effects of weak structural enforcement get out of hand.

Increasingly we also find that the campaigns explicitly focus priorities on matters of direct social concern and introduce forms of public participation in the campaigns. For instance, the 2002 environmental enforcement campaign emphasized that priority should be given to violations that were of most concern to the general public (Editorial 2002). It continued using input from citizens not only to find out which companies were violating regulations but also to check on the work of local-level enforcement bureaus by stimulating citizens to report transgressions during public hearings and through hotlines. The 2002 campaign also started to offer rewards for valid tips about secret nightly pollution discharges, a practice that built on local experiments in Jiangsu, Zhenjiang and Shanghai (van Rooij 2006: 341).

The effects of the campaigns have been mixed. While we noted earlier that there have been some short-term positive effects, in the longer term the effects on reducing violations of law and the related risks and causes for social unrest have been limited or simply undocumented (van Rooij 2009). When campaigns end, the incidence of violations tends to return. Campaigns might thus have a symbolic function (cf., Edelman 1987) serving national politicians as a way of public signalling that they are serious in addressing particular social concerns about violations of regulatory law. However, the ad hoc nature of the campaigns undermines the general power of the law as well as popular trust in the law, since laws are seen by both regulated firms and the general population to be enforced only cyclically.

Campaigns serve as a stop-gap measure to be used in response to escalating effects of weak structural enforcement. However, their experimental and short-term nature challenges campaigns to provide structural solutions to the complex structural problems of limited capacity and conflicts between national law and local contexts. Ironically, the ad hoc campaigns have become an institutionalized part of China's mode of governance that has developed in response to its fragmented nature and is operated through internal Party-state competitive cadre evaluation mechanisms. As such it has institutionalized a form of experimental governance that undermines the formal rational functioning of the actual laws it has sought to enforce.

UNREST AND SOCIETAL ENFORCEMENT OF RISK REGULATION

Over the last decade we have seen a change in the way regulation is implemented in China. As documented in more detail elsewhere (van Rooij 2012) and discussed briefly above, Chinese lawmakers and administrative enforcement authorities have increasingly provided space for citizens and civic organizations to aid in the implementation of regulatory law. Concurrently, citizens and civic organizations have increasingly developed the capacity and awareness that such space is necessary and have undertaken action to implement regulation that can protect them or their interests from harm.

There are three chief types of societal action: providing information to authorities about violations of law, initiating legal action in court against violators, and taking collective action in response to harm or potential harm by violators (van Rooij 2012). Over the last decade or so there has been a rapid increase in environmental complaints, rising steadily to about 700,000 in 2010 (van Rooij 2012). Similarly, many complaints are issued to the labour inspectorates relating to labour-related transgressions and violations, with labour inspectors receiving nearly 700,000 complaints in 2010 (van Rooij 2012). The use of legal options is more mixed. Labour-related court cases have increased very rapidly with up to 317,000 in 2009, compared with a mere 126,000 in 2006 (China Labour Bulletin 2010). Also, in the field of intellectual property rights, there has been an immense growth in the number of cases (Dimitrov 2009: 105).

In other fields, however, there has been much less litigation. Of the many Chinese farmers whose land has been taken without proper compensation, only 0.9 per cent of cases have been taken to court (Zhu et al. 2006). And in the field of the environment, where about 700,000 complaints are made annually to the authorities (Ministry of Environmental Protection 2010) compared with about 700,000 labour complaints (van Rooij 2012), the courts conduct only about 3,000 environmental cases per year (van Rooij 2010). This is only 1 per cent of the number of labour court cases. Over the last decade or so, collective forms of action, which often concern violations of regulatory law such as those related to land, environment or labour, have risen dramatically (Legal Daily 2012). The 78,000 large-scale protests in 2005 – the last year for which we have reliable data – much more than doubled in number to a reported 180,000 in 2011, according to an estimate by a Beijing-based sociologist (News 2011).

Some citizens taking action against violations of regulatory law have been notably successful. We know, for instance, that there is a positive correlation between citizen complaints and the number of administrative sanctions environmental regulators issue for pollution-related violations (van Rooij 2010). There is also anecdotal evidence of how particular information sharing in the national and international media by citizens and civic organizations has spurred action to end regulatory transgressions and their related risks. Two pre-eminent examples concern fake traditional cures and Apple-subcontractors using the poisonous substance n-hexane to clean iPhone and iPad screens (van Rooij 2012). Evidence indicates citizens have been able to win in court when suing enterprises breaking regulatory law; for instance 58 per cent of citizen plaintiffs have won in court against polluting firms (van Rooij 2012). There have also been landmark court cases, such as one in Fujian province, with 1,721 citizens successfully suing a local polluter and receiving both an injunction and damages.

Collective action has certainly produced some successful results. In 2010, for instance, workers at Honda factories in Guangdong and Hubei provinces were successful in having their demands for better wages and working conditions met, following a strike that spread rapidly to other plants. Following the strike, workers throughout the coastal area in similar production facilities were able to secure better pay and conditions. Other examples of successful collective action are the various demonstrations against new polluting projects in cities such as Xiamen, Shanghai, Beijing, Guangzhou, Qidong (Perlez 2012) and Shifang (BBC News 2012), forcing local regulators to reconsider and ultimately annul or relocate such projects (Johnson 2010, van Rooij 2010). Finally we can also think of rural successes of demonstrating citizens against illegal land takings in Wukan village in Guangdong Province in 2012 (The Guardian 2012).

These successful cases have particular characteristics. They enticed forms of citizen action that gained much attention, in either or both domestic and foreign media. They mostly involved a large number of participants. And in some of the cases protesters and those opposed to the protests clashed violently, resulting in human injuries or even fatalities. In his analysis of why activists in China are able to have their demands met, Cai (2010) has pointed at similar variables that can explain higher success rates. His work shows that the government operates on an institutionalized form of cost–benefit analysis, in which it weighs the costs and risks of meeting the demand against the costs and risks of activism at not meeting it. The action that creates more unrest – through a large number of participants, media attention, foreign involvement and casualties – is more likely than other recalcitrant action to have its demands met. In other words, more unrest leads to better citizen enforcement of regulatory law that was made to prevent and control unrest.

When their activism is successful, citizens can play a crucial role in enforcing regulatory law, either directly or by putting pressure on the administrative authorities, thus helping to prevent risks and sources of unrest. However there are severe limitations on what citizens can actually do and therefore on the effects of their actions in helping to enforce regulatory law and reduce risks that can cause further unrest. Some citizens are better able than others to gather and share information about regulatory violations and to take action to have these violations ended; generally citizens with better education, income, organizational capacity, social connections and leadership ability are better able to help enforce regulatory law (van Rooij 2010, 2012). And as noted above, some violations are more likely than others to secure enforcement through citizen activism, especially those that are highly visible, have immediate negative effects, or draw much media attention.

Maintaining a regulatory system that increasingly depends on and responds to citizens' activism for its implementation will therefore inherently create in China a bias towards the interests of richer and better-educated citizens and the outcomes and risks that they are most aware of and care about. Quantitative data indicate a strong correlation between environmental complaints and per capita GDP (van Rooij and Lo 2010). In 2009, while 37 per cent of all environmental complaints to government authorities concerned noise pollution, only 13 per cent concerned the more difficult and observable problems of water pollution (van Rooij 2012), which pose a much bigger economic and health risk to society.

Ironically, citizens' actions to help enforce the law and prevent unrest can be seen as forms of unrest in themselves, especially when they involve significant numbers of people, media coverage, foreign attention and violence (cf., Cai 2010). Once citizen action comes to be seen as a form of unrest, all of the Party-state's authoritarian mechanisms are put to work, and authorities at different levels of administration consider or actually take action to prevent or hinder citizens demanding the enforcement of regulatory law. Authorities can obstruct access to information deemed to be sensitive through barring citizens from accessing it, even when such information concerns violations of national regulatory laws (van Rooij 2012). Authorities have obstructed access to lawyers and courts in cases deemed sensitive, even when the cases concerned major violations of regulatory law such as the Melamine case. This action has ensured that aggrieved citizens could not successfully sue for damages and therefore would not take their action to court. Nonetheless, fear of instability sometimes inspires authorities to force a court to accept cases, perceiving resolution of the matter to be safer and more cost effective socially in the court than on the street (Su and He 2010).

Authorities have criminalized certain forms of petitioning and complaining. And with the increased sensitivity of, for instance, environmental and land-related complaints, a number of unfortunate petitioners have been detained in black jails and psychiatric wards or prosecuted criminally and sentenced to prison terms. Lawyers seeking to help citizens pursue court action over regulatory violations that authorities deem to be sensitive for social unrest have also found themselves in trouble. Consequences range from receiving frequent visits by internal security officials to losing their lawyer's licence or being detained for weeks or even sentenced to prison for years (van Rooij 2012).

Civic organizations that provide valuable support for citizens to understand regulatory violations and organize responses to enforce the law are limited by authoritarian restrictions on their financing, legal status and branch office operations. Some organizations working on highly sensitive issues ranging from food safety to women's rights have been forced to close. Some authorities view public interest lawyers and civic organizations as quite the opposite of necessary supportive institutions to help citizens enforce regulatory law and reduce both risk and sources of unrest. Rather these authorities see such sources of support as direct instigators of unrest, thus 'undermining social harmony and stability' (Guangdong Provincial CCP Politico-Legal Committee 2009).

Finally, authorities at different levels of administration have reframed forms of protest action by citizens to undermine citizens' belief that these actions can be fruitful. Aided by the media, authorities have portrayed citizens challenging regulatory violations as unruly elements or mentally deranged (van Rooij 2010). These messages to dissuade citizens from following through on their grievances convey that the Party-state's response will damage how participants in such protest actions are perceived in society. Authorities may also seek to emphasize that development trumps preventing and controlling risk, or that reducing such risk is impossible (van Rooij, Lora-Wainwright and Wu 2012).

Here we see that the Party-state has an uneven approach to stimulating and restricting citizens' involvement in the implementation of regulatory law, as it seeks outcomes most consistent with the national goal of achieving and maintaining social stability. In the process the Party-state is undermining popular trust in itself and in the legal system, as these preventive actions clearly give citizens mixed signals. Citizens learn it is risky and costly for them to try to help enforce regulatory law, even if their actions aim to directly address the harms and dangers that society faces.

Through their own actions and Party-state responses to these actions, citizens learn that only under certain conditions can they be successful in their complaints, court cases or collective action (van Rooij 2012). Matters must escalate to a certain threshold where large numbers participate in the action, a higher level of administration is drawn in, media coverage is large scale, foreign support is evident, and casualties are involved in the resistance action or in what motivated this action. Authorities have criminalized certain forms of petitioning and complaining, and have penalized or dissuaded other forms. Yet authorities have also forced courts to accept cases that they believe will be resolved in a socially more cost-effective way in the court than on the street. These mixed signals to the people have been institutionalized in an internal incentive structure replete with similar contradictions. It rewards cadres who keep petitions, disputes and collective action controlled and localized, but also stimulates cadres to give in to citizen demands should matters get out of control (Fu and Cullen 2007, Cai 2010, Su and He 2010, Liebman 2011). Here the Party-state has institutionalized an incentive structure that is likely to create more rather than less unrest.

CONCLUSION

Unrest and state regulation are clearly linked in China. Fear of potential unrest has spurred the development of regulatory law, creating ambitious rules that fail to take account of China's continued structural challenges with implementing law. While administrative enforcement remains difficult, regulatory laws fail to prevent violations that may breed unrest. In response, China has developed ad hoc enforcement mechanisms to deal with the most pressing or visible violations, especially those that may be sources of public unrest. However these mechanisms fail to have a sustained effect as they do not solve structural enforcement problems. Nowadays citizens have more space to encourage or even pressure authorities to enforce regulation, but fear of unrest has made the government both supportive and restrictive of such help, depending upon the extent of unrest this citizen help inspires. Thus citizens are successful in helping to implement regulatory law usually only when matters escalate and the government sees no option but to give in to citizen requests and take strong measures to end the violations that inspire these requests. In sum, unrest breeds regulation that itself can breed unrest; regulation seems to function best for the citizens to achieve their desired outcome when the damages as well as the scope of action taken by citizens escalate.

The result is a situation of regulation by escalation; both regulatory lawmaking and enforcement are directly spurred by and a cause of such escalation. From an authoritarian point of view this is quite worrisome as it means that attempts to decrease unrest only spur more unrest. It seems that regulation by escalation in China is the result of negative interaction among China's traits of authoritarianism. Fragmentation undermines the structural development and administrative enforcement of regulatory laws that were adopted to address unrest through formal rational means. In response a combination of experiments and responsively populist mechanisms such as campaigns and public enforcement actions have been deployed. Experiments directly undermine the formal rational and institutionalized nature of the laws and institutions developed in the first place. Societal mechanisms fail when the Party-state chooses control rather than freedom in its trapeze act of combining authoritarianism with societal responsiveness. The internal mechanisms for cadre evaluation that are used to assess China's increasingly competitive bureaucracy have institutionalized these failing experimental and responsive mechanisms and the overriding concern for preventing short-term social unrest over long-term risks that may ultimately also endanger regime stability.

REFERENCES

Aalders, M. (1984), *Industrie, Milieu en Wetgeving: De Hinderwet tussen Symboliek en Effectiviteit* (Industry, Environment and Legislation: The Nuisance Act between Symbolism and Effectivity). Amsterdam: Kobra.

Alcorn, Ted and Ouyang, Yadan (2012), 'China's invisible burden of foodborne illness', *The Lancet*, 379 (9818): 789–90.

Alford, William P. and Liebman, Benjamin L. (2001), 'Clean air, clean processes? The struggle over air pollution law in the People's Republic of China', *Hastings Law Journal*, 52 (March): 703–48.

An, Rongda (2009), 'Taizinai wan teshu daiyu, sizi cagai shengchan riqi' (Taizi milk plays a game of special treatment and itself changes the production date), http://www.jk3721.com/html/jiankangzixun/200901/05-18.html. Accessed 15 January 2013.

Andrews-Speed, Philip, Yang, Minying, Shen, Lei and Cao, Shelley (2003), 'The regulation of China's township and village coal mines: a study of complexity and ineffectiveness', *Journal of Cleaner Production*, 11: 185–96.

Asian Development Bank (2007), *National Food Safety Regulatory and Strategic Framework, Technical Assistance Completion Form* 2007. http://www2.adb.org/Documents/TACRs/PRC/37599-PRC-TCR.pdf. Accessed 10 February 2010.

Aubert, Vilhelm (1967), 'Social functions of legislation', *Acta Sociologica*, 10: 98–120.

Baldwin, Robert and Cave, Martine (1999), *Understanding Regulation. Theory, strategy and practice*. Oxford: Oxford University Press.

BBC News (2012), 'China factory construction halted amid violent protests', 3 July, http://www.bbc.co.uk/news/world-asia-china-18684895. Accessed 12 January 2013.

Brown, Lester R. (1994), 'Who will feed China?', *World Watch* (September/October): 10–19.

Cai, Yongshun (2004), 'Managed participation in China', *Political Science Quarterly*, 119(3): 425–51.

Cai, Yonghsun (2010), *Collective Resistance in China: why popular protests succeed or fail*. Stanford: Stanford University Press.

CCP Central Committee and State Council (1997), 'Zhonggong zhongyang, guowuyuan guanyu jinyibu jiaqiang tudi guanli qieshi baohu gengdi de tongzhi' (CCP Central Committee and State Council notice on further strengthening land management in order to realize the protection of arable land), no. 11, 15 April.

Chen, Xiaojun (ed.) (2003), *Nongcun tudi falüzhidu yanjiu, tianye diaocha jiedu* (Research on the village land legal system, an analysis on the basis of fieldwork). Beijing: Zhongguo zhengfa daxue chubanshe.

Cheng, Xiang (2011), 'The workload dilemma for Chinese street-level environmental regulators: better work vs. more work'. Paper presented at the 2011 Law and Society Association Meeting, San Francisco, CA, 4 June.

China Labour Bulletin (2010), 'China's labour dispute court cases increase by over ten percent in 2009', http://www.china-labour.org.hk/en/node/100706. Accessed 23 June 2011.

Cooney, Sean (2007), 'China's labour law, compliance and flaws in implementing institutions', *Journal of Industrial Relations*, 49(5): 673–86.

Dimitrov, Martin K. (2009), *Piracy and the State: the politics of intellectual property rights in China*. Cambridge: Cambridge University Press.

Edelman, Murray (1987), 'The construction and uses of social problems', *University of Miami Law Review*, 42: 7–28.

Edin, Maria (2003), 'State capacity and local agent control in China: CCP cadre management from a township perspective', *China Quarterly*, 173: 35–52.

Editorial (2001), 'Xie zhenhua juzhang zai quanguo kaizhan yansuchachu huanjing weifa xingwei zhuanxiang xingdong dianshidianhua huiyishang de jianghua' (Speech by minister Xie Zhenhua at the televised conference of China's strict inspections and sanctions campaign againgst environmental violations), *Huanjing gongzuo tongxun* (Environmental Work Report), 283: 2–3.

Editorial (2002), 'Yancha huanjing weifa xingwei weihu shehui daju wending guojia huanbaozongju bushu xin yi lun yancha xing dong' (Strict inspections of environmental violations protect the overal social stability, sepa deploys a new round of strict inspection campaigns), *China Environmental News* (Internet Edition), 29 May.

Editorial (2008), 'Shenjieshi huaner 3 si, yiqian bu jiance sanjuqingan' (Three infants died from kidney stones; no detection of melamine in the past), *Nanfang zhoumo* (Southern Weekend), 17 September.

Editorial (2011), 'Laodong jiancha zhikun: renyuan jingfei buzu xianzhi zhifa jianguan nengli' (Troubles in labour inspections: a lack of staff and resources limits enforcement and inspection capacity), *Sina* news, http://news.sina.com.cn/c/sd/2011-02-26/183022019877.shtml. Accessed 12 February 2012.

Fu, Hualing and Cullen, Richard (2007), 'From mediatory to adjudicatory justice, the limits of civil justice reforms in China', http://papers.ssrn.com/sol3/papers.cfm?abstract_id=1306800. Accessed 10 May 2008.

Guangdong Provincial CCP Politico-Legal Committee 2009 (2009), 'Investigative report of Guangdong Province on the Question of professional citizen's legal agents', http://www.clntranslations.org/file_download/93. Accessed 10 October 2010.

Guo, Xiaolin (2001), 'Land expropriation and rural conflicts in China', *China Quarterly*, 166: 422–39.

He, Baogang and Warren, Mark E. (2011), 'Authoritarian deliberation: the deliberative turn in Chinese political development', *Perspectives on politics*, 9(2): 269–89.

Heilmann, Sebastian (2008), 'From local experiments to national policy: the origins of China's distinctive policy process', *The China Journal*, 59: 1–30.

Heimer, Maria (2006), 'The cadre responsibility system and the changing needs of the party', in Kjeld Erik Brodsgaard and Zheng Yongnian (eds.), *The Chinese Communist Party in Reform*. London, Routledge, pp. 122–38.

Hu, Kangsheng (2002), *Zhonghua renmin gongheguo nongcun tudi chengbaofa shiyi* (Commentary on the PRC Rural Land Contract Law). Beijing: Falü chubanshe.

Johnson, Thomas (2010), 'Environmentalism and NIMBYism in China: promoting a rules-based approach to public participation', *Environmental Politics*, 19(3): 430–48.

Lampton, David M. (1987), *Policy Implementation in Post-Mao China*. Berkeley: University of California Press.

Landry, Pierre F. (2008), 'Decentralized authoritarianism in China: the communist party's control of local elites in the post-Mao era', *Recherche*, 67: 2.

Legal Daily (2012), '2012 nian qunti shijian yanjiu baogao' (Report on Mass Incidents in 2012), 27 December, http://www.legaldaily.com.cn/The_analysis_of_public_opinion/content/2012-12/27/content_4092138.htm. Accessed 7 February 2013.

Levitsky, Steve and Way, Lucan A. (2002), 'The rise of competitive authoritarianism', *Journal of Democracy*, 13(2): 51–65.

Levitsky, Steve and Way, Lucan A. (2010), *Competitive Authoritarianism: hybrid regimes after the cold war*. Cambridge: Cambridge University Press.

Li, Ling (2003), 'The sky is high and the emperor is far away: the enforcement of intellectual property law in China', *Boletín Mexicao de Derecho Comparado*, no. XXXVI (108): 951–1010.

Lieberthal, Kenneth (1992), 'Introduction: the "fragmented authoritarianism" model and its limitations', in Kenneth G. Lieberthal and David M. Lampton (eds.), *Bureaucracy, Politics, and Decision Making in Post-Mao China*. Berkeley: University of California Press, pp. 1–30.

Liebman, Benjamin (2011), 'A populist threat to China's courts?', in Mary Gallagher and Margaret Woo (eds.), *Chinese Justice: civil dispute resolution in post-reform China*. Cambridge: Cambridge University Press. pp. 269–314.

Liew, Leong H. (1993), 'Rent-seeking and the two-track price system in China', *Public Choice*, 77(2): 359–75.

Liu, Dong (2011), 'A safety net of holes', *Global Times*, 30 May, http://special.globaltimes.cn/2011-05/660197.html. Accessed 10 February 2013.

Liu, Ying and Jiang, Jianqui, (2009), 'Guanyu woguo tudi zhifa yu chengkun zaisikao', *Faxue zazhi*, 6: 121–214.

Lorentzen, Peter (2013), 'Regularizing rioting: permitting public protest in an authoritarian regime', *Quarterly Journal of Political Science*, 8: 127–58.

Lu, Xiaobo (1999), 'From rank-seeking to rent-seeking: changing administrative ethos and corruption in reform China', *Crime, Law and Social Change*, 32(4): 347–70.

Mao, Xuedan, Hu, Junfeng and Liu, Xiumei, (2011), 'Woguo xijunxing shiyuanxing jibing jibingfudan de chubu yanjiu' (Epidemiological burden of bacterial foodborne diseases in China: a preliminary study), *Chinese Journal of Food Hygiene*, 23 (2).

Mertha, Andrew C. (2005), *The Politics of Piracy: Intellectual Property in Contemporary China*. Ithaca, NY: Cornell University Press.

Mertha, Andrew C. (2009), 'Fragmented authoritarianism 2.0': political pluralization in the Chinese policy process', *The China Quarterly*, 200 (1): 995–1012.

Ministry of Environmental Protection, PRC (2010), *Zhongguo huanjing tongji nianbao 2009* (China Environment Statistical Report 2009). Beijing: China Environmental Science Press.

Minzner, Carl F. (2005), 'Xinfang: an alternative to formal Chinese legal institutions', *Stanford Journal of International Law*, 42:103–79.

Minzner, Carl F. (2009), 'Riots and cover-ups: counterproductive control of local agents in China', *University of Pennsylvania Journal of International Law*, 31: 53–123.

Morgan, Bronwen and Yeung, Karen (2007), *An Introduction to Law and Regulation, Texts and Materials*. Cambridge: Cambridge University Press.

Nathan, Andrew J. (2003), 'Authoritarian resilience', *Journal of Democracy*, 14 (1): 6–17.

News, Bloomberg (2011), 'China cracks down in wake of riots, bombings', http://www.bloomberg.com/news/2011-06-13/china-cracks-down-in-wake-of-riots-bombings.html. Accessed 15 February 2013.

Ngo, Tak-Wing and Wu, Yongping (eds.) (2009), *Rent Seeking in China*. New York: Routledge.

OECD (2007), *OECD Environmental Performance Reviews: China*. Paris: OECD Publishing.
Peerenboom, R. (2002), *China's Long March toward the Rule of Law*. Cambridge: Cambridge University Press.
Perlez, Jane (2012), 'Water Project is abandoned following protests in China's New York Times', 28 July, http://www.nytimes.com/2012/07/29/world/asia/after-protests-in-qidong-china-plans-for-water-discharge-plant-are-abandoned.html?_r=0. Accessed 12 January 2013.
Phan, Pamela N. (2005), 'Enriching the land or the political elite? Lessons from China on democratization of the urban renewal process', Pacific *Rim Law and Policy Journal*, 14: 607–56.
Pringle, Tim E. and Frost, Stephen D. (2003), 'The absence of rigor and the failure of implementation: occupational health and safety in China', *International Journal of Environment and Health*, 9 (4): 309–16.
Prosterman, Roy, Schwarzwalder, Brian and Ye, Jianping (2000), 'Implementation of 30-year land use rights for farmers under China's 1998 land management law: an analysis and recommendations based on a 17-province survey'. *Pacific Rim Law and Policy Journal*, 9 (3): 507–68.
Reilly, James (2011), *Strong Society, Smart State: The Rise of Public Opinion in China's Japan Policy*. New York: Columbia University Press.
Roth, Aleda V., Tsay, Andy A., Pullman, Madeline E. and Gray, John V. (2008), 'Unraveling the food supply chain: strategic insights from China and the 2007 recalls', *Journal of Supply Chain Management*, 44 (1): 22–39.
SEPA (2007), *Zhongguo huanjing tongji nianbao 2006* (China Environment Statistical Report 2006). Beijing: Zhongguo huanjing kexue chubanshe.
Shirk, Susan L. (1993), *The Political Logic of Economic Reform in China*. Berkeley: University of California Press.
Stockmann, Daniela (2012), *Media Commericalization and Authoritarian Rule in China*. Cambridge: Cambridge University Press.
Su, Yang and He, Xin (2010), 'Street as courtroom: state accommodation of labor protests in south China', *Law & Society Review*, 44 (1): 157–84.
The Guardian (2012), 'Wukan holds its election after protests that cowed officialdom', 3 March, http://www.theguardian.com/world/2012/mar/03/wukan-villagers-elections-protests. Accessed 12 January 2013.
van Rooij, Benjamin (2006), *Regulating Land and Pollution in China Lawmaking, Compliance, and Enforcement: theory and cases*. Leiden: Leiden University Press.
van Rooij, Benjamin (2009), 'The politics of law in China: enforcement campaigns in the post-mao PRC', Working Paper, 25 March, http://ssrn.com/paper=1368181. Accessed 25 March 2009.
van Rooij, Benjamin (2010), 'The people vs. pollution: understanding citizen action against pollution in China', *The Journal of Contemporary China*, 19 (63): 55–77.
van Rooij, Benjamin (2011), 'Regulating land and pollution at Lake Dianchi: lawmaking, compliance and enforcement in a chinese and comparative perspective', in Mattias Burell and Marina Svenson (eds.), *Making Law Work: Chinese laws in context*. New York: Cornell University Press, pp. 367–403.
van Rooij, Benjamin (2012), 'The people's regulation, citizens and implementation of law in China', *Columbia Journal of Asian Law*, 25 (2): 116–79.
van Rooij, Benjamin and Lo, Carlos H.W. (2010), 'A fragile convergence, understanding variation in the enforcement of china's industrial pollution law', *Law & Policy*, 32 (1): 14–37.

van Rooij, Benjamin, Lora-Wainwright, Anna and Yunmei, Wu (2012), 'The compensation trap, Chinese lessons about the limits of community based regulation', *Pace Environmental Law Review*, 29 (3): 701–45.

Wang, Alex (2013), 'The search for sustainable legitimacy: environmental law and bureaucracy in China', *Harvard Environmental Law Review*, 37: 367–430.

Wang, Yanhua (2010), 'Laodong jiancha zhifa "ba nan"' ('Eight problems' in the inspections and enforcement of labour law), *Zhongguo renli ziyuan shehui baozhang*, 8: 45.

Wedeman, Andrew H. (2003), *From Mao to Market: Rent Seeking, Local Protectionism, and Marketization in China*. Cambridge: Cambridge University Press.

Weller, Robert P. (2008), 'Regime responses, responsive authoritarianism', in Bruce Gilley, Larry Diamond and Weitseng Chen (eds.), *Political Change in China: Comparisons with Taiwan*. Boulder, CO: Lynne Rienner Publishers, pp. 117–38.

World Bank (2007), 'China's compliance with food safety requirements for fruits and vegetables, promoting food safety, competitiveness, and poverty reduction', *World Bank Report,* http://documents.worldbank.org/curated/en/2006/01/8021307/chinas-compliance-food-safety-requirements-fruits-vegetables-promoting-food-safety-competitiveness-poverty-reduction. Accessed 10 February 2010.

World Bank and SEPA (2007), *Costs of Pollution in China: economic estimates of physical damages* (Conference Edition). Washington: World Bank.

Wright, Tim (2004), 'The political economy of coal mine disasters in China: "your rice bowl or your life"', *China Quarterly*, 179: 629–46.

Xiaokang News (2012), 'Xiaokang diaocha: bacheng youlu "shejian" shang de anquan' (Xiaokang news survey: people in eight cities are most concerned about food safety), July Issue, http://xkzz.chinaxiaokang.com/xkzz3/newsview.asp?id=6079. Accessed 20 September 2013.

Xin, Chunying (2007), *Zhonghua renmin gongheguo laodong hetongfa shiyi* (Commentary on the PRC Labour Contract Law). Beijing: Falü chubanshe.

Xin, Chunying (2009), *Zhonghuarenmin gongheguo shipin anquanfa shiyi* (Commentary of the PRC Food Safety Law). Beijing: Falü chubanshe.

Xinhua News (2009) 'Chinese consumers concerned about food safety', http://www.chinadaily.com.cn/china/2009-03/27/content_7624158.htm. Accessed 10 January 2013.

Xinhua News (2010), 'Chinese consumers concerned about food safety 2009', http://www.chinadaily.com.cn/china/2009-03/27/content_7624158.htm. Accessed 10 February 2010.

Xinhua News Agency (2007), 'More than 1,000 rescued from forced labor in China', 21 August, http://english.people.com.cn/90001/90776/6238653.html. Accessed 12 May 2008.

You, Changqiao (2009), 'Ju'nenggai "shuangyangshui" weiji gongguan de sida shibai – 2004 weiji gonguan anli pandian zhisan' (Four deceptions in the public relations responses to the juneng calcium hydrogen peroxide crisis, a case study inventory of the 2004 public relations in crisis), *Quanqiu pinpaiwang*, 24 February, http://www.globrand.com/2009/162809.shtml. Accessed 12 January 2013.

Zeegers, Nicolle, Witteveen, Willem and van Klink, Bart (2005), *Social and Symbolic Effects of Legislation under the Rule of Law*. Lewiston: Edwin Mellen Press.

Zhang, Yizhong (2003), 'Zhifazhong baohuzhuyi chengyin yu fangfan' (Causes and countermeasures of protectionism in law enforcement), *Zhongguo Gongshang guanliyanjiu*, 5: 18–20.

Zhongguo, Rendawang (2008), 'Boqu "san lu" shijian jiaoxun caoan zhenduixing-qiang, fenzushenyi shipin anquan fa fayan shifa zhaideng' (Drawing lessons from the 'san lu' incident to strengthen the focus of the draft: published extracts of the speeches of small group members on the food safety safety draft consideration), http://www.npc.gov.cn/npc/zt/2008-11/10/content_1655901.htm. Accessed 12 January 2013.

Zhu, Keliang, Prosterman, Roy, Ye, Jianping, Li, Ping, Riedinger, Jeffrey and Ouyang, Yiwen (2006), 'The rural land question in China: analysis and recommendations based on a 17-province survey in 2005', *New York University Journal of International Law & Politics*, 38 (4): 761–839.

6. Mediating state and society: social stability and administrative suits

Michael Palmer

INTRODUCTION

A significant dimension of legal systems committed to important principles such as the rule of law and good governance is their use of the courts to make public officials in some way accountable for the manner in which their decisions affect individuals. This is especially so where such decision-making gives rise to a citizen grievance. In post-Mao China's legal development, one of the most serious difficulties has been the need for effective legal controls over the exercise of administrative powers by the state. The traditional, paternalistic authority of the Chinese state has been reinforced by a socialist dictatorship and the perceived need to protect rapid economic growth by ensuring a stable socio-political environment, so that China retains a very strong executive, albeit one still at the call of the Chinese Communist Party (CCP).

At the constitutional level in the People's Republic, a greater emphasis on the need for a regular legal framework for the exercise of authority has encouraged the introduction of important new values and rights.[1] But the impact of such progress is muffled by the fact that constitutional rights are not justiciable. A system of administrative litigation (*xingzheng susong*) was experimented with in the 1980s under the provisional civil procedure code, and was introduced in the form of a national code in 1990. It was to be a process by which the citizen (and other actors in civil society) might more effectively challenge state (mis)conduct, but in reality it has been transmuted by judicial practice favouring mediation. The process of administrative litigation is seen by many observers within and outside China as a critically important 'access to administrative

[1] Most notably, freedom of person (Article 37), governance in accordance with the rule of law (Article 5, as amended 1999), and the state protection of human rights (Article 33, as amended 2004).

justice' avenue that could not only vindicate rights but also promote lawful conduct and good governance by the Chinese executive.[2] The disguised meaning of the system of administrative litigation – and the relationship between this camouflaged meaning and official policies favouring socio-political stability and a 'socialist harmonious society' (*shehui zhuyi hexie shehui*) – is a very significant and ongoing story. Accordingly this chapter explores two key questions: what is the nature and significance of the role of mediation in administrative litigation in the PRC, and what are the most salient current developments in this unfolding tale.

WITHDRAWING SUIT

The most important recent development occurred in December 2007 when the Adjudication Committee of the Supreme People's Court of the PRC adopted new rules or *guiding* on the conduct of administrative litigation. These provisions came into force on 1 February 2008, bearing the title: 'Rules of the Supreme People's Court Concerning Several Problems in the Withdrawal of Administrative Suits' (*Guanyu xingzheng susong chesu ruogan wenti de guiding*) (Supreme People's Court 2008a). The Rules offer a rudimentary regulatory framework for the process of the plaintiff abandoning suit. Article 3 of the new system is especially important, containing as it does some basic procedural safeguards for withdrawal – that is, protection for the plaintiff is apparently needed when an administrative lawsuit is interrupted by the plaintiff's decision not to pursue her or his or its claim. Citizen suits, some pursued passionately, others perfunctorily, must come to an end through a dignified withdrawal, and with the parties expressing satisfaction at the apparently inchoate outcome. The provisions in Article 3 require the

[2] Moreover, the system of administrative litigation is now informed by the due process commitments China made to the WTO in the Accession Protocols of 2001 (Accession Protocols 1.2.D.1 and 1.2.D.2). In addition, China's obligations under the various UN international human rights covenants of which it is a state party mean that the ability of the aggrieved citizen or resident to sue the Chinese state for gross infringements of international human rights and failure to attain promised standards significantly depends on the provision of effective processes for securing access to justice. However, the UN Committee on Economic, Social and Cultural Rights has advised the PRC authorities that they must ensure more robust avenues for securing justice are made available to people in China for safeguarding the human rights that China has undertaken to guarantee under that Covenant (Choukroune 2005).

court to accept and approve the withdrawal if it determines that: first, the withdrawal of the suit represents the true intention of the plaintiff; second, any changes made by the defendant state agency to the specific administrative action that has given rise to the complaint are lawful, consistent with administrative regulations, within the competence of that agency, and damage neither the public interest nor the legal rights and interests of others; third, the court is notified of any such changes in writing; and, finally, no objection is raised by a third party (Supreme People's Court 2008a; also see Supreme People's Court 2008b.)

Effects of Withdrawing Suit

When the defendant state agency changes its specific administrative action, what does it do? According to Article 4 of the 2007 Rules it may do one or more of several things: it may agree to carry out certain actions or statutory duties requested by the plaintiff, or give compensation or take remedial actions. Or the court may give recognition to a settlement regarding a disputed administrative ruling (*xingzheng caijue anjian*) – that is, where a state agency has made an 'umpiring'-type decision with which the plaintiff disagrees, and the disagreement is subsequently resolved by a negotiated settlement, then the court may under the Rules choose to recognize that settlement.

Article 5 of the Rules allows the court considerable discretion in ruling on the approval of the withdrawal of the suit. Thus withdrawal may be approved once the state agency has completed its promised action. Or the abandonment of suit may be delayed and the trial even suspended when immediate performance is not possible. The court may also approve a withdrawal where there is an appeal or a petition for a retrial (Article 8). The Rules also stipulate that a court ruling that approves the withdrawal of a suit may expressly contain information about important aspects of the withdrawal – for example, identifying the main alterations made by the defendant to its administrative conduct, requirements regarding performance, and also indicate that certain aspects of the administrative conduct complained of do not, in the court's view, need to be enforced (Article 6). The People's Court is still expected to adjudicate the case and deliver a judgment if these conditions are not met, or if the plaintiff decides after all not to apply for a withdrawal (Article 7).

Taken as a whole, the 2007 Rules are a very strong and clear *encouragement to plaintiffs in citizen–state disputes to withdraw their complaints against the state* providing that certain conditions are met, namely, that withdrawal is a plaintiff's *true wish*, and the defendant state agency, in adjusting its conduct to meet the demands of the plaintiff, does so lawfully and without harming the rights of others. And as we shall see shortly, it is important to regulate better the withdrawal of suits, because this has become a widespread practice in courts in many parts of contemporary China hearing administrative cases brought by aggrieved citizens against the state. The 2007 Rules were introduced because the Administrative Litigation Law 1989 (or 'ALL'), which was seen at the time of its introduction as such a crucial development in China's emerging system of socialist legality, did not expressly deal with the phenomenon of the interrupted lawsuit. The Supreme People's Court therefore decided to regulate the process of withdrawal through these Rules. This of course raises the question: why did the practice of withdrawal of suit become so popular, so much so that the Supreme People's Court decided – more than a decade and a half after the ALL 1989 was promulgated – to regularize the process of abandonment of suit?

Transforming the ALL

The Rules are intended to guide the work of the administrative chambers of the people's courts. These chambers were introduced on a nationwide basis in the late 1980s better to handle citizen–state cases. These chambers were to be staffed by high-quality judges, and the special track of administrative procedures was introduced to enhance the effectiveness of citizen complaints in a politically sensitive context (Palmer 1989). After all, suing the state in a people's democratic dictatorship is an inherently risky affair. And yet, from at least the mid-1990s onwards, it is clear that unusual processes were at work because more and more administrative suits were commenced, but then withdrawn without any kind of explanation. Observers noted that in a number of instances of withdrawal, the plaintiff appeared to be satisfied with the outcome, even though she or he did not have their day in court, nor 'win' their case.

In 2005 an important news report in *Renmin fayuanbao* (People's Court Daily) pointed to a spiralling rate of withdrawal in administrative suits in many localities in China – as many as 60 per cent of all first instance administrative cases in some localities – and emphasized that this phenomenon did need careful analysis. Indeed, the author of this news report observed that it was really puzzling that the judges in the administrative chamber were themselves not perplexed by the high rate of withdrawal, given that the Administrative Litigation Law 1989 is silent on this course of action (Dai 2005). In this respect, the wording of the 2007 Rules is very unhelpful, for the text tells us very little about the phenomenon of withdrawal other than to indicate that it is now officially permitted and should take place within the fairly clear boundaries that we have considered above.

DECISION-MAKING IN THE ALL: THEORY, PRACTICE AND … MORE THEORY

Theory: No Mediation

In many cases the process of withdrawal is the result of a settlement between the parties that has reached a process of pre-trial mediation by the intended trial judge. In several recent publications (Palmer 2007, 2009, 2010) I have discussed this judicial practice of pre-trial mediation in administrative cases that come before the people's courts, and the legally difficult relationship between such practice and the forceful declaration at Article 50 of the ALL 1989[3] that mediation may not be used to determine the outcome of the substance of a claim brought against the state body under the Law. The ALL 1989 (at Article 67) permits the use of mediation in handling the issue of the compensation award to be made if the plaintiff succeeds in her or his or its claim. But in ruling on the lawfulness of the conduct of an administrative act, the court was not (and in formal terms is still not) permitted to attempt to mediate the differences between the parties in order to secure a settlement; the conduct complained of was in some way unlawful, or it was not.

Practice: Mediation

Since the mid-1990s, however, it had become increasingly apparent that despite the ban on court mediation, judges increasingly allowed themselves to serve as mediators in cases post filing but prior to the trial. Typically it has been the collegiate panel's leading judge (*zhushen faguan*) who conducts the mediation. The ban on mediation in the ALL 1989 and the absence therefore of appropriate procedural rules agreed upon and made publicly available for regulating this process was pithily expressed in the characterization of this process as 'mediation without the [written] mediation agreement' (*meiyou tiaojieshu de tiaojie*). Various techniques emerged that were consistent in name with the mediation ban

---

[3] Article 50 of the ALL stipulates firmly that 'the people's courts in hearing administrative cases may not use mediation'.

in the ALL 1989 and which provided some kind of normative corpus that guided the process.

Thus, for example, after a judge-mediated compromise outcome had been agreed, the defendant state agency might adjust the administrative act that gave rise to the action, or cancel and perhaps replace it with a decision that the plaintiff could agree to accept. In other cases the plaintiff might consent to the administrative conduct that created the grievance and claim, but secure certain concessions from the defendant that bore no direct relationship to the claim per se. Thereafter, the court typically approved a request for withdrawal by the plaintiff. To ensure enforcement, some of the mediated settlements in administrative suits were drawn up in written form. While for obvious reasons such agreements could not – as often happens in civil proceedings – become an order of the court, the defendant would sometimes require the plaintiff to notarize the written settlement. This was typically done at the request of the defendant – rather than, as might have been expected, at the behest of the plaintiff – because the defendant state agency wanted to bring closure to the case, and so prevent the plaintiff from resurrecting another claim based on the same grievance at some future time.

2007 Rules as a Legitimizing Fig-leaf

The 2007 Rules are in effect an acceptance of the practice of administrative suit judicial mediation and an attempt to bring some procedural guidance and legal certainty to the resulting settlements. They do not mention the sensitive name of 'mediation', however, because of opposition from the Standing Committee of the National People's Congress, which insisted that the term be excluded on the ground that its inclusion would be inconsistent with national law: namely, Article 50 of the ALL 1989.[4] So the Rules *silently assume* that in many instances a settlement outcome will have been achieved by mediatory intervention by a judge. And when reference is made to what happens in these cases, the expression 'settlement' (*hejie*) rather than 'mediation' is used. As we have seen, the Rules nevertheless offer a normative framework regulating withdrawal and attempt to ensure fairness in the treatment of the parties. Both before and after their introduction, these Rules have been justified in substantial part as contributing to the creation and maintenance of a socialist harmonious society within China. Mediation of administrative

---

4 Private disclosure, interview with Supreme People's Court judge, Beijing, July 2009.

cases will, it is argued, help to keep state and citizen closer together (Palmer 2009, 2010).

These efforts to infuse administrative litigation with mediation parallel similar developments in 'letters and visits' (*xinfang*), and administrative reconsideration (*xingzheng fuyi*), two other important avenues for securing (or otherwise) administrative justice. Mediation is a key process for ensuring that conflicts are contained, so that political and social stability prevails.[5] This vision continues to highlight the importance of the rule of law, but it also stresses the need for a close and harmonious relationship between the people and the state (Palmer 2009, 2010). And it is clearly a latter day expression, in some respects at least, of the Confucian values that infused traditional Chinese legal culture. Current policies promoting a harmonious society may also be seen as a part of the continuing reaction to the policies of continuous revolution (*jixu geming*) and disorder of the Cultural Revolution. Despite the widespread cynicism of ordinary people about the way that the current system of political authority is working, my sense is that when these central government promoted values of 'harmony' and 'stability' lock into local community norms they may well gain legitimacy and effectiveness.

Where I live currently – eastern Guangdong – is not only the site of several large local protests (notably over development projects at Wukang and Hailufeng), but also has a long history of violence and instability. However, in the past ten years villages in the area have seen the development of 'elders' associations' or 'elders' groups' (*laoren zu*) consisting of well-known 'seniors' drawn from various local lineages in the countryside – typically a village, but now also somtimes a suburban area of greater Shantou. In Mao's analysis of class oppression and exploitation, of course, the authority of lineage elders was considered to be one of the main systems of authority 'oppressing' ordinary members of Chinese society, and the land reform movement of the early 1950s was in part an attempt to eliminate such authority.

However, over the past decade or so these elders' groups, formed on the basis of a reviving lineage culture, have come to play an increasingly significant role in managing many important matters at the grassroots level. The social prestige of the elders enables them to resolve disputes between villagers – often in accordance with village regulations and agreements (*xianggui minyue*) – to facilitate reconciliation and maintain social order in the villages. These groups are characterized locally as non-registered civil associations (*minjian zuzhi*), and officially operate

---

5 See, for example, Lam (2004).

under the supervision of the Villagers' Committees. Single surname villages have refurbished their ancestral halls (*citang*), and prominent members of various local lineages often constitute the leading members of a local elders' association. It is perhaps not surprising that the region has only very low rates of litigation, including administrative litigation. And these traditional elders' groups are tolerated precisely because they promote local harmony and social stability. They are symbiotically related to the CCP's national policy of 'harmonious society'.

Justifications for Using Mediation in Administrative Litigation

But in most urban areas of China, such traditional forms of social control are absent, and citizens are more willing to bring suit against the government. Reliance on mediation for decision-making in administrative cases has accordingly been encouraged on a number of related grounds. It is argued (somewhat counterintuitively) within Chinese discourses on administrative justice that the government and the people no longer retain the confrontational, antagonistic relationships that they once did. Accordingly they should be looking to cooperate more with each other – both in their personal interest and for the greater good of harmony and stability in society. In addition, many administrative acts in present-day China do not necessarily contain a distinctively public element. They are increasingly matters of routine decision-making and so do not in themselves raise important rule of law issues. Further, it is emphasized that administrative law in China has become much more complex since the late 1980s. As a result, the rights and wrongs in administrative cases are often not as easily identified as they once were (Palmer 2009, 2010).

Recent Justifications

Indeed, in the past year or so, arguments in the Chinese legal press for allowing the formal introduction of judicial mediation in the administrative litigation process have become more and more insistent. Again, contrasts in social conditions between the time of the promulgation of the ALL in 1989 and the present day are stressed. The changed environment has given rise to a need for a shift in emphasis from assessing the legality of concrete administrative conduct to ensuring the realization of substantive rights, obligations and interests through mediation and settlement. In addition, it is again pointed out that much administrative conduct is increasingly of a quasi-private nature – for example, administrative contacts – and there is also increasing recognition that important decisions often take the form of 'abstract' administrative acts, so that disputes arising out of such conduct are therefore often best handled through the process of mediation. In effect, judicial mediation in administrative cases is lauded for its more sophisticated nature and capacity to produce better outcomes (Yuan 2011, Zhou 2011). In 2010 the Supreme People's Court issued a Notice on prioritizing mediation and on combining mediation and adjudication in handling cases, which specifically encouraged a gradual expansion of mediation in court handling of administrative cases (Supreme People's Court 2010).

Harmony and Law

Current policies promoting a socialist harmonious society are, of course, not only expected to promote harmony and social stability but also are intended to be consistent with the goals of creating a rule of law state. Indeed, 'adherence' to democracy and the rule of law are considered to be essential conditions for the creation of socialist social harmony because, inter alia, they help to promote social equity and justice. All citizens are equal before the law, and there must be respect for and protection of human rights, 'in accordance with the law', to ensure the rights and freedoms of citizens.

Nevertheless in the key Party document on the creation of a socialist harmonious society (CCCP 2006), law as an instrument of social control (rather than rights) is also emphasized. Thus, in addition to strengthening grassroots social security comprehensive management measures to 'ensure the overall stability of the social order', there should be a continuing process of cracking down 'in accordance with the law' on serious criminal activities and public security issues, to 'resolutely curb' the high incidence of criminal offences. Moreover, the overall drive to create a socialist harmonious society must of course be carried out under the leadership of the CCP. The twin concerns with social obedience and Party domination suggest a less than wholehearted embrace of 'rule of law' values. This too is reflected in the toleration of the widespread court practice allowing pre-trial mediation of administrative cases and the Supreme People's Court introduction of Rules that in all but name legitimize this practice despite the obvious conflict with the intention of the ban on mediation in the ALL 1989. In this respect it is interesting to note that while the CCP document on socialist harmonious society mentions administrative reconsideration, it makes no direct reference to administrative litigation.

RELUCTANT USE OF THE ALL 1989

Administrative Cases, Compared to Civil and Criminal

Party-state control over the local courts is thought to make success in administrative suits difficult to achieve, and mass petitions and protests have developed as alternatives. These both help to explain why the overall levels of administrative litigation have increased by less than 1 per cent per year on average since their high point in 2001 in the aftermath of the PRC's constitutional embrace of the principle of 'rule of law governance'. Over the past decade or so, civil case loads have remained fairly constant while criminal cases have been enlarging steadily. As in the 1980s, the courts are increasingly important sites for handling criminal cases. Official statistics on administrative, civil and criminal cases handled by the people's courts contained in the *China Law Yearbook* and the Reports of the Presidents of the Supreme People's Court thus show clearly that in the PRC rising popular discontent with perceived administrative misconduct is not matched by a significant increase in administrative litigation.[6]

Rise in Alternative Forms of Response

The limited enthusiasm for access to administrative justice through the ALL 1989 and related channels is paralleled by the rise in various forms of mass discontent. As Minzner (2006) pointed out, these manifestations of popular discontent often embrace an accumulation of grievances, and may be infused powerfully with expressions of anger against apparent injustice and maladministration such as corruption in the government, too much taxation, and violence carried out or ordered by cadres. These expressions of discontent include citizen unrest not only in the form of strikes (against employment restructuring, non-payment of wages and so forth), but also local protests against land resumptions (land grabbing, forced demolitions and unfavourable resettlement), collective action against environmental degradation, objections to unlawful taxation and meddling in village elections, and popular displeasure at court decisions that increasingly extends to web-based protests by netizens.

---

[6] See, for example, *Zhongguo Falü Nianjian 2012* (China Law Yearbook 2012), at pp. 181–3, p. 1066, and p. 1094.

TYPES OF ALL CASES

We have noted the general 'flatness' in levels of administrative litigation since the late 1990s and the rise in alternative, popular, forms of reaction. At the same time, there have been relatively few changes in the kinds of case that aggrieved citizens are prepared to pursue through administrative litigation; they may have already attempted unsuccessfully to secure 'justice' through other official avenues of complaint against administrative misconduct such as 'letters and visits', administrative mediation and administrative review. Thus, several important features stand out in the official statistics on administrative cases handled by the people's courts contained in the *China Law Yearbook* and the Reports of the Presidents of the Supreme People's Court. First, cases against the public security organs have maintained a steady rise during the past two decades and these are always one of the three most common types of case. Second, cases involving issues of 'industry and commerce' remain a limited form of suit. Third, cases on city construction experienced a dramatic leap at the beginning of the century, with the figures for 2002 almost twice those for 2001.[7]

REFORMING THE ALL 1989?

Twenty Years' Experience

The ALL 1989 has now been in force for more than 20 years, and various drafts of a refurbished version of the Law have been produced for more than a decade. In the 1989 ALL, Article 1 declares its intended functions:

> This Law is drafted on the basis of the Constitution in order to safeguard correct and timely adjudication of administrative cases; to protect the lawful rights and interests of citizens, legal persons and other organizations; and to uphold and supervise the exercise of administrative power in accordance with law by administrative organs.

It is not clear that the Law does indeed guarantee the prompt handling of complaints, safeguard the lawful rights of individual and groups, and scrutinize effectively the lawfulness of administrative conduct. Commentators within and outside China have noted many key limitations in the

---

[7] See, for example, *Zhongguo Falü Nianjian 2002* (China Law Yearbook 2002), at p. 1240.

ALL 1989, and I do not propose to deal with them here.[8] Suffice to say here that these include the limited jurisdiction of the administrative chambers in the people's courts, the restricted ability of the courts to address the issue of the true identity of the administrative decision-maker, and the problems courts face when they challenge the government.

Reforms

Radical reforms have been proposed accordingly to open up access to administrative justice through a refurbished system of administrative litigation. These reforms include broadening the jurisdiction of the courts in administrative litigation cases, allowing for a wider spectrum of proceedings (including, for example, public interest litigation and simplified procedures), and enhancing enforcement powers (see, for example, Zhan 2012: 213). Supporters of legislative reform also propose that a revised ALL should expressly give legal recognition to the role of mediation in administrative suits.[9] We can see this reflected in draft revisions of the Administrative Litigation Law, an entirely new Administrative Procedures Law, and various local experiments with administrative justice.[10] Commentators have expressly pointed to the 2007 Supreme People's Court Rules on withdrawal of suit as providing the foundations for the explicit recognition of a role for mediation in a revised ALL.

---

8 See, for example, Finder (1989), Potter (1994), Song (1994) and Pei (1997).

9 See, for example, Liu (2011: 206–7).

10 The development of a comprehensive Administrative Procedure Law designed to provide a broad normative framework for governmental conduct – rather than just dealing with complainants aggrieved by maladministration – is being facilitated on an experimental basis by local provisions for Shantou City. My colleague at Shantou University Law School, Professor Deng Jianguang, has played a major role in drafting the experimental legislation: Shantou Shi Xingzheng Chengxu Guiding (2011). Although these local rules do not deal with administrative litigation per se, there is a clear role given to mediation in the resolution of complaints brought against the government under the rules.

INTEGRITY OF PROCESS? DECISION-MAKING IN THE ALL 1989: THEORY AND PRACTICE

Fuller on Purity of Process

The emergence of mediation as an almost mandatory pre-trial stage in administrative litigation entails jurisprudential difficulties. The most fundamental of these was identified by Lon Fuller in a seminal series of general essays on the 'processual integrity' of differing modes of dispute resolution (1963, 1971 and 1978). In Fuller's view, particular processes and institutions of dispute resolution have their own specific integrity, logic and morality. His analysis recognizes a fundamental contrast between the two main forms of third-party intervention for dispute resolution: mediation and umpiring (adjudication and arbitration). The processes are so unlike in nature that they should never be combined.

The core value of mediation is the most advantageous settlement, with each party making compromises in order to secure a better overall outcome. The informal processes of mediation – such as caucusing with the parties separately – are thus directed at uncovering and expressing the interests of the parties, not at applying the law. For Fuller, mediation is orientated to the parties' relationships, and it is their mutuality, consent and reciprocity that informs and justifies the process. The morality of umpiring, on the other hand, lies in reaching and applying a decision according to the law (and the facts). The process of umpiring thus requires a fully detached and impartial third-party decision-maker to ensure appropriate procedures, by means of which the parties may present reasoned arguments and evidence to support their case and then to determine the outcome through strict application of the law. Combining the roles of mediator and umpire, Fuller warns, leads to 'confusion' and undermines the purity and clarity of role essential for the correct application of the contrasting processes to particular cases. In addition, adjudication is a public function, whereas mediation is ordinarily a private course of action, so it is important not to confuse the rights vindication role of adjudication with the kind of relationship readjustment that lies at the core of mediation.

Mixed Processes

In many jurisdictions in the world today, even in public law proceedings (including judicial review in some cases), there are hybrid or mixed processes in which mediation is combined in some way with adjudication. Processes are integrated in an attempt to perform a wide and effective variety of functions, including not only the determination of rights but also mending of relationships, resolution of disputes, reduction of social conflict and even administrative rulemaking – 'reg–neg' or regulation crafted by negotiation with relevant bodies such as NGOs – and public policy decision-making. This hybridization is thought to be better able to reflect the ever-increasing social complexities found in many societies (Menkel-Meadow 2000: 19–21), so the administrative chambers of the people's courts in the PRC are not alone in bringing together the differing processes of decision-making found in mediation and adjudication. China's approach is also justified in some ways that are part of the rhetoric of 'mixed processes' found elsewhere in the world. For example, it is true that the two processes share several common features like efficiency, cost savings (both time and money), apparently clear separation of proceedings into distinct stages, flexibility and a triangular structure of decision-making.

However, the central elements of the system in the PRC also differ in several important respects from hybrid processual innovations found elsewhere, such that it would be a mistake to characterize the PRC system of withdrawal after pre-trial mediation in administrative litigation as a legitimate 'mixed process'. First, in the PRC administrative litigation 'mixed process', an indispensable role for the neutral third party who encourages the participants to either reach their own settlement or make a disinterested decision is absent. Here the intervening third party is a judge who is under career pressures to secure a meditated outcome, and who has informal (or semi-formal) but strong public policy considerations necessarily informing her or his decision-making. Second, in the PRC approach, the idea that mediation may be started and proceeded with only under the parties' express consent so that the parties can abandon the mediation at any time is clearly absent. Under pressure from over-active judges and powerful state defendants, the plaintiffs are often mandated into a 'reconciliation' process. Third, the conduct of the mediation in mixed processes elsewhere in the world is often the responsibility of a mediator who is in some way independent of the court that may eventually come to try the case, whereas in the PRC's system of 'pre-trial mediation' in administrative litigation it is the trial judge who carries out the process of mediation. Finally, the general policy preference in the PRC for reconciliation between the parties as an outcome is not one that is necessarily found elsewhere in the world.

The Legal Culture Defence

One of the problems with the approach taken in the PRC is that Fuller's idea of integrity of process is largely absent from dispute resolution thinking and practice. The long-standing concern in Chinese society, at least at the ideological level, with harmony, restoration of relationships and indeed social stability, is such that combining dispute resolution processes is regarded as a quite natural fusion of the virtues of each process. Alternating between and mixing up mediation and umpiring (whether adjudication or arbitration) is the preferred strategy for many third-party decision-makers, and in particular mediating without the ultimate sanction of adjudication or arbitration (mediating with a 'club' as Fuller put it) is regarded by many specialists as weak and ineffective.

Luban and the Needs of the Legal System

Another consideration is the effectiveness of the legal system as a whole, a matter raised forcefully by David Luban (1995) in his partial defence of the critique of ADR by constitutional lawyer Owen Fiss. Fiss critiqued the process of settlement as one which, inter alia, undermines the role of the courts in creating new legal (and in due course, new social) norms and overlooks the role of the judge in protecting the procedural rights of weaker parties (Fiss 1984, 1985). Luban acknowledges that this is indeed one of the weaknesses of a system that places a great deal of weight on settlement rather than adjudication, and also that the courts will indeed be incapable of helping the law to develop if adjudication is avoided. Luban points out that courts are unlikely to be able to cope with their case loads if settlement is not allowed. Arguing that a legal system needs *both* settlement (achieved by negotiation or mediation) *and* adjudication, Luban claims the question is therefore how best to balance the two approaches. He also suggests that some of the jurisprudential concerns about the private nature of settlement might be met if mediated agreements are registered and made public where they involve the public interest.

In the case of the PRC, it seems to me that in striking such a balance it would be most appropriate to allow only *adjudication* in cases of administrative litigation. Not only is the case load for administrative cases relatively limited, as we have seen, but also the possibilities of mediation are strongly present in local people's mediation systems, the 'letters and visits' system, and, of course, administrative review. In such circumstances, to reserve the track of administrative litigation for adjudicative decision-making makes a great deal of sense from the point of view of both the public interest (rule of law; good governance) and the plaintiffs' desire for access to administrative justice.

CONCLUSIONS

Courts and the Polity

We have seen that in the PRC, concerns with social values including harmony, stability and reconciliation, have hollowed out through judicial practice the strict ban on mediation in the ALL 1989. I have put forward the argument that despite claims made for the benefits of giving formal recognition to pre-trial mediation of administrative litigation cases, the ban on mediation would be better enforced than relaxed. Of course, from a comparative viewpoint, it can be argued that it is not appropriate for an unelected body such as a court to challenge, and on occasion overturn, the decisions of a legislature or a government that is popularly elected and for which there may already be available other avenues of criticism or complaint, such as an ombudsman system (Tushnet 1999, Waldron 2006, Rubin 2008). At the very least, in firmly institutionalized democracies with robust multi-party political systems, strongly established rule of law values, a liberal and independent press and other media outlets, and an autonomous and vibrant civil society, such challenges may be seen as something of a double-edged sword.

In holding powerful public institutions and their decision-making to account, the court is conducting itself in a manner that raises significant concerns about the legitimacy of its decision-making authority. The situation is surely less worrying in transitional systems that are either abandoning socialism or, as in China's case, slowly modifying a system of Communist Party rule in order to meet the needs and challenges of economic and legal reform, globalization (including entry to the World Trade Organization) and greater engagement with the international legal community. In such circumstances, courts may indeed play a substantial role in helping to ensure that governmental conduct is at the very least lawful and also to provide an avenue of redress for those whose grievance is that their rights and interests have in some way been harmed adversely by unlawful or very unreasonable executive decisions. In the PRC, the system of political representation remains very stilted and controlled, civil society is only little by little shaking off decades of state penetration, and reluctant commitment of the authorities to rule of law values means that there is an important need for the courts to be allowed to function in a manner that promotes the legality of governmental decision-making, especially where decisions impact on the growing ranks of the socially disadvantaged.

Harmony Ideology

In pursuit of the goal of a socialist harmonious society and seeking to secure social stability at a time of very rapid economic change and social dislocation, the system of administrative litigation in the PRC has become something that the drafters of the ALL 1989 clearly intended it not to be. Mediation, although not mentioned by name, is increasingly tolerated and indeed now stressed as the preferred form of decision-making. The unmistakably stipulated norm that in handling the substantive issues in an administrative case, the court may not use mediation, has been subverted. However, harmony ideologies such as that proposed by the Party-state over the past few years often contain a strong element justifying dominance, coercion and an expression of communal identity against the outside world, as anthropologist Laura Nader (1990: 1–11) has emphasized.

Individual and institutional interests, ideology and cultural factors all have an important part to play in the Chinese resort to de facto judicial mediation in administrative cases. But it is difficult to escape the conclusion that a significant dimension in the transformation of the role of mediation in public law suits is pursuit of social order and control. In short, the ALL 1989 has thus become an instrument for controlling the citizen rather than the state. In many parts of China, the people's courts in practice now recommend and indeed mandate mediation in the shadow of the trial. And while this system of judicial mediation does have virtues from the point of view of the disputing parties and the political system, it also considerably disadvantages the weak and underprivileged, and limits the ability of the courts to act as a monitor of the legality of executive conduct.

Fusion of Party and State

This development is also linked to the political reality that law and legal development in China remain very much subject to Communist Party policy and institutional dominance. The Party has grown less concerned with the separation of Party and state that Deng Xiaoping and Zhao Ziyang advised to be such an important reform, and which helped to prepare the ground for the ALL 1989. Whereas Deng Xiaoping once insisted on reform in the direction of separating Party and state, the conservative leadership of the past few years has stressed the need to establish a 'socialist harmonious society' in which Party and state are firmly bonded. The difficulty of imposing standards of correct conduct on a political ruler is a significant problem of governance in most societies but the difficulty is compounded in the case of contemporary China by the fact that the real decision-making may take place in a Party context and then be implemented by a state organ. As a result, an aggrieved citizen who seeks redress has to do so against the agent rather than against the principal.

From a systemic point of view, this limits the potential of the process of administrative litigation to function as a mechanism of accountability and good governance. As we have also noted above, in the PRC's current state of political and legal development, this limitation may be crucial. Civil society has little ability to make effective protests, and governmental accountability to the legislature – despite China's doctrine of legislative supremacy – remains largely ineffective, as do the official processes of supervision. So while mediation may indeed have a role to play in administrative suits, adjudication should be allowed to regain its principal role. The very limited role that might be allowed for mediation should be given formal legal recognition and CCP decision-making that significantly impacts on administrative conduct itself should be brought into the jurisdiction of the administrative chambers of the people's courts.

REFERENCES

CCCP (2006), Zhonggong zhongyang guanyu goujian shehui zhuyi hexieshehui ruogan zhongda wenti de jueding (Decision of the Central Committee of the Chinese Communist Party regarding several important questions on the construction of socialism and a harmonious society), 11 October 2006, http://news.xinhuanet.com/politics/2006-10/18/content_5218639.htm. Accessed 30 October 2013.

Choukroune, Leila (2005), 'Justiciability of economic, social, and cultural rights: the UN Committee on Economic, Social and Cultural Rights' review of China's first periodic report on the implementation of the International Covenant on Economic, Social and Cultural Rights, *Columbia Journal of Asian Law*, 19(1): 30–49.

Dai, Weizhong (2005), 'Xingzheng susong tiaojie zhidu yinggai gaige' (The system of mediation in administrative litigation should be reformed), *Renmin fayuanbao*, (People's Court Daily), 28 August 2005: 4.

Finder, Susan (1989), 'Like throwing an egg against a stone – administrative litigation in the People's Republic of China', *Journal of Chinese Law*, 3(1): 1–28.

Fiss, Owen (1984), 'Against settlement', *Yale Law Journal*, 93: 1073–90.

Fiss, Owen (1985), 'Out of Eden', *Yale Law Journal*, 94: 1669–73.

Fuller, Lon (1963), 'Collective bargaining and the arbitrator', *Wisconsin Law Review*, 18: 3–47.

Fuller, Lon (1971), 'Mediation: its forms and functions', *Southern California Law Review*, 44: 305–39.
Fuller, Lon (1978), 'The forms and limits of adjudication', *Harvard Law Review*, 92: 353–409.
Lam, Willy (2004), 'Socialism with a harmonious face: Hu Jintao's plan for reform', *China Brief*, 4(20): 5–7.
Liu, Jianlong (2011), 'Administrative litigation in China: parties and their rights and obligations', *NUJS Law Review*, 4: 205–29.
Luban, David (1995),'Settlement and the erosion of the public realm', *Georgetown Law Journal*, 83: 2619–62.
Menkel-Meadow, Carrie (2000), 'Mothers and fathers of the invention: the intellectual founders of ADR', *Ohio State Journal on Dispute Resolution*, 16(1): 1–37.
Minzner, Carl (2006),'Social instability in China: causes, consequences, and implications', csis.org/files/media/csis/events/061205_mizner_abstract.pdf. Accessed 30 October 2013.
Nader, Laura (1990), *Harmony Ideology: justice and control in a Mexican zapotec village*. Stanford: Stanford University Press.
Palmer, Michael (1989), 'The revival of mediation in the People's Republic of China: (2) judicial mediation', in W.E. Butler (ed.), *Yearbook on Socialist Legal Systems 1988*. New York, Dobbs Ferry: Transnational Books, pp. 143–69.
Palmer, Michael (2007), 'Controlling the state? Mediation in administrative litigation in the People's Republic of China', *Transnational Law & Contemporary Problems*, 16: 165–87.
Palmer, Michael (2009), 'Compromising courts and harmonizing ideologies: mediation in the administrative chambers of the people's courts in the People's Republic of China', in Andrew Harding and Penelope Nicholson (eds.), *New Courts in Asia*. London: Routledge, pp. 194–214, 375–82.
Palmer, Michael (2010), 'Administrative suits and harmonious settlements: a twilight issue in the legal development of contemporary China', *Journal of Comparative Law*, 4(2): 71–8.
Pei, Minxin (1997), 'Citizens v. mandarins: administrative litigation in China', *The China Quarterly*, 152: 832–62.
Potter, Pitman (1994), 'The administrative litigation law of the PRC: judicial review and bureaucratic reform', in Pitman Potter (ed.), *Domestic Law Reforms in Post Mao China*. Armonk, NY: M.E. Sharpe, pp. 270–304.
Rubin, Edward (2008), 'Judicial review and the right to resist', *Georgetown Law Journal*, 97: 61–118.
Song, Bing (1994), 'Assessing China's system of judicial review of administrative actions', *China Law Reporter*, 8(1–2): 1–20.
Supreme People's Court (2008a), 'Zuigao renmin fayuan guanyu xingzheng susong chesu ruogan wenti de guiding' (Supreme People's Court rules concerning several problems in the withdrawal of administrative suits), adopted at the 1,441st Meeting of the Adjudication Committee of the Supreme People's Court, promulgated on 1 January 2008, and in force 1 February 2008, http://news.xinhuanet.com/legal/2008-01/16/content_7432440.htm. Accessed 30 October 2013.
Supreme People's Court (2008b), 'Guanyu renzhen guanche zhixing zuigao renmin fayuan xingzheng susong chesu ruogan wenti de guiding de tongzhi' (Notice on seriously carrying out the Supreme People's Court rules concerning several problems in the withdrawal of administrative suits), *Zuigao Renmin Fayuan Gongbao* (Gazette of the Supreme People's Court), 1: 19–20.

Supreme People's Court (2010), 'Zuigao renmin fayuan guanyu jin yibu guanche tiaojie youxian, tiao-shen jiehe gongzuo' yuanze de ruogan yijian' (Several opinions of the Supreme People's Court concerning taking forward the work principle of mediation takes priority, mediation and adjudication are combined), promulgated on 7 June 2010, http://www.court.gov.cn/qwfb/sfwj/yj/201008/t20100811_8489.htm. Accessed 1 January 2011.

Tushnet, Mark (1999), *Taking the Constitution Away from the Courts*. Princeton, NJ: Princeton University Press.

Waldron, Jeremy (2006), 'The core of the case against judicial review', *Yale Law Journal*, 115: 1346–407.

Yuan, Dingbo (2011), 'Sifa huanjing fasheng jubian: xingzheng shenpan faguan zui guanzhu sanda xiufa jiaodian – xingzheng susong bu shiyong tiaojie mingcunshi-wang jidai feichu' (Huge change in the judicial environment: judges adjudicating administrative [cases] are concerned mostly with three significant points of revision – mediation is not suitable in administrative litigation is a dead letter and needs to be abandoned quickly), *Fazhi ribao* (Legal System Daily), 1 July 2011: 5.

Zhan, Zhongde (2012), 'The amendment of the Administrative Procedure Law of China', *Frontiers of Law in China*, 7(2): 211–24.

Zhongguo falü nianjian bianjibu (eds.) (2003), *Zhongguo Falü Nianjian 2002* (China Law Yearbook 2002). Beijing: Falü chubanshe.

Zhongguo falü nianjian bianjibu (eds.) (2013), *Zhongguo Falü Nianjian 2012* (China Law Yearbook 2012). Beijing: Falü nianjianshe.

Zhou, Bin (2011), 'Daibiao huyu wei xingzheng susong changkai tiaojie damen, shijianzhong you silei xingzheng susong anjian ke yong tiaojie' (Representatives call for the great door of mediation to be opened in administrative litigation: in practice there are four types of administrative litigation case for which mediation may be used), *Fazhi ribao* (Legal System Daily), 14 March: 3.

7. Death sentencing for stability and harmony

Susan Trevaskes*

INTRODUCTION

Death sentencing may sound discordant with notions of stability and harmony. But the death sentence has an obscure place in the law–politics–stability nexus as it operates to stabilize and harmonize Chinese society. This chapter examines an important but largely overlooked aspect of the Chinese justice system; the use of exemplar cases promulgated by superior justice organs – the Supreme People's Court (SPC) and the Supreme People's Procuratorate (SPP) – to 'guide' judicial and prosecutorial decision-making in lower courts and procuracies. China's SPC has long used 'reference cases' (*cankao anli*), otherwise known as 'standard cases' (*dianxing anli*), to illustrate best practice and educate the local ranks in best-practice decision-making. This is a case referencing system whereby exemplar cases are promulgated to local jurisdictions to guide understanding of new judicial interpretations, sentencing guidelines, opinions, law or policy. In November 2010 the SPC and SPP announced the establishment of a new 'case guidance system' (*anli zhidao zhidu*). The SPC and SPP select reference cases and 'upgrade' them to guiding cases, giving them more authoritative clout: the crucial difference is that local courts are now compelled to cite guiding cases in the judgments of similar cases.

Both types of exemplar cases have been used by the SPP and SPC in recent years to steer judicial and prosecutorial decision-making in a way that fulfils Party-state goals of stability maintenance and social harmony-building while at the same time, attempting to improve the quality of decision-making by guiding judges in the application of the law through

* Research for this book was supported by a grant from the Australian Research Council [DP0985738] and from the Centre on China in the World at ANU.

these cases. By examining the medium and message of these cases, we see how the socio-political role of punishment is articulated top down from the SPP and SPC to prosecutors and judges in local jurisdictions. These cases are a key means that the central judicial authorities employ to convey socio-political agendas on death sentencing indirectly from the Party into the justice system as both legal understanding and judicial practice.

Standard and guiding cases are an important legal mechanism used to keep judicial eyes firmly on sentencing outcomes consistent with national socio-political goals. But on use of the death penalty, legal and socio-political goals are not necessarily compatible in practice. The overall legal motivation for case guidance is to help standardize decision-making in courts nationwide and to limit unwieldy judicial discretion, enabling and promoting development of a mature continental/civil law-type case system in China to enhance the legitimacy of the law (Jiang 2011a). For this legal goal, guided use of the death sentence is part of a legal process to produce a longer-term outcome for the state of the legal system. The overall socio-political motivation for case guidance at this particular juncture in China's development, to produce stability and harmony, is to satisfy short- and long-term outcomes for the state of Chinese society. The death sentence is to help harmonize social relations specifically to help avert further social disharmony and unrest in communities affected by homicide. These two motivations compel the judiciary to deliver simultaneously what politico-legal authorities call 'positive legal outcomes' and 'positive social outcomes'.

As our discussion on use of the death penalty reveals, through the use of these cases, superior authorities in fact pressure judges to conflate 'positive legal' and 'positive social' outcomes for what the political authorities recognize as the higher political causes of stability maintenance and harmony-building. This problematizes case guidance on death sentencing because the prescribed ways for the judiciary to simultaneously pursue the socio-political goals of death sentencing for stability and harmony are not fully compatible with the overall legal goal of case guidance in general, which is to improve the credibility of the judiciary (SPC Opinion 2013). Dominance of the former goal imposes a practice of judicial activism that effectively subverts the latter goal. In practice then, inherent incompatibility in ways to pursue the 'legal' and the 'social' outcomes complicates death sentencing in homicide cases, where judgments are literally matters of life and death and so have particular significance for social stability and harmony.

GUIDING CASES, STANDARD CASES AND DEATH PENALTY REFORM

Since the early 1950s the SPC has issued models of selected cases to courts nationwide to exemplify typical or representative judicial practice (Li 2009, Yu and Gurgel 2012). This system of promulgating standard cases was introduced as a guidance mechanism to help judges interpret how to apply new rules or new policies to meet new political directives and new legal developments (Zhou 2004). Since 1985 reference cases have been published regularly in *The SPC Gazette*, which is distributed to courts to inform and update members of the judiciary. These cases are chosen and published in an attempt to shape or reshape judicial decision-making behaviours but they have no legally binding authority (Li 2009, Zhou 2004). In November 2010, the SPC and SPP announced the establishment of a new 'case guidance system'. The SPC issued its first set of guiding cases in December 2011 and these 'guiding cases' now exist alongside the 'standard' or 'reference' cases.

Guiding cases are selected by the SPC and the SPP as examples of correct application of an important legal principle or newly enacted or complex law (Jiang 2011a, Hu 2012, Yu and Gurgel 2012). While the SPC is yet to institute a system of binding precedent (*stare decisis*) in China, nevertheless this new case guidance system is a significant legal reform. SPC deputy president Shen Deyong identified legal benefits, claiming the case guidance system is designed specifically to reform decision-making mindsets, limit judicial discretion and improve consistency in decision-making (Shen 2011). By examining the medium and the message of these cases, we see how the socio-political role of punishment is articulated down through the SPP and SPC to prosecutors and judges in local jurisdictions. These cases are a key means that the SPC and SPP employ to convey the political message on death sentencing from the Party into the justice system as both legal understanding and judicial practice.

Both guiding cases and standard cases on the death penalty illustrate how the SPC and SPP plant Party national policy into nationwide court practice as the two legal authorities instruct courts on how to respond to the political imperatives of stability maintenance and harmonious society-building articulated by the Hu Jintao government. The SPC and SPP use the cases to implant a more 'balanced' sentencing approach consistent with SPC policy in 2007 urging judges to 'balance leniency and severity' (*kuanyan xiangji*).[1] But this balanced approach has been a hard sell for the courts in communities where a violent death has wrecked social harmony. The argument put forward by reformers is that lenient death sentencing for some capital cases can help to harmonize social relations or at least avert further disharmony by preventing further escalation of violence by criminals or the families of offenders isolated from society through the stigma of harsh punishment. For other more heinous cases, however, 'immediate execution' should be used to punish offenders and to deter violent crime.

To avert social disharmony and stability in these communities the SPC and SPP have sought to reconcile or 'unify' what politico-legal authorities call positive 'legal outcomes' (*falü xiaoguo*) with positive 'social outcomes' (*shehui xiaoguo*). Certain homicide cases which were the product of a domestic or neighbourhood dispute have been earmarked as possible cases for which lenient death sentencing can apply. A way to soften the death penalty for these types of cases is to consider mitigating factors, in particular to recognize the defendant's act of offering financial compensation to the victim's family as a mitigating sentencing factor. By accepting compensation as a mitigating factor and giving the defendant a 'suspended' death sentence (subsequently converted to a life sentence), courts enter potentially contentious territory. This practice of 'exchanging money for a life' moves sentencing considerations well beyond the criminal circumstances of a case to rely on the acquiescence of the victim's family in order for the criminal to deserve a more lenient sentence, without running the risk of 'destabilizing' community sentiment in homicide cases.

The SPC's guidance work in relation to Party doctrine of social stability/harmonious society introduced in the mid-2000s has been primarily through standard cases. The SPC's most prominent attempt to guide lower court decision-making in death penalty issues relating to social stability-harmonious society came a year before the 2010 establishment of the case guidance system, in the form of a set of five standard death penalty cases that were promulgated in the national media in mid-2009. These 2009 standard cases aimed to guide lower court judges in delivering more lenient death sentencing in cases of homicide resulting from a personal dispute and they are still in place.

Below we consider three of these 2009 SPC standard cases and one 2010 SPP guiding case to see how they play their part in harmonizing social relations through averting further social unrest in communities

[1] On the policy of 'balancing leniency and severity', see Trevaskes (2010).

affected by a violent death. Since significant changes to use of the death penalty were introduced from 2007, we turn first to an outline of the post-2007 death penalty process and debate. This enables us to place the death penalty in general, and these cases in particular, in the context of China's political agenda of building a harmonious society and preserving social stability.

REFORM IN DEATH PENALTY USE FROM 2007

It is widely known outside China that the PRC is the world's no. 1 executioner of criminals. It is less well known that in recent years China's highest court has tried to institutionalize a less severe mindset for capital case decision-making, with the lowering of the execution rate.[2] In October 2006, nearly 25 years after the first 'strike hard' campaign, an amendment to the Organic Law of the People's Courts returned to the SPC exclusive authority to review and approve all death sentences from 1 January 2007. This precipitated an immediate drop in executions. The number of death sentences in 2007 was reduced by 30 per cent as a direct result of this reform, according to the SPC.[3]

Around this time social stability rhetoric found a new home in SPC discourse within the broad national imperative of 'building a harmonious society'. SPC reformers seeking to reduce use of the death penalty argued that in terms of criminal punishment, a 'harmonious society' could be achieved by severely punishing only an extremely small minority of society's most truly heinous criminals, while sparing the lives

---

[2] Numbers killed remain a state secret, but experts in Beijing now put the annual rate at around 3,000 to 4,000, which is a dramatic reduction. It contrasts sharply with the 'strike hard' period estimates of around 8–10,000 per annum in the early 2000s, around 15,000 in the mid- to late 1990s, and much higher before that; according to the *People's Daily* (1984) in the first eight months of China's first 'strike hard' campaign, over 24,000 people were executed These estimates for the early 2000s and the 1990s are from published Western sources. Johnson and Zimring estimated the figure to be around 6,000 per annum in 2006 and 2007 in the lead-up and start of the shift to leniency from 2007, and around 15,000 during the 1990s when anti-crime campaigns were prevalent. Experts in Beijing interviewed by the author put the figure today at around 3,000 annually. For an insightful discussion about estimations of the number of executions, see Johnson and Zimring (2009: 231–42).

[3] 'China Sees 30% Drop in Death Penalty', *Xinhua News*, 10 May 2008, http://www.chinadaily.com.cn/china/2008-05/10/content_6675006.htm. Accessed 13 March 2013.

of the vast majority of criminals who commit extremely serious crimes but do not deserve to be killed. This would help to harmonize social relations or at least avert further disharmony by preventing further escalation of violence by criminals or the families of offenders isolated from society through the stigma of harsh punishment.

The SPC reformers' strategy was to promote an alternative death sentence already in the Criminal Law but underutilized – a sentencing option that while still recognized as 'capital' punishment ultimately delivers a life sentence rather than execution in capital cases. This alternative, called *sihuan*, is a 'death penalty with a two-year reprieve' and is known as a 'suspended' death sentence. The sentence is almost always commuted to a life sentence after the expiry of the two-year probation period. SPC Chief Justice Xiao Yang announced at the end of 2007 that for the first time in PRC history, and as a direct result of the January hand-back of authority to the SPC to approve death sentences, the number of suspended death sentences handed down had outnumbered the number of executions in China.

The SPC's plan was to further reduce executions by taking advantage of harmonious society doctrine. Reformers in the SPC sought to guide lower court judges to 'harmonize social relations' in capital cases by handing down suspended death sentences in two types of case. These are assault resulting in death and homicide resulting from a personal (domestic or neighbourhood) dispute that escalated into violence. The SPC's guidance mechanisms soon began to play a vital role in promoting and achieving a more lenient capital punishment regime in the style urged by the national politico-legal authorities. Without major amendments to the 1997 Criminal Law, and with the Law's ambiguity built solidly into it, the SPC would use its guiding instruments to influence judges' interpretation and assessment in the sentencing process.

SPC Chief Justice Xiao Yang and a cohort of SPC colleagues began working actively to replace the 'strike hard' ethos with the more lenient 'kill fewer' ethos. In 2006 the SPC began promoting sihuan as the conduit through which lower courts could strictly control execution rates in keeping with the new 'kill fewer' ethos. On 7 November 2006 at the Fifth National Criminal Justice Work Conference, Xiao Yang announced that only in exceptional circumstances should a sentence of immediate execution be given in cases of homicide or cases of assault resulting in death that had escalated from domestic or neighbourhood disputes, or where the case involved legally recognized mitigating circumstances such as the defendant surrendering or performing a meritorious service. The sentence for typical cases of this kind should be *sihuan*.

The SPC then issued a number of directives in 2007 encouraging judges to apply a policy of 'balancing leniency and severity'. This was applicable in cases with statutory mitigating circumstances such as the criminal's voluntary surrender or where discretionary circumstances could apply. One such discretionary circumstance was the newly established practice of allowing defendants to financially compensate the victim or victim's family in exchange for the promise of the more lenient (*sihuan*) death sentence. Financial compensation to the victim's family through subsidiary civil action (*fudai minshi susong*) is an established legal provision in the Criminal Procedure Law whereby the victim or the victim's family can sue the defendant for material and psychological damage or loss resulting from the defendant's actions.[4] It was drawn into more common use in the early to mid-2000s in minor criminal cases such as drink driving or minor assault. With the introduction of the harmonious society doctrine in the mid-2000s, it was touted as a way of reducing 'social disharmony' in minor criminal cases through a process of mediation. The process requires the defendant not only to pay compensation to the victim or victim's family, but also to show remorse, and for the victim and/or family to forgive the perpetrator (Trevaskes 2009). From 2007 the SPC began to promote this practice in death sentencing, encouraging judges to offer defendants in cases of homicide and assault resulting in death the chance of a reduced sentence upon demonstrating necessary contrition in the form of showing remorse, receiving forgiveness and understanding from the victim and or family, and promptly paying civil compensation to the family. It was hoped this practice would promote social harmony in communities through reconciling those socially harmed by violent death. In many cases, the families of murder victims have lost the family breadwinner. Past judicial experience indicates that enforcement of court orders for offenders to pay compensation to victims' families is ineffective in relation to soon-to-be-executed prisoners. *Sihuan* has therefore become an option to offenders as a means of ensuring that they pay the family compensation.

One key means for the SPC to implement its judicial reform plan was by issuing interpretations and opinions directed at courts of first instance, as noted above. A second aspect of the reform process involved changing the mindsets of judges in provincial higher courts. After 2007, provincial courts were required to send death sentence applications for review and

---

4 Subsidiary civil action is dealt with in the Criminal Procedure Law. For an outline of supplementary civil compensation see McConville et al. 2011: 198–20.

approval to the SPC. In the politically more conservative context of the post-17th Party Congress period, the death penalty reform process became subject to conflicting political imperatives at national and provincial levels. In the context of a national 'stability maintenance' obsession, understandings of the need for and utility of severe punishment were contested. The SPC expected higher courts to embrace the new, more lenient 'kill fewer, kill cautiously' punishment ethos. Yet provincial Party authorities expected the courts to ensure maintenance of stability through effective crime control – read 'severe punishment' – in their provincial jurisdiction to achieve the social harmony and social stability now articulated as a top national priority.

THE 2009 SPC STANDARD CASES

Within this conflicted political context, the SPC continued to promote its main reform objective of 'killing fewer' by encouraging lower court judges to take into account a greater variety of discretionary mitigating factors in sentencing homicide cases that had escalated in intensity from already existing domestic or neighbourhood disputes. From 2007, the SPC encouraged courts to hand down suspended death sentences in such cases through attention to three main mitigating factors concerning the defendant: they had surrendered to police, admitted guilt, and shown remorse through willingness and ability to financially compensate the victim's family through subsidiary civil action. This mitigating factor of offering financial compensation was itself politically contentious since it moved beyond the criminal circumstances of a case to rely on the acquiescence of the victim's family, for the criminal to deserve a more lenient *sihuan* sentence, without running the risk of 'destabilizing' community sentiment in homicide cases. It required from a victim's family their agreement to accept the compensation offered by the criminal, to forgive the offender as part of the process of criminal reconciliation, and to accept the *sihuan* sentence rather than immediate execution. This agreement, it was argued, would provide the necessary lubricant to ensure 'harmonized' social relations within communities where a violent death had occurred.

SPC directives, notices, interpretations and opinions provided courts with a clear understanding of the SPC's broad politico-legal reform intentions. But these guidance instruments did not provide clear instruction to courts on how to implement the newly touted discretionary factor of compensation by the offender. This new part of the sentencing procedure required a degree of judicial activism since it required judges to persuade victims' families to accept a reduced sentence for the offender in exchange for compensation for loss or harm from the crime.

It is not surprising that some members of the judiciary were initially hesitant in employing the compensation card. Some judges in provincial courts feared a public backlash. Others were unsure about what specific kinds of crime circumstances the SPC would find acceptable or appropriate for applying this practice, which critics dubbed a 'pay for your life' scheme (*huaqian maiming*). The SPC publishes a series of standard cases on the same topic in a national newspaper to propagate a new approach and practice. This is what the SPC did in 2009 to clarify the case circumstances under which provincial courts should actively promote leniency in death sentences by encouraging financial compensation and apology from the defendant to obtain a *sihuan* sentence, as a way of harmonizing social relations and preventing potential social unrest in communities where a homicide has occurred.

In mid-2009 a series of five standard cases was published in the SPC's newspaper *Fazhibao* (hereafter referred to as *Legal Daily*). The SPC advised that these standard cases provided reference for judicial decision-making, promoted a more unified system of death sentencing standards, and clarified the kinds of cases where the SPC would not approve immediate execution (Jiang and Xu 2009a, 2009b). These standard cases offered a practical model for judges to actively promote financial compensation to the victim's family and achieve their reconciliation with the criminal through the judges' own mediation. Each of the 2009 standard cases listed below purports to demonstrate best practice in judicial decision-making by averting potential social instability and harmonizing social relations.

SPC Standard Case 1:	'Judge travels across three provinces to mediate case and bring Ma Tao'an back to life from the dead' (Legal Daily 2009a)
SPC Standard Case 2:	'The death penalty review and approval process can be likened to the delicate ladies' craftwork of embroidering' (Legal Daily 2009b)
SPC Standard Case 3:	'The review and approval process tests the abilities of SPC judges to deal effectively with the masses' (Legal Daily 2009c)
SPC Standard Case 4:	'The life or death decision on Feng Fu hangs in the (Review Process) Balance' (Legal Daily 2009d)
SPC Standard Case 5:	'How to save a life without negatively impacting on social stability' (Legal Daily 2009e)

Each of these cases seeks in its own way to clarify application of the law and to demonstrate correct practice in death penalty sentencing involving compensation to the victim's family. Each case demonstrates how the SPC encouraged judicial mediation between defendant and victim's family in an attempt to secure a compensation arrangement to qualify the defendant for a suspended death sentence. Hence, this new judicial activism required SPC and higher court judges to actively intervene in capital cases inside and outside the courtroom to try to secure the socio-political objective of harmonizing social relations. It was understood that the move would help to avert effects of death sentencing that were potentially socially destabilizing. Below are paraphrased accounts of three of the five cases published in *Legal Daily*.

Case 3: 'The review and approval process puts to the test the abilities of SPC judges to deal effectively with the masses'

On Chinese New Year evening in 2008, Chen Si knocked on the door of Chen Qin's residence with hammer in hand. In the altercation that followed, he ended up bludgeoning Chen Qin's son to death. Chen Si had come to Chen Qin's residence intending to exact revenge on him for a dispute about money. Chen Si had lent 500 yuan to Chen Qin's brother who had refused to repay him.

The personal conflict first began to escalate on a previous occasion when Chen Qin and his brother found themselves in a physical altercation with Chen Si. The village mediation committee had ruled on the matter and ordered Chen Qin's brother to repay the loan and to compensate Chen Si for his medical expenses in relation to the brawl. Yet Chen Si still wanted revenge.

On 14 August 2008 the Anqing Intermediate Court convicted Chen Si of intentional homicide and sentenced him to death with immediate execution. Chen Si appealed but was unsuccessful and on 6 October the case was sent to the SPC for review and approval. The three-person SPC collegial panel included assistant judge Li Jun who was to examine the case files and provide an internal opinion. Li noted that Chen Si had not fled the scene after the murder and had surrendered to police. He also noted that Chen Si's family had already given compensation of 9,000 yuan to the victim's family.

Li Jun visited Anhui to talk with Chen Si in prison and while on the trip also visited judges in the Anhui Higher Court who handled the appeal hearing. Li discussed with them some possible alternatives to execution in which more positive 'legal outcomes and social outcomes' could be achieved. Li and Anhui Higher Court judges visited Chen Si's family to see if they could persuade the family to offer 70,000 yuan more in compensation. Li Jun then returned to Beijing to visit with Chen Qin and his wife who had since relocated to Beijing. He attempted to persuade them to accept the compensation using the argument that 'people who live in the same small village cannot afford to keep grievances and refuse to forgive'. Eventually, the offender's family cobbled together the money required to compensate the family, and the victim's family accepted the compensation and the plea for forgiveness. On that basis, the SPC rejected the higher court application for execution and sent the case back to Anhui for resentencing to *sihuan*.

Case 4: 'The life or death decision on Feng Fu Hangs in the (review process) balance'

In February 2007 Feng Fu sold Zhao Xiao a piece of land where Zhao built a house. The land was located in between Feng's and Zhao's existing properties. A dispute over payment ensued between the two families on 13 May 2007, each party accusing the other of not complying with the signed contract. Feng Fu grabbed a knife from his home, stabbed Zhao Xiao to death, and injured two members of Zhao's family, one sustaining serious injuries and one minor injuries. Feng fled and was later apprehended. On 10 December 2007 the Taizhou Intermediate Court in Zhejiang province convicted Feng of intentional assault resulting in death and sentenced him to death with immediate execution. On 23 June 2008 the case was appealed by the defence in the Zheijing Higher Court but the appeal was rejected. The case was sent to the SPC for execution review and approval.

The case had led to disharmony in the community. Regardless of the sincerity of the defendant's family's anguish as expressed through their offer to pay 10,000 yuan for the victim's funeral costs, the victim's family mounted a petition in the village demanding that Feng be executed. The Taozhou Intermediate Court was under great pressure because the victim's mother had made herself a constant presence outside the gates of the court, protesting in her funeral garb. In this context, the SPC panel were under pressure to approve the execution application. But as the SPC saw it, the relationship between the two families had broken down only as a result of the dispute, before which it was a very close friendship. They had begun fighting only when each side developed conflicting understandings of the nature of the contractual conditions of the land sale.

After the conviction, Feng's family placed 150,000 yuan as (potential) compensation in the safe keeping of a law firm's trust account as a sign that they were immediately willing and able to pay compensation. SPC judge Li noted that in murder-robbery cases, it is difficult for judges to consider reducing a sentence to *sihuan* even if the defendant offered compensation to the victim. But in Feng Fu's case, the dispute was personal and in line with the 1999 SPC Minutes on using the death penalty cautiously in such cases, the SPC panel believed it was still possible to persuade the victim's family to accept compensation and agree to reduce the sentence to *sihuan* and therefore that it was worth the effort to pursue a compensation agreement between the families. Zhao's wife wrote a notice to the court saying that the 150,000 yuan was not sufficient and would not be accepted but if Feng's family compensated with 208,000 yuan deposited directly into her bank account, her family would forgive the offender and not oppose a reduced sentence and Feng Fu would be allowed to keep his life. Judge Li Yong approached Feng's family with his offer and they accepted. The SPC rejected the provincial court's application for execution citing the rationale that the 'sentence was inappropriate', requiring the Zheijiang provincial court to resentence the offender to *sihuan*.

Case 5: 'How to save a life without negatively impacting on social stability'

On 2 March 2007, Ge Bing made a suicide pact with his girlfriend when her family refused to allow them to marry. Ge slit his girlfriend's throat, killing her, then attempted to commit suicide but was unsuccessful. On 16 December 2007 the Hebei Higher Court upheld his conviction and sentence (immediate execution). The case was then sent to the SPC. In the SPC's review and approval process if one of the three-member collegial panel disagrees with the other two members, the case must be sent to the SPC's adjudication committee. In this case, a majority of the collegial panel believed that the general circumstances of the case were not extraordinary; that is, the consequence of the crime to society was not excessively grave, nor was the attitude of the defendant towards the crime out of the range of a normal homicide case. They believed that the social harm caused by the crime was not excessively grave or widespread and that the circumstances of the crime were relatively minor compared to other serious offences. The dissenting judge's opinion was that it was indeed a 'normal' homicide, that is, not inconsistent with the circumstances of other homicides that are given immediate execution. On the recommendation of their criminal tribunal head, the entire panel went to Wanquan village in Hebei province and along with judges from the Hebei Higher Court visited the parties to gain a better understanding of the particular circumstances of the case. All 235 villagers had signed a petition demanding that the defendant be executed. When the judges arrived at the village, they visited the victim's family who told them, 'our child died but the defendant's family's child ended up living, therefore we lost face in the village'. The judges discovered through their investigations that the 235 villagers had signed the petition only because the victim's father had personally called door to door asking them to do so, and they felt it would be unneighbourly not to sign and they would lose face with him if they refused. The case was eventually sent back to the provincial court for resentencing to *sihuan*.

The SPC cases discussed in this section contrast with the SPP's dilemma as demonstrated in the SPP guiding case promulgated in 2010, which we discuss below. This case relates to the issue of excessive leniency in death sentencing and its potential negative effect on social harmony and stability when heinous murderers are given suspended death sentences.

DEATH PENALTY REFORM AND THE 2010 SPP GUIDING CASE

Unlike standard cases, which have a decades-long tradition, the case guidance system is a newly established system in courts and procuracies. In 2009 at a national political-legal conference, Central Politico-legal Committee head Zhou Yongkang announced the imminent introduction of the new case guidance system to upgrade standard cases. In 2010 he published in the Party journal *Qiushi* a paper on social management and stability maintenance, extolling the value of the new system. He explained that the system is established 'in order to standardize judicial discretion' for certain criminal cases in which judgments commonly deviate from best practice or cases that are likely to attract a strong reaction from the masses (Zhou 2010). The case guidance system was established to improve consistency in sentencing across jurisdictions, so that 'similar judgments are made in similar cases' (*tongan tongpan*) (Zhang 2012, Hu 2011).

The SPP and SPC formally established separate guidance systems in 2010 and promulgated SPC and SPP Decisions formally establishing the system in November that year. Proponents of the SPC system say it has enabled the SPC to give a heightened 'interpretative' function to cases that the SPC chooses to use as standards of correct judicial practice (Hu 2011). While the SPC Directive on guiding cases issued in November 2010 makes it clear that lower courts '*shall* reference' (*yingdang cankao*) guiding cases when trying similar cases, the SPP does not compel prosecutors to use its guiding cases. It merely states they *may* (*keyi*) apply these cases to similar cases (Jiang 2011a). This makes SPP guiding cases less authoritative in scope. Compared to the importance placed on the emergence and development of the guiding case system in the SPC, the SPP issued its first batch of guiding cases in 2010 without great fanfare. Nevertheless, the SPP considers the new system to be a great improvement on the case referencing system (Jiang 2011b).

Chen Guoqing, Director of the Legal Policy Research Office of the SPP, explained in an interview with *Legal Daily* that although the procuratorate has had its own standard case system for decades, a noticeable lack of clearly specified and relevant mechanisms prevented these cases from working effectively to standardize decision-making across the nation (Jiang 2011b). The standard cases performed only a limited guidance function and a new system that would unify decision-making behaviours across jurisdictions was required. The purpose of a new case guidance system within national procuratorate organs was therefore to 'establish an integrated system and a platform which is operated in a unified, well-communicated, authoritative and efficient manner to improve the quality of case guiding practices, enhance the function of typical cases, unify the law enforcement standards, and maintain the fairness and authority of justice'.

Article 2 of the SPP Regulations Relating to the Case Guidance System stipulates that the case guiding system be established on the basis of practices that are representative of typical (i.e. unexceptional) court cases in nature and are significant for providing guidance on fact-finding, adopting evidence, applying laws and regulating discretion. The SPP Directive on Issues Relating to the Case Guidance System stipulates that the selection of cases is not limited to issues related to application of law but also addresses fact-finding, adoption of evidence and the practice of discretion. This includes (1) cases in which the application of law is not clearly specified; or cases that emerge as frequently occurring crimes; (2) cases that are often open to error in the process of law enforcement; and (3) high-profile cases that arouse strong public attention and social concern (Jiang 2011b).

Chen Guoqing noted that the SPP was then promoting 'three priority tasks' in the case guidance system. One is to 'use guiding cases to guide prosecutors in the process of legal supervision, to soften the impact of social conflicts throughout enforcement of the law'. The second is to 'enhance prosecutors' correct understanding and comprehensive implementation of the policy of balancing leniency and severity', and the third is to 'prevent the emergence of new conflicts in the community where a crime is carried out, so that social harmony and stability can be maintained to its full potential' (Jiang 2011b). By 2010, the national criminal justice policy of 'balancing leniency and severity' was well established in the discourse and operation of criminal justice work in China. Yet despite widespread acceptance that a new era of 'lenient' death sentencing was in force, contention remained over what type of criminal offences deserved 'immediate execution' and what type could be deemed less serious and therefore suited to a *sihuan* sentence.

Prosecutors, like judges, were also struggling with the issue of what kinds of violent crimes that resulted in the victim's death deserved the punishment of immediate execution and in what circumstances *sihuan* would be appropriate. From 2007, justice system reformers were developing ways to influence this discretionary space in a direction that created more positive legal outcomes by encouraging judges to use their discretion to recognize mitigating circumstances that can attract a *sihuan* sentence. Part of the task of preventing the emergence of new conflicts in a community in the aftermath of violent death involved averting scenarios where the murderer was given a sentence seen to be too lenient for the crime, especially when no specific reasoning for leniency was given in the judgment notice. The application of *sihuan* is not clearly articulated in law and is contentious in practice, especially when judges fail to provide adequate judicial reasoning for what some see as lenient sentencing. In this context, the SPP issued its first set of three guiding cases in December 2010. Two of the three guiding cases listed below (Case 1 and 2) focussed on how to 'harmonize' social relations to avoid socially destabilizing effects of sentencing decisions.

SPP Guiding Case 1: A case of affray by Shi and 16 others
SPP Guiding Case 2: A case of kidnapping by Xin Yuanlong
SPP Guiding Case 3: A case of judicial officer Lin Zhibin committing irregularities in the prison system

Here we discuss Case 2, which is the first death penalty guiding case issued by the SPP. Case 2 is a kidnapping-murder case that addresses all three of the priority tasks then outlined by SPP research office head Chen Guoqing in relation to the contentious problem of applying *sihuan* to heinous crimes. It also points to the issue of how prosecutors should respond to the use of vague and unacceptable judgment rationales such as the oft-used enigmatic rationale 'In light of the specific circumstances of the case'. This case is summarized below.

SPP Guiding Case No. 2: The Case of Kidnapping by Defendant Xin Yuanlong (SPP Notice 2010)

Case briefing: In an attempt to overcome financial difficulties, defendant Xin Yuanlong came up with plan to kidnap a child and blackmail the parents. Several times he travelled to Cixi City in Zhejiang Province to look for an appropriate location to commit a kidnapping and for possible victims. On the morning of 18 August 2005, Xin drove his private van from Ningbo City to arrive at Tuanquan Zhi Road, Cixi City, and there he waited for an opportunity. At around one o'clock in the afternoon, Xin saw a young girl, Yang. He tricked the nine-year-old into his van by telling her that 'Teacher Chen is looking for you'. He covered Yang with a plastic bathing basin and drove the van to the back of a hill in Qianhu Town, Ningbo City. At around ten o'clock, having obtained the telephone numbers of Yang's father and her home, Xin drove to an air raid shelter, suffocated Yang to death by covering her mouth and nose and buried her.

On 19 August Xin took a train to Guangde County in Anhui Province and bought a mobile phone. He called Yang's home at around midnight on 20 August, declared he had kidnapped Yang and urged Yang's father to go to Changxing County on 25 August to exchange his daughter for a ransom of 600,000 yuan. Xin then took a train to Wuhu, Anhui Province to make another call to blackmail Yang's father. However, he had lost the note with the family's phone number, and in error dialled a number ending with 7353 (the correct one ended with 2353). The person who answered the call had a Ningbo accent, while Yang's father spoke standard Mandarin. Assuming that the parents had involved the police, Xin stopped taking action. On 15 September 2005 Xin was apprehended by the police. He confessed and made statements and exculpations about the process of kidnapping and killing Yang. Accompanied by police, Xin identified where he had buried Yang's body. A human skeleton and two strands of hair identified as belonging to Xin were found at the crime scene. The police also seized Xin's mobile phone.

The prosecution process: The case was filed and investigated by Cixi City Public Security Bureau and was then transferred to the Ningbo People's Procuratorate for examination before prosecution on 28 November 2005. On 17 January 2006 the Ningbo Intermediate People's Court found that with the intent of blackmailing for money, the defendant illegally kidnapped and killed the victim. The Court found that his acts constituted a crime of kidnapping, the crime was conducted in a cruel manner, and the consequences were serious, therefore severe punishment should be imposed. He was sentenced to death with immediate execution.

Xin filed an appeal to the Zhejiang Higher Court. On 12 October 2006 the Zhejiang Higher Court also found that since the crime was committed in a very cruel manner, and the consequences were extremely serious, Xin should be subject to heavy punishment. However, considering 'the specific circumstances of the case' as the judgment notice put it, Xin should be sentenced to death but not executed immediately. Therefore the sentence was reduced to a suspended death sentence. On 25 June 2007 the victim's father filed a petition in the Zhejiang People's Procuratorate, requesting that the prosecution present a protest against the judgment of second instance. The provincial procuratorate reviewed the case and held that it was definitely incorrect for the Zhejiiang Higher People's Court to amend the first instance judgment by sentencing Xin to the death penalty with a two-year reprieve (*sihuan*). Therefore on 10 August 2007 the provincial procuratorate presented an appeal against the second instance judgment to the SPP in Beijing in accordance with the procedure for supervision of trial.

The SPP dispatched personnel to Zhejiang Province to examine and review the relevant circumstances of the case. The SPP Procuratorial Committee held that the facts of the case of kidnapping by defendant Xin were clear, and the evidence was reliable and sufficient. Defendant Xin should be sentenced to death with immediate execution. That the Higher People's Court of Zhejiang Province sentenced Xin to death penalty with a two-year reprieve 'in light of the specific circumstances of this case' was definitely an error and should be corrected accordingly. The SPP's reasoning for a sentence of immediate execution was as follows. First, Xin intentionally committed an extremely serious crime, and therefore should be sentenced to death. Xin planned the crime in a deliberate manner, which demonstrates extremely grave malicious intent. Xin deliberately schemed to kidnap a victim, repeatedly visited the location of crime in Cixi City, and chose a remote and deserted driving route. Second, the consequences of Xin's crime were extremely serious, and the harm to society was extremely grave. He killed nine-year-old Yang on the same day as he kidnapped her after he had obtained the family's phone number from the victim (showing that he had no intention of keeping her alive). After being apprehended, Xin displayed a very negative attitude. Xin did not confess immediately and did so only later. He fabricated a story about committing the crime with other offenders. Xin's criminal acts not only deprived the victim of her life, causing immeasurable pain to the victim's family, but also seriously impacted on the sense of safety of the local public. Third, the resentencing of the case to *sihuan* in the trial of second instance was deemed completely unacceptable by the victim's family and the local community. The relatives of the victim vehemently requested that Xin be sentenced to death with immediate execution. The local community felt it difficult to accept the judgment of the second instance, requesting that the court impose severe punishment on Xin.

On 22 October 2008 the SPP presented an official protest to the SPC in accordance with Article 205(3) of the Criminal Procedure Law. On 18 March 2009 the SPC ordered the Zhejiang Higher People's Court to form another collegiate panel to retry the case. On 14 May 2009 the Zhejiang Higher People's Court panel held that defendant Xin kidnapped and killed the victim with an intent to extort valuables. His acts constituted a crime of kidnapping. The criminal means by which he committed the act were extremely cruel, the circumstances were vicious, and the social harm produced by the crime was particularly grave. Xin showed no remorse for his crime, and should be subject to severe punishment. The SPC sustained the application from the procuratorate to correct the judgment of the second instance, rejecting its rationale for a more lenient sentence. The collegial panel of the Zhejiang Higher People's Court withdrew the *sihuan* sentence, affirmed that the original sentence of immediate execution was correct, and submitted the death sentence application to the SPC for review and approval. Xin was executed on 11 December 2009.

RECONCILING POSITIVE LEGAL OUTCOMES WITH POSITIVE SOCIAL OUTCOMES

Achieving the right balance in death sentencing by enacting a more lenient death penalty system without attracting the ire of a generally pro-death penalty public or conservative political leaders has been a fraught experience for the SPC and the SPP. Legal outcomes of cases that judiciaries hope will advance the cause of a more balanced death penalty regime often fail to take account of the potential negative social outcomes – socially destabilizing and/or socially disharmonious – that the sentence can attract. Senior jurists have called for judges to reconcile or 'unify' positive legal outcomes with positive social outcomes of cases. The SPP and SPC share the concern to reconcile fair legal outcomes with positive social outcomes, a concern that runs through all of the socio-political issues in the cases described above. At the heart of both the guiding and standard cases is a central message about the imperative of 'reconciling legal outcomes with social outcomes' of capital cases towards achieving the national political goals of social harmony and stability.

The 'legal outcomes'–'social outcomes' discourse first entered judicial circles in the early 2000s during the last national 'strike hard' campaign from 2001 to 2003. Politico-legal authorities began touting the importance of a central criminal justice goal of unifying the legal outcomes of cases with their social outcomes. Positive legal outcomes are essentially the outcomes of criminal trials in which due process has been observed and the law applied correctly. A positive social outcome relates to the perceived social utility of punishment: its capacity to deter crime and to deliver social stability. Until the end of 2003, many in Party and policing circles put their faith in the so-called deterrence effect of 'striking hard' as a positive way of attaining social outcomes embodied in the social stability required to support economic reform. Hence Party figures such as Luo Gan stressed the importance of social outcomes when exhorting criminal justice organs to 'severely punish' serious criminals. But an implication was that seemingly less valuable positive legal outcomes could to some extent be legitimately forsaken or 'simplified' in the interests of achieving positive social outcomes. A notorious example is the 'two basics' (*liang ge jiben*), a practice in anti-crime campaigns where the standard of proof used to determine guilt is diluted. Under the 'two basics' policy, judges need to be satisfied only that the basic facts of a case are clear, and that the basic evidence is sufficient (Trevaskes 2012).

In the early 2000s reformers such as SPC President Xiao Yang argued against this social outcomes reasoning; for them the most effective positive legal outcomes of case decision-making should be compatible with and supportive of positive social outcomes, but in pursuing social outcomes, due process should not be forsaken. Courts, they argued, can build a more socially stable system by providing robust and dependable legal scaffolding so that people can enjoy confidence in the Party-state's governance capacities.[5] Through proper adherence to due process of law, courts will be best placed to provide the structural mechanisms for maintaining social stability rather than relying on external policies and anti-crime crackdowns on what the Party deems to be socially destabilizing crimes.

The political appetite for severe punishment through striking hard at serious crime waned in the harmonious society era from the mid-2000s. Even so, justification for policy and practice in judicial and prosecutorial

---

5 See, for instance, Xiao Yang's reaction to the social outcomes argument during the 2001 Yanda Campaign when the Shanghai Party Committee Chief insisted on using 'social outcomes' to legitimize severe and swift punishment (Trevaskes 2002: 683).

circles continued to draw heavily on political discourse and reference to positive social outcomes just as it had done in the past. The Jiangxi Higher Court Vice-President Fang Xiaochun and his colleagues in the Jiangxi Procuratorate, for instance, reasoned that the act of paying compensation in death penalty cases not only leads to a reconciliation between the two parties, it also 'eliminates many social contradictions and removes hidden perils' in communities, and in this way 'reconciles legal outcomes with social outcomes of a case' (Fang et al. 2010: 12).

In a 2008 article he wrote on systematically unifying legal and social outcomes of sentencing, SPC Vice-President Zhang Jun claimed that this unification is a clear requirement of both the SPC and the Party. It is also an expectation of the general public in relation to the work of criminal justice organs. Courts are to seek social outcomes that 'fully protect and promote social harmony and stability'. At the same time, Zhang reasoned, this would enable courts to implement the policy of balancing leniency and severity, to protect the rights of defendants and victims alike, and to rely on the law in sentencing correctly (Zhang 2008). In an interview with *Legal Daily* in October 2009, Zhang Jun again exhorted judges in death sentencing to implement the policy of balancing leniency and severity and in doing so, to 'fully protect and promote social harmony and stability' (*quanli baozhanghe cujin shehui hexie wending*). In line with this goal, Zhang stressed the importance of reaching consensus in criminal cases to 'win the hearts of the people' and 'to obtain positive social outcomes' (*qude lianghao shehui xiaoguo*) (Legal Daily 2009f).

RECONCILING SOCIAL AND LEGAL OUTCOMES IN THE SPC AND SPP CASES

Authorities hoped that reconciling positive outcomes with social outcomes would promote social cohesion and stability. This intention shines through all three SPC standard cases described above. In Case 3, for instance, SPC judge Li Jun visited Anhui to discuss with the death row defendant the possibility of offering compensation to the victim's family. He also discussed with judges from the Anhui Higher Court some possible alternatives to immediate execution 'in which more positive legal and social outcomes could be achieved'. According to the SPC newspaper article outlining the case, the main experience gained from this process was that when sentencing, judges need to take into account the deep agony of the victim's family and the subjective and objective circumstances of the crime. Judges also need to grasp the essence of criminal justice policy and be skilled in the craft of meditation, but to do so within the existing framework of the law. At the same time, courts need to guide the families of the offender and victim in order to 'close the case and solve the problem' (*anjie shiliao*) (Legal Daily 2009f).

In Case 4, an acceptable social outcome was required to stop the victim's mother from petitioning outside the gates of the court, protesting in her funeral garb. The positive legal outcome of the case was that it applied the suspended death sentencing in a legally acceptable way. The judges noted that the case could be characterized as 'borderline' execution/*sihuan*, that is, the consequences of the crime were not so socially harmful that the court would 'have no alternative but to kill' (*feisha buke*). Hence, the outcome reflected the proper use of *sihuan* according to Article 48 of the Criminal Law (Legal Daily 2009d).

In Case 5, the SPC adjudication committee had convened on a number of occasions to deliberate the case.[6] The adjudication committee decided on 20 December 2008 not to approve the execution. Judge Dai presented the reasoning that in cases of murder-robbery, drug trafficking and other similar crimes, handing down a sentence of execution is not normally considered controversial in law. But this case began as a civil-neighbourhood issue. In such borderline (execution/*sihuan*) cases, choosing to kill, when a clear alternative exists, is a decision not consistent with the spirit of the law. Hence, the SPC fulfilled the imperative to obtain a positive legal outcome by choosing 'not to kill' since there was no legal imperative 'to kill'. The original sentencing considerations were heavily swayed by public opinion in the village, for instance, with the 235 villagers signing the petition. However, as Judge Dai noted, it was important to uncover the motive behind the signatures. In this case, the villagers had signed not out of popular indignation at the crime but because they thought they would lose face if they did not do so. The real motive for the petition needed to be clarified. Had the SPC simply ordered a resentencing to *sihuan* without first ascertaining the facts relating to the circumstances of the original sentence, such action may have led to an unharmonious negative reaction in the village. In that case, the standard case explanation notes, the SPC would have had to assume some responsibility for any subsequent social unrest (Legal Daily 2009e).

In the SPP guiding case, the lesson learnt was to avoid creating new social conflicts by allowing too lenient a sentence to be given in proportion to the gravity of the crime committed. Often in the past,

---

6 Because the three-person collegial panel was divided in its members' opinions on the case, it handed over the case to the SPC adjudication committee.

judges would accept the prosecution case despite unanswered questions or relatively minor holes in the evidence chain, giving a *sihuan* sentence rather than immediate execution in order to 'leave some leeway' (*liuyou yudi*). A *sihuan* sentence was given in these cases to avoid wrongful executions when some aspects of the case remained problematic or unanswered or where it was suspected that more than one offender was involved in the crime. The SPP considered the evidence in its guiding case to be sufficient, but when the case was first appealed, a number of very minor case details were in conflict with the rest of the evidence.[7] Hence, the case exemplifies prosecutorial action in disputing cases where there is no clear reasoning behind a *sihuan* sentence (SPP Notice 2010).

CONCLUSION: IMPROVING LEGAL OUTCOMES BY IMPROVING THE LAW

All of the cases discussed in this chapter demonstrate to some extent politico-legal reformers' intent to harness discretionary power for the political cause of stability. Post 2007, reformers did indeed seek to improve the legal outcomes of death penalty cases by reforming the discretionary alternatives to immediate execution. But they did so first and foremost to effect the socio-political objective of harmonious society-building, by encouraging judges to use *sihuan* in homicide cases where the defendant had offered compensation to the family of the victim. But this so-called 'cash for clemency' practice set the scene for an ethically and ideologically contentious sentencing process that fuses social outcomes with legal outcome objectives in what is arguably a morally contentious way. In many cases, controversy and 'contradiction' have been amplified, rather than diminished, by the political requirement that judges play their part in building a harmonious society through their role as judicial activists in justice practices, which are now permeated by

---

[7] The second instance resentencing to a suspended sentence was based on the belief that there were two uncertainties. One was that the serial number of the mobile phone found on the defendant was not the same as the number that the seller of the mobile phone had given police. The other was the testimony of two witnesses who claimed to have seen a middle-aged woman take a girl. There was therefore conjecture that there was a co-offender. Both the mobile phone issue and the witness issue were later investigated by the SPP and found not to be reliable. It was later found that the mobile phone serial number sold by a witness to the defendant was in fact the same as the one in the defendant's possession and the act described in the witness report of a middle-aged woman taking a girl was in fact not at the location of the kidnapping.

marketplace compulsions and motivations. Those who oppose the cash for clemency practice argue that providing a lifeline to only one section of the criminal community – those who can afford it – can never help bring about harmony in communities where poverty and lack of opportunity often not only cause the conflict that leads to violent crime but also prohibit offenders from taking advantage of the harmony–stability imperative to save themselves from execution.

In the post-17th Party Congress period of the late 2000s, the place of social stability as a central political imperative was cemented as a key justice system goal at roughly the same time as a new case guidance system in courts and procuracies was established. The standard and guiding cases published between August 2009 and December 2010 carry a strong 'social outcomes' message about the imperative of stability maintenance, and an arguably weaker 'legal outcomes' message about applying discretionary power to the most effective legal end. Through the prism of these stability-related homicide cases we can see how senior justice authorities in the SPC and SPP have attempted to standardize discretionary decision-making in homicide cases so that harmonious society and stability-related crime control and social control objectives are better achieved.

But we have also seen that the socio-political goal of stability maintenance problematizes case guidance on death sentencing because it is not fully compatible with the overall legal goal of case guidance in general, which is to improve the credibility of the judiciary. Thus, socio-political goals impose a practice of judicial activism that can subvert the long-term goal of improving the legitimacy of the legal system. Incompatible 'legal' and 'social' messages complicate death sentencing in homicide cases. Indeed, some scholars and practitioners in China now argue that social benefits of 'cash for clemency' are in many ways illusionary and the legal benefits are flawed (Liang 2010). To improve the 'legal outcomes' of cases, critics argue it would be much more appropriate to improve the law itself. This is effectively a call to trust the law to do its job. These critics draw attention to the imperative of building authority and legitimacy of law by prioritizing legislative reform, rather than prioritizing an ambiguous notion of positive legal outcomes. They see that the Criminal Law should be amended to redefine the standard for death penalty as a punishment, or at least to clarify the meaning of 'extremely serious crime' (Article 48) and to increase the kinds of discretionary circumstances under law for mitigated punishment, in addition to civil compensation.

These amendments would inherently lead to positive social outcomes. Law applied consistently and correctly, according to clear and precise substantive and procedural rules, of itself would promote public confidence in the Party-state and its judicial organs to deliver a stable society through institutionalizing rule-of-law values such as consistency and fairness. This alternative idea of attaining positive legal outcomes has developed in the death penalty debate in China today to acknowledge the need not only for legal propriety to ensure correct legal judgments are made strictly within the boundaries of the law, but also for the Criminal Law itself to be greatly improved through substantial amendments. Once again, we find the debate returning to the basic issue of building rule of law. This issue requires judges and legislators alike to drive the debate and the reform process rather than remaining in the default position of continuing to allow political rhetoric and its makers to drive future judicial reform.

REFERENCES

Fang, Xiaochun et al. (2010), 'Sixing anjianzhong de minshi peichang yu liangxing wenti sikao' (Reflections on the civil compensation system and the issue of sentencing in death penalty cases), *Renmin jiancha* (People's procuratorate semi-monthy), 7: 11–14.

Hu, Fengbin (ed.) (2012), *Zhongguo zhidao anli cankao anli panzhi zongtilian (xingshi juan er)* (Collection of judgment extracts and reference cases in China, criminal cases, Vol. 2), Beijing: Falü chubanshe.

Hu, Yunteng (2011), 'Ruhe zuohao anli zhidao zhidu de xuanbian yu shiyong gongzuo' (How to appropriately select and apply guiding cases), *Zhongguo shenpan zinwen yuekan* (China Trial), 67: 82–5.

Jiang, Anjie (2011a), 'Zuigao renmin fayuan yanjiushi zhuren Hu Yunteng – renmin fayuan anli zhidao zhidu de goujian' (Head of SPC research office Hu Yunteng on the establishment of the case guidance system), *Fazhi ribao* (Legal Daily), 5 January, http://www.legaldaily.com.cn/bm/content/201101/05/content_2427562.htm?node=20739. Accessed 2 November 2011.

Jiang, Anjie (2011b), 'Zuigao renmin jianchayuan yanjiushi zhuren Chen Guoqing: jiancha jiguan anli zhidao de guojian' (SPP head of research office Chen Guoqing on the construction of the case guidance system in the procuratorate), *Fazhi ribao* (Legal Daily), 5 January, http://www.legaldaily.com.cn/fxy/content/2011-01/05/content_2427651.htm?node=21211. Accessed 2 November 2011.

Jiang, Anjie and Xu, Wei (2009a), 'Shenyong sixing yinling zhongguo sifa geng lixing' (Cautious application of the death penalty is leading the way in developing a more rational justice system in China), *Fazhi ribao* (Legal Daily), 4 August, http://www.legaldaily.com.cn/bm/content/2009-08/05/content_1133596.htm. Accessed 2 November 2011.

Jiang, Anjie and Xu, Wei (2009b), 'Tegao: zhuming xingshi xuezhe cheng shenyong sixing yinling zhongguo sifa geng lixing' (Special report: famous legal expert states that cautious application of the death penalty is leading the way in developing a more rational justice system in China), *Fazhi ribao* (Legal Daily), 5 August, http://www.legaldaily.com.cn/0801/2009-08/05/content_1133954.htm. Accessed 2 November 2011.

Johnson, David and Zimring, Franklin (2009), *The Next Frontier: national development, political change, and the death penalty in Asia*. Oxford/New York: Oxford University Press.

Legal Daily (2009a), 'Faguan kuasansheng tiaojie Mao Tao'an qisi huishen, yifa bu hezhun sixing dianxing anli: zhi yi' (Judge travels across three provinces to mediate case and to bring mao tao'an back to life from the dead: standard case of non-approval of the death sentence: Case 1), 2 November, http://www.legaldaily.com.cn/misc/2009-10/30/content_1174648.htm. Accessed 22 March 2011.

Legal Daily (2009b), 'Sixing fuhe ru nuren xiuhua banjingxi: yifa bu hezhun sixing dianxing anli: zhi er' (The death penalty review and approval process can be likened to the delicate ladies' craftwork of embroidering: Case 2), 30 August, http://www.legaldaily.com.cn/zbzk/2009-08/30/content_1154119.htm. Accessed 22 March 2011.

Legal Daily (2009c), 'Sixing fuhe kaoyan faguan qunzhong gongzuo nengli' (The review and approval process tests the abilities of SPC judges to deal effectively with the masses), 30 August, http://www.legaldaily.com.cn/zbzk/2009-08/30/content_1154118.htm. Accessed 22 March 2011.

Legal Daily (2009d), 'Feng Fu shengsi banzhe sixing fuhe diedang' (The life or death decision on Feng Fu hangs in the review process balancing act), http://www.legaldaily.com.cn/0801/2009-08/03/content_1133997.htm. Accessed 22 March 2011.

Legal Daily (2009e), 'Ruhe baozhu yitiaoming, you bu yingxiang wending' (How to save a life without negatively impacting on social stability), 30 August, http://www.legaldaily.com.cn/zbzk/2009 08/30/content1154116.htm. Accessed 22 March 2011.

Legal Daily (2009f), 'Zuigaofa yaoqiu gedi guanche sixing zhengce zuohao fudai minshi tiaojie gongzuo' (SPC requires courts at all levels to implement death penalty policy in line with civil compensation mediation work), 15 October, http://npc.people.com.cn/GB/15177/123385/10197835.html. Accessed 22 March 2011.

Li, Shichun (2009), 'Anli zhidao zhidu de ling yi tiao silu – sifa nengdong zhuyi zai zhongguo de youxian shiyong' (Forging an alternative path for the case guidance system: the limited applicability of judicial activism in China), *Faxue* (Legal Science), 6: 59–64.

Liang, Genlin (2010), 'Sixing anjian bei xingshi hejie de shida zhengwei' (The ten big falsehoods about the idea of criminal reconciliation in death penalty cases), *Faxue* (Legal Science), 4: 3–21.

McConville, Mike et al. (2011), *Criminal Justice in China: an empirical inquiry*. Cheltenham UK/Northampton MA: Edward Elgar.

People's Daily (1984), '1984 10 yue 31 ri: yanda diyizhanyi chengguo xianzhu' (31 October 1984: The Fruits of Yanda's First Offensive are Outstanding), *Renminwang Ziliao* (People's Daily Resources On-line), http://www.people.com.cn/GB/historic/1031/3642.html. Accessed 1 November 2010.

Shen, Deyong (2011), 'Zuidu zhongshi anli bianxuan gongzuo chongfen fahui anli zhidao zuoyong' (Attaching the greatest importance to the work of case selection in order to bring into full play the guidance function of cases), in Zuigao fayuan zhongguo yingyong faxue yanjiusuo (eds.), *Liangxing guifanhua dianxing anli*

(Standard cases for the standardising of sentencing), Beijing: Renmin fayuan chubanshe, pp. 1–5.

SPC (2013), 'Zuigao renmin fayuan guanyu qieshi jianxing sifa weimin dali jiaqiang gongzheng sifa buduan tigao sifa gongxinli de rugan yijian' (SPC Several opinions on actual justice practice for the people, vigorously strengthening a fair judiciary and continuously increasing judicial credibility) Document No. 9, 6 September 2013, http://legal.china.com.cn/2013-10/28/content_30426034.htm. Accessed 30 October 2013.

SPP Notice (2010), Zuigao renmin jianchayuan guanyu diyipi zhidao anli de tongzhi (SPP notice on the release of the first batch of guiding cases), 31 December, http://www.chinalaw.gov.cn/article/fgkd/xfg/sfwj/201108/20110800348004.shtml. Accessed 15 November 2011.

Trevaskes, Susan (2002), 'Courts on the campaign path: criminal court work in China's "yanda 2001" anti-crime campaign', *Asian Survey*, 42(5): 673–93.

Trevaskes, Susan (2009), 'Restorative justice or mcjustice with Chinese characteristics?', in Mary Farquhar (ed.), *Twenty-first Century China: views from Australia*. Cambridge: Cambridge Academic Press, pp. 77–96.

Trevaskes, Susan (2010), 'The shifting sands of punishment in China in the era of harmonious society', *Law and Policy*, 32(3): 322–61.

Trevaskes, Susan (2012), *The Death Penalty in Contemporary China*. New York: Palgrave Macmillan.

Yu, Ping and Gurgel, Seth (2012), 'Stare decisis in China? The newly enacted guiding case system', in M. Wan (ed.), *Reading the Legal Case: Cross-currents between law and the humanities*. Abingdon, UK and New York: Routledge, pp. 142–58.

Zhang, Jun (2008), 'Nuli zhuiqiu falü xiaoguo yu shehui xiaoguo de youji tongyi' (Doing the utmost to pursue the systematic unification of legal outcomes and social outcomes), *Fazhi ribao* (Legal Daily), 30 April, http://www.legaldaily.com.cn/zbzk/content/2008-04/30/content_2280548.htm?node=25668. Accessed 7 August 2013.

Zhang, Zhiming (2012), 'Zhongguo fayuan anli zhidao zhidu gongneng de renzhi' (Understanding the value and function of the case guidance system in Chinese courts), *Xuexi yu tansuo* (Study and Exploration), 3: 65–70.

Zhou, Daoluan (2004), 'Zhongguo anli zhidu de lishi fazhan' (Historical development of the case guidance system in China), *Falü shiyong yuekan* (National Judges College Law Journal), 218: 3–8.

Zhou, Yongkang (2010), 'Shenru tuijin shehui maodun huajie, shehui guanli chuangxing, gongzheng kangjie zhifa, wei jingji shehui you hao you kuai fazhan tigao geng youli de fazhi baozhang' (Thoroughly promote the resolving of social contradictions, social management innovation and fair and clean enforcement of the law to enhance and further develop economy and society, and to create stronger guarantees for the rule of law), *Qiushi* (Seeking Truth), 4: 3–6.

8. Criminal procedure, law reform and stability

Guo Zhiyuan

The Criminal Procedure Law (CPL) is one of China's most important laws. Directly or indirectly it involves the rights and interests of all citizens, since any citizen can potentially be a suspect or victim of a criminal offence. A number of provisions in the CPL have a bearing on the fundamental rights of citizens as listed in the Constitution since they provide concrete mechanisms for implementing these abstract principles. The CPL has therefore long been considered China's 'mini Constitution', 'practical Constitution' or 'Constitution in action'. The first CPL was enacted in 1979, substantially revised in 1996 and overhauled again in 2012.[1] This chapter traces the development of these reforms to China's CPL, and explores how concerns for stability have impacted upon them.

In China establishing and maintaining order in society is considered the ultimate goal of both crime control and human rights protection. Social order is interchangeable with stability so it can be said that stability concerns underlie both the crime control and due process goals of criminal procedure. For legal reformers, reform proposals conducive to social stability will usually prevail. In this chapter I first introduce the background and process of law reforms relating to criminal procedure and follow with discussion of some key changes in the new CPL.[2] I then explore the reasons for these reforms, arguing that in the 2012 CPL

[1] English-speaking observers of Chinese law use different terms to account for the change to the CPL legislated in 2012. For some, this change is an amendment, for others it is a revision. Some reference the quality rather than the quantity of the change and speak of it as reform.

[2] A full English translation of the 2012 CPL courtesy of the Danish Institute for Human Rights is available at http://lawprofessors.typepad.com/files/130101-crim-pro-law-as-amended-en.pdf. Accessed 27 August 2013.

amendment, stability is the most important goal. In conclusion I anticipate the challenges that will confront China in implementing the new CPL.

CPL REFORMS IN THE LAST DECADE

Since the CPL was amended in 1996, circumstances for reform of both the CPL and the overall system of law in China have changed significantly. Both the overall national goal of 'managing state affairs according to the law' (*yifa zhiguo*) and the imperative that 'the state should respect and protect human rights' have been codified in the Constitution and made essential constitutional principles, indicating the increasing importance China has placed on the concepts of rule of law and human rights protection. Yet over the past two decades, newly emerging crime categories have precipitated the need to strengthen the capacity of crime control.[3] In this context the CPL has an obvious role in legal reform, to accommodate new requirements from judicial practice and society as a whole.

The imperative for CPL reform also originated from defects in the 1996 CPL. Some of the legal processes created by previous revisions to the CPL proved unworkable in practice and created problems in implementing the 1996 law. For example, extorting confessions by torture was not addressed appropriately in the 1996 CPL, leading to a number of wrongful convictions. The cases of She Xianglin (Liu 2005), Du Peiwu (Peng and Shi 2000) and Zhao Zuohai (Ji 2010) illustrate the numerous examples of such scandals. Another defect was the criminal defence system, which remained undeveloped even after the 1996 revision, and defence lawyers continued to encounter many 'difficulties' in fulfilling their responsibilities. For instance, it was still difficult for lawyers to access both clients who were criminal suspects and these clients' case files for review, and to collect evidence from witnesses on the victim's side. The CPL needed comprehensive revision not only to improve the letter of the law, but also to solve practical problems in its operation.

However this revision took much longer than anticipated. It was on the legislative agenda for the 10th National People's Congress (NPC) Standing Committee as early as 2003. By the end of 2004, the central government issued a series of judicial reform plans with many of their 35

[3] As terrorism crime has become a global problem, China is no exception. Yet corruption remains China's biggest crime headache and juvenile delinquency has become an ever more serious social problem.

goals involving revisions to the CPL. In 2006–07 the NPC Standing Committee's Legislative Affairs Commission convened several symposiums on CPL reforms. However the participants, including practitioners and academics, held divergent opinions on many issues such as the use of illegally obtained evidence in criminal trials and the standing of a defence lawyer in the investigative stage. The revision plan was therefore postponed until 2008 when the central government issued another set of judicial reform opinions that proposed 60 goals for judicial reforms, a number involving CPL reform. Only after this was revision to the CPL returned to the legislative agenda, this time for the 11th NPC Standing Committee in 2009.

During the 2000s, the CPL revision process was a constant focus of academic research and debate, and progress in other areas of law paved the way for formal amendments to the CPL. For example, the Supreme People's Court (SPC) took back the exclusive power to review all capital cases in January 2007 (Li and Cheng 2008). A revised Lawyers' Law took effect on 1 June 2008, and two sets of important evidence rules were enacted in 2010, including 'Rules on Examining and Judging Evidence in Death Penalty Cases' and 'Rules on Exclusion of Illegal Evidence in Handling Criminal Cases'. All of these judicial interpretations and regulations have been incorporated into the new CPL.

After intense preparations and discussions, on 30 August 2011 a draft of the amendment to the CPL was posted on the website of the NPC for public comment. This was the first time the Chinese legislature had invited the general public to comment on a proposed amendment to the CPL. The move opened another chapter in the struggle to protect society against crime while protecting individuals against arbitrary state power. By the end of September 2011, the legislature had received 80,953 items of comments or suggestions by 7,489 persons or organizations from all walks of life (Zhang 2011). The draft amendment originally contained 99 articles, but with comments from the public and experts, 111 amendments expanded the new CPL to 290 articles. The process presents clear proof of public participation in the legislative process.

On 14 March 2012 a 92 per cent majority passed the new CPL, to become effective on 1 January 2013.[4] The amendment overall concerns seven key areas: rules of evidence, coercive measures, criminal defence

---

4 Because it was legislated in 2012 and enacted in 2013, this version is commonly referred to as the 2012 CPL and as the 2013 CPL, depending upon the user. Either is taken as acceptable.

and representation, investigative measures, trial procedure, enforcement procedure and special proceedings. This amendment has a number of features.[5]

First, it consolidated the accomplishments of recent judicial reform by incorporating new SPC judicial interpretations or institutionalizing some successful pilot reforms. For example, the amendment absorbed some provisions from the 2007 Lawyers' Law and the 2010 Exclusionary Rules of Evidence. And for criminal mediation it also established special proceedings that had been piloted for a couple of years and proved to function well in practice.[6] Second, the amendment incorporated clauses of signed international conventions to demonstrate China's commitment to international treaties. For example, by referring to the United Nations Convention against Transnational Organized Crime and to the United Nations Convention against Corruption, the amendment adopted some measures to protect witnesses (Article 62), permitted but limited the use of technical investigations (Articles 148–152), and set up a special procedure to confiscate assets of corrupt criminal offenders (Chapter 3, Procedures for the Confiscation of Illegal Earnings in Cases Where the Suspect or Defendant Has Absconded or Died).

Third, some provisions were in response to hotly disputed issues in academic circles. For example, witness protection and economic compensation for witnesses have long been raised as proposed solutions to low witness attendance at trial. The idea of pre-trial conferences was also put forward as a way to prevent the formal trial from being interrupted by rushed defence or continual adjournments.[7] Fourth, the amendments incorporated some changes that meet practical needs or solve problems in

---

[5] Key features of the revised CPL in the view of some NPC members (*Focus on Ten Highlights of the 'Great Revision' of the Criminal Procedure Law*) are on the NPC website in Chinese at http://www.npc.gov.cn/huiyi/lfzt/xsssfxg/2012-03/09/content_1707024.htm. Accessed 24 August 2013; and in English on the Law Library of Congress website at http://www.loc.gov/lawweb/servlet/lloc_news?disp3_l205403080_text. Accessed 24 August 2013.

[6] The amendment did not include the pilot reforms, which drew divided opinions about their effects or proceedings such as sentencing procedure reform.

[7] Other examples include but are not limited to the following: the prosecutor should appear in court to support prosecution when a publicly prosecuted case is tried by summary procedure; larger roles should be given to both prosecutor and lawyer in death penalty review procedure. To prevent procedural backflow, the amendments revised the system of remanding for retrial, special procedure for juvenile cases, and special procedure for mandatory treatment of mentally ill criminals.

practice. For instance, Amendment 15 addresses the issue of transformation of evidence, allowing for evidence collected in the process of administrative law enforcement to be admitted as evidence in criminal proceedings. Finally, the amendments legalized already existing practice such as secret investigation and technical investigation, which have both long been in operation.

KEY CHANGES TO THE CPL

The 2012 CPL amendment involves 149 articles: 66 new, 82 revised and one deleted. It can therefore surely be regarded as an overhaul of the 1996 CPL. Below I briefly overview some of the key changes to the CPL through this amendment.

Anti-torture Mechanism

Prevention of torture has been contentious and a focus of law reforms in China for years. The first CPL in 1979 contained a black letter rule against torture,[8] and this rule has been retained after two rounds of substantial revisions. Since at least 1997, China has officially acknowledged that coerced confessions are a problem (United Nations 2006)[9] and authorities announced measure after measure in attempts to address it.[10] Yet there seemed to be little discernible progress, and the exposés of a series of wrongful convictions resulting from interrogational torture imposed greater pressure upon the Chinese legislature to continue striving to accomplish this mission. This is why a number of provisions in the new CPL are aimed at preventing torture.

---

[8] The relevant provision reads: 'The use of torture or extortion to obtain a confession and the use of threats, inducement, and deception and other illegal means to collect evidence is strictly prohibited …'.

[9] The government's willingness to acknowledge the pervasiveness of torture was confirmed when the Supreme People's Procuratorate (SPP) published *Xingxun bigong zui* (The Crime of Tortured Confession) in late 1997, which included China's first public official statistics on criminal cases of tortured confession. It reported an average of 364 cases per year between 1979 and 1989, upward of 400 cases per year for most years in the 1990s, and included the admission that 241 persons had been tortured to death over the two-year period 1993–94.

[10] A principle of excluding illegally obtained oral evidence including confession was established in judicial interpretation by both the SPC and SPP after the 1996 CPL was enacted.

First, Article 50 established the privilege against self-incrimination. This addition fails to provide suspects or defendants a clear right to silence, especially when combined with the lingering requirement in Article 118 that they must answer questions truthfully. Nevertheless in terms of torture prevention it is a great improvement. The privilege against self-incrimination is not intended to create a right to silence for the suspects or defendants, nor is it intended to flesh out the principle of presumption of innocence (although that is indeed a logical inference of this principle). Its only goal is to legally oblige police not to force suspects to incriminate themselves.

Second, the new CPL has incorporated a refined version of the exclusionary rules of illegally obtained evidence, which was enacted in 2010 in response to the Zhao Zuohai case. The new CPL spans four articles that address issues relating to the exclusionary rules. Article 54 defines the scope of illegally obtained oral and physical evidence and suggests a compulsory exclusion model for oral evidence but a discretionary exclusion model for physical evidence.[11] The other three articles concern the suppression hearing. Article 56 gives the parties and their representatives the right to apply for suppression but requires them to bear a slight preliminary burden of providing evidence or clues.[12] Article 57 imposes the burden of proof upon the prosecution and requires police to take the stand when legality of evidence needs to be proven.[13] Article

---

[11] Confessions by a suspect or a defendant obtained through torture and extortion and other illegal means, and witness testimonies and victim statements obtained through the use of violence, threats and other illegal means should be excluded. Where physical or documentary evidence is collected in ways violating legal procedures and severely affecting judicial justice, corrections should be made or justifications provided. Where no correction or justification is provided, such evidence should be excluded.

[12] Where, in a court hearing, an adjudicator believes that illegally obtained evidence under Article 54 may exist, a court enquiry should be conducted into the legality of such evidence. A party and their defender or an agent *ad litem* has the right to apply to the people's court to exclude evidence obtained illegally. Where exclusion of illegally obtained evidence is applied for, relevant information or materials about the illegal practice should be furnished.

[13] During a court enquiry into the legality of the evidence collection process, the people's prosecutor's office should prove the legality of the collection process. 'Where available evidentiary materials are not able to prove the legality of evidence collection, the people's prosecutor's office may request the people's court to notify relevant investigators or other persons to explain before the court; the people's court may also, at its own initiative, notify relevant investigators or other persons to explain before the court. The relevant investigators or other

58 imposes a standard of proof 'beyond reasonable doubt' for a suppression hearing by providing that although collecting evidence using illegal means cannot be excluded, the evidence collected this way should be excluded.[14]

Third, to prevent torture and coercive confession, a new Article 121 requires audio or video recording of questioning sessions to be compulsory for crimes punishable by life imprisonment or death and other serious crimes, and optional in all other cases.[15] Since the beginning of the 21st century, a series of pilot projects has explored feasible ways to ensure the legality of the interrogation process. Options including a lawyer's presence, audio recording and video recording had been tested for their effectiveness and feasibility across China. Many in the system found it premature to allow a lawyer to be present during police interrogation, but as alternative reform initiatives, audio or video recording of interrogations gradually became an accepted practice.[16] Here the new CPL marks another important achievement.

These new provisions not only impose supervision over the interrogators, but also can produce powerful proof relating to the legality of interrogation sessions. Involuntary confession was a prevalent assertion for many defendants when they later pleaded not guilty in the prosecution or the courtroom after they had admitted guilt during the investigation. Whenever this issue was raised, neither the prosecution nor the court had the means to confirm whether any improper methods were actually

---

persons may themselves ask to appear to offer an explanation. Relevant persons should appear upon the court's notification.'

[14] 'Where by means of a court hearing, evidence is determined to have been obtained illegally or where situations of collecting evidence using illegal means provided under Article 54 cannot be excluded, such evidence should be excluded.'

[15] 'When the criminal suspect is being interrogated, the investigator may record the interrogation process in audio or visual forms; for crimes punishable by life imprisonment or death and other serious crimes, audio or video recording of the interrogation process is mandatory.'

[16] In November 2005 the SPP issued 'Regulation on Whole-process Audio-recording and Video-recording during People's Procuratorate Interrogation of Suspects in Corruption Cases (Trial Implementation)', then subsequently issued another three regulations applying to it, on technical norms, technical working process and system construction norms. These indicate that the Procuratorate has begun to accept the supervision of audio and video recording. In the 2012 CPL, audio recording and video recording have been extended to all major crime cases including capital cases and cases punishable by life imprisonment. This means audio recording and video recording have been made compulsory for police action in major cases.

employed at interrogation. With audio recording or video recording now a required practice for major cases, the police have a useful tool to reject an assertion of torture by the defence.

Finally, the new CPL has also added some procedural requirements to reduce the possibility of torture and coercive confessions. For example, prompt transfer of criminal suspects to detention centres after being taken away is now required as a way of avoiding the torture sometimes conducted in police detention.[17] The CPL now provides that interrogation should be conducted within a detention centre once the suspect has been formally detained there.[18] The stricter supervision over detention centres will make it more difficult to torture suspects who are detained. Most torture is conducted by police of the local police station (*paichusuo*) or even by security guards (*zhi'an lianfangyuan*) after the suspect is taken away and before s/he is formally checked in at a detention centre. From their implementation in January 2013, these measures will hopefully play an important role in preventing torture before detention.

Investigation Reform

Investigation is a crucial phase of the criminal process. It has long been regarded in China as the most powerful weapon in the fight against crime, and as stated earlier, one purpose of the revisions was to strengthen the capacity of crime control. Investigation was thus one of the main areas of reform in the new CPL. Here reforms focused on two areas: coercive measures and special investigative measures.

Coercive measures

Two types of coercive measures against suspects shape the degree to which the suspect loses personal freedom. These are deprivation, which includes arrest and formal detention,[19] and restriction, which includes residential surveillance and obtaining a guarantor or bail pending trial. According to the legislature, the ideology guiding revisions to coercive

---

[17] Paragraph 2 of Article 83 has been amended to read: 'After being taken into custody, the person should promptly and no later than within 24 hours be delivered to a detention facility for custody.'

[18] A new paragraph is inserted as Paragraph 2 of Article 116: 'Where investigators interrogate a criminal suspect after s/he has been delivered into a detention facility, they should do so within the detention facility.'

[19] To avoid confusion the author uses substantial translation of technical terms. Arrest refers to *juliu*, a short period of temporary detention following arrest, and detention refers to *daibu*, a long period of detention following arrest.

measures is to protect suspects' rights by using the least coercive measures possible: reducing pre-trial incarceration and providing measures as alternatives to arrest and detention. Article 79 of the new CPL makes progress by both limiting and fleshing out the criteria for formal detention,[20] Article 86 reforms the detention review procedure,[21] and Article 93 establishes a periodical review system for detainees.[22] More importantly, the new CPL establishes clearer criteria for both residential surveillance and obtaining a guarantor pending trial, which in theory will expand the use of measures other than detention and arrest.

However, the amendments on coercive measures were broadly criticized when the draft was released on 30 August 2011. The most disturbing provisions concern residential surveillance in a designated location and the notification of family members or work unit after arrest,

---

[20] 'The suspect or defendant should be arrested where evidence proves facts for a crime and the suspect or defendant is punishable by imprisonment or a more severe sentence, and where bail, residential surveillance or other measures are inadequate to prevent any of the following risks to the public where the person may: (1) commit a new crime; (2) pose an imminent risk to state security, public security or social order; (3) destroy, falsify or conceal evidence or interfere with the witness or collude in giving a statement; (4) retaliate on the victim, tipster or the person making accusations against him; or (5) attempt to commit suicide or abscond. Where evidence proves facts for a crime and the crime is punishable by imprisonment of more than ten years; or where evidence proves facts for a crime and the crime is punishable by imprisonment or a more serious sentence, but the suspect has intentionally committed a prior crime or their identity is unknown, such person should be arrested. Where a suspect or a defendant released on bail or under residential surveillance breaches the provisions for release on bail or residential surveillance and the circumstances are grave, the suspect or the defendant should be arrested.'

[21] 'When a people's prosecutor's office reviews and approves an arrest application, it may question the suspect; questioning the suspect is mandatory in any of the following circumstances where: (1) doubts exist about whether or not the conditions for arrest are met; (2) the suspect asks to give a statement to the prosecutor face-to-face; or (3) the investigation may be in serious violation of the law. When reviewing and approving an arrest application, the people's prosecutor's office may question witnesses and other participants in the legal proceedings, and consider the opinion of the defence attorney; if the defence attorney asks to express their opinion, the opinion should be heard.' The previous CPL allowed only file reviewing.

[22] 'After the arrest of a suspect or a defendant, the people's prosecutor's office should continue to check the need for detention. Where detention is no longer necessary, this office should give advice to release the suspect or defendant or alter the compulsory measures. Within 10 days, relevant authorities should notify the people's prosecutor's office on how the advice is handled.'

detention or surveillance in a specified location. Under Article 73 in the draft amendment, in cases of crimes concerning national security, terrorism or serious bribery, defendants or suspects can be put under residential surveillance in places outside their own homes if surveillance in their home is likely to hinder an investigation. When suspects or defendants are held under surveillance outside their homes, within 24 hours family members are to be informed of the surveillance as well as the reasons and location, except when family members cannot be reached or this notice could hinder the investigation in cases involving suspected crimes of endangering national security or terrorist activities.

This article probably drew the most attention and the most criticism when the draft was released for comment. Critics found the definition of 'endangering national security' and 'terrorist activities' vague. And since police could easily claim that to notify family members of a suspect's arrest would be likely to 'hinder investigation', police could use this restriction as an excuse to not inform the family about the detainee or arrestee within 24 hours of the detention or formal arrest.

Some people were extremely worried that the draft article would only make it easier for the police to detain human rights lawyers and other human rights defenders without informing their families, on the pretext that the cases involve national security or terrorism. These concerns were not totally unfounded. Residential surveillance was initially intended to keep an eye on suspects outside detention centres to facilitate an investigation, but surveillance in a specified residence had already turned it into another form of detention, sometimes worse than formal detention. Some held that the change would leave suspects in such situations with less legal protection than if they were held in detention centres where there is at least some level of monitoring.[23] A good legal provision should leave no chance for enforcement agencies to abuse it at their discretion. This article clearly needed further specification and a monitoring mechanism. In response to the furious criticism, Article 73 in the new CPL reads:

> Where the suspect or arrestee has no permanent domicile, surveillance may be enforced at a designated place of residence. Where the suspect or arrestee is suspected of crimes of endangering state security, crimes of terrorism and *particularly* serious crimes of bribery, and residential surveillance at the domicile may impede the investigation, this surveillance may, upon approval by the next higher people's prosecutor's office or public security authority, be enforced at a designated place of residence.

---

[23] Beijing lawyer Liu Xiaoyuan held this view.

As for notification, Article 91 of the new CPL provides that family members should be informed within 24 hours of residential surveillance at a designated place of residence or a formal detention (*daibu*) except when family members cannot be reached. As for arrest (*juliu*), Article 83 provides that family members should be informed within 24 hours after the person is taken into custody, save where it is impossible to furnish a notice or where crimes endangering state security or crimes of terrorism are suspected and a notice may impede the investigation. When circumstances impeding investigation disappear, family members of the person in custody should be notified immediately. The new CPL has improved significantly in light of this notification rule, but critics continue to raise concerns that police notice to families about detentions might not include the actual location of the suspects or other crucial information (China Law and Policy 2012).

Investigative measures

In another big move the new CPL codified technical investigation and secret investigation, thus legalizing and regulating current practice. This sparked mixed reactions from legal experts. While some warned of possible abuse of these controversial measures, others argued that they will help further to protect human rights and that they conform with, rather than contradict, international conventions involving monitoring and undercover investigations.

Only five articles in the new CPL address technical investigation and secret investigation. In contrast to the complexity of these investigative measures and their potential to damage citizens' privacy and other rights and interests, the provisions in the new CPL are clearly too general and in some respects even vague. For example, investigators themselves are to decide whether a case falls within the scope of crimes for technical and secret investigative measures. More importantly, although the CPL was intended to keep technical and secret investigation under control, the provisions expose loopholes with the procedure. One concerns the approval procedure. The relevant provisions use vague language such as 'after passing strict approval requirements' but leave it unclear which authority is to approve the procedure and what kind of procedure meets strict approval requirements. The other problem concerns the time limit on applying such kinds of measures. Article 149 indicates there is no time limit; technical investigations can go on for three months and be extended unlimited times. And again, the criteria and procedure for approval are unclear.

Criminal Defence and Legal Aid

The most significant achievement of the new CPL is generally seen to be reforms relating to criminal defence, especially the legal aid system. Under the 1996 CPL, a suspect could retain a lawyer at the investigative stage, but the lawyer could only provide 'legal advice' as a 'consultant'. The retained lawyer could not act in the capacity of a defender until the prosecution began. The new CPL grants suspects the right to retain a defence lawyer (who can act as a defender) as early as the investigative stage. Hence, lawyers can now play a bigger role in protecting suspects at the crucial stage of investigation.

Second, the new CPL has sought to diminish the barriers defence lawyers confront in representing criminal clients. The criminal defence bar repeatedly complained of 'Three Difficulties' – arranging to meet with clients, accessing the prosecution's case files, and carrying out their own investigation and collecting evidence. Under Article 37 of the new CPL, lawyers can meet their clients without the approval of investigative agencies, except in cases involving national security, terrorism or particularly serious crimes of bribery. Meetings between lawyer and client/s are not to be monitored, and the defence lawyer can verify relevant evidence with the suspect/s and the accused. But this can occur only at the prosecution stage. At the investigation stage, a defence lawyer can only learn about case facts and provide legal consultation.

Lawyers now have broader access to the prosecution's case files. Under Article 38, 'starting from the date of the review by the people's prosecutor's office, a defence attorney may access, excerpt and copy filed materials of the case. Other defenders may also access, excerpt and copy such materials with the permission of the people's court or the people's prosecutor's office.' This suggests significant progress on the 1996 CPL where the defence lawyer could not review case files until the court registered the case. At the prosecution stage, Article 36 allowed the defence lawyers only to review some legal documents without substantial content. Unfortunately, the new CPL made no changes to the provision on defence lawyers' right to independent investigation, leaving it difficult for defence lawyers to collect evidence via independent investigation. Therefore the disparity between the prosecution and defence in their capacity to collect evidence is still enormous.

Third, the new CPL encourages defence lawyers to protect the procedural rights of the client (*susong quanli*), marking a shift in the lawyer's role in criminal cases. Under the 1996 CPL, the emphasis of legal representation was on the substantive rights and interests of the accused; defence lawyers tried their best to influence the guilt or innocence decision or at least persuade the court to reduce the sentence after the prosecution secured conviction.

The conviction rate in China remains high,[24] with police, prosecutors and judges all tasked with the common goal of punishing criminals. The later stage of criminal proceedings is designed to impose quality control on the case presented at the previous stages of the criminal process so it is rare for the court to find a defendant not guilty. Hence defence lawyers can play a very limited role in representing their clients. Professor Chen Ruihua and other scholars have argued that procedural defence (*chengxuxing bianhu*) should be defence lawyers' primary role in representing criminal clients. The new CPL's recognition of procedural defence paves the way for further development of the criminal defence system in China.

As for the legal aid system, its institutions may still not have sufficient resources to take on the increase in caseload, but doubtless the new CPL's greatest progress in criminal defence has been in improving the legal aid system. Progress is particularly evident in eligibility for legal aid and in the stage at which the accused gains the right to free counsel. Article 34 has enlarged the scope of defendants entitled to mandatory free counsel, from only defendants charged with a capital offence, underage, or suffering physical disability (blind, dumb or mute) to cases punishable by death and life imprisonment, or where the accused is physically or mentally disabled or is a minor. The new CPL has also extended the right to free counsel from as late as the trial stage under the 1996 CPL to the investigation stage, so that suspects and defendants have this right from the very beginning of the proceedings.

Special Proceedings

The 1979 CPL set out one type of regular procedure for all cases and the 1996 amendment added a summary procedure, but neither outlined procedures for special cases. The new CPL has set out four special procedures, here too signalling increasing sophistication. First, it diverts juveniles into a criminal procedure separate from the regular criminal procedure. It retains the special protections provided by the 1996 CPL,[25] and incorporates some provisions such as the Juvenile Protection Law

[24] According to judges at various levels whom the author interviewed across China, in recent years the rate of acquittal is as low as under 1 per cent.

[25] These include the right to have a closed hearing, to have proper adults present during crucial stages such as interrogation and trial, and to access free counsel.

from relevant laws and regulations. It has also adopted more protections for juvenile suspects and defendants – for example, juveniles may be granted conditional non-prosecution (Articles 271–273). It also establishes a confidentiality system for people under 18 who have committed a crime and received punishment of less than five years in prison; their criminal record is to be sealed and cannot be provided to any organizations or individuals (Article 275).

Second, the new CPL sets up 'Procedures for Reconciliation between Parties in Public Prosecution Cases'. In recent years, pilot projects have been conducted on criminal mediation, and the new CPL has legalized these practices by increasing the scope of the types of case for which criminal mediation can be used. However the Procedures contain only three articles and need to be fleshed out further using SPC judicial interpretations so that they can be properly implemented.

Third, the new CPL has introduced 'Procedures for the Confiscation of Illegal Earnings in Cases Where the Suspect or Defendant Has Absconded or Died' and 'Compulsory Medication Procedures for Mentally Ill Persons Excluded from Criminal Liability According to Law'. The latter is a special procedure similar to the commitment hearing in the United States and provides a judicial review for involuntary hospitalization and treatment in cases involving defendants deemed to be insane. The court can commit a mentally ill person to an 'ankang hospital' (*ankang yiyuan*) administered by the Ministry of Public Security for compulsory medical treatment through a formal hearing when the mentally ill person: (1) has committed a violent crime, endangered public security or caused death or injury to others; (2) was determined to be not guilty because of insanity after mental health assessment in accordance with law; and (3) poses a continuing risk that endangers public security. The new CPL also requires a periodical assessment and judicial approval for release of these mentally ill patients, and puts compulsory medication under the procuracy's supervision. These provisions seek not only to prevent mentally ill offenders from arbitrary hospitalization, but also to ensure that only those who are cured and pose no danger to the public can be released back into the community.

The discussion above has centred on some of the main improvements to the 2012 CPL. From here let us turn to consider the stability imperative, which arguably has driven many of the new provisions in the CPL.

STABILITY AND CPL REFORM

Stability has long been among China's most cherished values. The ruling class of every dynasty considered stability as the primary political ideal. Still today, with rapid economic growth and societal development, the Chinese government openly admits stability is the nation's overwhelming socio-political goal. The slogan 'building a harmonious society' and accompanying official commentary on the national goal of development vividly demonstrate the continuing importance of stability. Some observers claim harmonious society is the materialization of stability and constructing a harmonious society means attempting to achieve stability through all kinds of governance tools, of which law is undoubtedly the most important and powerful.[26]

The Dual Purposes of Criminal Process: A Theoretical Perspective

CPL reform is closely entwined with maintaining social stability in any jurisdiction; by its nature a criminal justice system is to deal justly with crimes and extreme anti-social behaviours that threaten social stability to maintain social order. In the history of modern criminal procedure we can perceive a gradual, sometimes interrupted, but obvious shift in understandings of criminal justice away from overwhelming emphasis on punishment towards emphasis on rights protection. All along, criminal procedure has continued to pursue the political goal of social stability through just punishment of criminals to prevent socially disruptive crime.

There is a consensus among Chinese academics that the CPL has dual goals: crime control and due process (or human rights protection as Chinese scholars prefer to call it) (Chen 2012). The former requires the CPL to be effective in punishing actual offenders to protect the general public from harm caused by crime. The latter requires the CPL to protect the accused from improper prosecution and ensure that they are afforded all procedural rights in the criminal process. In most cases, these two goals are compatible. Where they conflict, legislators need to strike a balance between crime control and human rights protection. A superordinate factor makes this difficult task easier. As some scholars have suggested (Song 1995), social order is that superordinate factor and thus

[26] Xinhua news website, 'Goujian shehui zhuyi hexie shehui' (Building a Socialist Harmonious Society), http://politics.people.com.cn/GB/8198/70195/index.html. Accessed 15 January 2013.

should be taken into account when a legal reform involves the contradiction between crime control and human rights protection.

In the academic discourse on Chinese criminal procedure, human rights refer to the rights not only of the accused but also of other parties to criminal proceedings, especially the victims. And since law in China has traditionally been perceived as an instrument to protect the majority, human rights in a broader sense include the rights of all citizens. When human rights are understood in this way, the order of society is the ultimate goal of both crime control and human rights protection. In this context, the order of society is interchangeable with social stability, which is the overlap between crime control and due process. Therefore, when a legal reform involves a dilemma between crime control and human rights protection, the proposal conducive to maintaining social stability will always prevail.

Take the exclusionary rule of illegally obtained evidence outlined above as an example. Compulsory exclusion of illegally obtained evidence is clearly conducive to human rights protection. But some argue that rigid enforcement of this rule can impair the goal of crime control because the real criminal offender may be set free due to inadequate evidence of guilt. In designing the rules excluding illegally obtained physical evidence, the Chinese legislature therefore did not adopt the US-style compulsory exclusion model but instead set up a discretionary exclusion model in Article 54. This reflects the preference for crime control over due process on this matter.

In the past, both scholars and the legislators in China have tended to think admitting illegally obtained physical evidence is harmless since the truth of this evidence is not corrupted by the illegal means used to obtain it. Yet many argue that the legislature cannot afford to allow real criminals to go free simply because of police misconduct. The new CPL has therefore adopted a compulsory exclusion model for one type of evidence: oral evidence. The rationale for this change is stability related. The legislature now acknowledges that the practice of interrogational torture and other illegal means to obtain evidence will lead to false confession, and admission of such evidence in the courtroom can cause wrongful conviction. In such cases, not only is the real offender still at large and can continue to pose a threat to society by committing new crimes, but wrongful convictions will cause further instability to society because the victims of wrongful convictions and their families will turn to all kinds of remedies to appeal. In the long run, exposure of wrongful convictions will weaken public confidence in the criminal justice system and lead to deterioration of the social order.

It can be seen that the pursuit of 'substantive fairness' (*shiti gongzheng*) – a term interchangeable with crime control in China's discourse – has played a key role in design of the exclusionary rule. The Chinese legislature values substantive fairness over procedural fairness because the former is more likely to maintain stability in society. Like Chinese society in general, China's criminal justice system has always attached more importance to the outcome than the process of criminal cases; it assumes that only those judgments reflecting substantive fairness can settle disputes. Hence, most CPL reforms still focus on achieving substantive fairness.

MORE EXAMPLES FROM THE 2012 REVISION OF THE CPL

Concern for stability has played an important role in the 2012 amendment of the CPL. The overview above of key changes in the new CPL has explained how the majority of legal reforms in the field of criminal procedure concern maintaining social order, i.e., stability. One could argue that all the anti-torture mechanisms will help to strengthen human rights protections by imposing more limitations on government organizations that have contributed to rights abuses. However the ultimate purpose of these measures is to prevent wrongful convictions. The same is true of measures to prevent coercive confession since this not only impairs procedural fairness, but also and more importantly leads to wrongful convictions. Given that Chinese society has exhibited increasingly lower tolerance of wrongful convictions, the Chinese legislature had no choice but to release a set of measures to eliminate interrogational torture or at least reduce it to a minimum.

The amendments to the compulsory measure and investigative measures outlined above clearly indicate their designers' intention to enhance the capacity for punishing crimes, the purpose of which is to maintain the stability of society. For example, residential surveillance, especially in a designated place, was conceived mainly to control suspects chargeable with financial crimes. And according to some commentators, the legislature also hopes to replace the practice of 'double designation' (*shuanggui, shuangzhi*)[27] with residential surveillance in a designated place.

---

[27] *Shuanggui* and *shuangzhi* are disciplinary measures taken by a committee of discipline investigation or a monitoring department towards Communist Party members or cadres involved in corruption cases.

Financial and surveillance corruption crimes threaten social stability, and improvements to residential surveillance are expected to help restore social order by punishing these crimes effectively.

Most of the new special procedures have also taken stability into account. Criminal mediation began to gain popularity with the advent of harmonious society as the main goal of societal development. With the new special procedure for reconciliation between parties in public prosecution cases, authorities are expected to handle criminal cases in a non-adversarial way so that harmony can be restored in the community as a result of reconsolidating relations between the victim and offender.

Another example of the influence of the social stability imperative is the establishment of compulsory medical treatment, also as a result of public pressure. More and more mentally ill persons have been involved in criminal cases in recent years; some have even committed violent crimes and pose great danger to society. But people with a minor mental illness or even mentally healthy people who were hospitalized had been forced to receive compulsory medication. These instances exposed a serious loophole in the mental health law. The new CPL has sought to at least partially solve this problem by setting up a procedure for compulsory medication. This special procedure guarantees that only those who satisfy certain criteria can be committed to a psychiatric hospital. It also ensures that only those who are cured and no longer pose a possible danger to the public can be released into their communities, through periodical assessment and judicial approval for release of mentally ill patients.

Juvenile delinquency is becoming a more serious problem for every society and China is no exception. To better serve the special needs of juveniles and fulfil the tasks of correcting their behaviour, the new CPL has separated the juvenile justice system from the ordinary criminal justice system. Again, concern for stability is at work here because handling juvenile cases appropriately is always a key to solving and effectively handling crimes in general in any legal system.

With concern for stability hovering over the CPL amendment process, the legislature has had to strike a balance between different interests from this perspective. Anecdotal reports indicate there were deep-rooted differences of opinion among stakeholders in the drafting process. Generally the 2012 CPL retains the structure of the previous version but expands the number of articles from 225 to 290. The revisions reflect the tension and compromises between the public security forces and more reform-minded academics and other individuals involved in the drafting process. It could be seen as generally appropriate to have an ultimate value to rely on to inform decision making when concerns for crime control and concerns for due process conflict. But sometimes preferring to maintain stability will cause contradictions between some legal provisions. For example, it is difficult to square Article 50 with Article 118: Article 50 establishes a preliminary privilege against self-incrimination that reads 'No person may be forced to prove their own guilt' while Article 118 retains the suspect's obligation to answer an interrogator's questions truthfully. So suspects must answer truthfully, but interrogators are limited in the measures they can take to force people to talk. At its base, this tension reflects the horse-trading under way in the drafting process. There were more reform-minded drafters who wanted a robust privilege against self-incrimination, but obviously the public security forces and other more heavily law-and-order factions would not let this through.

EXAMPLES FROM ADMINISTRATION OF CRIMINAL JUSTICE

Concern for stability has not only played a dominant role in the legislative process, it is also deeply rooted in criminal justice practice, and is often referred to in relation to 'the social effect or "outcome" (*shehui xiaoguo*) of a case'. For example, assessment of the potential social outcome has played an important role in decision making and has sometimes even been a priority consideration when police, prosecutors and judges are determining whether to grant a mental examination. Considering the potential social effect involves balancing the protection of rights between the defendant and the victim. In some cases, the victim and their family made every effort to prevent the official agencies from initiating mental examination of the offender because they were afraid the offender would go free if found to be insane.[28]

Consideration of social effect also involves the general public's attitude towards professional evaluations of insanity. In major criminal cases, especially where the offender is not obviously insane or where multiple victims are involved and there is public anger at the offender,[29] official agencies are subject to significant pressure from the public to punish the offender. This generally tends to discourage the agencies from requesting

---

[28] The victims and their families lack trust in both judicial agencies and psychiatrists, whom the victims and families assume the defence will bribe to give the opinion the defence wants.

[29] A major murder case in Nanping in Fujian is a good example. Despite reports that the killer might be mentally ill, he never secured a mental examination. See Chu 2010.

mental health assessments. The public's ignorance of mental illness coupled with the still prevalent philosophy of an 'eye for an eye' in Chinese society make it difficult for police, prosecutors and judges to strike a balance between judicial fairness, public opinion and social stability.[30]

CONCLUDING REMARKS: CHALLENGES FOR IMPLEMENTATION

As many have anticipated, practical hurdles stand between what the law says and what we will see in practice upon implementation of the new CPL in 2013. Quite a few of these obstacles stem from the compromises made about concern for stability.

Privilege Against Self-incrimination vs. Obligation to Truthfully Confess

As stated earlier, although it is a big move towards human rights protection for the new CPL to recognize the privilege against self-incrimination, the obligation to truthfully answer questions posed by interrogators will dramatically contradict the reform's potential. Questions have been raised about how one can reconcile the right against self-incrimination and the obligation to tell the truth if one does not have a right to silence. The obligation to truthfully answer questions posed by interrogators should have been abolished in the 1996 CPL amendment because it conflicts with the principle of presumption of innocence established in the same amendment. Over the 16 years since that amendment, Chinese law professors have taught their students that the suspects' obligation to honestly answer questions imposed by interrogators should and definitely would be cancelled in the next overhaul of the CPL. However, to many people's surprise, the new CPL still retains this provision. How to square the privilege against self-incrimination with the obligation to truthfully confess in practice will be an important challenge facing China's criminal justice system under the 2012 amendment.

[30] The case of Qiu Xinghua is a good example of killing one to pacify a dozen, even though this man was very likely to be mentally ill. See Ma and Zhu 2006.

Challenges for Implementing the Rule Excluding Illegally Obtained Evidence

When the exclusionary rules were passed, the scope of excludable evidence was arguably narrowed, and this was sheer coincidence. According to Article 43 of the 1996 CPL, 'It shall be strictly forbidden to extort confessions by torture and to collect evidence by threat, enticement, deceit or other unlawful means'. However the 2010 exclusionary rules provide that 'Illegal oral testimonies include confessions obtained through illegal means such as extorting confession through torture, as well as witness testimony or victim statements obtained through illegal means such as use of violence or threats'. The new CPL, by incorporating the scope of illegal evidence stipulated by the 2010 exclusionary rules, has actually diminished the scope of what is considered illegally obtained evidence established in the 1996 CPL. This raises the question of whether confessions obtained through threat, enticement and deceit fall under the scope of illegally obtained evidence and therefore should be suppressed. A preliminary empirical survey conducted by the author has confirmed these questions still have no answer in practice.

Supervising Interrogation

In spite of a series of anti-torture measures, the lawyer is still not entitled to be present when a suspect is interrogated. The Ministry of Public Security has a long-standing objection to the lawyer's presence during interrogation. Pilot projects on lawyers' presence have been conducted over a number of years, producing some positive outcomes, but the Ministry of Public Security still refuses to accept this proposal.

The Criminal Defence System

There are still some exceptions to a lawyer's right to meet his or her clients. As stated earlier, in cases involving state security, terrorism or extremely major cases of bribery, defence lawyers still need to obtain approval from investigative organs to meet with clients. This means that the Public Security organ still has the power to determine who can meet with their lawyer, and it may use the capacity for exception to restrict defence lawyers' rights to meet with detained human rights defenders charged with offences that fall into the category of 'endangering national security'.

Under the 1996 CPL, lawyers enjoyed the right to conduct independent investigation, but now there are many limitations restricting lawyers' ability to conduct their own investigation. For example, a defence lawyer must obtain permission from a witness before interviewing them and the lawyer cannot compel that witness to testify. These restrictions are untouched in the amendment to the CPL. Without capacity to conduct independent investigation, it is doubtful whether defence lawyers can fulfil their responsibilities and provide acceptable service to their clients.

All of the challenges I have identified here point to ongoing tension between the crime control and due process goals of criminal justice. Both of the goals and therefore the tension between them are particularly pertinent in the present era where maintaining stability is a primary goal of state power.

REFERENCES

Chen, Guangzhong (ed.) (2012), *Xingshi susongfa* (Criminal Procedure Law). Beijing: Peking University Press.

China Law and Policy (2012), interview with Seton Hall Law Professor Margaret K. Lewis, 29 September 2012, http://chinalawandpolicy.com/podcasts-on-china/revisions-to-chinas-criminal-procedure-law-will-defendants-have-rights/. Accessed 14 August 2013.

Chu, Baishan (2010), 'Fujian nanping fasheng jingshenbing huanzhe kansha xiaoxuesheng e'xing shijian' (In a major murder case in Nanping, Fujian, a mentally ill man killed primary school students), 23 March, *Renminwang* (People's Daily online), http://society.people.com.cn/GB/1062/11201539.html. Accessed 20 April 2011.

Ji, Beibei (2010), 'Innocent man spent 11 years in jail', *Global Times*, 10 May, http://www.globaltimes.cn/china/society/2010-05/529982.html. Accessed 24 January 2013.

Li, Wenhui and Cheng, Jinging (2008), '2007 nian: sixing fuhequan huijia' (In 2007 the authority to review and approve death sentences returned to its [rightful] home), *Jiancha ribao* (Procuratorial Daily), 23 July, http://newspaper.jcrb.com/dzb/fukan/page_26/200807/t20080723_39879.html. Accessed 15 January 2013.

Liu, Li (2005), 'Wrongly jailed man freed after 11 years', *China Daily*, 14 April, http://www.chinadaily.com.cn/english/doc/2005-04/14/content_434020.htm. Accessed 24 January 2013.

Ma, Lie and Zhu, Zhe (2006), 'Shaanxi "temple killer" loses appeal, executed', *China Daily*, 29 December, http://www.chinadaily.com.cn/china/2006-12/29/content_770282.htm. Accessed 15 January 2013.

Peng, Xiancai and Shi, Jiasan (2000), 'Du peiwu cuo'an de qianqian houhou' (The whole story of a wrong conviction: the Du Peiwu case), *Renminwang* (People's Daily online), http://unn.people.com.cn/GB/channel23/176/842/200011/08/6165.html. Accessed 15 January 2013.

Song, Yinghui (1995), *Xingshi susong mudi lun* (The Purpose of Criminal Process). Beijing: Chinese People's Public Security Press.

United Nations, Economic and Social Council Commission on Human Rights (2006), *UN Office of the High Commissioner for Human Rights Report of the Special*

Rapporteur on Torture and Other Cruel, Inhuman or Degrading Treatment or Punishment, 47, UN Doc. E/CN.4/2006/6/Add.6, 6 March 2006, http://daccess-dds-ny.un.org/doc/UNDOC/GEN/G06/117/50/PDF/G0611750.pdf. Accessed 24 January 2013.

Zhang, Weijie (2011), 'Xingsufa xiuzheng ni'e bigong zhi huo, bu zizheng qizui shou rentong' (Revision of Criminal Procedure Law aims to prevent the plague of interrogational torture, and privilege against self-incrimination has been recognised), *Gongren ribao* (Worker's Daily), 31 December, http://www.chinanews.com/fz/2011/12-31/3573992_3.shtml. Accessed 15 January 2013.

9. Stability and anticorruption initiatives: is there a Chinese model?

Fu Hualing*

INTRODUCTION

China is a highly corrupt state. The people's responses to corruption, as expressions of opposition or anger, are a real source of instability. Government responses to corruption are therefore also partly responses to this discontent – moves to prevent resistance action by the public to guard social stability. In considering state moves to create and maintain stability in Chinese society, it is therefore useful to consider the state's approach to addressing corruption.

Despite its entrenchment, corruption has not undermined China's economy and social stability, or the political legitimacy of the Chinese Communist Party. Corruption inches in, and the Party fights back. Corruption and anticorruption efforts have reached a stalemate (Wedeman 2012). One conventional explanation of China's ability to manage the impact of corruption is China's 'authoritarian resilience' (Nathan 2003). This term has gained currency and in different guises such as 'Beijing Consensus' or 'China model' has become a mainstream explanation of China's economic growth and political sustainability (Kennedy 2011, Zhao 2011). By that theory, China's authoritarianism is resilient because the Party is able to adapt to new circumstances without changing the political structure. While significant changes have taken place at ideological, institutional and operational levels, through innovation and adaptation the Party is able to face the challenges that China's rapid social and economic transitions have posed (Shambaugh 2008).

The concept of the China model (*Zhongguo moshi*) has crept into Party thinking and become a catchword to highlight China's social and economic achievement. In a positive spin, authoritarianism is cast as an

* The author would like to thank Professor Hilary K. Josephs for her comments on the chapter.

asset instead of a liability. The China model, as the concept is narrowly used inside China, focuses on the core authoritarian features of the political system and brushes aside its innovative and adaptive aspects. Since the global financial crisis in 2008, the Party has become more confident about its own political system and way of doing things, and more assertive in pushing away institutional designs that are regarded as 'Western'. This China model has also been used to explain the Party's willingness and capacity to control the spread of corruption.

A neglected aspect in the authoritarian thesis is the degree to which China is learning from international best practice based on the principles of transparency, rule of law and public participation (Rose-Ackerman 1999, Peerenboom 2007). To enhance anticorruption enforcement, the Party has done more than it is willing to admit in creating institutions that may in the long run pose serious challenges to its rule. In essential aspects, China appears to be on the track of the Eastern Asian Development mode, in the sense that a steady increase in GDP per capita has allowed more material resources for social development, institutional capacity building and social activism. In this East Asian development model, in response to economic and social development, the government becomes more inclusive and tolerant of different political views and allows the articulation and assertion of independent interests. With enhanced media supervision and mobilization of civil society forces, the government and the general public become less tolerant of corruption. In this model the social and economic changes ultimately lead to a degree of political liberalization, such as the development of rule of law, enhanced public participation, more competitive local elections and a more transparent and accountable government, all contributing to more effective anticorruption enforcement and thus also to social stability (Peerenboom 2007, Zhao 2011).

This chapter argues that anticorruption enforcement in China goes beyond relying on authoritarian measures, such as extra-legal detention and use of the death penalty. The fact that the Party can still hold on to its position in the battle against corruption can be better explained by the Party's ability to learn from overseas experiences and to introduce a series of anticorruption initiatives that are rule-of-law based, transparency centred and democracy driven. One of the best examples of China's extensive drawing from international best practices is China's active participation in the United Nations Convention against Corruption (UNCAC)[1] and faithful implementation of the relevant treaty obligations.

---

[1] The General Assembly of the United Nations adopted the UNCAC on 31 October 2003. The UNCAC calls for its signatory states to enhance the force of

Interestingly, while China pushes back any UN-based supervisory mechanism in the broadly defined human rights areas, it has followed in good faith the recommendations of the UNCAC. While a reform initiative may be doomed if it is introduced to improve citizens' civil and political rights, it becomes possible when introduced to enhance anticorruption enforcement. This quality of anticorruption measures makes them distinctive as a mechanism in the political quest for stability.

ANTICORRUPTION AND THE THESIS OF AUTHORITARIAN RESILIENCE

As an ideal type, the China model offers a three-fold argument in relation to corruption in China. First is the authoritarian efficiency thesis, which argues that China is able to maintain a stable political environment, sustainable economic growth and a high level of human development because of its authoritarian system. The identifiable characteristics include the absence of political opposition to the Party, the dominant role of the Party in state affairs, a parchment division of powers within the state and between the state and society, a rubber-stamp congress and a compliant judiciary, and above all, managed public participation. In spite of institutional adaptation and innovation, the political structure in its core remains intact and the Party remains in control (Naughton and Yang 2004). The concentration of political power allows the Party to make tough decisions and remain decisive in designing and achieving its policy objectives, and the decisiveness in decision making and effectiveness in policy implementation in turn allow the Party to better manage corruption and reduce the negative impact that corruption may otherwise have.

The structure of corruption differs in different regime types and correspondingly corruption may have a different impact on the political

---

combating corruption by promoting anticorruption education and prevention, enhancing criminal punishment and anti-corruption enforcement, and strengthening international cooperation. The Convention came into force on 14 December 2005. As of July 2012, 161 states were parties to the UNCAC, including China. 'Background of the United Nations Convention against Corruption', http://www.unodc.org/unodc/en/treaties/CAC/index.html. Accessed 10 September 2010; 'UNCAC Signature and Ratification Status as of 12 July 2012', http://www.unodc.org/unodc/en/treaties/CAC/signatories.html. Accessed 13 September 2012. China signed and ratified the UNCAC on 10 December 2003 and 13 January 2006 respectively.

and economic system (Wedeman 2012). Because of the effective macro-control, corruption in China is more 'managed' and less destructive and predatory than is the case elsewhere. There are variants in that argument, ranging from the view that corruption plays a facilitative role in China's unique economic transition; or that corruption is stable, regularized and can be absorbed effectively as part of the cost of doing business in China; to the view that the impact of the otherwise predatory corruption is back-loaded, with its destructive nature to be revealed only in a distant future. Despite the variation, the common thread that ties the argument together is that while corruption remains prevalent, it is well managed so as not to undermine the Chinese economy and social stability.

Authoritarianism allows the Party to take draconian anticorruption measures that are often unconstrained by law and unaccountable to the public. Commentators have pointed out the powerful Party disciplinary mechanism that wields extraordinary extra-legal power in investigating and disciplining Party officials, including extra-legal power of detention incommunicado, aggressive interrogation without legal representation, a compliant legal system to rubber-stamp the Party's decisions, periodical campaigns against corruption, and use of harsh penalties (Sapio 2010). Ultimately it is the disciplinary power of a Leninist Party and its disregard for laws and rights that matter most in anticorruption enforcement (Hsu 2011).

Second is the authoritarian benevolence thesis. According to that thesis, the Party is not only powerful but also claims to exercise power as guardian of the national interest. It is often said that China's one-Party state has an anti-democracy instinct, which co-exists with an anticorruption instinct. The Party gained its political power by overthrowing a corrupt regime, and has been vigilant in preventing and punishing corruption. As powerful as it is, the Party claims that it does not have any interest of its own and holds political powers merely to serve the best interest of the nation and the people (Nathan 1986).

The Party's claim has historical resonance. It has been said that state leaders in the Confucian tradition tend to be paternalistic and more self-constraining in exercising power, thus less prone to grand corruption as is often observed among dictators elsewhere. For all its authoritarian traits, Confucianism emphasizes a strong and meritocratic system of bureaucracy with personal ethics and moral obligations to be accountable to the people, which serve as external and internal controls over the rulers (Bell forthcoming, Fukuyama 1995, 2011). Being moderated by Confucian ethics, rulers in that tradition are self-limiting and self-correcting in the exercise of power, and a built-in self-regulatory mechanism serves to prevent excessive corruption and abuses. As corrupt as they may be, political leaders are committed to nation building and long-term growth (Hsu, Wu and Zhao 2011) and will not allow corruption to undermine their larger nationalist agenda.

Under that cultural tradition, corruption may be less predatory and less destructive to the economy (Wedeman 2012). In the Chinese case, the Party is ready to acknowledge the shocking degree of corruption within the political system and the potential political damage that corruption may inflict, and is determined to face up to the challenges. Importantly, Party leaders in China are not widely known to be predatory in enriching themselves, a trait that characterizes other high-corruption states. Simply put, China is not (yet) a kleptocracy.

Finally there is the authoritarian legitimacy thesis. Because of the combination of efficiency with benevolence, the authoritarian government receives wide popular support, with labour, entrepreneurs and the middle class all expressing a high level of trust in the regime (Bell forthcoming, Perry 2007, Wright 2010). Indeed this level of trust is so high that there is little need for mobilization and non-institutional participation. Manifestations of this high trust have two characteristics. One is that anticorruption activities are locally oriented with goals rarely beyond attracting the attention of higher authorities, punishing corrupt local officials and stopping egregious local practices. Petitioners, protesters and other stakeholders who demonstrate a high degree of deference to, and confidence in, the higher level authority's commitment and competence in solving the problem, are more prone to petition to higher authorities. In doing so, they expressly attribute the cause of the corruption squarely to the failure of policy implementation at the local levels and abuse by local officials in the process (Bell forthcoming, Li 2008). In sum, it is the bad apples that are to blame.

The second characteristic is that anticorruption activism is rule based and anticorruption protest does not reach beyond exercising rights as provided in Party norms and state laws. There is abundant 'rule consciousness' but a deficit of 'rights consciousness' independent of the Party rules and state laws (Perry 2007). Rights consciousness, where it exists, is based on, and derives from, rule consciousness (Lorentzen and Scoggins 2010). Perry (2007), doubting the possibility of a 'rights' discourse in China, goes as far as arguing that state proclamation of rights is not different from past state propaganda of 'class struggle'. Therefore protest in post-Mao China is not qualitatively different from that in Mao's China and both are regime supportive, sharing similar protest symbols, repertoire and goals. Extending the argument to its logical end, anticorruption enforcement is authorized and controlled by the state and operates according to the official rules of the game (Perry

2007: 21). As such, it is neither politically destabilizing nor regime subversive.[2]

ANTICORRUPTION INITIATIVES: FROM TRANSPARENCY TO PARTICIPATION

This section considers three examples of China's international learning: (1) auditing of government budget and expenditure to enhance fiscal accountability; (2) introducing an open government information (OGI) system to improve public access to government information; and (3) the rise of social media, which mobilizes anticorruption activism in civil society. These three examples are widely discussed in China and are chosen here for three related reasons. First, these examples represent anticorruption intervention at different levels. Government auditing represents a top-down intervention and works mainly inside government departments; OGI represents a dynamic interaction between civil society actors and the government; and social media offers both opportunity and incentives for spontaneous and bottom-up social mobilization.

Second, these examples serve as proxies for larger policy changes and point to the direction of future and further structural reform. Auditing and its accountability structure invite congressional oversight of government fiscal policies and therefore enhance the separation of powers in China's political system; OGI mechanisms demand transparency, accountability and rule of law in government decision making; and social media provides the best opportunity for democratic deliberation and political participation. Finally, all three mechanisms are concerned with access to information. An authoritarian system habitually misinforms its citizens and the best antidote for corruption, as supplied by the three reform mechanisms, is to place the government 'under the sunshine'.

---

[2] China's acceptance of authoritarian rule and tolerance of government corruption are often studied in the particular Chinese cultural setting in which corruption is practised. In this perspective, China's gift-giving culture and the imperatives of reciprocity in personal relationships provide fertile soil in which corruption grows. Indeed, corruption and gift-giving may be indistinguishable to a significant degree and it is impossible for the law to identify where gift-giving ends and where corruption begins. Cultural expectation of gift-giving and reciprocity desensitizes corrupt transaction and hostility towards it, and the way that corruption is embedded in cultural practice encourages society to absorb corruption's destructive impact. See Gold, Guthrie and Wank 2002.

Government Auditing

The structural problem in China's 'unusual' budgetary system and the lack of accountability in government expenditure (Wong and Bird 2008) have mattered significantly in explaining the prevalence of corruption and its resilience. On the budgetary side, it is well known that an extra-budgetary fund (EBF) is widely used to compensate for budgetary shortfall and to enhance government revenues. EBF includes fees, fines, levies and other hidden revenues that the government permits but does not effectively control. Local governments are too eager to explore extra revenue opportunities to meet their expenditure. On the expenditure side, there is little meaningful monitoring and accountability and individual departments have wide discretion in the fiscal process. The combination of discretion in revenue collection and the lack of control in expenditure naturally led to widespread misconduct and corruption. Officials keep part of the money they have collected in their own pockets before handing it over to the departments, and departments with a fee-generating capacity set up their own secretive 'small treasuries' and spend the money they collect for their own benefit (Fu and Choy 2004, Wedeman 2000).

A significant first step in the fiscal reform undertaken by Zhu Rongji as Premier was to remove the power to collect fees and levies from individual officials, with the ultimate goal to create a clear separation between revenue gathering and expenditure in the fiscal system. Before Zhu's reform, for example, traffic police were required to issue tickets to drivers for violating road traffic rules and collect fines on the spot. Not surprisingly, officers were eager to issue as many tickets as possible and personally keep as much of the fines as they could. After the reform, fines would be paid directly into a government banking account and money would no longer change hands between police and drivers. A simple mechanism of payment changes the landscape of police corruption on the streets (Fu and Choy 2004).

Having placed individual-level corruption under some control, the government moved to the next target of 'small treasuries'. The principal tool in policing illicit 'small treasuries' and illicit spending is government auditing. Constitutionally, auditing agencies are accountable directly to the corresponding people's congress. In 1983 the first national audit office, the China National Audit Office (CNAO), was established with the responsibility of investigating the accounts of government departments. In 1995 the Audit Law was promulgated and the first comprehensive auditing was undertaken in 1996. Under the Audit Law, the auditing offices review the budget implementation of all government entities and all public funds and assets are the targets of audit. As Li Jinhua, a former Auditor General of the CNAO said, the CNAO is the 'watchdog' of state assets, with the duties to ensure a degree of fiscal rule of law and fiscal transparency (Bao 2004).

The CNAO's first serious audit in 1999 revealed widespread irregularities, wastage and abuses on the part of the central ministries, including delayed preparation of budgetary plans, lax fiscal management, misuse of EBF, and diversion of EBF for profit-making activities. The Standing Committee of the National People's Congress (NPC) received the report favourably. Although the report and the reporting process were not well covered in the media, it was the first time that China rigorously audited central ministries and state-owned enterprises (SOEs), and reported the auditing results to the NPC's Standing Committee (NPCSC) (Bao 2004).

Aggressive publicity of audit reports was inspired by the US Government Accountability Office (GAO). In 2001, while Premier Zhu Rongji was receiving David Walker, the US Comptroller General and Head of the GAO, the guest mentioned the audit information disclosure system used in the US. Knowing that such a system existed in China, the Premier made the decision that as long as information is accurate, it should be reported truly and comprehensively to the NPCSC (Bao 2004).

The decision to publicize auditing reports was implemented in 2003 after Wen Jiabao became Premier. On 25 June 2003 Li Jinhua submitted to the NPCSC the 2002 audit report of the central government organs. This was a critical report that named and censured powerful ministries in public. Its wording was direct and sharp, and its allegations were made clearly and supported by evidence. With this report made public widely, Li Jinhua as CNAO auditor-general started the so-called 'audit storm', which swept through the central ministries.

The CNAO auditing uncovered a shocking level of corruption and waste in both central and local governments and in both government departments and SOEs. Its revelations also led to certain disciplinary and legal actions against officials directly involved in the corrupt practices. While there were some reservations about the long-term impact of the audit storm, the CNAO is duly credited for its courage in confronting and unveiling long-standing problems.[3] Since 2003 the scope of audit has gradually been expanded from auditing income and expenditure to covering the effectiveness of government fiscal management, including

---

[3] The auditing page on the People Net website provides detailed information. See http://finance.people.com.cn/GB/8215/34856/index.html.

unreasonable budget estimations, slow progress in project implementation and inappropriate policies in the SOEs. Attempts are also made to extend the audit storm to local governments, although auditing at local levels proves to be more difficult. At the central level, the CNAO continues to conduct rigorous audits, publicize the names of offending organs and recommend solutions, despite the resistance of some central ministries.

Open Government Information

The Open Government Information Regulations (OGI Regulations) took effect in 2008. Under law all administrative agencies, subject to certain conditions, are required to publicize or make available information they have created or obtained in the course of carrying out their duties and to provide information to members of the public upon request. There is a statutory requirement for government departments to supply certain information to the public through government reports, official websites, press conferences, broadcasting, television and so forth, and to send certain information to designated archives and public libraries for public access. Regarding disclosure on application, applicants may apply for disclosure of information only if it relates to their 'needs for production, livelihood activities or scientific research'. An administrative organ may refuse to disclose government information on the grounds that the information is a state secret, commercial secret, or involves the privacy of a third Party. With promulgation of the OGI Regulations, Chinese citizens enjoy a limited legal right to know.

While the OGI system is mandated by the UNCAC, it also drew broadly from international experiences against corruption and reflected a domestic need for transparency and accountability. OGI is part of China's ongoing open government initiatives, which include earlier programmes on 'transparency in government affairs', and other OGI initiatives. While there are significant legal, political and cultural hurdles to implementing the OGI Regulations successfully (Fu 2009, Horsley 2010), the OGI Regulations provide an additional stimulus to enhance transparency, strengthen accountability and improve governance. The Administrative Litigation Law allows citizens to file complaints in courts against a specific violation of the law or dereliction of duty on the part of the government. If that law provides a shield for citizens to protect their rights from official infringement, the OGI Regulations are potentially swords for citizens to monitor the government more proactively and effectively.

There is also a strong demand for OGI in China's emerging civil society. Activist lawyers, reporters and other informed members of society are mobilizing the law to push for a more open government. Most noticeably, green NGOs have been working to increase both the supply of and demand for government information. On the supply side they have organized training for officials in environmental protection agencies and assisted in drafting more detailed and meaningful local rules on accessing environmental information. On the demand side they have worked with lawyers and activists in requesting information and bringing the authorities to court when their requests are denied (Horsley 2010).

Activist lawyers and rights advocates have indeed seized the opportunity to exercise the right to know upon promulgation of the law. Xu Zhiyong and *Gongmeng* (the 'Open Constitution Initiative') have been active in identifying cases to test the OGI Regulations. Another veteran lawyer, Hao Jinsong, is also actively involved in OGI cases. There are encouraging signs of academic activism on access to government information, and more law professors are filing applications for information disclosure and bringing cases to public and media attention. Tsinghua University law professor Chen Jie filed an application requesting information related to the Wenchuan earthquake from the State Earthquake Administration; and three Peking University law professors battled with the Beijing Highway Administration regarding information on the use of highway levies. Shenyang resident Wen Hongxiang requested in an online posting that the Finance Bureau of Shenyang City disclose government entertainment expenses. It is cheerful news in virtual space but embarrassing for the city government. Others followed suit immediately and started to make similar demands in other cities related to other information. Demand for information regarding officials' income soon turned to queries about the budget and government spending. After the central government announced a four trillion RMB economic stimulus plan, Shanghai lawyer Yan Yiming immediately requested publication of the details.

To the credit of the government at all levels, a large amount of government information has already been publicized within the short history of the implementation of the OGI Regulations, and the system has improved in spite of limitations in its institutional design and implementation. Indeed, the government has also used the OGI mechanism to enhance bureaucratic control and ensure faithful implementation of central policies. By providing information through official websites, press conferences and other means in a timely fashion, the government can guide, shape, and, in the end, control public opinion.

Generally the amount of information disclosed voluntarily by the central and provincial governments has been increasing since 2008, while that disclosed by city governments has remained largely unchanged. On the other hand, the number of OGI-based requests for information from city governments has increased rapidly, although the situation with information requests to the central and provincial governments has changed little. Another healthy sign is the increase in judicial review applications in spite of judicial caution and passivism (Chen 2012).

The performance of different areas varies greatly and some places are performing much better than others. It is important to assess this performance closely to develop a clear understanding of what makes the difference. A large-scale study by Lorentzen, Landry and Yasuda (2010) assessed the OGI performance of 113 cities according to eight dimensions. The overall performance was disappointing: with 63 points out of a total of 100 as basic compliance, the mean score was 31.06 and the median was only 26.6. The lowest reached 10.2. But an otherwise critical review also pointed to the potential of OGI in China. The highest score in the survey attained 72.9 points. The best predictor for good performance was the wealth of the city: better developed infrastructure and institutions for the OGI system, better managed and more open government and better educated and informed residents with greater demand for open government. Wealthy cities also tend to rely less on SOEs and have a more diversified economy. Other factors contributing to better OGI in a city included the educational background of its mayor – cities administered by mayors with legal training performed better than others; and the length of service of the mayor – the longer the service, the better the OGI system. OGI is thus likely to improve when cities accumulate wealth, diversify their economy and choose their leaders wisely.

Like the rule of law in general, the OGI Regulations are a double-edged sword. They empower and legitimize the government through information management and control, but they are also a useful tool in the hands of the citizens who have developed the potential of these regulations to constrain government power (Horsley 2010). As part of the ongoing reform to liberalize governance in China, the new OGI Regulations have potential to help drive the development of a more transparent, responsive and accountable government. The litmus test in the decade to come is whether the government can be forced through litigation, public opinion or other means to publicize information that is inconvenient, embarrassing or even outright offensive to the government.

The Rise of Social Media

A free and independent press is often regarded as a necessary condition for clean government, and countries with a higher level of press freedom tend to have a lower level of corruption. Since corruption is mostly a consensual crime carried out in the dark, a free press with its probing investigative journalism is regarded as indispensable to bring corruption to light. In democracies, making the public aware of corruption scandals can mobilize public support, generate pressure that forces corrupt officials to resign, and ultimately bring electoral defeat of the political Party that is implicated in corruption (Rose-Ackerman 1999).

The Chinese press does not have the major characteristics that define a free press. In China there is little open political competition, a low level of public participation, and weak protection of civil and political rights, in particular the freedom of speech. To the contrary, the press is owned and controlled by the Party and the Party has historically placed severe restrictions on investigative reporting, especially about negative events such as corruption.

Yet for a combination of reasons the press in China has been playing a significant role in exposing certain corruption and forcing the Party to take more action against corruption. First is the agency problem; because of information asymmetry, central authorities need to rely on the press to expose local corruption to discipline local officials more effectively. Economic reform has led to increase not just in local political powers but also in local corruption and violation of central rules. In this new context, the media as a controlled forum is well placed to serve as 'representatives and trustees of the public, translating raw public opinion into a collective, supervisory role' (Cheung 2007: 363). In doing so, the media develops potential to become an influential actor in monitoring the government (Liebman 2005).

Second, in the reform era the media has developed self-interest in aggressive news reporting. Forced to be financially independent, the media is managed as a business and so needs to follow business logic. Like its counterparts in a market economy, the media in China relies on advertising revenue, which in turn relies on circulation and reader preference. Corruption scandals are provocative and popular news among readers and there are sufficient incentives in the media for journalists to launch their own investigations, as illustrated by the popularity and resilience of investigative journalism in China (Cullen and Fu 1998).

Finally, formal education, in conjunction with opportunities and incentives, nurtures an emerging professional identity within the community of journalists. Inspired by some exemplary reporters who covered controversial cases courageously and strategically, and influenced by global media, a new generation of reporters has emerged and they are no longer satisfied with the status quo. Without challenging the political system directly, many of these journalists have developed a strong sense of social responsibility; they are passionate about social justice issues and are prepared to expose the dark side in business and government. Indeed, major scandals in the past decade, ranging from the death of Sun Zhigang[4] to the melamine-tainted milk formula,[5] have been exposed by courageous reporters who are willing to take the risk to reveal corrupt behaviour.

Of course, state media is under the tight control of the Party, and within the authoritarian political structure it is unlikely to become an independent watchdog (Cheung 2007, Keller 2003). Weak state monitoring and control over officials has led to a more society-based activism in exposing corruption through naming and shaming on the Internet. A particularly significant development in China since the 1990s is undoubtedly the emergence of social media and vibrant online activism. The advance of information technology enables almost instantaneous reporting on corruption despite widespread censorship. In a society well known for its tight press control and censorship, social media provides an alternative source for information and a new platform for action. Since the Party's promotion of the Internet as a supervisory tool in 2008 (and the famous online chat between then Party General Secretary Hu Jintao and members of the public), Chinese netizens have developed a culture of cyberactivism in which ordinary citizens expose misconduct and scandals. Through a coordinated search commonly referred to as 'human flesh search' (HFS) (Downey 2010),[6] they also identify and hunt down corrupt officials.

---

[4] Sun Zhigang was a migrant work whose death in 2003 after his arrest for failure to produce a residence permit received massive attention in newspapers and on the Internet in China and caused a national outcry. See Hand 2006.

[5] This 2008 food safety scandal involved milk, infant formula and other food materials and components adulterated with melamine, apparently to give the appearance of a higher protein content. By November 2008 China reported an estimated 300,000 victims, with six infants dying from kidney stones and other kidney damage, and an estimated 54,000 babies hospitalized. http://en.wikipedia.org/wiki/2008_Chinese_milk_scandal. Accessed 31 October 2013.

[6] Downey (2010) defined the term:

> Human-flesh search engines – *renrou sousuo yinqing* – have become a Chinese phenomenon: they are a form of online vigilante justice in which

Examples abound in which netizen-led action has led to successful publicity, investigation and prosecution. An official from Nanjing was photographed when making a speech criticizing developers for selling property at below-market value. The speech was controversial and attracted public attention. He was hunted down and later identified as Zhou Jiugen, a district housing management bureau chief. In the photograph he was smoking an expensive brand of cigarette ('95 Supreme', which sells at 1,500 RMB per carton). From a pack of cigarettes, netizens through HFS discovered Zhou's expensive watch, car and in general a luxury lifestyle. The continuous exposure finally led to an official investigation. Zhou was subsequently sentenced to 11 years' imprisonment for taking 1.2 million RMB in bribes.[7]

In another case an official who was pictured smiling at a tragic traffic accident scene angered netizens. Through collective vigilantism, they identified the person as the Shaanxi Safety Inspection Bureau Chief, Yang Dacai. Further HFS revealed that Yang wore different watches, all expensive ones, on different occasions. All the photographs were posted online with highlights on the watches and calls for further investigation. In response, Yang was removed from his post and subsequently sentenced to 14 years' imprisonment for corruption (Kaiman 2013).

The intrusive HFS has on many occasions degenerated into online mob rule – 'a 21st century version of the medieval "stockade"' (Eberlein 2008). But when the search aims at corruption, the intrusion and aggression prove to be the most effective anticorruption tool, 'a 24-hour-a-day nightmare for government officials across China' (Mackinnon 2012). HFS organizes otherwise isolated individuals into a collective action and facilitates the creation of online anticorruption communities. Through their online activism and offline mobilization, dedicated members of the public have exposed wrongful death in custody and condemned police abuse of power, forced the judiciary to respond to public opinions and revise their decisions, and brought the vivid image of corrupt and abusive officials before the public. Through online mobilization, HFR nurtures a civic anticorruption culture and influences the official media. Social media therefore sets the agenda in inter-media relations and anticorruption information flows from the social media to state media. Because of the aggressive HFS, corruption scandals and

---

Internet users hunt down and punish people who have attracted their wrath. The goal is to get the targets of a search fired from their jobs, shamed in front of their neighbors, run out of town. It's crowd-sourced detective work, pursued online – with offline results.

[7] http://baike.baidu.com/view/2057114.htm. Accessed 31 October 2013.

critical reflections first appear in social media. They are followed up, usually with some reluctance, by the official media if only as an attempt to remain relevant and to mould the public mood. With over 500 million Internet users keenly watching the government, the Internet is bound to be an influential political actor that is hard to rein in.

In response, the Party has become more responsive to cyberactivism by taking effective remedial actions. Typically, as in the case of Zhou Jiugen and many others, the Party orders a prompt investigation once it detects collective wrath from the public and, not surprisingly, finds sufficient evidence that warrants disciplinary action or criminal punishment. The official action is often swift and both the officials and the issue involving them vanish from public view. Beyond the individual cases, the government stays engaged with the online forces of civil society. Auditing may be distorted, and OGI-based application may be denied, but the battle against corruption has been fought in the court of public opinion through public mobilization. In the end, the Party is forced to take the pulse of public opinion carefully and to treat it seriously.

Authoritarian Resilience and Anticorruption Initiatives

The anticorruption efforts described above have had a certain positive impact on anticorruption enforcement in China. First, they signal the commitment and determination of the Party to control the further spread of corruption. Party leaders have on countless occasions openly admitted existential challenges posed by corruption, often framed in life or death terms. Former Premier Zhu Rongji was well known for his tough talk on anticorruption. Presidents Hu Jintao and others have repeatedly warned that the Party and the nation will collapse if corruption cannot be brought under effective control. It is, of course, the Party's own decision to allow the CNAO to publicize shocking mismanagement, embezzlement and stealing of public funds within the central ministries; to allow citizens to ask probing questions; and to tolerate HFS, which has produced many embarrassing moments for the Party. In the past two decades, the Party has regularly supplied new anticorruption mechanisms, and the discussion surrounding them has generated a positive policy environment that enhances people's trust in the central authority and encourages institutional participation. Those new initiatives make anticorruption a live issue. They supply the much needed oxygen into routine anticorruption efforts and make anticorruption a sustainable enterprise.

Second, the continuous supply of anticorruption measures engages the public and incorporates the elite into institutional reforms. Political reform remains a taboo issue and is not open to serious public discussion.

However when an anticorruption, good governance reform is initiated, it blows fresh air into otherwise suffocating political circumstances. Most of the reform measures have attracted tremendous public interest and scrutiny, and regularly involve a large number of experts, professionals and the general public in the legislative and policymaking process from consultation and promulgation to implementation and evaluation. Government officials in charge are eager to promote the new initiatives; scholars and experts as a matter of routine are invited to give their views and to put the reform in a proper historical and comparative perspective. Lawyers and other activists test the feasibility of a new scheme and scrutinize undertakings made by the government. The deliberation on the potential of those measures captures the imagination of an otherwise frustrated audience.

These mechanisms are not merely empty talk or window dressing. They deliver in part and create their own winners and losers. Each anticorruption initiative opens its own space and opportunities for legal action and political reform. The mechanisms may be structurally defective in design and poor in their implementation, and as such they attract waves of criticism that they deserve. But after all the criticisms are voiced, people continue to go back to the mechanisms for future improvement. The audit reports could be more effectively implemented; courts should have been more active in creating and enforcing the right to know in OGI-based judicial review; and coordination between online activism and offline mobilization in anticorruption activities could be improved. As defective as they are, however, these mechanisms do not generate wholesale rejection and cynicism, which may lead to radicalism.

For many NGOs working on the ground to advocate for social justice, the OGI and other innovative measures are much needed tools to engage the system. Imagine an environmental NGO trying to enforce environmental accountability against polluting factories, such as the well-known case of the Yunnan-based environmental NGO, *Lüse Liuyu* (Green Watershed) in its tough battle against the Luliang Chemical Industry Co. Ltd for dumping highly toxic chromium residue into the Nanpan River, causing cancers and other diseases among villagers residing nearby (Yu and Chen 2012). The OGI law was one of the few institutional tools available to Green Watershed to engage the authorities and compel them to act. Through online mobilization, Green Watershed successfully drew wide public attention to the case. After all, the toxic residue has effectively produced a cancer village near the Nanpan River, which happens to be the source of the Pearl River in Guangdong. But online activism cannot replace offline action and when it comes to offline mobilization, the OGI system offers the best available tool to initiate an action. Armed with the OGI Regulations and the implementing rules, Green Watershed has tried to approach the provincial environmental protection department, the bank that finances the enterprise and the banking regulatory agency for a wide range of information. OGI-based action is clearly a tempting and useful stepping stone into government offices.

Thirdly, anticorruption initiatives offer hope that corruption can be solved through incremental institutional innovation, and the accumulated effect of small changes may ultimately reach a tipping point in the political system. Institutional innovation may be ineffective to control grand corruption at the higher echelons of government, but it is effective in putting the routine and petty corruption that directly affects the daily activities of ordinary people under some effective control. Ordinary citizens are most vigilant in monitoring front-line representatives of the Party-state, such as tax collectors, police officers, judges and urban management personnel, and it is not surprising that Chinese social media is full of reports on abuse and corruption in matters that concern the daily lives of ordinary people. When corruption at the lower end is controlled, corruption is removed from public view. While undoubtedly continuing, corruption has been hidden and made a more remote issue for ordinary citizens. Tighter control and discipline of lower-level civil servants generates more public confidence in the system and could solidify the system at its foundations.

At the same time, anticorruption initiatives offer hope for more structural reforms. Aggressive auditing offers some hope of top-down anticorruption reform within the government ministries. Regular auditing and the revelation of systematic misuse of public funds and embezzlement appear to be an excellent entry point to political reform at a structural level. The fact that a ministry could keep and misuse millions of dollars raises a series of questions relating to financial accountability, budgetary process, congressional oversight and, ultimately, tax payers' rights. In direct response to the auditing storm, the NPC, as potentially an alternative power house, strengthens its grip over the fiscal process by setting up an independent Budget Committee. Further legislation to place the revenue and spending powers of the government organs under more effective congressional control has also been discussed.

OGI offers a similar opportunity at a deeper structural level. Since promulgation of the OGI Regulations, ordinary people have developed a keen interest in knowing government entertainment budgets and assets of Party officials. The new OGI Regulations, the subsequent legal actions, and lively online discussions surrounding the matter are nurturing a healthy dose of cynicism about officialdom, from which a culture of political accountability could arise. Pressure is now mounting for legislation to compel Party and state officials to disclose their personal assets.

Finally, the Internet offers the best accountability mechanism and the best forum of democratic participation in China. Undoubtedly, with its strong Chinese characteristics, HFS is a convenient and effective instrument in the ongoing popular war against corruption. The collective online vigilance galvanizes public support, puts officials on notice and compels the Party to take effective and visible remedial actions. Significantly, the Internet is creating an alternative community of voices and an alternative source of power in the virtual world in competition with those in the real world. The Internet is set to continue to offer forums and possibilities for more institutionalized public deliberation and political participation (Jiang 2008, Yang 2011).

THE LIMITS OF AUTHORITARIAN ADAPTATION

China's authoritarian resilience has its limits and the authoritarian thesis mentioned at the beginning of this chapter is substantially weakened upon closer examination. First, the benevolent thesis is being falsified in front of the eyes of the general public. The Bo Xilai affair and its aftermath reveal the uglier side of the political system and the shocking scale of violence, corruption and moral decay among political elites. The scandal challenges the myth of Chinese exceptionalism and lays bare how, despite the tough rhetoric, the Party is unable to control the spread of corruption. Corrupt interests are institutionalized and entrenched. Contrary to the Party's claim of benevolence, political corruption is reaching, and is seen to reach, the Party's political core and is running out of control.

While China no longer has a single despot and will not resemble other kleptocracies in the structure and pattern of corruption, it is developing its own predatory corruption. Increasingly the Party itself is seen as part of the problem instead of the solution. For some, China practises 'crony communism' (Dickson 2011) in which predatory Party leaders rob the nation of its wealth (Pei 2006). Greed and corruption exposed by the CNAO and the petty corruption that the HFS exposes are slowly eating away at the Party's credibility.

Without the anticorruption credibility it claims, the authoritarian system is not as efficient and effective as it appears when confronted with powerful interests and a massive corruption problem. The shortage of political will aside, China's authoritarianism is highly fragmented and the complicated policy process, which relies heavily on building vertical and horizontal consensus through negotiation, renders implementation of anticorruption policies extremely difficult (Lieberthal 1995). After all the tough rhetoric against corruption, the Party's investigations rarely lead to criminal prosecution, and indeed only a tiny percentage of the officials investigated for corruption by the Party's disciplinary machinery are later prosecuted in court. China runs a soft anticorruption regime in which criminal law remains marginal despite the recent amendment and expansion. The Party's soft law prevails and the Party largely internalizes its own corruption problem (Fu 2013). While the Party will continue to prosecute egregious cases, it will also try to make sure that prosecution does not sabotage the political loyalty of its members. The political imperative necessitates highly selective investigation and prosecution.

Many of the anticorruption initiatives are innovative, but they tinker at the margin of politics and are diluted during implementation. Innovative measures such as auditing, OGI and media exposures may not be able to tame the corrupt impulse within the Party, and the piecemeal institutional reform may not have the potential to serve as a catalyst for further structural change. Take audit for example. Realistically what the auditors can achieve beyond the naming and blaming of some individual offenders is highly doubtful. As a subordinate organ of the State Council, the CNAO's power is limited because it faces a problem common to the entire government. Central ministries are powerful. Financial irregularities, and for that matter corrupt practices, are not regarded as politically risky business. At the end of the day, a few officials may receive Party discipline or criminal punishment, but the same institutional corruption resurfaces every year. As *Renmin wang* (the People's Net) – the official website of *Renmin ribao* (People's Daily), the Party's official newspaper – conceded in one of its online editorials, it is difficult to uncover problems, but even more difficult to solve them (Chen 2004).

It is not surprising that anticorruption initiatives tend to be launched in a highly ritualistic fashion but fall far short in their implementation. The Party is decisive in making new policies one after another, but it is far less resilient in implementing these policies because of the nature of authoritarian decision making (Cox and McCubbins 2001). The anticorruption policy process has a relatively short time span, and it rises and falls at short intervals. When a new programme is initiated, there is no shortage of goodwill and determination to make it work. Each initiative could potentially have a significant impact in a particular policy area and offer a possible entry point into the larger political system. After all, initiatives such as auditing, OGI and many others have worked in other societies and could be made to work in China, but only if implemented properly.

Because of the initial political support, especially the personal endorsement of top leaders such as Zhu Rongji in his support of auditing and Wen Jiabao's endorsement of OGI, and Hu Jintao's famous online chat with netizens, initial policy implementation is normally smooth. Reformers within the government or civil society sectors are able to score a few initial victories and those successes are then widely reported, discussed and endorsed within the policy circle, among academia and through the media. Success generates hope and reformers inch forward and move deeper into the political system, until they encounter more structural difficulties and are pushed back. Can OGI applicants ask anything about the Party's spending power and the real operation of the system? Can the NPC punish ministers for financial irregularities and outright corruption? And to what degree can corruption be fully investigated and reported on the media? These are challenging questions that do not have easy answers in China's political system.

Given the political constraints, institutional innovation is bound to be 'shallow' and only scratch at the surface, even though it is continuous. Anticorruption reform has been most active in the past decade, but it shifts from one policy area to another without creating sustainable results. Some anticorruption initiatives are of course more resilient than others, but each initiative on its own does not bite and it is impossible for isolated mechanisms to coalesce into a comprehensive anticorruption momentum. Anticorruption enforcement appears like hit-and-miss guerrilla warfare and does not develop a systemic, deep-level engagement. At the end of the day, anticorruption enforcement creates shocks more than hope and offers surprises more than remedies. Examples of short-term fixes with little long-term planning abound.

Finally, the authoritarian state may have encountered more difficulties than the conventional theories admit in its search for legitimacy (Bell forthcoming). The base of legitimacy, according to the China model, lies in part in trust in the Party to control corruption. Accordingly while people loathe local corruption, they have faith in the Party to sort out the problem. The logic of Chinese authoritarianism is reliance on the central patriarch as a panacea to end all the local abuses. As a result, petitions regarding local grievances go to Beijing for a quick fix (Minzner 2006). But that design ironically weakens the level of trust and undermines Beijing's legitimacy, as the petitioners soon find out local officials do not cause all the miseries on their own and the central authorities are also part of the problem. When that happens, people may suspend their deference to the central authority, challenge the credibility and legitimacy of the system and resort to assertive, disruptive and radical mobilization (Li 2008, Pils 2012). As Li (2008: 222) puts it, 'High trust in the centre induces petitioning, which then may devastate that trust and thereby induce more aggressive popular actions'.

People's trust in the Party and deference to authorities in general may be waning when the people are less economically reliant on the government than they used to be. Generally economic freedom leads to political freedom in which economically independent people are more demanding of their government and less tolerant of government abuses and corruption (Inglehart and Welzel 2005, Fukuyama 1995). Rule consciousness and rights consciousness among the people may be a distinction without significant difference for their understanding of the struggles for rights in their daily life (Li 2010, Wong 2011). As manifest in organized rallies and demonstrations, people's concerns are more than about egregious practice and petty corruption; their petitions often go beyond the implementation of existing rules as such. As HFS-exposed scandals appear to show, people are curious about petty corruption but they also cast significant doubt on the legitimacy of the system. Beyond immediate grievances, citizens are demanding the right to know, the right to be heard, the right to express and, above all, the right to participate. In the online and offline mobilization against corruption, official rules that are tolerant of misconduct are hardly relevant.

If the popular faith in political and legal institutions is fading, will people continue to channel their grievances through the institutions in which they no longer have faith? Will lawyers and other civil society forces continue to rely on institutional means and implement incremental reforms? How will society react when citizens who report corruption and misconduct are harassed by the government, sued by officials for defamation, or detained by the police (van Rooij 2012)? To use the Green Watershed example again, OGI Regulations empowered the NGO in the initial stage of the engagement by allowing a dialogue with department agencies. But all the departments declined to intervene and denied the application on dubious legal grounds: the bank cited commercial trade secret; the regulatory body pushed the applicant to the Environmental Protection Administration (EPA), and the EPA said it lacked the technical capacity to fulfil its duty. Something was clearly operating behind the scenes to frustrate the exercise of a legal right, but there was little that the NGO could do to initiate meaningful action. Will the Green Watershed or any other NGO continue to rely on the OGI system in demanding rights and advocating changes or engaging in more direct political activism?

CONCLUSION

It is evident that most of China's reform on corruption in the past decade has been geared directly or indirectly towards enforcing anticorruption, and despite political inertia the government has produced significant institutional changes in the anticorruption field. At least the Party has faced up to the challenges and has kept the anticorruption momentum going forward. While corruption is spreading and becoming entrenched, the Party is also digging in. The tough battle against corruption continues.

Conventional understanding has it that China fights against corruption in its own authoritarian way by relying on draconian measures to showcase its commitment and determination. It was said that instead of transparency, separation of powers and the rule of law, which are tested international best practices, the concentration of powers in one authoritarian Party best explains the Party's control over corruption. Its draconian measures are said to have achieved a high degree of efficiency in containing the further spread of corruption and legitimacy among the ordinary people.

This chapter argues that authoritarian efficiency is not the whole story in explaining anticorruption policies in China. It may not even be the main story. China has been active in learning from international best practices and indeed most of its anticorruption policies closely follow the formula provided by the UNCAC and other bodies including the World Bank, the Organisation for Economic Co-operation and Development (OECD) and Transparency International. Because the Party remains in charge of the anticorruption agenda, the anticorruption measures it uses are not hostile to the concepts of a limited separation of powers, transparency and public deliberation and participation – all building blocks for democratic governance. The continuation of China's anticorruption campaign relies as much on continuously adapting liberal-oriented institutions as on one-party authoritarianism.

The new institutional reforms discussed in this chapter signal the Party's commitment to adapt and learn, and evidence makes clear that the Party has adapted and learned a lot. Whether the Party can buy enough time to reform itself and pre-empt a corruption-generated political crisis is unknown. Corruption certainly exists in every political system and democracy per se does not offer a panacea. There is strong evidence that corruption can be effectively controlled under authoritarianism, but China's authoritarian system faces a massive corruption problem that is deeply entrenched and intrinsically tied to the operation of the system.

The Party may not be able to change itself in a significant way and if so, corruption will continue to spread and deepen. Without deeper-level political reform, institutional innovation and adaptation will be too marginal, too slow and too little to have an impact.

This chapter therefore argues that, for the time being, implementation of international anticorruption best practices in China has contributed to the Party's political stability and authoritarian resilience. The future remains uncertain and is unfolding as we speak. With its cessation seemingly impossible, corruption will continue to present a threat to stability in China, especially while it is entrenched systemically and the Chinese people are aware of this. The anticorruption initiatives that the government has pursued over recent years signal the Party-state's concern about corruption and about public responses to it. The latter is inevitable while stability remains a foremost national concern. So as discussion in this chapter conveys, rather than the question, 'Is there a Chinese model', a more revealing question seeks to uncover what the Chinese approach to anticorruption, whether a model or not, can reveal about the authoritarian Party-state's moves to ensure stability within Chinese society and by extension stability of its own hold on running the nation.

REFERENCES

Bao, Dike (2004), 'Who gives the auditor general Li Jinghua the "imperial sword"?', *Renminwang*, http://www.people.com.cn/GB/jingji/1045/2617567.html. Accessed 31 October 2013.

Bell, Daniel (forthcoming), *Political Legitimacy in China: a Confucian approach*, unpublished manuscript in author's possession.

Chen, Yongxi (2012), 'A right to know that has little to know with supervision', in Fu Hualing and Zhu, Guobin (eds.), *Constitutional Rights and Constitutionalism: research on contemporary constitutional problems in China.* Hong Kong, Hong Kong University Press.

Chen, Yun (2004), 'What to expect after the auditing storm', http://www.people.com.cn/GB/jingji/1045/2603574.html. Accessed 31 October 2013.

Cheung, Anne S.Y. (2007), 'Public opinion supervision: a case of media freedom in China', *Columbia Journal of Asian Law*, 20(2): 357–84.

Cox, Gary W. and McCubbins, Mathew D. (2001), 'The institutional determinants of economic policy', in Stephan Haggard and Mathew McCubbins (eds.), *Presidents, Parliaments, and Policy.* Cambridge: Cambridge University Press, pp. 21–63.

Cullen, Richard and Fu, Hua Ling (1998), 'Seeking theory from experience: media regulation in China', *Democratization*, 5: 155–78.

Dickson, Bruce J. (2011), 'Who consents to the "Beijing consensus"?: Crony communism in China', in Hsu, S. Philip, Wu, Yu-Shan and Zhao, Suisheng (eds.), *In Search of China's Development Model: beyond the Beijing consensus.* London and New York: Routledge, pp. 189–203.

Downey, Tom (2010), 'China's cyberposse', *New York Times*, 3 March. http://nytimes.com/2010/03/07/magazine/07Human-t.html?pagewanted=all. Accessed 31 October 2013.

Eberlein, Xujun (2008), 'Human flesh search: vigilantes of the Chinese internet', *New America Media*, http://news.newamericamedia.org/news/view_article.html? article_id=964203448cbf700c9640912bf9012e05. Accessed 31 October 2013.

Fu, Hualing (2009), 'Can OGI take off in China?' *China Rights Forum* 1: 98–102.

Fu, Hualing (2013), 'The upward and downward spirals in China's anti-corruption enforcement', in Mike McConville and Eva Pils (eds.), *Comparative Perspectives on Criminal Justice in China*. Cheltenham UK and Northampton, MA, USA: Edward Elgar, pp. 390–410.

Fu, Hualing and Choy, Pinky D.W. (2004), 'Policing for profit: fiscal crisis and institutionalized corruption of Chinese police', in Stanley Einstein (ed.), *Policing, Security and Corruption*. Office of International Criminal Justice, USA.

Fukuyama, Francis (1995), 'Confucianism and democracy', *Journal of Democracy*, 6(2): 20–33.

Fukuyama, Francis (2011), *The Origin of Political Order: from prehuman times to the French revolution*. London: Profile Books.

Gold, Thomas, Guthrie, Doug and Wank, David (2002), *Social Connections in China: institutions, culture, and the changing nature of guanxi*. New York: Cambridge University Press.

Hand, Keith (2006), 'Using law for a righteous purpose: the Sun Zhigang incident and evolving forms of citizen action in the People's Republic of China', *Columbia Journal of Transnational Law*, 45: 114–95.

Horsley, Jamie P. (2010), 'Update on China's open government information regulations: surprising public demand yielding some positive results', http://www.freedominfo.org/2010/04/update-on-china-open-government-information-regulations. Accessed 31 October 2013.

Hsu, S. Philip, Wu, Yu-Shan and Zhao, Suisheng (eds.) (2011), *In Search of China's Development Model: beyond the Beijing consensus*. London and New York. Routledge.

Hsu, Szu-Chien (2011), 'Strengthening the soft discipline constraint: limited reform in curbing leading cadres' power', in Hsu S. Philip, Yu-Shan Wu and Suisheng Zhao (eds.), *In Search of China's Development Model: beyond the Beijing consensus*. London and New York: Routledge, pp. 224–45.

Inglehart, Ronald and Welzel, Christian (2005), *Modernization, Cultural Change, and Democracy: the human development sequence*. Cambridge: Cambridge University Press.

Jiang, Ming (2008), 'Authoritarian deliberation: public deliberation in China', http://papers.ssrn.com/sol3/papers.cfm?abstract_id=1672887. Accessed 31 October 2013.

Kaiman, Jonathan (2013), 'China's "brother wristwatch" Yang Dacai jailed for 14 years for corruption', *The Guardian*, 5 September.

Keller, Perry (2003), 'Privilege and punishment: press governance in China', *Cardozo Arts and Entertainment Law Journal*, 21(1): 87–138.

Kennedy, Scott (2011), 'The myth of the Beijing consensus', in Hsu, S. Philip, Wu, Yu-Shan and Zhao, Suisheng (eds.), *In Search of China's Development Model: beyond the Beijing consensus*, London and New York: Routledge, pp. 27–44.

Li, Lianjiang (2008), 'Political Trust and Petitioning in the Chinese Countryside', *Comparative Politics*, 40(1): 209–26.

Li, Lianjiang (2010), 'Rights consciousness and rules consciousness in contemporary China', *China Journal*, 64: 47–68.

Lieberthal, Kenneth (1995), *Governing China: from revolution through reform*. New York: W.W. Norton & Company, Inc.

Liebman, Benjamin (2005), 'Watchdog or demagogue: the media in the Chinese legal system', *Columbia Law Review*, 105(1): 3–157.

Lorentzen, Peter, Landry, Pierre and Yasuda, John (2010), 'Transparent authoritarianism? An analysis of political and economic barriers to greater government transparency in China', http://papers.ssrn.com/sol3/papers.cfm?abstract_id=1643986. Accessed 31 October 2013.

Lorentzen, Peter and Scoggins, Suzanne (2010), 'Rising rights consciousness: undermining or undergirding China's stability?', http://papers.ssrn.com/sol3/papers.cfm?abstract_id=1722352. Accessed 31 October 2013.

Mackinnon, Mark (2012), 'Do China's bloggers threaten or bolster communist rule?', *The Globe and Mail*, 9 September.

Minzner, Carl (2006), 'Xinfang: an alternative to formal Chinese legal institutions', *Stanford Journal of International Law*, 42: 103–79.

Nathan, Andrew, J. (1986), *Chinese Democracy*. New York: Knopf.

Nathan, Andrew, J. (2003), 'Authoritarian resilience', *Journal of Democracy*, 14: 6–17.

Peerenboom, Randall (2007), *China Modernizes: threat to the West or model for the rest?* Oxford: Oxford University Press.

Pei, Minxin (2006), *China's Trapped Transition: the limits of developmental autocracy*. Cambridge, Mass: Harvard University Press.

Perry, Elizabeth J. (2007), 'Studying Chinese politics: farewell to revolution?', *The China Journal*, 57: 1–22.

Pils, Eva (2012), 'Charter 08 and violent resistance: the dark side of the Chinese weiquan movement', in Jean Philippe Beja, Fu Hualing and Eva Pils (eds.), *Liu Xiaobo, Charter 08 and the Limits of China's Political Reform*. Hong Kong: Hong Kong University Press, pp. 229–49.

Rose-Ackerman, Susan (1999), *Corruption and Government: causes, consequences, and reform*. Cambridge: Cambridge University Press.

Sapio, Flora (2010), *Sovereign Power and the Law in China: zones of exception in the criminal justice system*. Boston and Leiden: Brill.

Shambaugh, David (2008), *China's Communist Party: atrophy and adaptation*. Washington, DC: Woodrow Wilson Center Press.

van Rooij, Benjamin (2012), 'The people's regulation: citizens and implementation of law in China', *Columbia Journal of Asian Law*, 25(2): 116–79.

Wedeman, Andrew (2000), 'Budgets, extra-budgets, and small treasuries: the utility of illegal monies', *Journal of Contemporary China*, 9(25): 489–511.

Wedeman, Andrew (2012), *Double Paradox: rapid growth and rising corruption in China*. Ithaca: Cornell University Press.

Wong, Christine P.W. and Bird, Richard M. (2008), 'China's fiscal system: a work in progress', in Loren Brandt and Thomas G. Rawski (eds.), *China's Great Economic Transformation*. New York: Cambridge.

Wong, Linda (2011), 'Chinese migrant workers: rights attainment deficits, rights consciousness and personal strategies', *The China Quarterly*, 208: 870–92.

Wright, Teresa (2010), *Accepting Authoritarianism: state-society relations in China's reform era*. Stanford: Stanford University Press.

Yang, Guobin (2011), *The Power of the Internet in China: citizen activism online.* New York: Columbia University Press.

Zhao, Suisheng (2011), 'The China model of development: can it replace the Western model of modernization', in Hsu, S. Philip, Wu, Yu-Shan and Zhao, Suisheng (eds.), *In Search of China's Development Model: beyond the Beijing consensus.* London and New York: Routledge, pp. 45–64.

10. The impact of the 2009 People's Armed Police Law on the People's Armed Police force

Murray Scot Tanner*

INTRODUCTION

For the past two decades a major objective of China's state legislative work has been drafting a body of legislation to define the organizational structure of China's armed forces and law enforcement services, and to provide a legal basis for their activities. Key civilian legislation has included the portions of the Criminal Law defining crimes against national security, and the People's Police Law (1995), which codified the structure and legal activities of China's civilian police forces. On the military side, the National People's Congress (NPC) and the NPC Standing Committee have passed 18 laws and decisions on the People's Liberation Army (PLA) and military affairs (Chen and Zhang 2012).

Legislating the organization, leadership and missions of China's People's Armed Police (PAP) force is among the most important and institutionally challenging tasks for the Chinese legal system as it attempts to legalize and regularize control over its security forces. The PAP perform a uniquely important and broad set of roles in China's social control, internal security, and civil affairs systems. For the Chinese Communist Party-state, the PAP's defining mission is to provide, when needed, a disciplined and decisively powerful armed force that can repress almost any level of social protest or rioting when the regular public security forces require back-up, and thereby allow the regular PLA to limit its involvement in social control. And since the 1989 Tiananmen massacre, they have performed this mission relatively well, and have

* The views in this chapter are entirely those of the author, and should not in any way be interpreted as representing the views of the CNA Corporation, its corporate officers, or its sponsors.

permitted the PLA to keep the known number of cases in which they have had to participate in anti-protest activities to a relative handful. But in addition to social stability operations, the PAP have also been tasked with contributing to a wide array of social order, security and civil affairs activities – including border security, body-guarding senior leaders, protecting key Party and government facilities, fire-fighting and hazardous materials crisis response, disaster relief, special weapons and tactics police operations, and protecting China's forests, hydropower facilities and gold-mining operations. It is no exaggeration to say that the PAP's many contributions make it indispensable in maintaining social order in China, and in permitting the public security forces to focus on their professionalization as a law enforcement and criminal investigation force, and in permitting the regular PLA to limit its contributions to domestic security and focus on military modernization. Consequently, the issue of who can legally mobilize the PAP, which PAP units, and for what purposes and operations is a critical legislative question for China's social control system.

Because many of these items of legislation have been adopted in one of China's more open policy fora, the NPC, they have occasioned relatively public debate over some of the more sensitive issues of national security in the Chinese system. In 2009 Chinese legislative officials revisited one of the most enduring debates in the Chinese security community – what is the most appropriate balance of Central versus local power in control over China's security forces? The focus was the passage of the People's Armed Police Law, intended to provide legal definition for the command structure and the activities of the PAP in the same way the People's Police Law had done for civilian public security organs. For PLA officials, passage of the PAP Law was regarded as an important landmark in efforts to structure a complete military legislative framework, and permit China's armed forces 'to fulfil their missions effectively' (Chen and Chen 2013, Zhang 2010, Sun et al. 2011).

The 14-year process of drafting the PAP Law from 1995 to its passage in 2009 revived serious disagreements concerning the authority of local officials, in particular county Party and government leaders, to mobilize the PAP for security missions in their area. The debate also became an opportunity for criticism of the abuse of state coercive power by some local officials. Between April 2009 when the NPC Standing Committee debated the law's penultimate draft and the law's final passage in August 2009, the draft was revised significantly, removing language that reaffirmed the long-standing authority of local officials to mobilize local PAP forces. This research draws on NPC debates and other sources concerning the passage of the law to clarify why the draft PAP Law was revised, and what implication, if any, it has for the ability of local authorities to mobilize these forces to deal with local protests and other emergencies (State Council Information Office 2002).

HISTORICAL BACKGROUND

The locus of command and control over China's paramilitary internal security and border defence forces has been a recurrent source of debate in the Chinese Communist security system since before 1949, and the debate over the PAP Law underscored that down to the present day authorities have been unable to reach a politically stable equilibrium regarding which officials at which levels should exercise control. Even in the wake of the law's passage, debate continues about abuse of these forces by local officials (Chan 2012). China's current paramilitary police forces, the People's Armed Police force – established in 1983 – had numerous institutional predecessors before 1949.

Party officials have repeatedly reorganized control over these forces, readjusting the balance of leadership power among Central and local Party and government leaders at various levels, and between civilian public security forces and the PLA. From 1983 until the post-Tiananmen years, the PAP employed a leadership and cadre management system that officially gave government and military leaders 'dual leadership' over the PAP, but in reality was largely dominated by local Communist Party officials and their local public security departments. The system was called 'One Unified and Two Divisions', and under it the State Council and the CCP's Central Military Commission (CMC) jointly exercised unified leadership (*tongyi lingdao*) over the PAP forces at the Central level. At local levels throughout the system, local public security units at each were in charge of management (*guanli*) and command (*zhihui*) over the PAP, which included management over PAP cadres' recruitment and promotion. While on its surface this appeared to be a system that balanced central and local leadership, local Party leaders and public security units actually exercised the dominant control over these PAP units. As one police analyst describes the system at this time, 'the People's Armed Police accepted dual leadership (*shuangchong lingdao*), but with the "two divisions" [e.g., local leadership] as the main element' (An 2009, Tanner 2002).

In the wake of the PAP's failure to perform effectively during the 1989 protests, leadership and management over the PAP were reorganized. A major part of the official critique of the PAP system was that it had failed as a fighting force because it lacked both sufficiently centralized control and strong military discipline. Through the early 1990s PLA leaders assumed the leading role in the PAP's political work, even though China's successive Ministers of Public Security continued to hold the concurrent post of First Political Commissar of the PAP. Studies of Chinese military affairs after Tiananmen have often oversimplified these reforms by claiming the PLA or the CMC largely took over control of the PAP soon after the 1989 uprising.

But the major formal reorganization of civilian–military and central–local control of the PAP leadership and management was set forth almost six years later in a March 1995 joint directive by the State Council and the CMC, entitled 'Decision of the State Council and the Central Military Commission on Adjusting the Leadership Structure of the Chinese People's Armed Police Corps'. The directive 'further strengthened the CMC's leadership over the Armed Police forces' and made the PAP no longer 'a constituent part of the public security departments' (An 2009, Tanner 2002). The directive transformed the former leadership and management system from the more decentralized 'One Unified and Two Divisions' (or 'unified planning, with management and command divided by levels'), to a new system summarized as 'Two Unifieds and One Division'.

Under the new system, in addition to carrying out 'unified leadership' over the PAP, the State Council and CMC now also carried out 'unified management'. The most important aspect of the change in management was that PAP cadres were removed from the public security system's more decentralized system (dominated by Party committees and governments at the same levels) to the PLA's more centralized management system. Public Security departments at all levels of society would no longer manage PAP personnel, but they did continue to carry out command (*zhihui*) of the PAP at each level (An 2009, Tanner 2002). But under the 1995 directive, local Communist Party Secretaries and governments at the provincial, prefectural/municipal, and county levels retained important forms of influence over the PAP's funding, logistics, command and deployment.

From the standpoint of local Party and government officials faced with what we now know were rising levels of social unrest, one of the most important aspects of the 1995 State Council-CMC Directive was that it continued to assert the local Party and government officials' authority to mobilize some PAP forces in the event of emergencies. The forces over which they maintained authority were limited to the PAP forces that were stationed within their region, and would not, for example, include the former PLA mobilized divisions that would be transferred over from PLA to PAP unit numbers in the mid- to late 1990s. But for the locally based PAP forces, local Party and government authorities were authorized to mobilize these units in the event of major unrest or other crises, and could place these PAP forces under the command of their local public security forces, which maintained operational control over social stability operations. It was this joint directive of the CMC and the State Council, and not any basic organizational law reviewed and adopted by the NPC, that defined the main PAP leadership system for at least the 14 years from 1995 until 2009 when the Law of the People's Republic of China on the People's Armed Police was adopted (An 2009, Tanner 2002).

THE DEBATE OVER THE PAP LAW

Only a few of the basic facts of the drafting history of the People's Armed Police (PAP) Law are presented in the published Chinese materials. And the most detailed materials consulted for this chapter were from the 2009 debates (NPC Standing Committee Delegate Discussions 2008–09). But these materials are enough to suggest that the debate about the leadership system of the armed police continued almost from the moment that the 1995 CMC-State Council Directive was issued. Additional research must be done to better understand the disagreements over the Law and the Armed Police leadership structure between the late 1990s and 2008, and owing to the relative openness of legislative debates in China (as compared with debates on PLA and public security), these discussions over the legislation might prove to be an unusually fruitful avenue for better understanding the usually opaque politics of China's paramilitary forces.

The first formal proposal for drafting the People's Armed Police Law was submitted to the NPC in 1995, according to one source. Whether or not this precise date is correct, many other legislators who spoke in the debate over revision of the law in 2009 indicate that the process of drafting the law took more than a decade. As early as November 2002 a formal proposal for drafting the law was submitted by the PAP Party Committee to the CMC (PAP Commander 2009, NPC Standing Committee Delegate Discussions 2008–09).

Some time after that, a drafting committee was organized by the PAP Headquarters, presumably with PAP HQ as chair. The committee reflected both the broad nature of the PAP as a multifunctional force, and the legislative system's general tendency for broad inclusion of concerned bureaucracies. It reportedly included officials from across the civilian political-legal system, the regular PLA, and the NPC's core legislative drafting organs – specifically the CCP Central Political-Legal Committee, the CMC's Legal Affairs Bureau, the NPC Standing Committee Legal Committee, and the NPC Standing Committee Legislative Affairs Commission, the State Council Legal Affairs Bureau, and the Legal System Bureau of the Ministry of Public Security. Unfortunately, little information about the activities of the drafting committee and its internal debates has been located thus far.

At the beginning of 2003 the PAP Law was placed on the legislative plan of the CMC. The proposal was first included in the State Council's legislative plan in 2007, and was first added to the annual legislative drafting plan of the NPC Standing Committee in 2008. The draft law received its first reading and review at the Eighth meeting of the Eleventh NPC Standing Committee in April 2009. This meeting saw widespread agreement on the necessity of passing a law to govern the PAP, but also strong disagreement on several institutional issues, including what authority local Party and government officials should be granted for mobilizing PAP units. These debates prompted a significant revision of the draft, which ultimately kicked this critical issue down the road for the State Council and the CMC to deal with at a later day. The final version of the law was passed by the Standing Committee on 27 August 2009 (PAP Commander 2009).

General Wu Shuangzhan, at that time the PAP Commander, contended that China needed to draft the PAP Law so that the PAP's organization and activities would have a clear, coherent and legal basis. Wu elaborated the PAP's lack of a legally defined structure, noting that in the years since the modern PAP was established in 1983, its command organization and duties had been defined only in 'Party Central Documents, PLA- and PAP-related regulations, and some relevant regulations within a few State-promulgated laws'. Wu noted rather frankly that many of the PAP's existing regulations were relatively highly classified – in particular the PAP's sensitive directives regarding such topics as when and how it might use firearms during mass protests and riots. General Wu argued that it was important to codify some of those regulations and clauses into formal legislation that could be published openly (PAP Commander 2009).

Debates over leadership and control over the PAP became more public when the April 2009 draft was reviewed and discussed by the NPC Standing Committee. The April draft, in contrast to the 1995 State Council-CMC directive, contained only a few relatively brief clauses concerning which units of government had the authority to mobilize PAP units in response to a crisis. As the debate among the NPC Standing Committee delegates made clear, the law was never intended to fully replace CMC and State Council regulations as a detailed guide for mobilizing the PAP.

The April draft contained important wording regarding the power of local authorities. It largely preserved the system used in the 1995 CMC-State Council regulations, specifying that governments down to the county level could mobilize the PAP when needed (NPC Standing Committee 2009a and 2009b). In doing so, however, the draft used language that was less explicit than either the 1995 or 1980s regulations. The April 2009 draft noted that there would be times when government and police authorities at the county level and higher would need to activate the PAP. The April 2009 draft language, however, made reference to other directives from the State Council and CMC, presumably unpublished, that existed or would be issued in the future, and that these would more clearly define the circumstances and authority relationships required for activating the PAP than would the text of the PAP Law. Article 7 emphasized that local authorities would have to comply with these directives when they needed to mobilize PAP units.

The April draft also subtly warned against the tendency of some authorities to abuse their powers by issuing illegal orders to police. In keeping with other directives issued to civilian public security forces in recent years, the draft PAP Law attempted to strengthen the authority of PAP forces to resist such orders, authorizing these units to refuse illegal orders and report them up their chains of command.

Article 7 of the April draft read as follows:

> At times when county-level or higher People's Governments and their Public Security organs must activate [*tiaodong*] and employ [*shiyong*] People's Armed Police Forces to carry out security protection duties, they [e.g. local authorities] must act strictly in accordance with the limits of authority for approval [*pizhun quanxian*] and procedures [*chengxu*] as regulated [*guiding*] by the State Council and the Central Military Commission.
>
> No organization or individual is permitted to activate or employ People's Armed Police forces in violation of regulations. In the event that any [organization or individual] illegally activates or employs the People's Armed Police forces, the People's Armed Police forces should refuse to carry out [these orders], and should immediately report this to superior levels.

Article 7 sparked significant debate and several calls for revision among the NPC Standing Committee delegates, according to online NPC records of the April 2009 meeting (NPC Standing Committee Delegate Discussions 2008–09). Some delegates supported the wording as is. But several clearly objected to this authority being granted to officials at the county level. Some argued that China was facing enormous numbers of mass protests, most of which were motivated by legitimate popular grievances ('contradictions among the people'), and they feared that county officials might be tempted to misuse the PAP to suppress these protests in ways that would only exacerbate these protests and make local tensions even worse. These delegates cited long-standing official Central policy on the handling of 'mass incidents' to the effect that, while the state needed the capability to respond to dangerous riots and protests with force when necessary, the preferred way of dealing with such incidents was by encouraging local officials to consult with protestors, deal with real problems, and engage in patient, non-violent, educational and propaganda work. If it were too easy for county-level officials to mobilize PAP forces, these delegates insinuated, local officials would be too likely to rely on force as their first option.

One delegate, Bai Keming, captured a number of these themes in his comment on the draft:

> Regarding this question of whether or not it is necessary to mobilize the police forces, we must certainly be careful. Because right now a large number of [incidents] are contradictions among the people; concerning mass incidents, the overwhelming majority are also contradictions among the people. Regarding these contradictions among the people, when we handle them, we must to a greater degree do ideological work and educational work; but at times when it is necessary, we must also decisively use police force, and prevent these situations from turning more evil. From the standpoint of our work practice, we must decide with great care whether or not to deploy police force. I believe it is not good to take such an authority and devolve it to the level of the county [authorities]; the authority for mobilizing police force should be retained at the two levels of the province and the municipality [district]. These days, communications and information [flows] are extremely developed, and the two levels of the province and the municipality [district] can very quickly get a grasp of what is going on with an incident that occurs suddenly. So entrusting the decision on whether or not to mobilize police forces to a somewhat higher [administrative] level is a little more stable and appropriate (NPC Standing Committee Delegate Discussions (2008–09)).

Some NPC Standing Committee officials cited more narrowly administrative and organizational objections to the draft language in Article 7. They noted that the State Council, the CMC and PAP Headquarters had over the years already adopted a number of relatively detailed regulations governing the deployment and mobilization of the PAP. At least one delegate noted that the draft law was not specific enough about which local government units would actually have the authority to deploy PAP units – the local government collective leadership, the county government head, the county public security chief, etc. Broadly, the largest number of delegates whose comments were reported favoured drafting the authority to mobilize the PAP much more narrowly and strictly, and granting it only to government officials at the provincial and perhaps the municipal/district level, but not to county-level officials (NPC Standing Committee Delegate Discussions 2008–09).

When the NPC approved the final draft of the PAP Law in August, these arguments were taken on board, and the version of Article 7 contained in the April draft had been dropped (NPC Standing Committee 2009c). In its place was an Article 8 that omitted the wording that had made clear that county-level governments and public security departments had the authority to activate and employ PAP units, as had been the case in the 1980s and the 1995 State Council-CMC directive. In its place, the PAP Law asserted that any deployment or employment of PAP forces had to be carried out in accordance with 'the principles of strict review and approval and law governed policing'. But the law did not indicate the legal documents or Party-state directives in which these 'principles' were defined. And most importantly, in lieu of a clear or even implicit grant of authority to local government officials to activate and employ PAP, the Law issued a vague promise that the State Council and CMC would issue 'specific approval powers and procedures'. As claimed in Article 8:

> The principles of strict review and approval and law-governed policing shall be adhered to in deploying and using PAP units to carry out security tasks. Specific approval powers and procedures shall be prescribed by the State Council and the CMC.
>
> No units or individuals may deploy or use PAP units in violation of rules and regulations. In the event they are deployed and put to use in violation of rules and regulations, PAP units shall refuse to carry out tasks and immediately report the situation to higher levels.

While the law did not authorize local governments to mobilize PAP units on their own, it did reassert the authority of county and higher-level officials to deploy PAP units and command them in support of operations organized by public security, State Security, and other units within their region (NPC Standing Committee 2009c).

Article 10 of the final law, like Article 9 of the April 2009 Draft, enumerated several types of actions that PAP units would be permitted to carry out when acting as part of 'deployments' (*bushu*) planned by county-level and higher local governments and public security units:

> Article 10: PAP units may take the following measures when carrying out security tasks according to plans made by the public security agencies of people's governments at or above the county level:
>
> 1. Inspecting personnel, articles and conveyances in security areas and stopping those that are not permitted to enter or exit pursuant to rules and regulations and taking necessary measures to stop those that forcibly enter or leave the areas;
> 2. Questioning on the spot or checking the documents of people suspected of breaking the law or committing crimes and inspecting suspicious articles and conveyances during armed patrols with the consent of their commanders on the scene;
> 3. Assisting in enforcing road traffic control or control on the scene;
> 4. Taking necessary measures to stop or disperse crowds that gather to endanger social order or the security of targets of protection services; and learning related information from relevant units and personnel or conducting necessary surveillance on the scene as required for the performance of duties (NPC Standing Committee 2009c).

In the final draft, as in the April draft, PAP units were authorized to refuse illegal orders and to report such orders to higher levels. Beyond these clauses, the law did not specify central–local command relationships, and authoritative commentators did not clarify these issues. PAP Commander Wu Shuangzhan, speaking after the law's passage, stressed that local governments and their public security forces would be permitted to 'reasonably' employ PAP forces when they were needed (Xinhua 2009). But a CCP Central Party School specialist told Xinhua that in an era when mass protests were widespread, the law's command relationships would help prevent local governments from capriciously or wantonly making use of the PAP (Xinhua 2009).

Article 8 made clear that the real impact of the law on central–local command relations would be determined in large part by the regulations or directives issued or employed to clarify implementation. Chinese legislative practice for major laws like the PAP Law usually means that the detailed rules for implementing or enforcing the law would typically be embodied in separate implementing regulations (*shishi tiaoli*) or directives drafted by the key responsible bureaucracies in the months or years following the law's promulgation. In this case, those would be the State Council and the CMC. Following the law's passage, some legal specialists called for the drafting of detailed regulations to clarify the authority of various government levels to mobilize the PAP and the circumstances under which these forces could be ordered into action (Xinhua 2009). Because major Chinese laws are typically drafted very broadly, critical issues of implementation and enforcement are often left to be addressed later, and the drafting process for implementing regulations can be lengthy.

My research has not yet uncovered any evidence that new State Council-CMC directives have been issued since the PAP Law's passage clarifying government authority for mobilizing PAP forces. One plausible explanation is that any such regulations are secret, while another is that authorities may have had difficulty reaching agreement on any new regulations on mobilizing the PAP.

A review of local government plans for handling mass protests and other emergencies that authorities have promulgated since the passage of the PAP Law reveals some of the rules under which local authorities are permitted to activate the PAP, or must seek higher-level permission for doing so. These plans indicate that instead of drafting new regulations on the activation of the PAP, localities are being ordered to strictly comply with existing regulations, which in some cases were issued more than ten years ago.

Emergency response plans issued since the 2009 PAP Law in some counties and municipalities require local government authorities who need to activate PAP forces to strictly abide by existing directives issued in 1997. These are the 'Notice of the CCP Central Committee General Office and the State Council General Office on Circulating "Regulations Regarding Permission Authority for Deployment of People's Armed Police Forces and Activation and Use of Forces" and "Regulations Regarding Permission Authority for Deployments of People's Armed Police Forces and Activation and Use of Forces in the Beijing Area"'. These documents were issued as CCP Central Committee General Office Document No. 2 [1997], and so far as I have been able to determine, the documents are not available. But these documents are referenced and summarized in part in a number of local regulations that govern the activation and mobilization of PAP forces (Ankang City 2010, Beipiao City 2011, Hengshan County 2010, Jingkou Town 2011).

A review of some of these local directives, however, indicates that these Central Documents set out criteria for mobilizing PAP forces that prescribe different administrative levels of the political system that can authorize the mobilization of these PAP units.

Hengshan in Shaanxi, for example, directs that officials who must activate the PAP strictly abide by CCP Central General Office Document 2 (1997). Specifically, if local authorities must activate a squadron (*zhongdui*) or fewer than 100 PAP, the City Party Committee and City Government must approve the activation, and this must be reported to both the Shaanxi Provincial Public Security Bureau and the Shaanxi PAP General Corps (Hengshan County 2010).

Ankang Municipality (also Shaanxi) directives prescribe criteria under which central public security and PAP forces must be notified in the event of very large PAP deployments. Authorities must also abide by General Office Document 2 (1997). If they need to activate a squadron or fewer than 100 police, the City Party Committee and City Government must approve the activation, and local authorities must report the case to the Provincial Public Security Bureau and the Shaanxi PAP General Corps. To activate a group (*dadui*) or more than 300 police requires approval by the Provincial Public Security Bureau, and the activation must be reported to the Provincial Party Committee, the Provincial Government and the Shaanxi PAP General Corps. Activation of a PAP detachment (*zhidui*) or fewer than 1,000 police requires not only the approval of the Provincial Party Committee and Provincial Government, but also reporting of it up to Central level to the Ministry of Public Security and the PAP Headquarters (Ankang City 2010).

Local directives in Zhejiang also require officials to follow these Central Documents if they believe it is necessary to mobilize PAP forces. These directives go a step further than others reviewed for this chapter, noting procedure if especially violent criminal behaviour, including smashing cars or wielding weapons, occurs. Local officials can then set up, with approval of the local command department, special assault groups armed with lethal weapons to await orders in secret near the scene. If city officials need to mobilize additional PAP forces, city public security officials can apply to higher levels, following both Central directives and Zhejiang Public Security Bureau regulations on standardizing procedures for employing public security and PAP forces in social order incidents (Qingtian County 2011).

Local directives also suggest that the rules for activating the PAP reflect the multiple types of emergency response units of which the PAP is formed. The State Council and CMC have issued different regulations concerning the authority for the mobilization of PAP Gold, Hydropower, Forestry and Transportation units. The full text of this document also is apparently unavailable. But the available excerpts indicate that in the event of extreme emergencies, and if the number of forces does not exceed a group in size, localities may first deploy these units and inform the higher levels at the same time, a more flexible response standard than is used for some of the social unrest cases (Panzhihua City 2005).

CONCLUSIONS

Chinese leaders' decision to define the structure and tasks of the PAP in an organizational law meant that the long-running debate about Central vs. local control over China's paramilitary forces would be revived in the course of drafting of the 2009 People's Armed Police Law. For some officials involved in the drafting process, an important consideration was whether county-level leaders could be counted upon not to abuse their authority to mobilize PAP forces while putting down demonstrations. Between the April 2009 draft of the PAP Law and the final version of the law adopted in August 2009, the law was revised so that it did not explicitly provide county officials with legal authority to mobilize PAP units for social control operations in their region.

While the PAP Law suggested that the State Council and CMC might issue new directives on mobilizing the PAP, this author has not found any evidence that such directives have yet been issued. Instead, faced with apparent concern that lower-level local officials might abuse their authority over the PAP, it appears that many provinces and municipalities are opting instead for strict enforcement of a system passed in 1997 that requires county and municipal officials to seek higher-level Party and public security authorities' approval before they can mobilize even relatively modest-sized PAP units. On balance, therefore, the 2009 PAP Law has provided principles and broad directives that limit the explicit authority of the lowest-level local officials to mobilize these units. But the formal legal system still remains far from becoming the institutional forum in which Chinese political and security officials resolve the recurrent issues of PAP leadership, and through which they provide the system's most detailed, and authoritative regulations regarding who controls China's most powerful paramilitary units, and under what circumstances.

REFERENCES

An, Zheng (2009), *Zhongguo jingcha zhidu yanjiu* (Research on China's police system). Beijing: Zhongguo jiancha chubanshe.

Ankang City (2010), 'Ankgangshi gong'an jiguan chuzhi quntixing zhi'an shijian gongzuo yu'an' (Ankang municipality public security organs' work plan for controlling mass social order incidents), issued 8 July, at Ankang Government website, http://yjb.ankang.gov.cn/Article/class4/class20/201007/55.html. Accessed 30 September 2012.

Beipiao City (2011), 'Beipiaoshi chuzhi daguimo quntixing shijian yingji yu'an' (Beipiao municipality emergency response plan for containing large scale mass incidents), 25 August, Beipiao Government website, http://www.bp.gov.cn/news/?id=9443. Accessed 30 September 2012.

Chan, Minnie (2012), 'Officer warns against misuse of paramilitary forces', *South China Morning Post*, online edition, 6 June, www.scmp.com. Accessed 30 September 2012.

Chen, Chuangdong and Chen, Xiaojing (2013), 'Military legislation makes remarkable achievements during term of office of 11th Standing Committee of NPC', *Liberation Army Daily*, online 11 March, http://english.pladaily.com.cn. Accessed April 2013.

Chen, Chuangdong and Zhang, Mingjun (2012), 'Junshi lifa qude lishixing chengjiu – fang zhongyang junwei fazhiju juzhang wang lihong' (Historical achievements in military legislation – interview with Wang Lihong, Director of Legal Affairs Bureau of the Central Military Commission [CMC]), Jiefangjun bao (Liberation Army Daily), online edition, 24 October 2012, http://www.chinamil.com.cn/jfjbmap/content/2012-10/24/content_17437.htm. Accessed 29 October 2012.

Hengshan County (2010), 'Hengshanxian chuzhi tufa gonggong shijian yingji yu'an' (Hengshan county response plan for handling sudden public emergency incidents), 28 August, at Hengshan County Government website, http://hengshan.678114.com/Html/zhengfu/zhengwu/20100828CE3B1FFF.htm. Accessed 20 October 2013.

Jingkou Town (2011), 'Jingkuozhen quntixing zhi'an shijian yingji chuzhi yu'an' (Jingkou town emergency response plan for mass public security incidents), 9 October, http://www.bobai.gov.cn/(S(yrmiqs45xqizlum2pprtgg55))/Government/PublicInfoShow.aspx?Id=3527. Accessed 29 October 2013.

NPC Standing Committee (2009a), 'Apparent Text of PRC Armed Police Law Adopted at NPC Session 27 August 2009', Beijing, Xinhua Domestic Service in Chinese, 27 August, Open Source Center translation.

NPC Standing Committee (2009b), 'Renmin wuzhuang jingchafa (cao'an) quanwen ji shuoming' (People's Armed Police Law (Draft), Full text and legislative explanation), date of issue 28 April 2009, *Zhongguo renda wang* (NPC China People's Congress Network), posted at Qingdao City People's Congress Standing Committee website http://rdcwh.qingdao.gov.cn/n8146584/n8152591/n8153590/8381107.html. Accessed September 2009.

NPC Standing Committee (2009c), 'Apparent text of PRC armed police law adopted at NPC session 27 August 2009', Beijing Xinhua Domestic Service in Chinese, 27 August, Open Source Center translation.

NPC Standing Committee Delegate Discussions (2008–09), NPC Standing Committee delegate discussions of the draft People's Armed Police law, multiple reports, posted on National People's Congress website (Fall 2008–Spring 2009), at the following addresses: http://www.npc.gov.cn/huiyi/lfzt/fzjzf/2008-11/18/content_1458795.htm; http://www.npc.cn/huiyi/lfzt/rmwzjcf/node_9948.htm; http://www.npc.gov.cn/huiyi/lfzt/rmwzjcf/2009-04/16/content_1497940.htm; http://www.npc.gov.cn/npc/xinwen/2009-04/29/content_1500320.htm; http://www.npc.gov.cn/npc/xinwen/2009-04/29/content_1500323.htm; http://www.npc.gov.cn/npc/xinwen/2009-04/29/content_1500325.htm; http://www.npc.gov.cn/npc/xinwen/2009-04/29/content_1500327.htm; http://www.npc.gov.cn/npc/xinwen/2009-04/29/content_150 0328.htm; http://www.npc.gov.cn/npc/xinwen/2009-04/29/content_1500329.htm; http://www.npc.gov.cn/npc/xinwen/2009-04/29/content_1500332.htm. Accessed November 2009.

Panzhihua City (2005), 'Panzhihuashi renmin zhengfu bangongshi guanyu fahui wujing senlin budui zhinengyong de yijian' [Panbanfa 2005 54 hao] (Panzhihua city people's government general office opinion on giving full play to the capabilities of the people's armed police forestry corps: Panzhihua Government Circular No. 54, 2005), http://www.67863.cn/news/show.php?itemid=7766. Accessed 20 October 2012.

PAP Commander (2009), 'Wujing budui silingyuan jiu "wujing fa" zhiding deng wenti da jizhe wen' (People's armed police commander answers reporters questions on the 'armed police law' drafting and other topics), 27 April, http://www.gov.cn/gzdt/2009-08/28/content_1403586.htm. Accessed 20 September 2012.

Qingtian County (2011), 'Qingtianxian chuzhi quntixing tufa shijian yingji yu'an' (Qingtian county emergency response plan for containing mass sudden incidents), issued August, http://www.qingtian.gov.cn/zwgk/zfwj/qzbf/201109/t20110921_67120.htm. Accessed 29 September 2012.

State Council Information Office (2002), *China's National Defense in 2002*. English translation at Chinese Government website, http://english.gov.cn/official/2005-07/28/content_17780.htm. Accessed 12 October 2012.

Sun, Guanzhu, Wang, Jianrong, Zhang, Jianjie and Sun, Yafeng (2011), 'Hu Jintao wujing budui jianshe sixiang yanjiu' (Research on Hu Jintao's thinking regarding the building of the armed police forces), *Zhongguo junshi kexue* (China Military Science), 4: 37–44.

Tanner, Murray Scot (2002), 'The institutional lessons of disaster: reorganizing China's people's armed police after Tiananmen', in James Mulvenon and Michael Swaine (eds.), *The People's Liberation Army as Organization, V.1.0.*, Washington, DC: RAND Corporation, pp. 587–635.

Xinhua (2009), 'Wujingfa er shen ji tongguo, lifa fang difang lanyong wujing' (The PAP Law, after second reading, is passed, the legislation prevents local governments capriciously using the PAP), Xinhua, 29 August, reprinted in http://bzrb.newssc.org/html/2009-08/29/content_667711.htm. Accessed 30 October 2013.

Zhang, Mingjun (2010), 'Military legislation system with Chinese characteristics perfected', Liberation Army Daily online, 16 November, http://english.pladaily.com.cn. Accessed 12 September 2012.

PART 3

Framing the discourses of stability

11. Detention, stability and 'social management innovation'

Elisa Nesossi

INTRODUCTION

Since 2009, pre-trial detention institutions have appeared in the official and scholarly reformist discourse, opening up one of the last bastions of secrecy in the Chinese criminal justice system.[1] Before then, under the strict control of the public security authorities, pre-trial detention facilities were rarely the object of external scrutiny and were surrounded by an epistemically almost impenetrable wall. Discussions about amendment of the 1996 Criminal Procedure Law (CPL) addressed specific aspects of the legislation that could be improved during the pre-trial stage of proceedings. However, the discussions did not tackle directly the issue of pre-trial institutions, thus avoiding any direct challenges to the Ministry of Public Security (MPS) administering them (Nesossi 2008). This meant that while there could be public debate about the legislation – except where it concerns local regulations on detention centres, which are still treated as mainly internal matters open only to an inner core of the politico-legal circle (*neibu*) – the institutional and structural arrangements of these facilities could not be questioned.

This situation seems to have changed dramatically. A neglected area for a long time, pre-trial detention institutions quickly hit the headlines of national media after being finally nudged into China's official discourse in 2009. In February of that year, media reportage on the '*duo mao mao*' (hide and seek) accident involving the death of young Li Qiaoming in the Jinning detention centre in Yunnan Province projected the problems of

[1] The pre-trial detention centres I refer to in this discussion are primarily *kanshousuo* ('post-arrest' pre-trial detention centres). They are mainly institutions within the criminal justice system – that is, they are not used to detain people for other reasons such as administrative detention.

criminal detention centres into the spotlight.[2] Indeed, between 2009 and 2010 national media reported more than ten other 'unnatural deaths' (*fei zhengchang siwang*), raising public indignation and fuelling intense debates (China Daily 2009). Scholars and officials from the MPS and the Supreme People's Procuratorate (SPP) have been mobilized to make specific suggestions on how to strengthen the existing legal framework of such institutions and improve the conditions for those held within detention centres.

Such proposals and discussions, triggered by contingent instances of violence and abuses in places of detention, have continued to flourish since. They have been variously linked to wider discourses on reforms of criminal justice legislation and institutions, protection of criminal suspects' human rights, stability maintenance (*weihu wending*), social management (*shehui guanli*) and – more or less explicitly – political legitimacy. Scholars and officials offer intriguingly complex perspectives on both theoretical and empirical approaches to stability and its relationship with 'social management innovation' (*shehui guanli chuangxin*) in the context of criminal justice.

One of the premises of the analysis in this chapter is the subtle relationship between political structures and criminal justice. Damaška (1986) explained this relationship more specifically as between the institutional environment and the political purposes of the administration of justice. Of the two state models Damaška described – the activist and the reactive state – the activist model more closely resembles the Chinese state. This model is inspired by interventionist political doctrines that actively involve state authority in all spheres of social life and in the management of society, which 'as it exists … is defective and in need of improvement' (Damaška 1986: 80). The activist state legitimizes its power through 'a shared sense of citizenship', through 'harmony and cooperation rather than dissonance and conflict' so that 'individual autonomy is far from sacrosanct … what citizens want becomes increasingly what the state intends them to want' (Damaška 1986: 81).

In the activist state, results are of paramount importance and decisions are legitimated by the correct outcomes they embody; the correct outcomes of legal suits realize state policy. Without recognizing the value of procedures per se, the activist state prefers to avoid procedural safeguards that reflect distrust of its officials and to provide its officials with wide discretionary power to act. The authorities responsible for

---

[2] The '*duo mao mao*' accident has been widely reported on national media. See, for example: China Youth Daily 2009 and Luo 2009.

administering justice are encouraged to cooperate through a system of superior audits and incentives for promotion on a hierarchical scale. It is expected that officials whose individual aspirations may obstruct the harmonious functioning of the organization, and, more broadly of the state, will be bypassed for advancement (Damaška 1986: 21). In this context, the involvement of 'outsiders' in the criminal justice system is looked upon suspiciously and discouraged.

While models can be helpful explanatory tools, politics and systems of justice as they are actually lived are not static and closed entities. Their internal dynamics and interrelationships constantly change and evolve, at times becoming more sophisticated as they follow socio-historical developments manifest in local legal cultures and in contingent legal arrangements. Changes may be open or subterranean, gradual or abrupt, imposed or inherent. They may be triggered by internal factors like instinctive adjustments to the domestic legal and political systems, or by external influences as a by-product of globalization and other external circumstances (Nesossi 2012: 12).

Relying mainly on recent publications and proposals for reform by the MPS, the SPP and Chinese criminal justice scholars, this chapter offers a preliminary assessment of the type of change and 'innovation' (*chuangxin*) that is possible within the current framework of 'social management innovation'. It explores how typically Western concepts like transparency and accountability have been co-opted into the Chinese legal-political discourse on 'social management' and criminal justice 'socialization' (*shehuihua*) to support the line of stability and legitimacy maintenance. In particular, it considers the nature of the debates surrounding pre-trial detention reforms and the scope and significance of changes brought about in the name of attributes like openness (*kaifang*), public participation (*gongzhong canyu*) and transparency (*toumingdu*).

Overall, the chapter argues that the introduction of these new principles well serves the purposes of a wider project of 'social management' and social engineering pursued by the Party-state. The current politico-legal discourse may lead to formal alignment of China's criminal justice system with internationally recognized principles of criminal justice and, perhaps, to improving the conditions of detention centres in some parts of the country. Even so, that would hardly be indicative of a substantive change in the nature of the activist Chinese state, its bureaucratic structure and the criminal justice system as a whole.

This chapter has two main sections, followed by a Conclusion. The first section overviews the concept of 'social management innovation' and its implications for criminal justice. It delves into the issue of criminal justice 'socialization' and related discourses on the relationship between 'legal outcomes' (*falü xiaoguo*) and 'social outcomes' (*shehui xiaoguo*), finding that such concepts may assume various meanings and may easily be used to justify illegal or extra-legal practices. In the second section, these debates are contextualized and assessed empirically through the lens of 'innovation' in pre-trial justice and the discourses concerning official supervision over institutions of pre-trial detention. The Conclusion draws together these two sections, arguing that 'innovation' is crucial to the maintenance of stability and the power of the Party-state and it does not impinge upon the very nature of the criminal justice system and the main features of the activist state.

SOCIAL MANAGEMENT, STABILITY MAINTENANCE AND CRIMINAL JUSTICE SOCIALIZATION

From its very outset, in the context of the Chinese activist state, the concept of 'social management innovation' grew out of a purely political discourse on harmony and stability. Tensions generated within society by serious social inequality and rights violations that have become more prominent during the last 20 years, and the emergence of new social phenomena beyond the traditional remits defined by the state have made the Chinese government increasingly aware of the need to modernize its methods of control over society. The growing instability and social complexity seriously called into question the capacity of the Party-state to continue managing society efficiently, while simultaneously preserving control over it in a legitimate way. Tensions within society demonstrated that the forms of social management that characterized the early years of reforms needed to be reformed, improved and – using a term increasingly dear to various social and political sectors within China – 'innovated'.

During the 2011 Forum on Social Management and Innovation, Hu Jintao emphasized that social harmony could be achieved only through adequate social management strategies that could coordinate social relationships and behaviours, promote social justice and stability, and manage social risk. Accordingly, 'the main objective of strengthening and innovating social management is to preserve social order, promote social harmony, and ensure that people live in peace and work contently, in order to create a better environment for the work of the Party and the state' (Yan and Wang 2011: 92).

Notwithstanding the numerous official statements and debates on the meaning, scope and practical implications of 'social management innovation',[3] the concept remains somewhat nebulous. As such, it has the potential to be used and moulded opportunistically on the basis of very contingent Party-state needs as well as longer term-priorities. Pieke (2012: 159) argues that:

> Within the discursive space created with the concept of social management, many political agendas and images of China's future compete with each other. These include ruling China according to the law, strengthening and modernizing public and national security, developing a non-state, self-governing public sector, the retreat of the state from society and the economy, the strengthening and centralization of the state, and the promotion of the Party as the pivot of the nation … Social management is therefore somewhat of a magic wand, the cure to the many ills that plague Chinese society and government …

Theoretically, social management stemmed from the idea that economic development had caused dramatic social changes. However, since society remains defective, in order to be stable and harmonious, it needs to be perfected and brought to a higher level – where quality standards are defined by the state. Such understanding is indeed based on two

---

[3] In 2002 the Sixteenth Party Congress mentioned social management as one aspect of maintaining public order; similar references were made in the 2004 CCP Central Committee Decision on Strengthening the Party's Governing Capability and the 2005, Communique of the Fourth Plenary Session of the Sixteenth Central Committee. In 2005 Hu Jintao explained the main functions of the government are economic and market regulation, social management and public service. These functions, he added, would have to be carried out strictly according to the law. In 2007 the Report to the Seventeenth Party Congress reiterated the need to 'perfect the structure of social management'. In April 2010 *Qiushi* (Seeking Truth) published an article by Hu Jintao on 'Shengru tuijin shehui maodun huajie, shehui guanli quangxin, gongjian lianjie zhifa' (Promoting the Harmonization of Social Contradictions, Innovating Social Management and Fairly and Honestly Implementing the Law) and, one year later another similar article expressing Zhou Yongkang's main views on social management innovation. In February 2011 Hu Jintao delivered a series of speeches to provincial Party leaders on social management innovation expressing what is considered his orthodox view on this issue. Such official views have been formalized in the *Guanyu jiaqiang he chuangxin shehui guanli de yijian* (2011 CPC and State Council Opinions on Strengthening and Innovating Social Management). That year, the Twelfth Five-Year Plan included social management as one of its eight 'key targets', mentioning public service, democracy and legal system, a 'social management system for greater social harmony', and the use of volunteers.

assumptions. One is that society, independent of its internal complexity, may be changed and 'statized' – swallowed by the state (Damaška 1986) – that is, completely aligned with the interests of the state. The other is that the very same social energies (*shehui liliang*) that cause instabilities may be also used, or perhaps exploited, to recreate the lost harmony.

Whilst acknowledging the complexity of contemporary Chinese society, its increased sophistication and internal pluralism, Chinese political leaders looked at external models of public administration and social governance for inspiration on how to manage social phenomena appropriately. As Pieke (2012) explained, the Western discipline of 'public management' was introduced into the curricula of Chinese universities, translating the language of business administration into public administration and creating a new class of capable and pragmatic managers that would have the skills to similarly manage society as well as business. Reformers look at foreign models to identify alternative avenues of political success. In practice, this leads to the incorporation of foreign concepts – or at least foreign terminology – into the Chinese political vocabulary, together with possible ideas on how best to work with society to maintain and strengthen political legitimacy. In doing so, Chinese leaders have tried artfully also to please the West and its constant quests – rhetorical or in practice – for democracy, human rights and the rule of law.

Indeed, the Western discourse on the rule of law offers a fairly convenient avenue to link purely political needs with allegedly legal requirements. Thus, the Chinese government asserts that to promote stability the state should rely on the rule of law (*fazhi*), guarantee basic human rights, and promote pluralism and diversity within society. Social management mechanisms developing outside the realm of the law should be brought into such a framework and 'legalized'. Thus, the law should be improved with amendments to fit the objectives of social management and, as a result, it should prove instrumental to social harmony and stability (Gao and Chen 2012: 54). Rephrasing the idea of 'social management innovation' within the contours of the law not only confers legitimacy upon such a project inside and outside China, but also offers a tool for professionalizing, standardizing and – at least apparently – depoliticizing it. In this conception, traditional tactics for the maintenance of law and order should be legalized, made more scientific and professional, and rephrased using the modern and mild terminology of transparency, accountability, openness and public participation. Criminal justice is by no means an exception and perfectly fits the purposes of this ambitious project, since it is conceived as both an instrument to manage society and an area for experimenting with new principles.

Social Management, Criminal Justice Institutions and Legislation

In the hierarchy of officialdom that generally characterizes the activist state in Damaška's model (1986: 21), the institutions involved in administering criminal justice are all called to work jointly, in harmonious relations, to realize a socialist system of justice and stability. This is true in the project of 'social management innovation' in contemporary China, with the public security authorities called to improve their ability to preserve public safety and social stability. Both Zhou Yongkang and Meng Jianzhu[4] have stressed the crucial role of the MPS in preserving public security and, in particular, 'in solving three main problems: the management of services for the floating population; the management of the system of "help and education" of special groups; and the management of public security in some focal areas' (Song 2011: 31).

The courts are equally considered active players in strengthening and innovating social management to achieve social stability and, accordingly, 'judges should not only apply the law strictly but, through their work, they should also be able to re-adjust and manage social relationships' (Wang 2011). In their decisions they should act as both fair and highly efficient justice administrators, and as social managers (*shehui guanglizhe*) (An 2010: 1). When deciding a case, they should keep in mind social management priorities like the maintenance of stability and the harmonization of social conflicts.

Within the current institutional arrangement, the procuratorate is mainly considered complementary to the other organs of justice, in that it exercises legal supervision of the authorities directly responsible for taking measures for stability maintenance (Zhao and Li 2011). In one of his 2009 speeches on stability and the related duties of the political-legal authorities, Zhou Yongkang emphasized the crucial role of the procuratorate in supervising the implementation of projects aimed at realizing 'social management innovation' (Wu and Chu 2010). Such a crucial role is spelled out clearly in the 2011 '*Guanyu chongfen fahui jiancha zhineng canyu jiaqiang yu chuangxin shehui guanli de yijian*' (SPP Opinions on Fully Realizing the Procuratorate's Ability to Participate and Strengthen Social Management Innovation), which explicitly says that

---

[4] Zhou Yongkang was Secretary of the Central Political-Legal Committee of the CPC from 2007 to 2012 and was Minister of Public Security from 2002 to 2007. Meng Jianzhu is Secretary of the Central Political-Legal Committee, succeeding Zhou.

supervision is functional to 'social management innovation' as it contributes to harmonizing social contradictions and realizing social stability and fairness within society.

Under this project of institutional harmony and cooperation, when agreement among the *gongjianfa* authorities[5] fails or is difficult to reach, the highest harmonizing authority – the Politico-Legal Committee of the Chinese Communist Party (CCP) (*Zhongguo gongchangdang zhongyang zhengfawei*, generally called *zhengfawei*) – steps in to mediate (*xietiao*) the various positions and impose politically correct views on matters at stake.[6] Thus, despite ongoing internal debates about reform of the *zhengfawei*, the obsessive call for harmony and mediation of conflicts may raise interesting questions about possible future changes and the eventual dilution of power of this organ that is still so crucial to the entire administration of criminal justice in the context of a potentially harmonious but unstable Chinese society.

Criminal laws have been drafted and amended to accommodate these higher political and institutional priorities. As Guo's chapter in this volume elaborates, the more recent amendment of the 1996 CPL is a clear example of an institutional compromise inscribed into the pronouncements of the law.

'Socialization' of Criminal Justice

Another basic idea that the project of 'social management innovation' builds upon is that society is an organic unit comprising 'social people' (*shehuiren*).[7] In the activist state, relationships among 'social people' are based on 'a strong sense of citizenship, on harmony and cooperation rather than dissonance and conflict. People should be linked by their efforts to achieve common goals, each subordinate to the overriding state interest' (Damaška 1986: 81). Here criminal justice should contribute to building such harmony among the 'social people' by solving existing

---

[5] In Chinese, the term *gongjianfa* is generally used as an acronym of the Chinese terms for the police (*gong'an*), the procuratorate (*jiancha*) and the court (*fayuan*).

[6] The role of *zhengfawei* is defined in the 1980 Notice on the Establishment of the Central Political-Legal Committee, issued by the Central Party authorities.

[7] The expression *shehuiren* was used by Zhou Yongkang in a 2006 statement in which he was arguing that the 'working unit people' (*danweiren*) have transformed into 'social people' (Pieke 2012: 158).

contradictions (*maodun*).[8] With the ultimate aim of merging state interests with social interests and needs, criminal justice should be adapted to social changes and become 'socialized', a process made possible by the relative flexibility and malleability of both criminal justice and society.

In keeping with the multifarious concepts of social management and stability maintenance, the process of 'socialization' of criminal justice simultaneously implies multiple things. To start, it designates a relationship of mutuality between criminal justice and social development. As explained by Li and Shi (2011: 36), this implies that social development guides changes in criminal justice laws, policies and institutions, and provides the directions for criminal law reforms. In turn, criminal justice has the power to mobilize social forces and to provide the input for social changes and development.

The Chinese legal literature generally considers at least three examples of this mutual dependence. First, the rapid social changes that have followed economic development led to the emergence of new, particularly complex forms of crime. The 1997 Criminal Law has been amended to deal with these novel forms of crime, with new legislation and new institutions at different levels. New laws and institutional arrangements are aimed at addressing crime among specific social groups and preventing the recurrence of related social problems.

Second, Chinese society has become more open to external influences and is increasingly aware of law and rights. Such knowledge and increased consciousness has led legislators to change criminal laws with an eye to satisfying people's moral and social expectations. Today, the law must emphasize the protection of human rights and ideas of openness and transparency, and it seeks the involvement of social groups in the administration of criminal justice. Thus, changes in legal terminology and, at least apparently, in the spirit of the law, may in turn raise social consciousness about the law and create awareness of the complexities inherent in administering criminal justice.

Third, the increased pluralization of society and the incipient strengthening of civil society are leading the government to create new laws and new social structures to support implementation of the law, for example, programmes of restorative justice, crime prevention or involvement of social groups in the oversight of places of detention. Such experiments and new areas of law will likely strengthen, in a corporatist fashion,

[8] Trevaskes (2012) explains clearly the significance and implications of the recent use of the Maoist-inspired 'theory of contradictions' in relation to stability maintenance in contemporary China.

mostly mass organizations that are responsible for such activities to support the idea of 'interactive governance' (*wudong zhili linian*) (Li and Shi 2011: 38) promoted by the Party-state.

Crucial to the project of socializing criminal justice is harmonizing 'social outcomes' with 'legal outcomes'. Trevaskes (2012) details the genesis and the implications of the official discourse on the relationship between social and legal outcomes. Informed by Supreme People's Court (SPC) documents and considering both 'strike hard' (*yanda*) policies and official views on the death penalty, she convincingly argues that 'social outcomes is a byword for the perceived social utility of capital punishment, its deterrence effect, and its capacity to deliver social stability'. Its conceptual counterpart – legal outcomes – was coined more recently by legal reformers 'to acknowledge the need for legal propriety to ensure correct legal judgments are made strictly within the boundaries of the law' and that 'building authority and legitimacy of the law into the judicial system by prioritizing positive legal outcomes would in itself lead to positive social outcomes'. For these reformers, 'making social and legal outcomes mutually compatible required rebalancing the law–policy nexus to improve the quality of legal outcomes' (Trevaskes 2012: 6–7).

Overall, the project of harmonizing the two outcomes entails minimizing the risks of social tensions that may result from decisions by justice authorities or from laws that are not congruent with shared social values and moral principles. As Trevaskes (2012) implies subtly, the difficult relationship between social and legal outcomes makes the administration of justice not only challenging but also particularly dangerous, as it tends to blur the line between objective legal consideration and subjective assumptions.

Discourse on the correlation between legal and social outcomes has been developed mainly with regard to court decisions. Yet the difficult relationship between these two outcomes is also relevant to other areas in the administration of criminal justice, including the work of the public security authorities and the procuratorate. For example, as procuratorate and legal scholar Xiang Zexuan expounds:

> The procuratorate should conduct its legal supervisory functions aiming to reach equilibrium between the two possible outcomes. It should be fully aware of the legal outcomes resulting from its supervisory activities, which should be conducted according to the law. However, it should also know whether such supervisory activity conforms to the parameters imposed by the social needs of development and stability. (Xiang 2011: 33)

Judicial decisions by the justice authorities are often marred by vague use of such 'outcomes' concepts, which may be used to justify illegal or extra-legal judicial practices. Conduct such as torture by investigative authorities may be cannily condoned by the idea of achieving positive legal outcomes, which in some circumstances may be socially accepted as well. Here the process of supervising administration of criminal justice becomes particularly difficult – a matter of subjective balance between the two outcomes. Some instances of physical violence or other violations inflicted in the conduct of criminal justice have become publicly known, as in cases of death in custody or miscarriages of justice. These hamper the already fragile balance established between the legal and the social spheres, calling into question basic shared assumptions about the law and the institutions administering it and creating new social tensions and expectations. Public disclosure of instances of violence or other abuse by the public authorities has at least two purposes that concern knowledge and legitimacy. It enables the central government to identify problems at the local level and purge the so-called bad apples who cause them, and provides the authorities with a credible excuse to demonstrate their goodwill in problem solving and responding to the need to reform the system by introducing new principles.

Finally, the process of 'socializing' criminal justice also entails promoting its educational role. In fact, the Party-state requires institutional actors to set principles and examples for society at large to uphold and observe. Court doors are to be open wide and judicial decisions made publicly available, injustices are to be denounced widely, and places of detention are to be accessible to the outside world. Certain segments of society are also mobilized to play an active role in projects of openness and transparency, as discussion of criminal detention centres in the section below reveals.

PRE-TRIAL DETENTION, 'SOCIAL MANAGEMENT INNOVATION' AND 'CRIMINAL JUSTICE SOCIALIZATION'

Criminal detention centres in the PRC are places of detention at the county level or above, administered by the MPS's Bureau for Managing Prison and Criminal Detention Centres (*Gong'an bu jiansuo guanli ju*).[9]

---

[9] Under Article 5 of the 1990 'Regulations on Criminal Detention Centres', the State Security Bureau may also administer these detention centres at different

The people's police are responsible for law enforcement (*zhifa*) in these centres. Such centres are regulated not only by the 1996 CPL, but also by the 1990 *Zhonghua renmin gongheguo kanshousuo tiaoli* (Regulations on Criminal Detention Centres) (hereafter 1990 Regulations) and its *Zhonghua renmin gongheguo kanshousuo tiaoli shishi banfa* (Methods of Implementation) issued in 1991, and by specific rules, regulations and measures concerning particular aspects.

Article 2 of the 1990 Regulations identifies the types of people for whom criminal detention centres are to serve as custodial institutions: suspects prior to or after arrest, offenders sentenced to less than one year fixed-term imprisonment, offenders with less than one year left to serve and 'offenders whom it is inconvenient to send for reform through labour camps'.[10] Offenders sentenced to death also may be detained while awaiting execution.[11] In some major and difficult cases, with the joint formal approval of both the head of the local public security bureaus (PSB) and the director of the local criminal detention centre, and with the agreement of the people's procuratorate, criminal detention centres may also detain offenders with more than one year left to serve (Article 56, 1991 Methods of Implementation). In addition, under Article 2 of the *Kanshousuo liusuo zhixing fa zuifan guanli banfa* (2008 Methods for Administering Prisoners Retained in Detention Centres for Executing their Sentence), people sentenced to criminal detention (*juyi*) should be detained in criminal detention centres rather than in prisons.[12]

---

levels, including provincial, autonomous region and municipalities directly under the central government. Criminal detention centres at higher levels may also be established and administered by the authorities responsible for the railways, traffic, forestry and aviation.

[10] Neither the 1990 Regulations nor the 1991 Methods of Implementation clarify the term 'inconvenient' (*bu bian*).

[11] According to Article 15 of the 1994 Prison Law, 'Before a criminal is handed over to prison authorities for the execution of criminal punishment, if the remaining term of their sentence is no more than one year, criminal punishment will instead be executed by the criminal detention centre'. A similar provision is contained in Paragraph 1 of the 1987 SPC, SPP, MPS and MoJ (Ministry of Justice) *Guanyu zuifan zai kanshousuo zhixing xingfa yi ji jianwai zhixing de you guan wenti de tongzhi* (Notice on Issues Concerning Criminal Offenders Serving their Sentence within Criminal Detention Centres and Outside Prison under Surveillance).

[12] Criminal detention is one of the principal punishments defined by the 1997 Criminal Law, in Articles 42–44. The term of this detention is to be not less than one month but no more than six months.

The detention centres are still fairly closed and unscrutinized, but during the last 30 years a number of official mechanisms for supervising places of detention have been gradually incorporated into legislation and administrative regulations.[13] Indeed, following transformation of the police force from a mere instrument of the Party to a law enforcement agency, authorities soon recognized that law enforcers themselves had to be subject to law in exercising their powers, and a number of legal constraints were put in place to deter and punish abusive practices. As argued by Biddulph (2007: 277):

> Development of the legal system has expanded from a view that law is something that the police enforce, to include a requirement that the law enforcers themselves are subject to law in the exercise of their powers … social stability increasingly depends not only upon the exercise of the state's coercive powers, but also upon the state controlling arbitrary and abusive uses of power by state officials through strengthening legal control over them. The police themselves recognize this.

The PRC has progressively developed internal (*neibu*) and external (*waibu*) mechanisms of supervision (*jiandu xitong*) over law-enforcement organs and places of detention, through which state actors are held accountable for their conduct. Under the internal system of supervision, the authorities in detention centres are answerable to superior levels of their own segment of the bureaucracy and to the Central Commission for Discipline Inspection of the Communist Party (*Zhongguo gongchandang zhongyang jilü jiancha weiyuanhui*). Under the external system of supervision, they are accountable to the same level of national people's congresses or the Chinese People's Political Consultative Committee Conference (CPPCC),[14] the

[13] The system of supervision is based on principles contained in the 1982 Constitution (Article 27), the 1996 CPL (Article 224) and the 1995 Police Law (Articles 42–43).

[14] See the 1997 MPS *Gong'an bu guanyu zhudong jieshou renda, zhengxie dui kanshousuo gongzuo jiancha jiandu wenti de tongzhi* (Notice on Actively Accepting the NPC and CPPCC Supervision over the Activities of Criminal Detention Centres), and the 1993 NPCSC *Guanyu jiaqiang dui falü shishi qingkuang jiancha jiandu de ruogan guiding* (Provisions on Strengthening Inspection and Supervision of Law Enforcement). The external system of supervision is something of a meta-supervisory institution: a formal system of supervision over the legal framework governing places of detention, and over law enforcement and supervision of the detention system. Under the 1982 Constitution (Article 104) and the 2007 Law on Supervision of Standing Committees of People's Congresses at Various Levels, people's congresses have the constitutional and legal power to exercise supervision over state authorities.

Ministry of Supervision and the State Council,[15] the procuratorate,[16] and the general public.[17] The two distinct forms of control have their own peculiarities and priorities and are intended to be mutually complementary, meeting the differing but equally important needs of the detention institutions.

Promoting Transparency and Strengthening Supervision

In 2008 strengthening supervision of police stations (*paichusuo*) and detention centres, and improving their legislative framework were listed among the priorities of criminal justice reform. In January 2009 the MPS was made responsible for amending the 1990 Regulations[18] and a few months later the debate on reforms was already reaching its apex. Cases of abuse and 'unnatural death'[19] that populated the media during 2009 and 2010 helped project criminal detention centres into the spotlight, animating the reformist discourse among legal scholars and government officials as well as raising concerns among the general public. Many observers saw such cases as simply confirming shared images of violence within these obscure places where detainees are deprived of their liberty and are subject to the worst forms of abuse perpetrated by guards, case

[15] This form of supervision is mainly over administrative laws and regulations concerning places of detention (Wang 2006: 63). The Ministry of Supervision and its subordinate agencies have the authority to receive citizens' complaints against the public security authorities and to investigate unlawful acts.

[16] As indicated by the 1982 Constitution (Article 129), the people's procuratorate is the 'state organ of legal supervision' acting on behalf of the state in exercising control over public security organs and the courts. The procuratorial Department for the Supervision of Places of Detention (*jiansuo jiancha bumen*) is also the main organ responsible for supervising the application of custody measures and punishment. Article 8 of the 1990 Regulations confers upon the people's procuratorate a supervisory role over detention centres.

[17] According to the 1995 Police Law, the police must voluntarily accept citizen and society supervision (Article 44). According to Article 46, social supervision implies citizens' rights to make recommendations and suggestions to law enforcement agencies, to file complaints against the police – through the procuratorate or the Ministry of Supervision – and to bring lawsuits against the police.

[18] Notice of the General Office of the State Council on Issuing the Legislation Plan of the State Council (2009).

[19] This term was initially defined in the 1962 MPS *Guanyu ruhe huafen zhengchang siwang yu fei zhengchang siwang jiexian wenti de dafu* (Reply on the Issue of How to Differentiate between Natural and Unnatural Death).

investigators or fellow cellmates behind tightly closed doors. For reform-minded scholars and officials, the cases presented the perfect opportunity to put forward related proposals for legal and institutional reforms.[20]

Official statements and publications have associated the discourse on detention centres and their reforms with two main issues: the concepts of stability and social management, and debates about openness and transparency. In developing such ideas, they have produced a discourse that firmly links (in)stability to the recurrence of violence and institutional legitimacy, and ideas about supervision, transparency and accountability. Both the official and academic debates indicate that cases of abuse hamper social stability since they undermine the educational and restorative mission of the detention institutions. They also produce a serious discrepancy between the expected 'social outcomes' generated by justice administrators and 'legal outcomes' required by law, thereby challenging institutional legitimacy at its core.

Scholars have advocated for specific changes to management of the detention centres and their legislative framework, inserting their arguments into wider debates concerning criminal justice reforms and human rights. They sought amendment of the obsolete 1990 Regulations and issuing of a new law to replace them. They also pushed for authority over detention centres to be passed from the MPS to the Ministry of Justice (MoJ).[21] The proposals focussed on both the form and substance of the text of the 1990 Regulations. They called for rejuvenation of its language

---

[20] In April 2009, just a few months after the '*duo mao mao*' accident, the MPS and the SPP officially launched a five month campaign for revision of all the national criminal detention centres, aiming to strengthen internal and external supervision over detention centres and improve the procedures for reporting accidents. That same month, the SPP issued a paper, *Guanyu jianguan changsuobei jianguan ren siwang jiancha chengxu* (Several Opinions on Undertaking Legal Assessment in Cases of Unnatural Death); in May, the MPS published *Kanshousuo yufang he daji 'lao tou yu ba' shi tiao guiding* (Ten Regulations on Watching Out For and Combating Bullying in Detention Centres), and the *Guanyu kanshousuo nüxing zai yarenyuan shixing jizhong guanya guanli de tongzhi* (Notice on Centralizing the Management of Women Detainees in Detention Centres). A few months later, the MPS and the Ministry of Health promulgated the *Guanyu qieshi jiaqiang he gaijin gong'an jianguan changsuo yiliao weisheng gongzuo de tongzhi* (Notice on Strengthening and Promoting the Public Security and Supervisory Organs that Work on Medical Treatment and Health in Detention Centres).

[21] In 2003 scholars and local authorities had already advanced a proposal concerning passage of authority over criminal detention centres from the MPS to the MoJ. See Huang 2009.

and suggested a number of substantive changes to be standardized through a law issued by the National People's Congress Standing Committee (NPCSC) (Jiang 2010, Chen 2011). In their view, the law should introduce new and more specific procedures addressing issues related to the admission of detainees into criminal detention centres; the formalities governing meetings among lawyers, family members and detainees; medical assessment; procuratorial supervision; and interrogations (Xue 2007: 538–9). Once properly studied and systematized, such proposals for reforms informed the NPC 2011 motion to the MPS and the State Council calling for the promulgation of a national-level law.[22]

The reformist discourse advanced by Chinese legal scholars has been accompanied by an increased official emphasis on stability and security within institutions of detention. In 2010, through the *Guanyu zonghe zhili kanshousuo anquan guanli gongzuo de yijian* (Opinions on the Comprehensive Management of the Security Work in Detention Centres),[23] security work in detention centres was officially inserted within the framework of comprehensive management of public order.[24] According to the 2010 Opinions, 'problems related to the security work in detention centres have a direct impact on mechanisms for guaranteeing security within society'. Accordingly, the authorities administering such institutions and the procuratorate have been called upon to play a greater role in 'social management innovation' within detention facilities. The 2010 Opinions paper asks them to raise the level of security, minimize the risk

---

[22] *Quanguo renmin daibiao dahui neiwu sifa weiyuanhui guanyu di shiyi jie quan guo renmin daibiao dahui di si ci huiyi zhuxi tuanjiao fuzhengyi de daibiao tichu de yi'an shenyi jieguo de baogao* (Report on the National People's Congress Internal Affairs Committee on 'Review of the Motions Lodged by Delegates to the Presidium of the Fourth Session of the Eleventh National People's Congress' 31 December 2011), http://www.npc.gov.cn/npc/sjb/2011-12/31/content_1688779_3.htm. Accessed 1 January 2012. See also Chen 2012.

[23] *Quanguo renmin daibiao dahui neiwu sifa weiyuanhui guanyu di shiyi jie quan guo renmin daibiao dahui di si ci huiyi zhuxi tuanjiao fuzhengyi de daibiao tichu de yi'an shenyi jieguo de baogao* (Report on the National People's Congress Internal Affairs Committee on 'Review of the Motions Lodged by Delegates to the Presidium of the Fourth Session of the Eleventh National People's Congress' 31 December 2011), http://www.npc.gov.cn/npc/sjb/2011-12/31/content_1688779_3.htm. Accessed 1 January 2012.

[24] Such a framework is defined by the 2002 *Guanyu jin yi bu jiaqiang shehui zhi'an zonghe zhili de yijian* (Several Opinions on Continuing to Strengthen the Building of Comprehensive Management of Public Order), http://cmzz.mca.gov.cn/article/zcfg/zyfg/201201/20120100077335.shtml. Accessed 1 January 2012.

of 'unnatural deaths', and improve the system of legal supervision through the existing office of the on-site procuratorate (*zhusuo jian-chayuan*), with the overall aim of protecting social harmony and stability.

To complement the 2010 Opinions, in February 2011 the MPS issued the *Guanyu tuijin kanshousuo guanli jizhi chuangxin de tongzhi* (Notice on Promoting the Innovation of the Management Mechanisms in Detention Centres).[25] The introduction says:

> Over the years … detention centres have duly contributed to the fight against crime and the maintenance of social stability. However, recently new circumstances and problems have emerged. First, the management of detention is very challenging and difficult. At present, what makes it an arduous task is the persistence of internal contradictions among the people, the high rate of crime, and complex struggles against the enemies. This situation creates difficulties for daily management of the detainees; the instruments used to confront those who oppose management or try to escape need to be constantly innovated … Second, the construction of the national legal system is becoming progressively more sophisticated and the masses' legal consciousness and knowledge of rights has increased. As a result, protecting the rights and interests of detainees has become the focus of widespread concern in society. Third, the Internet has transformed into the main source of information and divulging of publicly shared opinions. During the last two years, detention centres have generated negative views within the public opinion. These negative views on law enforcement and management problems can easily become widespread online and they could harm the image of the public security authorities, the Party committee and the government, and damage social stability. In this context, the innovation of working ideology and mechanisms, and the effective improvement of the level of law enforcement and management of detention centres will raise confidence in the Party and the government, and will contribute to social harmony and stability. Thus, the public security and the supervisory departments should promote further the 'three priorities' and the 'three buildings' in a full understanding of the prominent problems existing today in detention centres. Thus, they need to sum up their experience, continue to explore innovative mechanisms, improve and perfect a management system that conforms to the developments in society, and fully raise the ability and quality of the public security and supervisory departments responsible for protecting social stability.

This MPS Notice is very significant as it clearly locates the work of detention centres within a wider project of stability maintenance and 'social management innovation' in the context of criminal justice socialization. Indeed, this introductory statement defines the framework for all the initiatives to be taken inside detention centres to promote innovation

25 www.gov.cn. Accessed 1 January 2012.

of their management style and advance social stability both within and outside the walls of the institution, while protecting the rights of detainees and the interests of society – and by reflex, of the state.

While it is generally recognized that policing of places of detention requires a fair amount of individual discretion, Chinese official commentators today openly admit that independent monitoring and supervision are generally crucial to institutional transparency, accountability to society, and the protection of human rights.[26] Chinese authorities are more heavily emphasizing external supervision of detention centres to strengthen already existing mechanisms and create new ones. The 2010 Opinions paper notes that 'in view of their nature and institutional features, detention centres become the focus of public concern and media attention'. This official statement constitutes the theoretical framework for recent debates and experiments on supervision of detention centres by both the procuratorate and the public.

During the first half of 2010, the head of the Bureau for the Management of Prison and Criminal Detention Centres, Zhao Chunguang, formally announced MPS support for initiatives promoting openness in places of detention under MPS supervision. He also issued the *Guanyu quanmian tuikai kanshousuo dui shehui kaifang gongzuo de tongzhi* (Notice on Fully Promoting Work on Opening Up Detention Centres to Society).[27] This Notice contributed to standardizing the various 'sunshine' (*yanguang*) initiatives[28] launched officially in a number of detention centres around the country.[29] The Notice promoted the idea of 'sunshine detention centres' (*yanguang jiansuo*) open to external scrutiny, in particular to detainees' families, journalists and certain groups

---

[26] It is interesting to note that the two Chinese National Human Rights Action Plans issued by the State Council in 2009 and 2012 include a full section on the rights of detainees, which was almost a taboo area in the public discourse until just a few years earlier. They also place greater emphasis on transparency and accountability in this area, to be realized through a well-developed system of supervision (State Council 2009, State Council 2012).

[27] Similar notices supporting 'sunshine' initiatives were also issued in relation to 'compulsory drug rehabilitation centres' (*qiangzhi geli jiedusuo*), 'pre-arrest detention centres' (*jiuliusuo*) and 'shelter and education centres' (*shourong jiaoyusuo*) (Yu 2010: 5).

[28] The 'sunshine policy' (*yanguan zhengze*) promoted in public discussion on politics and law in China refers to a number of initiatives taken in very different contexts to promote openness in various government areas to discourage corruption and illegal activities by public officials.

[29] See http://www.9ask.cn/zhuanti/shidian/20100515_531.html. Accessed 30 October 2012.

of citizens. Specifically, the Notice stresses the importance of three types of supervision that should be strengthened in detention centres: internal supervision by the MPS itself, supervision by the procuratorate and social supervision.

In June 2011 a joint notice *Guanyu gonghui, gongqingtuan, fulian zuzhi canyu zonghe zhili kanshousuo anquan guanli de tongzhi* (Notice on Participation of Trade Unions, the Communist Youth League and the All Women's Federation in the Comprehensive Management of Security Work in Detention Centres) was issued, aiming to formalize the intervention of mass organizations in detention work.[30] It encourages mass organizations to participate in managing security work within detention centres according to aims established by the political authorities and the public security organs. In this sense, the 2011 Notice is extremely emblematic as it represents the perfect combination of elements pertaining to the discourses on 'comprehensive social management', 'comprehensive management of public order', 'social management innovation' and participation and transparency as officially interpreted by the Chinese government. Thus, it promotes the principles of openness and public participation, but only within the limits imposed by the work of comprehensive social management, and these principles are to be realized through traditional mass organizations.

Preventing or avoiding recurrence of accidents inside detention centres has been approached not just through more thorough or innovative policing measures, but also through the regular presence of personnel from the procuratorate inside places of detention. Generally, supervision is exercised through both an on-site procuratorial office established as a permanent fixture within criminal detention centres[31] and an external procuratorial office (*paichu jianchayuan*). The on-site office of the procuratorate acts as a formal check on the work of the police in an attempt to counterbalance police power within such institutions. According to the 2008 *Renmin jianchayuan kanshousuo jiancha banfa* (SPP Methods for Procuratorial Work in Criminal Detention Centres), the procuratorate is responsible for supervising the legality and accuracy of procedures carried out upon detention (*shouya*) and release (*jiefang*) of pre-trial detainees, time-limits and the administration of detention, the

[30] The Notice was jointly issued by the Office of Central Committee on Comprehensive Management of Public Order, the MPS, the All-China Federation of Trade Unions, the Communist Youth League and the All-China Women's Federation.

[31] The on-site procuratorate offices were established through the 2007 SPP Decision on Strengthening and Improving the Procuratorate Supervisory Work.

education and 'reform' of detainees, and the investigation activities of the police. The 2008 SPP Methods together with the central government authorities' increased emphasis on supervision have fortified the official desire to have a system in place to supervise policing work in places of detention, thus working towards reinforcing and standardizing the role of the procuratorate. Notwithstanding the limits imposed by the weak authority of on-site procuratorates and the challenges they face working within detention centres (Nesossi 2012: 92–4), various mechanisms aimed at strengthening their role have been developed at the local level.[32]

Initiatives involving the procuratorate, mass organizations and the general public, which have proliferated in detention centres around China during the last few years, appear to demonstrate that promoting openness, transparency and accountability is both functional and complementary to the wider project within detention centres of maintaining stability and re-establishing public confidence (Zhao 2010). Indeed, official views support the idea that the new legislative framework and the 'sunshine' initiatives that have seen more than 1,500 detention centres opened up from mid-2009 to mid-2011 (Ministry of Public Security 2011) have reduced bullying and abuse in detention centres and have fully overcome public distrust of them. This sentiment is captured in a report from the MPS Bureau of Management of Prisons and Detention Centres (2011):

> Many people who visit detention centres generally express 'I never imagined' three times. I never imagined that ordinary people could access detention centres and could understand their real situation. I never imagined that the environment in the cell area could be so clean and bright and the detention facilities so modern. I never imagined that the style of managing police enforcement could be so civilized, as my general impression had been that detention centres are dark, damp and violent places.

CONCLUSION

This chapter presents an attempt to delve into possibilities for change in the current Chinese politico-legal context, aiming to identify the kind of 'innovation' that is feasible within the existing framework of 'social management innovation' given its constant preoccupation with stability. In theory, the idea of stability and innovation may seem incompatible. However, as this chapter demonstrates, in practice there is no contradiction between the obsessive emphasis on stability and the prominence

---

[32] An informed account of such initiatives is offered in Bai 2009.

given to innovation. Reforms within the institutions responsible for pre-trial detention demonstrate how this combination is possible in the present Chinese politico-legal context, and they may offer input for wider consideration about the complex dynamics unfolding in other areas of the Chinese legal system. The recent changes involving pre-trial detention facilities are therefore considered emblematic as they bring together discourses on 'social management innovation', stability, criminal justice socialization as well as institutional legitimacy and accountability, to prove how such theoretical and somehow contradictory and vague concepts may be harnessed to support actual reforms and innovation.

Various initiatives realized within detention centres in the last few years have stressed the importance of supervision – by the people's procuratorate, by mass organizations and by the public. The procuratorate is asked to check upon the work of the police and to strengthen its institutional structure and working procedures to perform such a role systematically. This form of supervision – albeit crucial in enhancing police accountability – may prove not to be extremely significant in changing policing practices within detention centres. Indeed, in a purely activist fashion, the police and the procuratorate should work together towards institutional harmony and the broader aim of social stability.

As explained in the second section, public and social supervision is to be realized through two main channels: mass organizations and the general public. Supervision by mass organizations, as supervision by the procuratorate, does not constitute a novelty in itself; indeed, what is new is the emphasis and publicity put on such work, and systematization of it through legal channels. Supervision by *mass organizations* is sometimes presented as supervision by *social organizations* (indicating NGOs and not-for-profit organizations). However, when performed by official representatives of the trade unions, the Communist Youth League and the Women's Federation, it may be considered as not the expression of a lively and pluralistic civil society.

Supervision by the general public, which the official discourse presents as a clear manifestation of public participation in the Chinese context, is by far the most interesting development in supervision of detention centres, albeit difficult to explain. The 'sunshine' initiatives promoted by the Chinese government may be approached taking into account the discourse on 'socialization of criminal justice'. First, they rely on the energies of society – or, at least, of citizens of good repute – in order to scrutinize the performance of the institutions of detention, with the aim of reassuring all members of society that those facilities are properly managed according to basic principles of humanity and shared morality. Thus, positive feedback coming from within society may help the system to regain its legitimacy and the general public to overcome its mistrust of the justice authorities. While the opinions of visitors may not have an effect on the possible recurrence of abuses or on the daily running of the facilities, they may nevertheless provide a stimulus for officials administering the detention centres to improve the quality of their work, at least in very contingent matters like food and hygiene, for example. Considered within the framework of public and social management, 'sunshine' initiatives exemplify ways in which Western concepts like transparency and accountability have been used within the Chinese legal–political vocabulary to rebuild social trust in the existing institutions and enhance political legitimacy.

Overall, an improved system of supervision that involves multiple social and institutional actors may prove very significant. It may generate changes at the very local level and, perhaps, if legalized – that is, if inserted into the national legislation – have a wider impact upon institutional relationships and social approaches towards the law and its representing authorities. Scholarly perspectives on the mutuality of law and society changes have argued to this effect. However, change and innovation may be possible only within existing parameters fixed by higher political priorities, which define the framework for all the activities possible within society. Indeed, the doors of detention centres could be opened widely to the public, but this action should be done to serve the project of stability and 'comprehensive social management' as requested by the 2010 Notice. All the social and legal activities should be performed with this clear-cut framework in mind.

The structure of the legal–political system may show a number of cosmetic changes and shifts. However, arguing that calls for transparency, openness and respect of human rights demonstrate changes in the wider approach of politics towards society and the law would likely prove to be quite simplistic. While new concepts are learned, re-interpreted and tossed about in the existing life of society, the political frame remains the same. Innovation and increased sophistication are, however, crucial to the Party-state for maintaining stability and continuing to exercise power. Changes do not substantially impinge upon the very nature of the criminal justice system, as the main features of the activist engineering state in fact remain the same.

REFERENCES

An, Keming (2010), 'Wang Shengjun zai guanche luoshi quanguo shehui zhi'an zonghe zhili gongzuo huiyi jingshen dianshi dianhua huiyi shang qiangdiao:

chongfen fahui renmin fayuan zhineng zuoyong, jiji tuiding shehui jianshe he shehui guanli chuangxin, weihu shehui hexie wending' (In a conference call on the meeting on the national implementation of the work on the comprehensive management of social order, Wang Shengjun emphasized: he needed to fully use the skills of the people's courts, actively promoting the construction of society and social management innovation, and protect social stability), *Renmin fayuanbao* (People's Court Daily), 9 July, http://npxfy.chinacourt.org/public/detail.php?id=41. Accessed 20 December 2012.

Bai, Quanmin (ed.) (2009), *Paizhu jianchaguan zhifa jiandu jishi* (Record on the on-site procuratorate supervision on the implementation of the law). Beijing: Zhongguo jiancha chubanshe [For internal circulation only].

Biddulph, Sarah (2007), *Legal Reforms and Administrative Detention in China*. Cambridge: Cambridge University Press.

Chen, Liping (2012), 'Fazhiban zhengzai shencha tiaoli xiugaigao' (The State Council Legislative Office is examining the proposal for the amendment of the detention centres regulations), 2 February, http://old.chinacourt.org/html/article/201202/02/474526.shtml. Accessed 18 September 2012.

Chen, Qiao (2011), 'Daibiao jianyi zhiding kanshousuo fa bimian liqi siwang shijian' (Representative proposed a method to avoid mysterious deaths in criminal detention centres), *Jinghua shibao* (Beijing Times), 14 March, http://news.sina.com.cn/c/2011-03-14/021222107993.shtml. Accessed 18 September 2012.

China Daily (2009), 'State cleans house over detentions', 20 April, http://www2.chinadaily.com.cn/china/2009-04/20/content_7693434.htm. Accessed 25 April 2009.

China Youth Daily (2009), 'Yunnan jingfang tongbao duo mao mao shijian. Cheng Li wan youxi fasheng yiwai' (Yunnan Police notify about the accident of hide and seek. A guy called Li had an accident while playing), 21 February, http://news.sina.com.cn/c/2009-02-21/032717258307.shtml. Accessed 20 December 2011.

Damaška, Mirjan R. (1986), *The Faces of Justice and State Authority: a comparative approach to the legal process*. New Haven and London: Yale University Press.

Gao, Mingxuan and Chen, Ran (2012), 'Lun shehui guanli chuangxin zhong de xingshi fazhi wenti' (Discussing the issue of the rule of law in criminal matters in the context of social management innovation), *Zhongguo faxue* (China Legal Science), 2: 54–66.

Huang, Xiuli (2009), 'Kanshousuo gaige, 26 nian hou ke zai chongqi. Zhuanfang Zhongguo fanzui xuehui fu mishu zhang, Zhongguo zhengfa daxue jiaoshou Wang Shun'an' (The reform of criminal detention centres restarts after 26 years. Interview with Wang Shun'an, Vice-Deputy Secretary General of China Crime Academic Society and professor at the Chinese University of Politics and Law), *Nanfang zhoumo* (Southern Weekend), 26 March, http://www.infzm.com/content/26106. Accessed 20 December 2012.

Jiang, Anjie (2010), '"Kanshousuo tiaoli": "da xiu" haishi "lifa"?' ('Criminal detention centre regulations': 'great amendment' or a 'new law'?), *Fazhi ribao* (Legal Daily), 24 February, http://www.legaldaily.com.cn/bm/content/2010-02/24/content_2063599.htm?node=20737. Accessed 20 December 2012.

Li, Ziping and Shi, Juban (2011), 'Shehui guanli chuangxin yu xingfa shehuihua' (Social management innovation and criminal law socialization), in Mingxuan Gao (ed.), *Shehui guanli chuangxin yu xingfa biange* (Social management innovation and reforms of the criminal law). Beijing: Zhongguo renmin gong'an daxue chubanshe, pp. 34–41.

Luo, Jieqi (2009), 'Guanfang tongbao "duo mao mao" shijian diaocha jieguo' (Officials notify about the results of the 'hide and seek' accident), *Caijing* (Finance and Economics), 27 February, http://www.caijing.com.cn/2009-02-27/110075141.html. Accessed 20 December 2011.

Ministry of Public Security Bureau of Management of Prisons and Detention Centres (2011), 'Gong'an bu jianguanju shouci tongguo meiti quanmian xitong gongbu jinnian lai quanguo gong'an jianguan gongzuo fazhan quanmiao' (The Bureau of Management of Prisons and Detention Centres of the Ministry of Public Security for the first time presented through the media a full description of the development in the work of the National MPS Bureau of Management of Prisons and Detention Centres during the last few years), 16 August, http://www.mps.gov.cn/n16/n1252/n1777/n2497/2897196.html. Accessed 20 September 2012.

Nesossi, Elisa (2008), 'Reforming criminal justice in the People's Republic of China? the black hole of pre-trial detention', *Journal of Comparative Law*, 3(2): 305–15.

Nesossi, Elisa (2012), *China's Pre-trial Justice: criminal justice, human rights and legal reforms in contemporary China*. London: Wildy, Simmonds and Hill Publishing.

Pieke, Frank (2012), 'The Communist Party and social management in China', *China Information*, 26(2): 149–65.

Song, Jianqiang (2011), '"Shehui guanli chuangxin" dui xingshi fazhi de jiben yiyun' (The basic implications of 'social management innovation' on the criminal law system), in Gao, Mingxuan (ed.), *Shehui guanli chuangxin yu xingfa biange* (Social management innovation and reforms of the criminal law). Beijing: Zhongguo renmin gong'an daxue chubanshe, pp. 26–33.

State Council Information Office (2009), 'Guojia renquan xingdong jihua (2009–2010 nian)' (National human rights action plan 2009–2010), 13 April, http://www.gov.cn/jrzg/2009-04/13/content_1283983.htm. Accessed 20 March 2010.

State Council Information Office (2012), 'Guojia renquan xingdong jihua (2012–2015 nian)' (National human rights action plan 2012–2015), 11 June, http://news.sina.com.cn/c/2012-06-11/152524573325.shtml. Accessed 28 July 2012.

Trevaskes, Susan (2012), *The Death Penalty in Contemporary China*. New York: Palgrave Macmillan.

Wang, Anguo (2006), 'Qianlun dui gong'an jiguan renmin jingcha de zhifa jiandu' (Simple discussion on the legal supervision over public security people's police), *Tiedao jingguang gaodeng zhuangke xuexiao gong'an guanli xi* (Journal of the Railway Police College), 16(4): 63–4.

Wang, Shengjun (2011), 'Laoji shiming yifa lüzhi nuli zai jiaqiang he chuangxin shehui guanli zhong de youxin zuoyong' (Keep firmly in mind the new accomplishment in the mission of strengthening and innovating social management), 6 February, www.court.org.cn. Accessed 20 September 2012.

Wu, Yuqi and Chu, Anhuai (2010), 'Jiancha jiguan tuijin shehui guanli chuangxin de diaocha yu sikao – yi falü jiandu de shijiao' (Investigation and reflection on the promotion of social management innovation by the procuratorial authorities, considering in particular legal supervision), *Dangdai faxue* (Contemporary Legal Science), 6: 140–45.

Xiang, Zexuan (2011), *Falü jiandu: linian, jizhi yu gaige* (Legal Supervision: ideology, mechanisms and reforms). Beijing: Zhongguo jiancha chubanshe.

Xue, Weihong (2007), *Jiya zhidu chuanxin redian wenti – yanjiu yu falü shiyong* (New Fundamental Issues on the System of Detention – Analysis and legal application). Beijing: Renmin fayuan chubanshe.

Yan, Shaofeng and Wang, Junqi (eds.) (2011), *Jiaqiang he chuangxin shehui guanli – dangyuan ganbu xuexi duben* (Strengthening and Innovating Social Management – Reader for Party Officials). Beijing: Renmin ribao chubanshe.

Yu, Nayang (2010), 'Gong'an jianguan changsuo dafang kaifang – San ji yi shang (han) juliusuo shourongsuo quanbu kaifang' (Great openness of detention centres by the public security – 'pre-arrest detention centre' and 'shelter and education centres' at the third level or above are completely open), *Fazhi ribao* (Legal Daily), 18 May, http://epaper.legaldaily.com.cn/fzrb/PDF/20100518/05.pdf. Accessed 24 September 2012.

Zhao, Chunguang (2010), 'Gong'an jianguan bumen ruhe zai shehui guanli zhong fahui geng da zuoyong' (How can the Bureau of Management of Prisons and Detention Centres of the Ministry of Public Security play a greater role in social management innovation?), *Fazhi ribao* (Legal Daily), 10 October, http://www.legaldaily.com.cn/bm/content/2010-10/10/content_2311412.htm?node=20730. Accessed 24 September 2012.

Zhao, Xinqiang and Li, Yingmin (2011), *Jiceng jiancha jiguan canyu shehui guanli chuangxin de sikao yu tansuo* (Reflections and examination of grassroots' procuratorate participation in social management innovation), *Zhongguo jianchaguan* (China Procuratorate), 5: 10–13.

12. The invisible hand of government: the conceptual origins of social management innovation

Flora Sapio

INTRODUCTION

In an obscure passage of *Anti-Dühring*, Friedrich Engels referred to the abolition of the state as the 'future conversion of political rule over men into *an administration of things* and a *direction of processes of production*' (Engels 1970: 292). More than 100 years after *Anti-Dühring* was written, in the 21st century across the globe the state has been hollowed out of many of its functions. Public services have been privatized, outsourced and contracted out in the belief they are best provided by markets. Bureaucrats have been turned into managers, who *administrate* and *direct* the creation of value. Citizens have been equalled to shareholders in the *management* of public affairs (Horner and Hazel 2005).

New Public Management (NPM) and Public Value Theory, nowadays taught at Chinese universities, have been made the new orthodoxy of public administration in China. Together with stability maintenance, they have been morphed into the policy of social management innovation (*shehui guanli chuangxin*) (Pieke 2012).[1] This so-called innovation rejuvenates the old science of *sotsialnoe upravlenie*, a discipline born in the Soviet Union that applied the laws of socialism to the lives of individuals. In contemporary China, the laws that the Party state claims will best ensure human development and therefore must be applied to the

[1] In this chapter I use 'social management' instead of 'social governance' because *guanli* is best translated as 'management', while governance is usually referred to as '*zhili*'. In fact, in the debate on the most appropriate reach of the state, critics of state intervention are using 'social governance' (*shehui zhili*) to convey their ideas, sometimes contrasting 'social governance' with 'social management'. See Chen (2013) and He (2013).

lives of citizens are now those of supply and demand through the market. Where once communities shared responsibility for the welfare of their members, now private provision of welfare is seen as a matter of personal success or failure. The cornerstone of any 'agreement' that may ever have existed between state and citizens has been replaced by a claim to rule based on the state's ability to guarantee equality of opportunities and protection from threats real and constructed.

In Western societies, the social dislocations and existential angst induced by the shift from 'government' to 'governance' have contributed to a rise in punitiveness (Garland 2001). In China, economic reform has unleashed gaping income inequality.[2] Dissatisfaction and the ensuing social unrest have prompted renewed emphasis by the Party state on stability maintenance. Social management innovation in China is intended to both reduce social unrest and remedy inequalities by introducing further economic deregulation. However, the 'small state, big society' model pushed by scholars of public administration, economics, political science and even law excludes any meaningful change in the relationship between power and individual.

The idea of social management is premised on a political paradigm of 'general will', holding that individuals should subordinate their own will and wishes to those of an abstract, supra-individual entity. It then follows that views not conforming to the consensus of the best model of social and economic development are by definition alien to the interest of the public. Hence such views are to be renounced or suppressed. The same is true of all conduct that expresses dissatisfaction with economic policies: only seemingly depoliticized protests and collective grievances pose a living threat to the current model of development. The Party state counters such threats using the stability maintenance component of social management, which involves an extensive internal security apparatus, early warning mechanisms, responsibility systems and, of course, the criminal law.

Quite obviously, the paradigm whereby individuals should yield to the general interest of the people originates from the philosophy of Marx and Engels. Marxism, however, was born in an intellectual atmosphere without strict separation between politics, theology and philosophy. Its notion of collective interest was influenced by the theology of evil, a theodicy ideated to ensure that individuals accept evil and suffering without ever doubting that the current state of the world was the best possible one. This idea reverberated in revolutionary-era China, and was

2 China's Gini coefficient was at 0.474 in 2012 (Yao and Wang 2013).

used much later to justify adopting social management innovation and the surveillance and social control measures we find in stability maintenance operations.

Intellectuals who introduced Marxism to China were not aware of how – nor even that – the same theological paradigm had influenced not only Marx and Engels, but also thinkers such as Adam Smith, Montesquieu and Rousseau, whose ideas the Chinese intellectuals used to change their country. The paradigm foregrounding general will was thus received and disseminated until it became, at different stages in the intellectual history of the PRC, a small but very powerful part of political orthodoxy.[3]

After 1978 the idea gained credit that the free pursuit of one's economic interest could benefit the whole of society. Inspired by Adam Smith, this idea bore the same intellectual debt to the theology of evil. It is therefore unsurprising that contemporary scholars of public administration would define their discipline as an 'amalgam of organization theory, management science and the concept of *the public interest*' (Henry 1975: 378). Inability to recognize and neutralize paradigmatic ideas hidden in otherwise very different political philosophies has contributed to an enduring emphasis on social stability maintenance, surveillance and social control.

After outlining stability and its connection to social management innovation in the first section below, I explain how the Party state rationalized the policy using the concept of the 'interest of the public' in the second section. In the third section I explain how the 'interest of the public' was at the core of Soviet-style social management, which by the end of the 1990s the Party state had effectively left behind. The fourth section links ideas of the Chicago School, which are now widely taught in China, with those of Adam Smith, showing how both Smith and his intellectual followers digested the idea of the 'good of the whole' from

[3] Christian theology never played a prominent role in Chinese politics as it did in European politics. It was therefore perfectly natural for intellectuals such as Yan Fu and later Chen Duxiu, Li Dazhao, Hu Shi, Liu Shipei, Gao Yihan and others to ignore it, and instead focus on the ideas of equality and democracy that they found much more attractive. Nevertheless, by sketching how this paradigm was transmitted to China, how it was never changed substantially, and how it can be still seen at work today, I do not claim that the theological influence visible in Marx, Engels and Adam Smith was the only force that has shaped ideas in China about the general interest. Other intellectual traditions, particularly Confucianism, have interacted with the idea of general interest and eased its reception, and the thought of Rousseau, Montesquieu and other early modern thinkers played various roles in introducing the general will paradigm to China. These issues require extensive analysis, which is beyond the scope of this chapter.

Christian theology. In the fifth section I argue that the very same intellectual debt was shared by Marx and Engels, whose works exerted a fundamental influence on Chinese Marxism. Finally, in the sixth section I explain how the dilution of Maoist ideology in post-Mao China has strengthened the ideological hold of the general will paradigm, which the Party state presented initially under the guise of Dengist pragmatism and subsequently through the doctrines of the Three Represents, the Harmonious Society and the Eight Musts. The contemporary quest for social stability in China is thus to be understood as an attempt by the Party state to make the behaviour of citizens conform to the general will paradigm, by giving up all those claims and demands that according to the Party state are against the general interest of the public.

STABILITY DISCOURSE

In February 1989, shortly after his inauguration as US President, George H.W. Bush travelled to Beijing. In the Great Hall of the People, addressing Deng Xiaoping, Li Peng, Zhao Ziyang and Yang Shangkun, Bush the Elder invoked the motive of 'respect for the individual as well as the integrity of the state' as the basis for the bilateral relationship (Bush 1989). Deng Xiaoping opened his address with the now famous phrase 'the need for stability overrides all other problems in China'. His speech continued that if protests, marches and demonstrations were held 365 days a year, economic reform would not take place. Deng never articulated a fully blown political theory, yet these and other pronouncements made the point clearly that GDP growth was more important to the nation than the needs, will and aspirations of individual citizens.

An opportunity to articulate the nexus between stability maintenance, survival of the CCP and economic development came the following year, in the aftermath of the so-called Tian'anmen incident and the disaggregation of the Soviet Bloc. Political and policy-making elites framed what happened on Tian'anmen Square using *legal categories*, which was to make the facts of Tian'anmen appear to be part of an endless series of counter-revolutionary crimes. Reliance on the concepts of crime and counter-revolution in turn determined what kind of response the Party would make, and who would be tasked with the imperative of ensuring the survival of the state.

A Central Committee Notice issued shortly after martial law had been lifted explained stability as 'comprehensive governance of public order' (*shehui zhi'an zonghe zhili*), and so identified the agency responsible for stability maintenance as the Central Political-Legal Committee. The

Notice explained that coupled with the Tian'anmen disruptions, the nation's rising crime rate called for capillary control and strengthening of administrative monitoring systems. Local political-legal organs were instructed to launch a few 'concerted actions' (*jizhong tongyi xingdong*) every year, and through swift and severe punishment of crime, and public order responsibility systems, guarantee that protest, demonstration and disorder be contained at grassroots level.[4]

The inadequacies of this stability maintenance approach, conceived mostly in terms of crime control and public order, became apparent during the subsequent decade, as industrial workers, peasants and urban dwellers affected negatively by SOE (state-owned enterprises) reform, heightened levels of taxations, land requisition and relocation projects would express their dissatisfaction with these and other economic policies by taking to the streets. Again the Party state's response was to reinforce coordination among the Political-Legal Commission, the military, police and state security, this time through creating the Central Leading Group on Stability Maintenance. One of the first initiatives of the new Leading Group was to commission a nationwide analysis of mass incidents (*quntixing shijian*).

Analyses of protests and demonstrations revealed to provincial political-legal committees that the primary cause of the increase in social unrest was the fallout of economic policies. Addressing this nexus between economic growth and social protest was difficult because political orthodoxy postulated *both* that social stability depends on economic development, *and* that economic development depends on social stability. By this orthodoxy, China's rising GDP rates should have led to gradual diminution, rather than relentless growth, of unrest. But instead the opposite phenomenon came about. Even so, the political demands voiced through protests did not reach the point of calling for a regime change.

In conveying their findings, analysts in the Political-Legal Committee Research Office abandoned the legal categories of crime and counter-revolution to articulate the stability maintenance discourse through political-philosophical concepts. Their most immediate referents were still Mao Zedong and his theory of contradiction. Framing protests as a

---

[4] *Zhonggong zhongyang guanyu weihu shehui wending jiaqiang zhengfa gongzuode tongzhi* (Notice of the Central Committee of the Chinese Communist Party on maintaining social stability and strengthening political-legal work), 2 April 1990.

kind of non-antagonistic contradiction allowed the Research Office to suggest the adoption of a more nuanced approach to stability maintenance.

Analysts held that different kinds of interests (*liyi*) exist in society and diversification of interests is a normal consequence of economic reform. Therefore, side by side with common interest (*gongtong liyi*), various social groups and their members hold sectoral and individual interests. Economic reform will eventually produce a harmony of collective and individual interest but along the road to such an ideal end-state, interests could easily diverge and sometimes be in conflict (*chongtu*). Mass incidents are therefore not a public order problem, but actual examples of conflict over diverging interests. They are preceded by tell-tale signs, and hence predictable and manageable. According to the Research Office, the most appropriate responses are to contain these incidents at grassroots level through early warning and responsibility systems, resolve them through mediation and other legal channels and use police forces cautiously, alongside wide-ranging structural reforms (Central Political-legal Committee Research Office 2001).

This shift in rhetoric from using legal categories of crime and counter-revolution to using political-philosophical concepts, alongside references to Party cadres as 'managers' (*guanlizhe*) of the masses, and to the conciliation of conflicting interests, was a fundamental change. Appeals to the idea of 'interests' (*liyi*) allowed a gradual coupling of the policy of stability maintenance with a set of structural reforms aimed at easing social tensions. Within a few years, this hybrid of increasingly sophisticated policing techniques and neoliberal economic measures would become known as social management innovation.

SOCIAL MANAGEMENT INNOVATION

If the policing component of social management innovation includes a gradual divestment of the *yanda* campaigns of the 1990s and early 2000s,[5] the introduction of crowd control mechanisms, reforms in population monitoring and so forth, the economic component involves changing the roles of government, NGOs and citizens. The rationale is that government bodies should pass on many of their former responsibilities to the non-state sector by expanding the scope of services delivered through the market, and focus on macro-economic coordination and

---

[5] In Chapter 7 in this volume, Susan Trevaskes offers some detail on *yanda* campaigns to 'strike hard' against serious crime. See also Trevaskes (2010).

supervision. Yet the market cannot always ensure provision of those services that do not yield profits. And access to the market is limited by one's income level or capacity to pay through other means, with the result that not everybody can obtain education, healthcare or justice if these are delivered at a price through the marketplace.

These failures of the market are to be addressed by NGOs and by citizens, who should use available mechanisms – local elections, grass-roots organizations (*minjian zuzhi*) the non-profit sector and so forth – to take an active part in ensuring the delivery of services they could otherwise not enjoy, and to convey their requests to government. This change in the respective roles played by public administration, NGOs and the public in delivering essential and non-essential services is not meant to impact upon the power of the Party or to induce a loosening of controls on the non-profit sector, which is already captured in a quasi-corporatist relationship with the state (Pieke 2012).[6] Rather it is to strengthen state capacity. This is what is meant by constructing a social management system 'under the leadership of Party committees, the responsibility of governments, with coordination by society and participation of the public'.[7]

Releasing the delivery of services from the public sector into the marketplace through social management innovation is not just risky but is unlikely to induce levelling of economic inequality any time soon. Increasing reliance on markets to distribute goods and services hitherto provided by the state could further inflate social unrest when (public–private partnerships aside) citizens realize they are paying higher prices to receive services of much less quality, they can no longer access goods or services they once enjoyed, they find that the state does not guarantee fair market competition and so forth. These so-called reforms in public administration through social management innovation are therefore introduced hand in hand with strengthening of the social stability apparatus.

---

[6] Anthony Spires' (2011) criticism of international cooperation, despite being framed from the perspective of 'civil society', highlights the same trend.

[7] In Chinese: *Dangwei lingdao, zhengfu fuze, shehui xietong, gongqun canyu*. A detailed illustration of reforms in different areas is contained in Central Document 11/2011, (Central Committee of the CCP, State Council 2011). This document has not been published to date, but it is known that the policy of social management innovation includes 50 reform measures involving the economic system, the surveillance apparatus and the legal system (New Capital Daily 2011).

Without the latter, popular discontent over declining quality of life would challenge the Party state's application of this imagined economic wisdom.

Since first articulated in 2004 (Central Committee of the CCP 2004), this shift in the role of government has attracted interest from various quarters. The public security apparatus began to claim – and post 2007 obtained – a bigger role in social management (Hu 2007). Before that, social management-inspired public administration reforms largely involved the creation of a social security system, with social stability maintenance mentioned only in broad and general ways (Chinese Communist Party 2004). Ongoing reforms of the public and internal security apparatus were not originally articulated in social management rhetoric as an integral part of a comprehensive policy of social governance.

After the conservative political turn following the 17th Party Congress in 2007, the unstable social and political environment – expressed in increasingly widespread unrest across the nation – inspired a reformulation of politico-legal rationales based on newly espoused political requirements of social management. By 2011 the Party state had changed the political rhetoric, reformulating one by one most of the tasks that formerly belonged to the political-legal apparatus to fit the rationales of social management innovation (People's Republic of China 2011). This move was necessary to bolster the stability maintenance policy then just introduced after the severely punitive '*yanda*' approach to social stability had been abandoned.[8]

Under this policy population monitoring, production safety, emergency response, control of demonstrations/protests, public order defence, comprehensive management of public order, community policing, crime control, state security, administrative and criminal law, Party building, clean governance and structural reform in the political-legal system were made *as important as* the reduction of economic inequalities and the forging of public–private partnerships. Signalling the substantial stake that public security organs had acquired in social management, the name, role and composition of the Committee for the Comprehensive Management of Public Order were changed. The renamed Committee for the Comprehensive Governance of Social Management coordinates the social management work of 40 government departments (New Capital Daily 2011), while still based within the CCP's Political-Legal Commission.

As soon as the public security apparatus acquired a substantial stake in social management, its voice could be heard bashing non-governmental

---

8 See Trevaskes (2010, 2012): 159–62.

organizations existing outside the state's legislative framework.[9] These NGOs were seen to be attempting to subvert state power or to foster political change, thus inspiring the call for a tightening of public order and social control policies (Fewsmith 2011).

While, on the one hand, the public security apparatus saw social management innovation favourably, a vocal source of opposition came from the New Left, whose members rejected the economic policies of this new approach, if not its social control measures. New Left members found themselves and their advocacy of neo-Keynesian economic policies, spearheaded by Bo Xilai, disgraced by political associations. Strategic discrediting used Bo's association with his wife's involvement in the Neil Heywood murder to overshadow debate about the integrity of the economic policies they proposed. The debate around neoliberalization and the role of the public security apparatus appears to continue. A broad consensus on social management was, however, reached in the spring of 2011, as the discussion below explains.[10]

MANAGING MEN

The connection between the economic reform and stability maintenance arms of social management rests on the concept of general will. Arguments in favour of a Chinese breed of neoliberalism and stability maintenance were presented using the general interest paradigm in a set of 13 *People's Daily* editorials and three cadre manuals (see Appendix). The general interest paradigm holds that the 'interest of the public' as a whole should always prevail over the interest of individuals or minorities. In theoretical terms, this paradigm is exceptionally hard to falsify, because it allows the proponents of disparate ethical and legal-philosophical positions to agree on its most basic premise, and hence what follows from it. It also appears to be sufficiently de-ideologized to bridge widely different political positions (Ginbar 2008).

---

[9] Non-governmental organizations can register with civil affairs departments and exist legally only if they obtain sponsorship by a government agency. Groups not allowed to register exist without formal legal status, or register as business entities. See Spires (2011).

[10] The events that marked achievement of this consensus were the Provincial and Ministerial Level Leaders' Social Management Innovation Seminar, held at the Central Party School in February 2011, and a Politburo Meeting convened on 30 May 2011.

The general interest, or, as these materials say, 'the interest of the public', is embodied by the government. As a public institution, the government has no will of its own other than the will of the people. Social stability is maintained, and society exists in a condition of stability whenever the will of the government and the will of the people are one. But when citizens do not see their will mirrored in the state's will and translated into policy, social instability increases, hence petitioning, self-immolations and demonstrations become endemic. Achieving and maintaining a unity of will between the state and the people is difficult, because a variety of different interests exist within society. Individuals, social groups and enterprises may agree on the broad goal of economic development but their different perspectives will result in their making different choices.

As the official explanation continues, to forge a healthy relationship between the interests of individuals, groups and the state, individuals have to be 'managed'. Social management therefore seeks to influence individual volition and individual action; it requires individuals to abstain from all conduct that satisfies their own interest but does not at the same time contribute to the interest of society as a whole.

This moral dictate applies to public officials and citizens alike. For instance, in their work Party cadres and public officials are expected to promote economic development rather than their own career advancement. Health professionals who work in a privatized, therefore profit-driven healthcare system must provide treatment for the sake of public health, not to maximize business profit. Even those engaged in humbler trades, such as 'gangmasters' (*baogongtou*) who recruit construction workers for a fee, should not deduct any part of their fee from workers' salaries. And at large, citizens should understand how change in Chinese society is unavoidable, and while they do enjoy a right to air their grievances, they are to do so lawfully, without putting their individual interest ahead of the higher good of public order and social stability.

Before 1978, the structure of interests in Chinese society was more homogeneous. Economic reform has since given life to a more complex social structure. Throughout the 1980s and 1990s subsequent waves of economic reform dismantled piece by piece the socialist-era system of social management centred on the work unit (*danwei*), central economic planning and cradle-to-grave welfare. By the early 2000s that system essentially ceased to exist. In the process the state had taken on a new role, one that needed to provide a credible response to the angst that in the meantime came to pervade Chinese society. The new role of the Party and of the state is to act as arbiter between competing interests. Nowadays they have restricted their responsibility to providing only those goods and services that they proclaim are most efficiently and effectively allocated by the public sector. These goods and services are dominated by the Party state's security- and justice-related concerns, which include litigation and alternative dispute resolution, public order and stability.

THE SCIENCE OF MANAGEMENT: *GUANLIXUE* AND *UPRAVLENIE*

Despite their very different means of implementation, social management in Mao-era China (*shehui guanli*) and in Soviet-era Russia (*upravlenie*) relied on the same paradigm. *Upravlenie* has no precise equivalent in English. Depending on context it can mean 'regulation', 'guidance', 'steering' or 'governance' (Schwartz 1973: 233). As the Russian state upheld at the time, regulation, guiding and governance were needed because people have an autonomous will which, if they follow it blindly, causes them to act against the laws that shape change in the economic and social system. The Communist elite laid a two-fold claim to superior mastery of these laws and to achievement of true class consciousness. True knowledge and true consciousness justified the state's moves to shape human life and economic activity according to the laws of scientific socialism. The results were economic planning and social management: *sotsialnoe upravlenie*.

In China, until the 1990s *upravlenie* was known as the 'science of management' (*guanlixue*), and social management was its sub-discipline. The works of Soviet theorists of public administration – A.M. Omarov (1987), M. Markov (1988) and Afanasev (1983) – were translated and used as textbooks. Throughout the 1980s Chinese public administrators attempted nothing less than to create a new *form* of human existence, a perfect human who thought and acted in accordance with the laws of socialism (Bakken 2000, Dutton 1992). But they soon realized that individual members of society had their own wills and wishes determined by forces other than socialism, so social stability could be maintained only if the will of individuals could be guided and coordinated (Tong 1991). They claimed there is a hierarchy of interests in which the will and interest of abstract, collective entities – the majority of the people (*guangda renmin*), the 'collective' (*jiti*) or the state (*guojia*) – precedes the interest of concretely identifiable entities as social groups and individuals. Individuals should therefore yield to the general will of society whenever their needs and desires are not compatible with the needs of the majority of the people as defined by their 'representatives'. Since the correct interpretation of knowledge lay only with the Party, and all sources of alternative knowledge were premised on an imperfect awareness of reality, no other arrangement would have been possible. Regulation of individual behaviours could not be limited to the public sphere. It had to be extended to the sphere of private life too, because the conscious choice of individuals could not distinguish between the public and private spheres.

Social management thus came to be developed with two distinct components. One consisted of government techniques inspired by socialism, such as economic planning and planning what could or could not be done at different times of life, such as marrying or conceiving a child. The second component was the general will paradigm. It gave life to a politics premised on something that could not be seen, touched or otherwise proven to exist in material reality, but was deemed to be all the more real and worthy of protection. The 'will' or the 'interest' of the people – an abstract entity that could neither talk nor make its own decisions – was made the yardstick for managing individual behaviours and determining what was, in absolute terms, harmful or beneficial.

A rhetorical reliance on the general will paradigm has allowed for the anointing over time of radically different models of economic development as the best and only possible one. A first important consequence was that the validity of *any* model had to be proven by actual improvements in the real world and in the lives of the people. Evidence to the contrary, such as starving peasants in the 1950s or those killed by over-abundant, poisonous food 50 years later, had to be removed from view. Surveillance, censorship and repression were thus justified to deal with these and other *anomalies*. Being supra-ideological, the general will paradigm has also enabled another important outcome. It has been used to justify circulating and using in the realms of higher education, economic theory, public administration and legal theory the ideas of economics luminaries such as Frank Knight (2009), Gary Becker (2000), Ronald Coase (2007), Eugene Fama,[11] Milton Friedman (2004), Robert E. Lucas (2003), Richard Posner (2012), and George Stigler (1990) among others.

A RISING TIDE LIFTS ALL BOATS

It is known widely that the Chicago School and its followers proceed from the assumption that the maximization of one's interest – market

[11] See, for instance, Cheng (2001).

rationality – is normatively good. By pursuing their individual interest, individuals behave in accordance with the laws of the economy, which dictate that interest maximization benefits the *whole of society*. This assumption is inspired by the thinking of Adam Smith. Yet Smith drew the idea of general interest from theology; God rules the natural world and society through general and immutable laws (Smith 2002, VI: 3). The human being has no power to determine or alter these laws but can act in the domain that God has left to human volition: she can care for her own happiness.[12]

The pursuit of individual happiness obeys divine will and takes place for 'the good of the whole'. The good of the whole of society is something the individual should not violate, so at times individuals should sacrifice their interest to the public interest of their society:

> The wise and virtuous man [sic] is at all times willing that his own private interest should be sacrificed to the public interest of his own particular order or society. He is at all times willing, too, that the interest of this order or society should be sacrificed to the greater interest of the state or sovereignty, of which it is only a subordinate part. He should, therefore, be equally willing that all those inferior interests should be sacrificed to the greater interest of the universe, to the interest of that great society of all sensible and intelligent beings, of which God himself is the immediate administrator and director. (Smith 2002, VI: 4)

Adam Smith, and others with him, did not use the words 'God' and 'divine will' as metaphors. To early modern thinkers, God acted in the world not through a direct intervention. The divine rule of the world took place through the laws of physics, biology and society. Confidence in the natural order was such that human-made rulers such as the state had to 'let do and let pass' (*laissez faire, laissez passer*), avoiding interference in laws that were the best possible, as they were chosen by the Creator of the Universe. At the same time, human rulers had to 'manage' society, to correct individual behaviours that violated these natural laws, going against the interest of society.

Patrick Riley (1978) has explained how the idea of the 'good of the whole' originated from early modern theological debates over grace and divine justice, and particularly from the work of the French Cartesian Nicolas Malebranche. Malebranche's theology of evil inspired not only

---

[12] 'To man is allotted a much humbler department, but one much more suitable to the weakness of his powers, and to the narrowness of his comprehension: the care of his own happiness', *The Theory of Moral Sentiments* VI: 3 (Smith 2002).

Smith (Hill 2001), but also Hegel and indirectly Karl Marx and Friedrich Engels, thinkers whose works have had a more than substantial influence on modern political thought in the PRC. To simplify, the problem of grace is rooted in a scriptural contradiction: God wills all people to be saved (1 Tim 2:4)[13] but not all of them will be saved (Matthew 7:13–14).[14] The exclusive nature of grace poses a conundrum because the logical conclusions it led to amounted to nothing less than blasphemy. If God was the Absolute Good, by creating human beings in the knowledge the majority of them were destined to eternal damnation he then acted in an evil way.

A solution to the problem was attempted by holding that God does not possess a single volition. Rather, the will of God can be distinguished into a general will and a particular will. In this view God normally acts in the world through his general will because he determined himself to create a universe that could be governed through the simplest laws (Malebranche 1992, I.XII, XIII), even though he could have created the world other than it is. This world is still imperfect, in that excessive rain can fall where it is not needed, and defective births can occur. God can avoid each one of these imperfections but doing so would require making the laws of nature more elaborate, which would go against God's determination to act in the simplest way possible. God made the laws of nature immutable, 'general for all times and for all places' (Malebranche 1992, II. XVIII), and He also foresaw all that would follow from them. God therefore wills everything that occurs, even droughts, floods and the birth of monsters (Malebranche 1992, II. XVIII). These phenomena do not result from God's particular will to cause harm (Malebranche 1992, II. XIX), but from the laws of nature. God could eliminate all evil from the world if He chose to do so. He could perform a miracle. But, He has chosen to obey the laws of the physical world (Malebranche 1992, II. XXI). If God performed a miracle to eliminate each and every single injustice in the world He would have to multiply his will *ad infinitum*. Then, the 'Rule of Law' He created and promised to follow would no

---

13 The relevant passage of Paul's First Letter to Timothy reads: 'First of all, then, I urge that supplications, prayers, intercessions, and thanksgivings be made for all people, for kings and all who are in high positions, that we may lead a peaceful and quiet life, godly and dignified in every way. This is good, and it is pleasing in the sight of God our Saviour, *who desires all people to be saved and to come to the knowledge of the truth*' (author's emphasis).

14 'Enter by the narrow gate. For the gate is wide and the way is easy that leads to destruction, and those who enter by it are many. For the gate is narrow and the way is hard that leads to life, and those who find it are few.'

longer be valid (Malebranche 1992, II. XXII), and the world would fall into a state of disorder.

Under Adam Smith's moral philosophy, and all conceptions of politics inspired by it, individual interest can never override the general interest of society, exactly as the particular will of God can never prevail over His general will. Individuals are free to pursue their desires only insofar as such pursuit benefits the whole. When it differs, they are to be educated as to where their true interest lies. Should education fail, they are to be disciplined.

COMMUNIST RELIGION

While I do not intend to construct an argument à la Talmon (1985), claiming that Marxism is a secular religion, Marxism too is premised on the general will paradigm. The paradigm reached Marx and Engels through the two channels of Hegelianism and theology. Hegel, who had lectured on Malebranche between 1821 and 1831, attempted to find his own solution to the problem of evil through the idea of Universal Reason – the Ultimate Design or Rational Process, which shapes and governs the world. Such Rationality, or Freedom embodied, provided a foundation for the existence of the state (*as an idea*).

Hegelian rationality is a seamless unity between individual will and universal will. The unity between the will of individuals and the will of the state is important because individuals' embracing of the general will is a signal of their complete development. No longer driven by wants and desires, which are subjective, socially constructed and external to reason, individuals are to make their choices in accordance with pure reason, letting the spark of the universal will in them shine. Once they learn to follow universal will, each of them will desire along the lines of this will and refuse what goes against it. Each one of them will acknowledge universal volition as their own volition, and thus live their life not as a slave of socially constructed desires, but as a human being free to pursue universal ends (Hegel 2008, para. 260).

In eighteenth-century Germany, theology was the main ground on which political and cultural battles were fought (Boer 2012: 9). Marx and Engels were active against Wilhelmine attempts at restoring a Christian state, and they waged their battle through the weapons of the Bible and theology, which they knew well. The general will paradigm, as well as concepts of first causes and efficient causes, subordination to the will of God etc. are staple ideas of Christianity. Engels, who had abandoned religious practice in his youth (Engels 2003a), knew about these ideas because he kept his interest in theology. Being troubled by the question of grace (Engels 2003b) brought him to the works of German theologians David Friedrich Strauss, Friedrich Schleiermacher, Christian Märklin, and Johann August Wilhelm Neander. In the political philosophy of Schleiermacher, a consciousness of the general will was a necessary stage in the development of a homogeneous people (*Volk*) and in the foundation of the state.

Marx and Engels saw all too well how this deist paradigm, once applied to politics, would automatically lead to authoritarianism. This peril was particularly visible in the ideas of a German socialist, Eugen Dühring, whose conception of politics and justice Marx, but particularly Engels, set out to criticize. Dühring saw the fundamental problem of politics as involving the relationship between the will of individuals and the will of society. His use of these ideas to think about politics led him to a foreseeable conclusion: every individual would agree with any other individual that the best remedy for unjust offences was mutual aid. Aggregation of their wills would produce coercive power, which was not 'the superior strength of the many against the individual or of the majority against the minority' (Engels 2003b: 352), but an actualization of the general will of society. The general will allowed individual will to find its maximum expression. But it also meant that individuals would be subject to 'absolute compulsion by the state' (Engels 2003b: 352), which was justified by natural justice.

On the one hand, Engels ridiculed this conception of politics. On the other, he was unable to offer a real alternative – a version of politics founded upon the idea of neither 'People' nor any other pseudo-divine, abstract and collective entity. In setting out to criticize Dühring he too relied on the general will paradigm.

To Marx and Engels the only possible solution to the injustice and inequalities of their time lay in a communion between individual and general volition. This communion could be achieved only after the abolition of social classes. Before the stage of Communism, individuals identified with the will of the class to which they belonged, with the exception of proletarians, who behaved individualistically as they were the prey of a false consciousness. The task of the Communist Party was then to educate proletarians, making them aware of where their true interest really lay, and of what they should want. The achievement of true class consciousness would then result in the natural alignment of the will of individuals with the will of a Communist society.

Closing the Circle

Because of its accessibility and systematic illustration of Marxism, *Anti-Dühring* was one of the core texts in the formation of Chinese Communism (Knight 2005). In disseminating Communist ideology, Chinese Marxists overlooked the flaws in Marx and Engels' thought. Just as those who, much later, used the conceptual heirs of Adam Smith to reform public administration, not one of them cared to explore Christian theology and its place in Marxism, which precluded them from the possibility of noticing and understanding the analogies sketched above. They had noticed how Marxism recognized the individual as somehow prey to larger forces. But they understood this feature of ideology in light of the problems of their own time and place. To them the most urgent problem was the role individuals could play in revolution if, despite their sacrifice, society would in any case make a transition to Communism.

Qu Qiubai sought a solution to this problem by once more using the general will paradigm, which he drew from Marxism–Leninism and from Hegel. Very similar conclusions were reached by Ai Siqi, Li Da and Mao Zedong (Knight 2005). By the time Mao Zedong thought was raised to the status of political orthodoxy, ideas about general will and particular will shaped the ideological apparatus that sustained Party rule and justified the friend/enemy divide. After the Mao era, various indigenous 'developments' in what is still claimed as Marxism demolished the edifice of Karl Marx's thought without touching the concepts that lay at its foundation. Reconciling radically different visions of human being, society and history was an aporetic task that post-Mao political philosophy solved by invoking one of the few surviving components of Marxism – the general will paradigm.

The Mao–Deng transition saw political philosophers grapple with a three-fold problem. They had to trace the origins – philosophical, social and structural – of ultra-leftism to avoid its resurgence (Misra 1998). But more importantly, they also had to justify regulation of agricultural and industrial production by the market, through gradual privatization, outsourcing and contracting out.

Four philosophical controversies – over the criterion for practice, feudalism, the source of knowledge and primacy of matter, and the stages of socialism – enabled the Mao–Deng transition (Misra 1998). They were used to introduce a *ti-yong*-style[15] separation between the ends to be

---

15 *Ti-yong* refers to the belief of late-nineteenth-century Confucian reformers that China should maintain its own style of learning to keep the 'essence' of

pursued by the government – stability and economic development – and the means through which these ends could be best achieved – economic reform. Such a separation between ends and means could not itself show that having a market economy was just or right. To do so, the 'interest of the people', understood as their material welfare, was once more invoked. The general will paradigm at the same time made it possible to avoid a relaxation of ideological conformity or of social control because it called for consensus. As Deng made clear: 'there exists a basilar unanimity between the interest of the state, the interest of the collective and the interest of individuals, and *if there are contradictions, the interest of individuals will submit to the interest of the state and collective*' (Deng 1980) (author's emphasis).

Ironically, the validity of the general will paradigm was reinforced even by advocates of political 'reform' such as Zhao Ziyang. As much as he called for a separation between the Party and the state, Zhao held that the will of the people was the ultimate source of sovereignty and that such will was embodied in the People's Republic of China. He claimed that given the guiding role the Party had played in founding the PRC, the Party should have focused on providing political guidance. It should have ruled China by means of general rules – its line (*luxian*), guiding principles (*fangzhen*) and policies (*zhengce*) – rather than by issuing detailed instructions. The Party's standpoint (*zhuzhang*) should have become the will of the state (*guojia yizhi*) by means of statutory procedures (*fading chengxu*). To ensure order and stability, the Party too should have submitted to the general rules it had adopted to guide itself and the country – Party discipline and state law. The similarities between Zhao's view of politics and Malebranche's theodicy are perhaps not a matter of chance.

The history of what followed is the history of how the idea of general will gained weight the more ideology was diluted, with thanks to a renewed interest in the works of Rousseau, Montesquieu, Voltaire, Locke and other early modern philosophers by contemporary Chinese political philosophers. This trend can be seen in the formulation of the Three Represents, which took the basic interest of the greatest majority of the people (*guangda renmin genben liyi*) as the foundation of political legitimacy. A similar invocation of the People's Masses underlies Hu Jintao's Harmonious Society Doctrine. A dominant role for the People has likewise been envisaged by the Eight Musts. Naturally, the people are

society, while using Western learning for 'practical application' to develop infrastructure and economy.

not intended to play a truly active role in politics – they are to *consent* to, and be mobilized, organized and led by the Party (Xi 2012, Central Party School Teaching and Research Department 2013), which represents their interest and is to act in the interest of the People of the World (Ling 2013).

Through all this time, the idea of the general interest of the people has been intertwined with the pursuit of social stability. The conceptual underpinnings of Social Management in a Harmonious Society, or the 'getting rich first' metaphor enable inequality, land disputes, heavy pollution and food safety concerns to be construed not as consequences of breakneck economic growth. Rather they result from individual *ir*responsibility, be it the responsibility of individuals for their own economic achievements, or legal persons' responsibility to obey the law on land, environmental protection and food safety.

Pursuit of social stability calls for the people's acquiescence to this state of things and to this refurbished ideological perspective. Through this 'general interest of the people' lens, accepting the externalities of economic development at a personal as well as a public level is in the interest of everybody at large. However the state has failed to mould docile depoliticized persons who accept a declining quality of life and what they perceive as injustice in the name of the 'interest of the people'. Concealing itself behind the small-government recipe and strong economic performance data, backed up with an extensive, technologically advanced stability maintenance apparatus has been a way the Party state has 'innovated' on social management to try to remedy this failure.

CONCLUSION

Behind its feel-good façade, the concept of social management innovation is premised on a political paradigm that subordinates the will, interest or good of individuals to the will, interest or good of abstract, collective entities. This paradigm derives from a theodicy aimed at making individuals accept evil and suffering as a necessary part of existence. Transposing it to a secular context has not changed the way it works (Agamben 2011). If in religion the general will paradigm is to induce individuals to accept suffering as part of the natural order of the universe, in politics this paradigm is intended to induce consensus on the proposition that the state interest, security, order and stability of the popular collective at all political levels are more important than individual well-being.

Readers may wonder to what extent political theology is relevant to the People's Republic of China, where theology never played a prominent role in the fields of law and politics, and where an autonomous philosophical tradition exists. Paradoxically, it is the assumed irrelevance of Christian theology to China that allowed *some* ideas to slip undetected into what dominates China's modern political philosophy. A paradigm of theological derivation was certainly not the *only* influence that shaped ideas about the why and how of 'social management' in contemporary China, including the concept of stability maintenance. China's intellectual tradition is too solid and complex to be displaced by a single idea, regardless of the prestige of this idea in Western philosophy and its long-standing utility for social management in practice. Together with other currents of thoughts, ideas about general volition have contributed to shape a politics where the disruptive effects of individual free will justify the need to maintain social stability at all costs.

REFERENCES

Afanasev, B.R. (1983), *Persons in Social Management* (Shehui guanlizhong de ren), Beijing, Zhishi Chubanshe.

Agamben, Giorgio (2011), *The Kingdom and the Glory: for a theological genealogy of economy and government*. Stanford: Stanford University Press.

Bakken, Børge (2000), *The Exemplary Society: human improvement, social control and the dangers of modernity in China*. New York: Oxford University Press.

Becker, Gary (2000), *Kouweide jingjixue fenxi* (An economic analysis of taste). Beijing: Shoudu jingji maoyi daxue chubanshe.

Becker Gary S. and Kevin M. Murphy, (2000) *Social Economics: market behavior in a social environment*. Cambridge MA: Harvard University Press.

Boer, Roland (2012), *Criticism of Earth: on Marx, Engels, and theology*. Boston and Leiden: Brill.

Bush, George W. (1989), 'Toast at the Welcoming Banquet in Beijing', The American Presidency Project, 25 February, www.presidency.ucsb.edu/ws/?pid=16694. Accessed 25 October 2013.

Central Committee of the CCP (2004), Zhonggong Zhongyang guanyu jiaqiang dangde zhizheng nengli jianshe de jueding (CCP Central committee decision on strengthening the party's governing capability), 19 September, http://www.china.com.cn/chinese/2004/Sep/668376.htm. Accessed 24 October 2013.

Central Committee of the CCP, State Council (2011), Zhonggong zhongyang, guowuyuan guanyu jiaqiang he chuanxin shehui guanlide yijian (The opinion of the Chinese Communist Party Central Committee and State Council on strengthening and innovating social management), 5 May.

Central Party School Teaching and Research Department (2013), 'Bage bixu ningju gongshi', (The Eight Musts embody consensus), 16 January, http://cpc.people.com.cn/n/2013/0116/c64387-20224497-4.html. Accessed 23 October 2013.

Central Political-legal Committee Research Office (2001), *Weihu shehui wending shishang diaoyan wenji* (Collected essays on investigations in maintaining social stability). Beijing: falü chubanshe.

Chen, Jiagang (2013), 'Cong shehui guanli zouxiang shehui zhili' (From social management to social governance), *Zhongguo Gongchandang Xinwenwang* (News of the Chinese communist party), 22 October, http://theory.people.com.cn/n/2012/1022/c245417-19341622.html. Accessed 25 October 2013.

Cheng, Yehua (2001), *Xifang huobi jinrong xueshuode xinfazhan* (New developments in Western monetary and financial science). Chengdu: Xinan caijing daxue chubanshe.

Chinese Communist Party (2004), Zhongguo gongchandang di shiliu jie zhongyang weiyuanhui disi ci quanti huiyi gongbao (Communique of the Fourth Plenary Session of the XVI Central Committee), 19 September, http://www.people.com.cn/GB/shizheng/1026/2793949.html. Accessed 24 October 2013.

Coase, Ronald (2007), *Qiyede xingzhi* (The nature of the firm). Beijing: Shangwu yingshuguan.

Deng, Xiaoping (1980), *Dang he guojia lingdao zhidude gaige* (Reforming the leadership system of the Party and the state), Xinhuawang (New China Net), 18 August, http://news.xinhuanet.com/ziliao/2005-02/04/content_2547080.htm. Accessed 24 October 2013.

Dutton, Michael (1992), *Policing and Punishment in China: from patriarchy to 'the people'*. Cambridge: Cambridge University Press.

Engels, Friedrich (1970), *Herr Eugen Dühring's Revolution in Science*, Emile Burns transl. New York: International Publishers.

Engels, Friedrich (2003a), 'Engels to Marx in Brussels', 17 March 1845, in Karl Marx and Friedrich Engels, *The Collected Works of Marx and Engels, Volume 38*, Charlottesville: Intelex Corporation.

Engels, Friedrich (2003b), 'Letter to Friedrich Graeber', 26 July 1938 and 27 July 1839, in Karl Marx and Friedrich Engels, *The Collected Works of Marx and Engels, Volume 2*, Charlottesville: Intelex Corporation.

Fewsmith, Joseph (2011), 'Social Management as a way of coping with heightened social tensions', *China Leadership Monitor*, 36: 1–11.

Friedman, Milton (2004), *Zibenzhuyi yu ziyou* (Capitalism and Freedom). Beijing: Shangwu Yingshuguan.

Garland, David (2001), *The Culture of Control: crime and social order in contemporary society*. Oxford: Oxford University Press.

Ginbar, Yuval (2008), *Why Not Torture Terrorists? Moral, practical and legal aspects of the 'ticking bomb' justification for torture*. Oxford: Oxford University Press.

He, Zengke (2013), 'Cong shehui guanli zouxiang shehui zhili he shanzhi' (From social management to social governance and good governance), Zhongguo gongchandang xinwenwang (Chinese communist party news network), 28 January, http://theory.people.com.cn/n/2013/0128/c49154-20347731.html. Accessed 24 October 2013.

Hegel, Georg Wilhelm Friedrich (2008), *The Philosophy of Right*, S.W. Dyde transl. New York: Cosimo Books.

Henry, Nicholas (1975), 'Paradigms of public administration', *Public Administration Review*, 35(4): 378–86.

Hill, Lisa (2001), 'The hidden theology of Adam Smith', *The European Journal of the History of Economic Thought*, 8(1): 1–29.

Horner, Louise and Hazel, Louise (2005), *Adding Public Value*. London: The Work Foundation.

Hu, Jintao (2007), 'Zai dangde shiqida shangde baogao' (Hu Jintao report to the Seventeenth Party Congress), Xinhuawang (New China Network), 24 October, http://news.xinhuanet.com/newscenter/2007-10/24/content_6938568_7.htm. Accessed 24 October 2013.

Knight, Frank (2009), *Fengxian, buquedingxing yu lirun* (Risk, uncertainty and profit). Beijing: Shangwu yinshuguan.

Knight, Nick (2005), *Marxist Philosophy in China: From Qu Qiubai to Mao Zedong, 1923–1945*. Dordrecht: Springer.

Ling, Xiaolin (2013), 'Qiushi zhuming wenzhang: jianchi Zhongguo tese shehuizhuyi budongyao' (Seeking Truth signed article: uphold Socialism with Chinese characteristics without swaying), Zhonghua renmin gongheguo zhongyang renmin zhengfu (Central government of the People's Republic of China), 15 January, http://www.gov.cn/jrzg/2013-01/16/content_2312986.htm. Accessed 24 October 2013.

Lucas, Robert E. (2003), *Jingji zhouqi moxing* (Models of business cycles). Beijing: Zhongguo Renmin Daxue Chubanshe.

Malebranche, Nicolas (1992), *Treatise on Nature and Grace*. Patrick Riley transl. New York: Oxford University Press.

Markov, M. (1988), *Shehui guanlixue* (The science of social management). Shanghai: Tongji daxue chubanshe.

Misra, Kalpana (1998), *From Post-Maoism to Post-Marxism: the erosion of official ideology in Deng's China*. New York: Routledge.

New Capital Daily (2011), 'Zhongyang zongzhiwei gengming bing zengjia 11ge chengyuan danwei' (Central Committee for the Comprehensive Management of Public Order renamed, increased by 11 units), 9 October, http://news.163.com/11/1009/03/7FT64GVS00014AED.html. Accessed 23 October 2013.

Omarov, A.M. (1987), *Shehui guanli mouxie lilun yu shijian wenti* (Some theoretical and practical problems of social management). Wang Sibing transl. Hangzhou: Zhejiang renmin chubanshe.

People's Republic of China (2011), 'Guomin jingji he shehui fazhan di shi'erge wu nian guihua gangyao' (Outline of the XII five years plan on national economic and social development), 16 March, http://www.gov.cn/2011lh/content_1825838_10.htm. Accessed 23 October 2013.

Pieke, Frank (2012), 'The Communist Party and social management in China', *China Information* 26: 149–65.

Posner, Richard (2012), *Falüde jingji fenxi* (An economic analysis of law). Beijing: Falü chubanshe.

Riley, Patrick (1978), 'The general will before Rousseau', *Political Theory*, 6(4): 485–516.

Schwartz, Donald V. (1973), 'Recent Soviet adaptations of systems theory to administrative theory', *Administration & Society*, 5: 233–64.

Smith, Adam (2002), *The Theory of Moral Sentiments*. Knud Haakonssen (ed.), Cambridge: Cambridge University Press.

Spires, Anthony (2011), 'Contingent symbiosis and civil society in an authoritarian state: understanding the survival of China's grassroots NGOs', *American Journal of Sociology*, 117: 1–45.

Stigler, George (1990), *Jingjixuejia he shuofuzhe* (Knowledge and persuasion in economics). Beijing: Sanlian shudian.

Talmon, Jacob (1985), *The Origins of Totalitarian Democracy*. Boulder: Westview Press.

Tong, Xing (1991), *Shehui guanlixue gailun* (General theory of social management). Nanjing: Nanjing Daxue Chubanshe.

Trevaskes, Susan (2010), *Policing Serious Crime in China: from strike hard to kill fewer*. London: Routledge.

Trevaskes, Susan (2012), *The Death Penalty in Contemporary China*. New York: Palgrave.

Xi, Jinping (2012), 'Quanmian guanche luoshi dangde shibada jingshen yao tuchu zhuahao liuge fangmian gongzuo' (To fully implement the spirit of the XVIII Congress one must have an outstanding mastery of work in six areas), *Qiushi* (Seeking Truth), 15 November, http://www.qstheory.cn/zxdk/2013/201301/201212/t20121227_202448.htm. Accessed 24 October 2013.

Yao, Kevin and Wang, Aileen (2013), 'China lets Gini out of the bottle: wide wealth gap', *Reuters*, 18 January, http://www.reuters.com/article/2013/01/18/us-china-economy-income-gap-idUSBRE90H06L20130118. Accessed 23 October 2013.

APPENDIX PUBLICATIONS ARGUING FOR A CHINESE BREED OF NEO-LIBERALISM AND STABILITY MAINTENANCE

13 *People's Daily* Editorials (10 February 2011–26 May 2011)

People's Daily Commentator (2011), 'Shuli gongxin cong xuehui qingting zuoqi' (Public trust is obtained by listening attentively), 10 February, http://opinion.people.com.cn/GB/13884723.html. Accessed 24 October 2013.

(2011b), 'Rang gongxingli zai yangguangxia shengzhang' (Let credibility grow in the sunlight), 17 February, http://opinion.people.com.cn/GB/13937594.html. Accessed 24 October 2013.

(2011c), 'Weihu qunzhong liyi caiyou gongxing' (Credibility is gained only by protecting the interest of the masses), 24 February, http://opinion.people.com.cn/GB/13995338.html. Accessed 24 October 2013.

(2011d), 'Yong zhidu shouhu gongxingli chengzhang' (Use institutions to protect the growth of credibility), 3 March, http://opinion.people.com.cn/GB/14048720.html. Accessed 24 October 2013.

(2011e), 'Ganbu zuofeng shi gongxinglide shengmingxian' (Cadres' work style is the lifeline of credibility), 17 March, http://opinion.people.com.cn/GB/40604/14163129.html. Accessed 24 October 2013.

(2011f), 'Rang "liyi ganggan" qiaojie shehui maodun' (Let the lever of interest prise social contradictions), 24 March, http://opinion.people.com.cn/GB/40604/14221209.html. Accessed 24 October 2013.

(2011g), 'Lishun jiegou cai neng shuhuan shehui jiaolu' (Social angst can be relieved only by rebalancing social structure), 21 March, http://opinion.people.com.cn/GB/14286261.html. Accessed 24 October 2013.

(2011h), 'Yi shehui gongshi hanyang gongxu liangsu' (Maintain public order and standards of decency through social consensus), 7 April, http://opinion.people.com.cn/GB/14327956.html. Accessed 24 October 2013.

(2011i), 'Rang shehui zuzhi zhutui shehui hexie' (Let social organizations promote social harmony), 14 April, http://opinion.people.com.cn/GB/14390232.html. Accessed 24 October 2013.

(2011j), 'Xintai peiyu zhizhengzhe de yidao kaoti' (Cultivating mentality – exam questions for those in power), 21 April, http://opinion.people.com.cn/GB/14449044.html. Accessed 24 October 2013.

(2011k), 'Yi baorongxing duidai yizhi siwei' (Treat unusually different thoughts with a tolerant heart), 28 April, http://opinion.people.com.cn/GB/14505701.html. Accessed 24 October 2013.

(2011l), 'Yong gongping zhengyi xiaojie ruoshi xintai' (Use fairness and justice to dispel a mentality of weakness), 5 May, http://opinion.people.com.cn/GB/8213/211790/14553685.html. Accessed 24 October 2013.

(2011m), 'Zhuiqiu lixing cong nali qibu' (Where does the pursuit of an ideal start?), *Renmin Ribao*, 19 May, http://opinion.people.com.cn/GB/40604/14675949.html. Accessed 24 October 2013.

(2011n), 'Zhizhengzhe yao cong qunzhong xuanhuazhong qingting chenmoude shengyin' (Those in power must lend an ear to the voice of those drowning in people's rioting), 26 May, http://politics.people.com.cn/GB/30178/14743565.html. Accessed 24 October 2013.

Three Cadre Manuals

Editorial Group of the Reader on strengthening social management (2011), *Jiaqiang he chuangxin shehui guanli xuexi duben* (A reader on strengthening and innovating social management), Beijing: Guojia xingzheng xueyuan chubanshe.

Editorial Group of Typical case studies and experiences in strengthening and innovating social management (2011), *Jiaqiang he chuangxing shehui guanli dianxing shili jingyan yu qishi* (Typical case studies and experiences in strengthening and innovating social management), Beijing: Renmin ribao chubanshe.

People's Daily Commentator (2011), *Jiaqiang he chuangxin shehui guanli dangyuan ganbu xuexi cankao* (Party cadres' reference materials on strengthening and innovating social management), Beijing: Renmin ribao chubanshe.

13. Framing the stability imperative

Susan Trevaskes, Elisa Nesossi, Flora Sapio and Sarah Biddulph

INTRODUCTION

The activist disposition of China's legal institutions in the era of Harmonious Society and Stability Maintenance enabled the Party-state to legitimize important changes in the practices and policies of courts, governments and security organs. These changes were based on a certain political narrative about the relationship of social stability to China's economic development and its reform path. According to the Party Central Politico-Legal Commission, China's law and order (including Stability Maintenance) policies aim to promote three key elements of China's modernization drive: stability, development and reform (Lin 2004). At the 17th Party Congress in 2007, China's senior authorities declared 'development is the priority task and stability the foremost responsibility' (Kelly 2011, He 2012). But why was law drawn into this picture – as part of the reform programme and in the service of stability and development? Why was it the type of legal reform that has further politicized the legal system as we have seen through the chapters in this volume? And why was the stability imperative seen to be so pressing that it has acquired such major political proportions at this juncture in PRC history, overtaking the highly important longer-term goals of legal reform to further legitimize the law and develop a mature legal system in China.

In this concluding chapter we address these questions by drawing from lessons in the studies presented across the book. We trace the Party-state's journey towards construction of 'stability' as the overriding national imperative in the late 20th and early 21st centuries and incorporation of polemical legal measures into the reform programme to address this imperative. First we briefly reflect on the re-politicization of Party power after 1989. We then interrogate how stability has been tied into the two other key elements of China's modernization goals: institutional reform and economic development, pulling legal measures into the reform package. How the Party-state has perceived the interrelationships here is important for understanding the law–stability nexus in the first decade of the 21st century – why national stability has been foregrounded as the nation's central political concern and why law has been put explicitly at the service of this imperative as the Party-state construes it. The legal measures to achieve stability make a life for law that is still at the firm hand of Party, politicians and national policy, and so create a very potent politics of law and stability in 21st-century China.

We find among senior leaders a disabling mix of unwillingness and inability to ease tensions between the demands of turbo capitalism and the need for lasting structural reform, which many developed countries' experiences indicate is the most effective way to manage social tensions. Leaders were prepared to accept some degree of social discord, which they assumed would accompany rapid economic growth, but they would not allow social unrest at such levels as to threaten China's prospects for a moderately prosperous society (*xiaokang shehui*). In the early 2000s the new Hu Jintao leadership recognized that in the longer term the state would need to take institutional reform, particularly legal reform, seriously. This reform would be the ultimate mechanism to 'govern the country according to the law', curb corruption, improve China's weak governmental and legal oversight mechanisms and sustain the prospects for a moderately prosperous – and stable – society. But Hu's leadership also recognized an inherent difficulty. A strong legal system working to apply and enforce the law across the nation would be the ultimate guarantee for long-term social stability, but building up and sustaining such a system would not be possible in the short term. In deploying the 'stability overrides everything' imperative, law was a mechanism drawn into securing stability for short term political gain. Plans for genuine systemic legal reform were overtaken, further eroding public confidence in the law and so deferring establishment of a strong and effective legal system to a more distant future. We therefore end the book on a cautionary note about the consequences of mobilizing the law to meet the stability imperative: weakening public confidence in law's legitimacy in China today.

BRINGING THE PARTY BACK IN

Party-state preoccupation with stability began to form in the late 1980s, even though threats to social stability through crime and other sources had been a continuous concern since the early 1980s. Deng Xiaoping and his Party colleagues initiated a programme of socialist rule-of-law reforms in the early 1980s to provide the broad legal scaffolding for economic development to take hold and to protect society from the kind of political chaos experienced during the Cultural Revolution. Senior authorities sought to establish a gradual separation of powers between Party and state, freeing up the Party to focus on policy issues and enabling administrators and legislators to deal with routine governance matters without constant Party interference. But with the 1989 Tiananmen incident and the collapse of the Soviet Union, the Party abandoned this aspiration to separate from the state, instead reasserting direct control over legislative and governmental organs (Chen 2013, He 2012, Feng 2013). The first buds of obsession with stability became evident in the early 1990s, with a change of political heart by the Communist Party.

Party leaders saw that avoiding the kind of deep-rooted collapse experienced in the former Soviet states in the early 1990s after the collapse of the Soviet Union required fundamental rethinking of governance, thinking that coupled more efficient political control over public officials with the continued commitment to economic development. This move towards re-embedding Party presence in government and legislative affairs primarily involved strengthening the Party's political influence over justice and security organs. This was achieved through reintroducing in 1991 at each administrative level in all courts, procuratorates, police and other security organs the Party's powerful politico-legal committees (*zhengfa weiyuanhui*), headed by the Party's Central Politico-legal Commission in Beijing (Lam 2009, Fu 2013).[1] Conceptually this did not entail a fundamental shift in the jurisprudential orientation of law in Chinese jurisprudence; PRC law, socialist in nature, was still conceived as an instrument to implement Party policies. Politico-legal committees in all justice and security organs both required and enabled the free flow of policy dissemination from Beijing on to the provincial, municipal and county levels.

Politico-legal orientations and priorities relating to crime control in the early 1990s found expression in the policies of 'Striking Hard' and

[1] The Central Politico-legal Commission of the CCP (Zhonggong Zhongyang Zhengfa Weiyuanhui) in Beijing sets the policy agenda for the nation's courts and prosecution, as well as for the police apparatus. Its sub-national committees at province, municipal and county level implement the Commission's policies. The Commission in Beijing has higher authority than other Central Committee departments. The Organization Department, the Propaganda Department, the United Front Department and other departments have advisory and coordinating powers, but the Commission enjoys the power to lead (*lingdao*) judicial and law enforcement organs (Lin 2004: 23–4).

'Comprehensively Managing Public Order', which were the focus of the Central Politico-legal Commission in Beijing. But towards the turn of the century it was becoming increasingly apparent that the scale of disputes and civil conflicts required a new approach to public order. In the early 2000s, China's politico-legal committees were gradually populated with police chiefs at the helm. The dual roles of many, also as deputy majors in jurisdictions around the nation, facilitated the smooth implementation and enforcement of national stability policy (Fu 2013) and subversion of legal concerns by overriding political concerns and actions.

In 2000 the Party established a 'Central Leading Group on Maintaining Stability' to operate within the auspices of the Politico-legal Commission (Fu 2013). This completed the gradual broadening of the Central Politico-legal Commission's attention beyond the exclusive focus on crime to also include disputes, collective protests and petitioning. While '*weihu wending*' (Stability Maintenance) was used in internal circles in the late 1990s, only in the early 2000s was the abbreviated catchcry *weiwen* fully embraced in the policing vernacular. With this it officially became the new focus of politico-legal organs, which formulated and implemented related policies (Trevaskes 2013).

STABILITY, REFORM AND DEVELOPMENT

Around the early 2000s, moves were made to make *weiwen* integral to national policing discourse, as the Central Politico-legal Commission set about realigning its stability-related work to address three main national tasks identified in the 16th Party Congress Report in 2004: stability, reform and economic development (Jiang 2003). This Party Congress Report made it clear that to enable the tasks of reform and development in China, the Party would need to maintain a social environment free from conflicts and discord (Lin 2004). *Weiwen* would be instrumental here as the Commission began further realigning its justice and security policies to address how authorities would successfully integrate the three main national tasks of socialist modernization: to enable institutional reform, encourage development and maintain social stability. The rhetorical glue essential for legitimizing the links inside this tripartite relationship came in the form of two agendas articulated by the Hu Jintao leadership. First was the 'Harmonious Society' agenda in the mid-2000s, and after 2007 the 'Stability Maintenance' agenda, both of them used to frame and rationalize stability by emphasizing it as a precondition of reform and development.

'Stability Maintenance' and 'Harmonious Society' provided the legitimizing context for action. The 2006 'Resolution of the CCP Central Committee on Major Issues Concerning the Building of a Socialist Harmonious Society' formally adopted Harmonious Society as the key Party line. The ideological goal of social harmony would inform the Party's response to the realities of inequality caused by the social and economic externalities of rapid economic development. This response had various arms: addressing development gaps between urban and rural areas and between various regions; establishing a social security system; and improving public services, social order, ideological and moral standards, scientific and cultural quality, and healthcare. Harmonious Society developed into the Party's dominant political ideology of the decade and a general blueprint aimed at binding fractured relations between the people and elites.

The 2006 Resolution was the final result of a process that had been developing over four years from 2002. The close rhetorical connection of social harmony to the three elements of modernization – reform, development and stability – had been publicized in a 2005 pronouncement by President Hu Jintao, where he declared that China had entered a critical juncture on the road to modernity and identified the logic of this connection. Chinese authorities had expected that as with all rapidly developing economies, some degree of social discord and disorder would accompany rapid economic growth, but these should not be permitted to threaten economic development. In this pivotal period in China's development, sustaining social order was essential to maintaining the momentum of economic growth; 'economic stagnation and protracted social upheavals' (Hu cited in Tanner 2012: 89) would follow from any failure to curb social unrest.

Hu's strategy embodied three understandings of political process that are crucial to understanding why the law became so important to the stability imperative (Tanner 2012). The first is that continued economic growth – which Hu insisted would need to be in the long run both socially and environmentally sustainable – is the ultimate guarantee of social peace. The second is that economic growth of itself is insufficient to sustain Party legitimacy. The Party therefore would need to reform its institutions of power, to improve its capacity to govern by directly addressing the governance failures that cause public frustration and disquiet. Government and justice organs would therefore need to work cooperatively and harmoniously, to develop more robust regulatory oversight and accountability mechanisms. The third understanding, for this book the most important element of Hu's Harmonious Society strategy, concerned containing social unrest. Given the acute level of social contradictions China had been experiencing during this pivotal period of economic transition, social instability would need to be decisively contained. So, while acknowledging that only rule-of-law building through institutional reform can lead to an orderly and harmonious society in the long run, during the interim period of market transition, politico-legal intervention would be required to control the social fall-out of economic reform (Tanner 2012).

Unacknowledged in Hu Jintao's speeches, however, is the extent to which a key method of attaining high-speed economic growth contributed to social unrest. The Party's insistence on maintaining the momentum of high-speed economic growth has produced a vicious cycle of unrest caused by pressure placed on local governments to continuously produce revenue by developing enterprises that require land acquisition and in many cases produce environmental contamination. Weak oversight and weak regulatory mechanisms to control local governments have enabled the high-speed development. Indeed, as He Qinglian argues, crony capitalism of local government has been revealed as the real culprit in disputes and protests. As she explains:

> The main cause of China's social conflicts is excessive extraction of resources by government at all levels, creating a vicious cycle between stability maintenance and economic development. Local officials need GDP growth to demonstrate their effectiveness, and are compelled to undertake a large number of projects. The most profitable projects are real estate and polluting industries (because China has very lax oversight on environmental pollution, and one can pay very little, or even nothing, for polluting). However, real estate development involves land acquisition and property demolition, and industrial pollution triggers environmental rights defense actions by local residents. The more the economy develops, the more conflicts there are between government officials and the people, and the more stability maintenance is needed, requiring greater expenditures (He 2012).

He Qinglian describes the Stability Maintenance regime using the analogy of an industrial chain, with the government at the top of the industrial chain 'plundering through land requisition, property demolition, and industrial pollution' as a way of maintaining tax and financial revenues. She identifies quite plainly here the missing ingredient in the stability–development–reform formula; structural reform replete with oversight mechanisms. Whilst reform might slow down turbo capitalism in the short term, it is needed to produce long-term confidence in the economy and in state institutions in the long run (He 2012).

REINSTITUTING MAOIST MASS-LINE JUSTICE

This viewing ground of the industrial chain of Stability Maintenance enables us to appreciate the role of law in this period. Without structural reform, law and judicial activism would need to be deployed as mechanisms to enforce a political morality premised on GDP growth as the basis for continuity of the current political arrangement. This chasm between long-term goals and short-term realities required politico-legal authorities to regulate conflict and contradiction through means justified by invoking the rhetoric of Maoism. Maoist practices – particularly mediation and campaigns – were returned to the political picture in the early to mid-2000s since it was understood that they had proven in the past to be an effective short-term mechanism for managing unrest. Enhancing the activist disposition of justice and security organs through the 'combat power' (*zhandouli*) of criminal trials, civil and criminal mediation, parapolicing operations and re-education through labour were stop-gap mechanisms for containing unrest, if not for achieving long-term harmony and stability. With political rhetoric sent into overdrive, and more than 600 billion yuan (approximately US $100 billion) annually poured into maintaining social stability, the stability imperative had overtaken plans for justice system reforms. The move further eroded public confidence in the law, thus undermining the fiduciary turf needed for reform of the legal system.

Indeed, the Party-state had once again 'slipped into the grooves that Mao had carved' (Chen 2013: 59), articulating social conflicts as the result of 'contradictions among the people'. Two senior policing researchers working on an internal report commissioned by the Central Party Committee in the mid-2000s represented the state of unrest in China as an expression of social contradictions between six main groups in society: rich and poor, government officials and the masses, labour and capital, people from urban and from rural areas, Han and various ethnic minorities, and people from different regions within China (Tian and Ren 2005). They argued that the central reason for the continuing presence of social contradictions in post-Mao Chinese society comes down to a clash between disparate interests (*liyi*), as manifest in the fundamental and deep conflict between all six types of dichotomous social groups. This incongruity of interests – particularly between the masses and the state itself – generated the increasingly hostile atmosphere of 'struggle' (*douzheng*) evident in the antagonistic way that people seek to protect their own interests through protests, disputes and legal challenges to government decisions (Tian and Ren 2005: 73–4). Yet rather than tackling social contradictions head-on through structural reform, in the mid-2000s the leadership mounted the Stability Maintenance craze entailing a rigid approach to justice and security to counter all areas of dispute and dissent. This would be the new short-term resolve, despite the costs it would yield for long-term stability through a well-functioning legal system.

POLITICIZING SOCIAL CONTRADICTIONS

Alarm at the number of collective protests exceeding 100,000 annually after the mid-2000s propelled social stability to the status of the number one socio-political imperative driving law and governance agendas. By this time, the political authorities had deeply embedded the concept of Stability Maintenance in politico-legal discourse. Unlike Harmonious Society, Stability Maintenance was never formally endorsed through a Party resolution as a national political goal. Nevertheless, this imperative was developed as a major policy, particularly after the conservative turn at the 17th Party Congress in 2007.

Stability Maintenance was developed into an umbrella term for handling all things public order related – a rhetorical mechanism for binding together a disparate array of legal levers that could be used to 'harmonize' disharmonious social relations, resolve disputes, control dissent and manage unrest. And with the dramatic rise in mass incidents in the post-2007 period, the main political agenda was gradually turned from one that purported to 'build' a certain type of society (a harmonious one) to one that required society to be protected from those who dissented against political or governmental authority. Hence, the stability agenda originally justified under the banner of developing harmony morphed into what scholar Yu Jianrong called a 'rigid' stability model (Yu 2010). Protecting society from the effects of instability had two sides: coercive tactics aimed at a minority of protest ringleaders, and 'persuasion and education' for the vast majority of people involved in disputes (Tanner 2007).

Even though by 2007 *weiwen* (Stability Maintenance) was ubiquitous in policing and more generally in political discourse, it did not emerge spontaneously as a mature and developed concept. As mentioned above, 'protecting social stability' (*baohu shehui wending*) had for decades been a leading rationale for policing crime, yet the catchword *weiwen* is relatively new to the policing repertoire. It appeared in late 2003 in the 20th National Public Security Work Conference – known in Chinese police jargon as the '20-*gong*' – a national policing conference that

Chinese policing circles now regard as 'historic' (Trevaskes 2013). During the 20-*gong* Minister of Public Security (MPS) Zhou Yongkang for the first time explicitly encouraged policymakers to adapt Maoist rhetoric to the policing of mass incidents, social protests and disputes. In his keynote speech, Zhou declared that all strength and effort would be given to the 'political struggle' for the important 'strategic opportunity' that *weiwen* presented to the nation:

> We must in a practical and realistic way, strengthen this work and make it a priority task for Party committees at each level. This is an important political task [*zhongyao zhengzhi renwu*] of the public security in China … Maintaining stability is intimately connected to the entire plan of building a harmonious society (Liu 2006: 227).

This rationalization illustrates how the Party saw Stability Maintenance as an intensely political project. Marketing Stability Maintenance in such a highly politicized way expanded its scope well beyond *weiwen* policing, to incorporate a wide array of legal mechanisms and justice practices. Mao-inspired discourse sought to bolster the political firepower for the policing of stability-threatening activities, but it also had another political motive. It was to revive the mass-line identity of politico-legal organs.

After the 20-*gong*, the Party's propaganda machine was given the imprimatur to sell the idea of politico-legal organs as bastions of mass-line justice. It was to promote mediation rather than litigation of civil and administrative disputes, aiming to avoid further exacerbating social instability at the expense of institutional reform. Even though courts and other justice agencies may have been sympathetic to addressing blatant injustices inflicted upon citizens in cases of forced evictions, land-taking and other civil and administrative disputes, they were reluctant to allow these cases to go to trial. Out-of-court mediation rather than litigation enables local authorities to deal with contested issues locally and prevents citizens from exercising their legal rights through court appeal or through petitioning to central authorities in Beijing. The Party's strategy to bring back Mao-style pre-emptive mechanisms such as mediation worked to help curtail unrest because it gave local governments and courts greater control over the outcomes of disputes and capacity to resolve issues at the local level in a timely manner, ensuring that successful appeal or petitioning to higher authorities would be difficult if not impossible. As Fu Hualing observes:

> A key strategy of general intervention is the promotion of aggressive mediation and the imposition of a duty on all government departments to end

> disputes proactively, as quickly as they occur. Courts in particular are encouraged to mobilize available resources to bring conflicts to an effective end at any cost. The interventionalist and proactive style of dispute resolution aims at preventing conflicts from forming, escalating and solidifying, regardless of their political orientations (Fu 2013).

While this form of dispute resolution may promote the short-term harmonizing ethos favoured by the current political system, it can also disadvantage the weak and underprivileged in society, and dilutes the courts' power to monitor the legality of acts of administrative agencies. Reluctance to allow cases to be addressed inside the courtroom through litigation is related to, among other things, the issue of judges' professional performance ratings; judicial decisions can be measured unfavourably against stability-related performance criteria (Minzner 2009). If the aggrieved party takes the disputes further up the appellate chain, or petitions outside government or the court at a higher administrative level, or worse still, travels to Beijing to petition, judges can take the political fall. Judges and other justice and security personnel in post-Harmonious Society China remain hobbled by the stability imperative since the new 18th Party Congress leadership was installed in November 2012.

Post 2012, we find a number of subtle shifts in Party policy towards stability. The new Party leadership under Xi Jinping opposes political liberalism. Yet it recognizes that the excesses of Stability Maintenance that encroached on the legal system, justice and state-sanctioned rights have damaged public trust in the law. After November 2012, the new Party leadership began realigning the politico-legal agenda by retreating from the hard stance on Stability Maintenance and emphasizing return to building a 'rule of law'. However, this is unmistakably a socialist rather than a Western-liberal-oriented rule of law. Moreover, the new leadership is yet to articulate how or even if it will endeavour to better manage tensions between reform, development and stability.

CONCLUSION: LAW'S UNSTABLE LEGITIMACY

Managing the tensions between reform, development and stability was integrated into the political rationale for legal reform in China in the late 20th and early 21st centuries, guiding the direction and changes made to politico-legal operations. This chapter has examined why and how judicial and security practices came to be framed within the political discourse around the imperative of protecting social stability. It has addressed why the stability imperative was made so prominent at this time in PRC history by examining the path of stability's rise to prominence through political programmes and rhetoric linking stability to the national imperatives of economic development and institutional reform.

This chapter has examined how and why law has been drawn into its present relationship with national stability, explicitly to dissuade, prevent and punish destabilizing activities through legal activism in the service of stability and economic development. In choosing this approach, authorities arguably recognized that further politicizing the legal system in this way would come at the expense of developing the legitimacy of the legal system and so its capacity to meet long-term stability needs. But they saw stability as the primary imperative at this juncture in PRC history since it was a prerequisite for continuing the nation's strong economic development. Familiar Maoist-style judicial and security practices were thus remobilized into service, now framed within the political discourses of Stability Maintenance and Harmonious Society, which foreground the imperative of protecting social stability.

This volume has not focussed on policing and *weiwen* per se, but the discussion above on why the stability imperative emerged and how social conflict was politicized through the Stability Maintenance agenda helps deepen our understanding of why and how law was tangled into revival of the mass-line in the political pursuit of social stability. Put simply, law became embroiled in Maoist-style activism because many areas of law in China have never been given the enforcement teeth to enable an alternative to Maoist-style activism to operate effectively. The Party-state has not breathed life into the idea of governing the country (strictly) in accordance with the law. It has not cultivated the jurisprudential underlay, the institutional arrangements, or the public understanding and trust that would sustain such a legal system. Law and the legal system have been kept in an elastic state, ready and able to respond to political sways.

What the Party-state had created was a legal system in some ways structured for weak enforcement at the sub-national level. The Party-state had indeed developed laws to regulate and oversee economic development, but strict enforcement of these laws was apparently not encouraged in sub-national jurisdictions. Through various top-down measures for assessing their performance and compliance, to serve its own interests the central government had vested the interests of local governments in protecting state-owned and privately owned development. The local governments recognized that strictly enforcing regulation could potentially slow the momentum for economic growth in their locality and thus their own performance indicators. It would also close down opportunities for them to exercise power in relations with developers and other dealers, and opportunities for personal reward through venal behaviour now commonplace at that level. Local governments therefore allowed development in a socially and environmentally unsustainable way. The imperative was to keep up the momentum of rapid market expansion that stringent enforcement of regulation and safeguards against the excesses of turbo capitalism would curtail. This situation enabled state and privately owned enterprises to prosper at the expense of citizens who, without protection of law, lacked the capacity to protect themselves from deregulated market forces.

The institutionalized structure for non-enforcement of law at the local level generated new popular understandings not just about the distribution of power between governments at national and sub-national level and the new landscape of vested interests in local development, but also about the legitimacy of law. Effectively, disempowering the law from protecting the citizens was to undermine the legitimacy of the law at a time when the Party-state recognized, but failed to prioritize, the importance of strengthening the legal system for longer-term economic and social goals, including economic development and stability. The moves, particularly in the first decade of the 21st century, to further politicize the law to serve the stability agenda have further eroded law's legitimacy. But law's legitimacy was the price that Hu Jintao and colleagues were willing to pay to secure short-term stability. They recognized that building the law's legitimacy through embedding due process, legal consistency and fairness into all levels of the legal system would require a long-term commitment from all levels of government to the proper enforcement of regulatory laws and oversight structures. It would require the Party-state to remove the conflict for local governments between their responsibilities to both maximize economic growth and enforce the law simultaneously within their jurisdiction. This was a task too difficult to achieve without risking short-term slowdown in China's turbo-capitalist economy.

'Localization' of justice practices over the last 15 years or more has meant that Party and government involvement in meeting the stability imperative through adjudication and dispute resolution has further entrenched existing power relations at the local level. This makes judicial fairness difficult to achieve in those areas where local governments have a vested financial interest in supporting the cause of local enterprises over the rights of local residents or transient workers, as is evident in cases of land, labour and environmental disputes. This entrenchment of local power relations, which has blocked enforcement of law to protect citizens, has had all the more impact on stability in politically sensitive disputes where citizens are disadvantaged by limited legal knowledge and limited or no access to lawyers, and thus have nowhere to go but on to the streets to protest. Use of the rhetorical tools of Harmonious Society and Stability Maintenance to cultivate legitimacy for the priority given to stability measures at the expense of legal propriety has made it possible for local authorities to argue that any deviation from the ethics of consensus and harmony defined by the Party-state poses a challenge to a morally absolutist politics that demarcates rights and wrongs in society. The general experience for China's citizens is that values and worldviews in conflict with those of the Party-state are allowed, but these must not be acted upon through collective or individual protest that will challenge this absolutism. Any legal or non-legal action expressing a lack of consensus with Party-state morality confronts the moral foundations of governance, inducing the use of the Party-state's coercive response.

Post-2012, with the ascension of the new Party leadership, 'rigid' Stability Maintenance rhetoric seems to have been pulled back somewhat. Yet intolerance of dissent remains and so, largely, do the politico-legal circumstances that inspire this dissent. Social stability continues as the number one socio-political imperative driving the law and justice agenda and the annual Stability Maintenance budget remains at over 700 billion yuan. Meng Jianzhu, the new head of the Central Politico-legal Commission, has implored justice agencies to 'civilize' their practices, conduct their work 'on the basis of the rule of law', and 'standardize' justice practices across the nation to ensure that the law is enforced properly. This is consistent with the nation's legal goals for long-term stability, if not with the short-term stability strategies articulated in Stability Maintenance and Harmonious Society. Here his insistence on standardizing practices is more a reaction to the rampant localization of justice practices in the 2000s than a signal of the national government's commitment to dramatically reforming China's politico-legal institutions.

In Xi Jinping's China, law remains an increasingly compelling force to meet citizens' demands for justice and protection of their rights. But law also remains captive to the stability imperative. Before Xi's ascension to China's presidency, Premier Wen Jiabao described instability and the unrest that it brings as the product of 'unbalanced, uncoordinated and unsustainable' economic growth (Fewsmith 2012: 2). Unbalanced, uncoordinated and unsustainable economic growth remains a steady undercurrent in state–society relations in China today because the legal levers of enforcement, oversight and other regulatory mechanisms that might deliver more sound governance practices are not well developed and so far there is no sign that the new leadership has the political will to tackle genuine structural reform. The Party-state therefore continues to recognize the importance of upholding law's legitimacy in the long term, but still supports the adoption of practices such as 'aggressive' mediation and anti-corruption campaigns in the short term as a way of trying to thwart unrest.

This conflictive situation is of course not unique to China. Indeed, tension in meeting major national goals may be inevitable as a nation passes through the type and scale of transition China is now undertaking. But as the studies in this volume have revealed, in China a political atmosphere that obsesses over stability and pathologizes social disorder has intensified tensions between the agendas of social order and social justice. This has stimulated a wider societal antipathy towards the prospects for genuine systemic reform, since such a commitment requires the Party-state to give due prominence to procedural propriety over stability concerns. Such antipathy leads back to the wider issue of law's long-term prospects for delivering the kind of legitimacy that is essential for the future prospects of Party rule.

REFERENCES

Chen, Xi (2012), *Social Protest and Contentious Authoritarianism in China*. New York: Cambridge University Press.

Chen, Xi (2013), 'The rising cost of stability', *Journal of Democracy*, 24(1): 57–64.

Feng, Chongyi (2013), 'Preserving stability and rights protection: conflict or coherence?', *Journal of Current Chinese Affairs* 42(2): 21–50.

Fewsmith, Joseph (2012), 'Social management as a way of coping with heightened social tensions', *China Leadership Monitor*, 36, http://www.hoover.org/publications/china-leadership-monitor/article/104226. Accessed 13 June 2013.

Fu, Hualing (2013), 'Politicized challenges, depoliticized responses: political monitoring in China's transitions', University of Hong Kong Faculty of Law Research Paper no. 2013/014. http://papers.ssrn.com/sol3/papers.cfm?abstract_id=2250073. Accessed 27 September 2013.

He, Qinglian (2012), 'China's stability maintenance system faces financial pressure', *Human Rights in China*, December issue, http://www.hrichina.org/crf/article/6415. Accessed 20 September 2013.

Jiang, Zemin (2003), 'Building a well off society in an all-around way and creating new conditions in building socialism with Chinese characteristics', *Xinhua*, 11 November.

Kelly, David (2011), 'Stability and social governance', *East Asia Forum*, 3(2): 12–13, http://www.eastasiaforum.org/2011/09/13/stability-and-social-governance-in-china/. Accessed 15 September 2013.

Lam, Willy (2009), 'The politicisation of China's law-enforcement apparatus', *China Perspectives*, 2: 42–51.

Lin, Zhongliang (2004), *Geji danwei zhengfawei de zhineng ji hongguan zhengfa gongzuo* (The functions and macroscopic tasks of the politico-legal affairs work of politico-legal affairs committees at all levels of government). Beijing: Chang'an chubanshe.

Liu, Baoxiang (ed.) (2006), *Gong' an gongzuo yu hexie shehui* (Public security work and harmonious society). Beijing: Qunzhong chubanshe.

Minzner, Carl (2009), 'Riots and cover-ups: counterproductive control of local agents in China', *University of Pennsylvania Journal of International Law*, 31: 53–123.

Tanner, Murray Scot (2007), 'Chinese Communist Party strategies for containing social protest', Paper delivered at 2nd Berlin Conference on Asian Security (Berlin Group).

Tanner, Murray Scot (2012), 'Internal security', in Chris Ogden (ed.), *Handbook of China's Governance and Domestic Politics*. Florence, KY: Routledge, pp. 88–96.

Tian, Quanhua and Ren, Hongji (2005), 'Xin xingshixia wo guo shehui maodun de yanbian dui shehui wending de yingxiang' (The evolution of social contradictions and influences on social stability in the new terrain in China), in Ershigong jingshen lilun yanjiu wenji bianweihui (eds.), *Lun zhanlue jiyuqi gongan gongzuo de gaige yu chuangxin: ershigong jingshen lilun yanjiu wenji* (Reforms and innovations for strategic opportunities of public security work: collected papers on the spirit of the 20-gong conference). Beijing: Zhongguo renmin gong'an daxue chubanshe, pp. 73–102.

Trevaskes, Susan (2013), 'Rationalizing stability preservation through Mao's not so invisible hand', *Journal of Current Chinese Affairs*, 42(2): 51–77.

Yu, Jianrong (2010), 'Holding tight and not letting go: the mechanisms of "rigid stability"', *Global China*, 5 (2), http://www.globalasia.org/V5N2_Summer_2010/Yu_Jianrong.html. Accessed 2 July 2012.

Index